Desert Rats at War

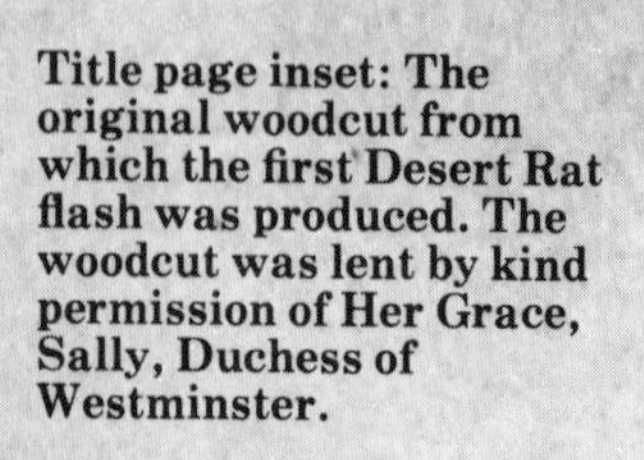

Title page inset: The original woodcut from which the first Desert Rat flash was produced. The woodcut was lent by kind permission of Her Grace, Sally, Duchess of Westminster.

Desert Rats at War

North Africa
Europe

George Forty

LONDON
IAN ALLAN LTD

This book was originally published as two volumes:
Desert Rats at War, North Africa
Desert Rats at War, Europe

© 1975, 1977 George Forty
© 1980 Ottenheimer Publishers, Inc.
All rights reserved. Printed in U.S.A.

ISBN: 0-89009-361-X

Contents

1939 1945

AFRICA

WESTERN DESERT
EL ALAMEIN TOBRUK BENGHAZI
TRIPOLI MARETH TUNIS

ITALY

SALERNO NAPLES VOLTURNO

FRANCE

NORMANDY THE SEINE ROUBAIX

BELGIUM

OUDENARDE GHENT MALINES

HOLLAND

EINDHOVEN TILBURG THE MAAS

GERMANY

THE RHINE AHAUS SOLINGEN
NIENBURG SOLTAU HAMBURG

BERLIN

When the 7th Armoured Division entered Berlin in the summer of 1945, they erected a stone monument at the end of the Autobahn and Avus. The monument, which is a record of the

in the area of the monument made it necessary for it to be taken down and moved to England where the Staff College has provided a lasting and final site for it near the 30 Corps Memorial

TO ALL DESERT RATS WHO MARCHED FROM MERSA MATRUH TO BERLIN

A MARCH UNSURPASSED THROUGH ALL THE STORY OF WAR

Foreword

on North Africa . . .

Field Marshal Sir Michael Carver,

GCB, CBE, DSO

Desert Rats at War paints a vivid picture of what it was like to serve in 7th Armoured Division between its formation in Egypt in 1939 and its victorious entry into Tunis at the end of the North African campaign in May 1943. I myself was privileged to serve in the division for almost the whole of that period, a lieutenant in 1st Royal Tank Regiment in 1939 and when we reached Tunis, a lieutenant-colonel commanding the regiment, one of the few units to serve with the division from the time of its formation not only until the end of the North African campaign but right up to the end of the war on the outskirts of Hamburg. It will awaken many memories among that gallant and cheerful band of desert veterans who proudly wore the red jerboa as their sign, and it will give a younger generation a clear idea of the conditions under which we fought. It was an exciting time for a young man and in many ways it was a clean war. There were almost no inhabitants to suffer from the destruction and suffering which war brings in its train. But however clean, war is an ugly business and we must beware of endowing it with too much romance.

Michael Carver FM

on Europe . . .

General Sir John Mogg,

GCB; CBE, DSO

The book will serve not only as an historic record of the division's triumphant progress, but it has the advantage of describing the victorious path to Berlin in a simple, human, light-hearted, easy-to-read style, lavishly illustrated with excellent action photographs.

The question "What was it like?" is difficult to answer after so many years. This record of first hand accounts, as seen through the eyes of the soldiers, the NCO, the young officer and the senior officer does much to describe the "feel of the battle," at the same time bringing out the characteristics of courage, staunch fighting spirit, light-hearted comradeship, discipline, and devotion to duty and the Cause, all of which contributed to the indomitable spirit and professional ability of the Desert Rats.

Having served in the division both in peace and war and with a son so recently in its successor, the 7th Armoured Brigade, it has given me great pleasure and immense pride to write this foreword and I hope that all who read this book will be inspired by the example of courage and proud achievement that it portrays.

Introduction

A Formation of All Arms

"An armoured division is a formation consisting of all arms.

Tanks by themselves cannot win battles, and the unarmoured units of the armoured division are indispensable, whilst the administrative services play roles no less vital and equally dangerous in maintaining supplies of all kinds, and in dealing with casualties to men and vehicles.

Each arm or branch of the service is a member of a team and has its vital part to play. Mutual understanding and confidence, based on experience during training and during action, form the keystone to success."*

This quotation, taken from a wartime Military Training Pamphlet, describes very clearly what this book is all about. Every single member of the 7th Armoured Division had a vital part to play in ensuring that the Desert Rat flash was, and still is, one of the most famous and respected formation signs to be found in any army anywhere in the world. I have tried, by means of photographs and first-hand accounts, to explain some of the many and varied wartime tasks undertaken by the men of these famous Divisions.

It has of course been a great privilege for me to write this book. When I was commissioned from the Royal Military Academy, Sandhurst, in July 1948 I joined the 1st Royal Tank Regiment, who were then part of 7th Armoured in Germany, so the first Divisional flash I ever wore was a Desert Rat and I can therefore fully understand the pride felt by all those original Desert Rats who served with the Division during its glorious and triumphal progress from Mersa Matruh to Berlin.

*Extract from Military Pamphlet No. 41 dated July 1943.

My first task in obtaining material for the book was to try to get in touch with as many ex-members of the Divisions as possible. The *Daily Telegraph,* the *Sun* and the *Daily Mirror* all allowed me to publish letters in their columns, and appeals were put out on my behalf by Charlie Chester on BBC Radio 2, local radio and newspapers, regimental magazines and many other agencies; indeed, I was even interviewed on BBC TV "South Today". I am ever in the debt of these many kind people, because the results they achieved on my behalf were truly staggering. I received a flood of letters and offers of help from over 700 ex-members of the Divisions and amassed such a wealth of material that it was soon evident I could not contain it all within the covers of a single book. Consequently, I have had to divide the story into two parts. The first part of this book deals only with the exploits of the Division in North Africa, from its formation in Mersa Matruh to its eventual victory in Tunis. The second part of the book deals with those who served in Italy and North West Europe.

It is unfortunately impossible for me to catalogue the names of all those Desert Rats who have freely given me so much help and advice. I have received so many treasured mementoes, photographs, reminiscences and anecdotes that many have had to be left out. For this I apologize, but I hope sincerely that the selection which I have managed to include is truly representative of all members of these great Divisions. One message has come over loud and clear from all who have written to me, and that is their pride in having served with the Divisions. The comradeship, loyalty and devotion to duty of all who wore the Desert Rat is something which is difficult for many people to understand in this self-centered age.

I must particularly thank Ted Flatters and Alan Atkins for the tremendous help and advice they have given me with the photographic material which forms such an important part of this book; my thanks also to Michael Haine who drew all the maps and diagrams; Mrs Nancy Rogers, my typist, without whom nothing would ever have got down on paper; Martin Brice of the Department of Photographs at the Imperial War Museum for his invaluable assistance and patient understanding; Jon, for his kindness in allowing me to reproduce his unforgettable "Two Types" cartoons; Terence Cuneo, George Davy and David Shepherd for giving permission for me to reproduce their marvellous paintings; finally my wife and sons who have encouraged and assisted me throughout the long months of preparation. I hope they will all think that the end product is worthwhile.

Floreat Jerboa!

George Forty
January 1975
Lulworth Camp, Dorset

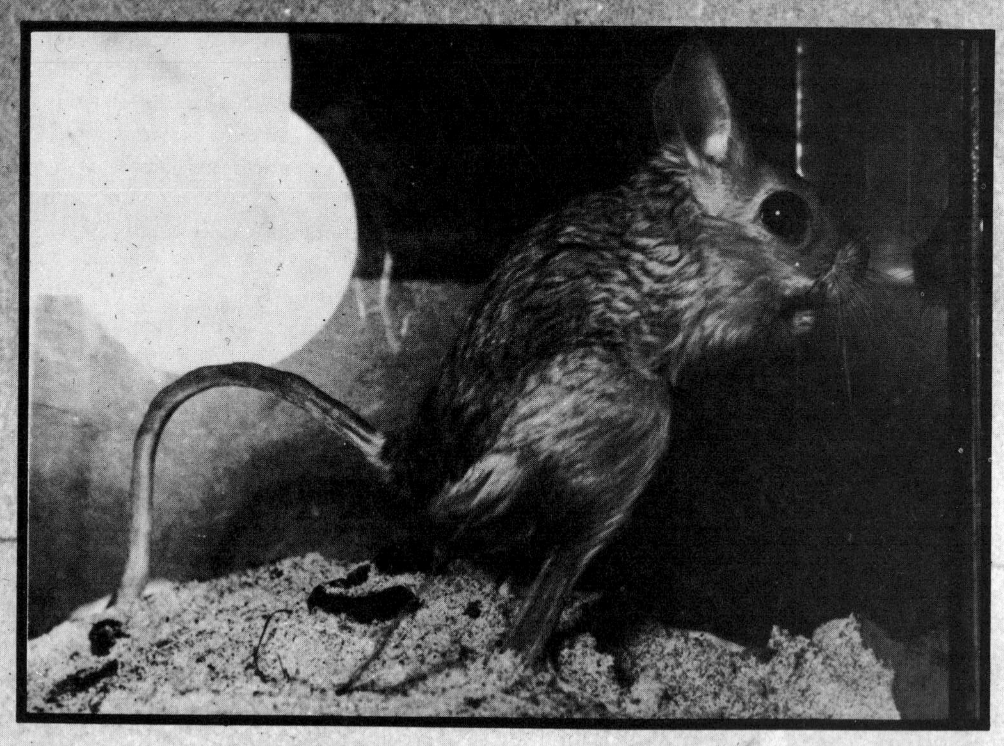

The Greater Egyptian Jerboa (Jaculus Orientalis).

Jock Campbell and Strafer Gott at Benghazi, December 29th, 1941.

The Desert Rat

During the last war the term "Desert Rat" was used to serve two purposes, one animal and one human.

The Animal Desert Rat
There are twenty-five species of jerboas alive today. Twenty-two of these are confined to Asia, but three occur in North Africa (The Egyptian Four-toed Jerboa, *Allactaga tetradactyla;* The Lesser Egyptian Jerboa, *Jaculus jaculus;* and The Greater Egyptian Jerboa — the "Desert Rat" of the Second World War — *Jaculus orientalis*). This species is found in the desert lands of Arabia. Like all jerboas it has pale, sandy-coloured fur, large eyes and ears, minute front legs and huge back feet.

Although only a few inches long it can jump as much as 6 feet in a single bound. The long balancing tail has a characteristic black and white tuft at its tip. This is no doubt used as some form of signalling device in jerboa sign language. When they are standing still the tail acts as a prop.

Despite the fact that they live in intensely hot desert regions, jerboas cannot endure high temperatures for any length of time. They survive by retreating during the day to their comparatively cool underground tunnels. The hot air is kept out by [illegible] plugging the entrance to the burrow. This is done in the early morning after their nightly food forays, before the arrival of the hot sun.

They sleep standing up, but rolled forward into a ball, with the ears folded down. They become rather cramped in this position and their first action on breaking through the entrance barrier is to roll and stretch on the sand. They clean themselves vigorously, grooming each of the large hind toes individually.*

The Human Desert Rat
Homo Sapiens, the human species of Desert Rat, was originally a member of the Mobile Division which, on 16th February 1940, was officially redesignated as the Seventh Armoured Division. The Jerboa was adopted as the Divisional sign and its soldiers became known as Desert Rats, a nickname which has stuck to every member of this famous Division and has subsequently been loosely attached to any member of the forces who served in the Western Desert.

Who better to symbolise the "Human Desert Rat" than two of the Division's greatest soldiers — Strafer Gott and Jock Campbell.

*Extract from *The Mammals* by Desmond Morris — reprinted by kind permission of the author and Hodder & Stoughton Ltd.

Setting the Scene for North Africa

The Western Desert has been somewhat cynically described as a place fit only for war. And yet the vast majority of British soldiers who lived and fought there found a strange fascination in the stark beauty of this barren landscape. Those who served "on the Blue" will never completely forget what it was like, so strong is the desert's hold on the minds of men. That famous explorer of deserts, Wilfred Thesiger, once wrote: "No man can live this life and emerge unchanged. He will carry, however faint, the imprint of the desert, the brand which marks the nomad; and he will have within him the yearning to return, weak or insistent according to his nature. For this cruel land can cast a spell which no temperate clime can match."*

The Bedouins say that the desert is a fortress to him who knows it, but a grave to him who does not. So perhaps we should do well to heed their warning and devote a few lines at least to describing the ground — in any event, didn't a famous general once say that time spent in reconnaissance is seldom wasted?

Running alongside the sparkling blue waters of the Mediterranean coast of Africa is a broad sandy plain with an average width of about 30 miles. It stretches from the Cairo-Alexandria road to the Cyrenaican frontier at Sollum. Here it narrows to a bare few hundred yards, where the escarpment almost

*_Arabian Sands_, Prologue.

reaches the sea. Here also in 1940 you would have seen the start of the rusted barbed-wire fence ("The Wire") which ran southwards along the frontier, down to the far-off wastes of the Great Sand Sea.

The escarpment is several hundred feet high, with few motorable tracks up it, one of the most important being the rough, winding path through Halfaya Pass about five miles south east of Sollum.

Beyond the escarpment to the south lies the desert proper, sand, stones and rock, with a few good tracks linking the occasional *bir* (Arabic — well), which are the only source of fresh water. Much of the area is sparsely covered with scrubby camel-thorn and supports little life beyond snakes, scorpions and other venomous insects, lizards, a few tough little rodents such as the now famous Jerboa, and the occasional black tents of the nomadic Bedouin. A compass is as vital in this terrain as it is to a sailor at sea. The climate ranges from scorching heat by day to extreme cold by night. The Khamsin, a hot, dry wind blowing from the south, whips up great clouds of dust and sand which finds its way into every crack and crevice, every eye, ear and nostril, until life is almost unbearable. Once experienced it is never forgotten, as this extract from a diary written by Kenneth Watt of 3 RHA vividly shows: "We had a very intense Khamsin wind with a heavy dust storm 'straight from the centre of Africa' today. I managed to rig up a tarpaulin against the windward side of the truck somehow or other, with two chaps, although it left us quite exhausted. We even managed to brew up some tea and force ourselves to eat a bit, before slithering under the truck to lie panting while the wretched thing vented its ill humour at us. The Khamsin is just like a blast from hell and completely saps all energy out of friend and foe alike. This particular one gave way in the evening to our customary off the sea breeze, and we were able to emerge and to remember that there was a war on".

It is easy to see why the Arabs say that after five days of it even murder can be excused!

If you were to have followed the coast road from Alexandria all those years ago and your work ticket had withstood the searching gaze of the MP on duty, then you would motor on past El Alamein, soon to take its place in history, stop perhaps for refreshment at the Noah's Ark NAAFI at El Daba, past Mersa Matruh where the Mobile Division was first assembled, and on westwards to "The Wire" and beyond it "up the Blue"!

Part of the Mobile Division at Charing Cross circa 1939.

Right: Directional signs.

Far right: This signboard was located on the outskirts of Alexandria.

Below: Looking down on the Quatarra Depression.

Below right: The "Noah's Ark" was a tented NAAFI canteen at El Daba circa 1942. There were also the "Ship Inn" at Mersa Matruh and the "Two Bees" at Buq Buq.

ROAD DISTANCE	MILES
SIDI BARRANI	95
BUQ BUQ	120
SALUM	145
BARDIA	165
TOBRUK	243
GAZALA	285
DERNA	358
BARCE	490
BENGHASI	550

E.W.J. 443

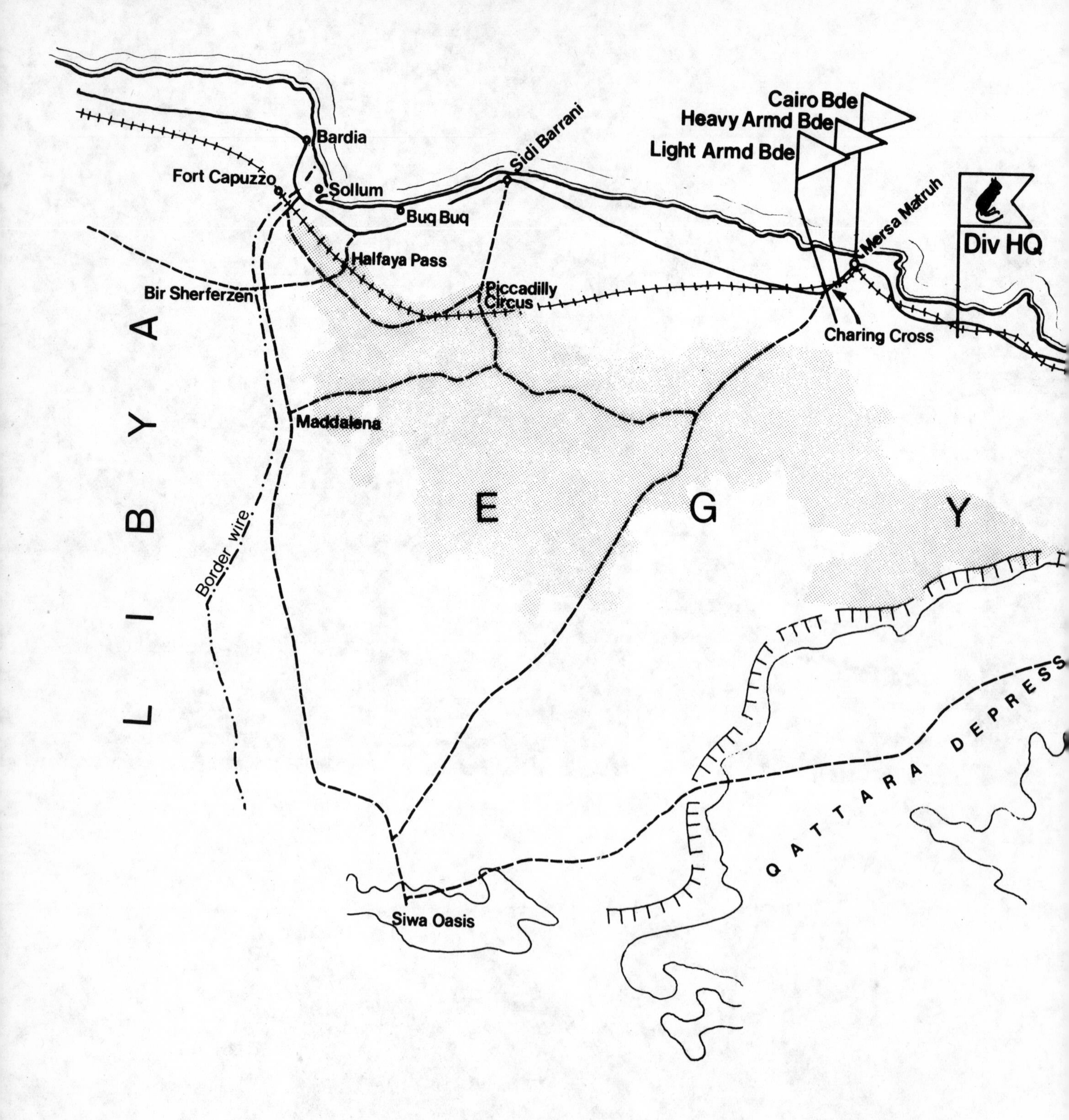

Cairo Bde
Heavy Armd Bde
Light Armd Bde
Div HQ
Bardia
Sidi Barrani
Fort Capuzzo
Sollum
Buq Buq
Mersa Matruh
Halfaya Pass
Bir Sherferzen
Piccadilly Circus
Charing Cross
L I B Y A
Maddalena
E G Y
Border wire
QATTARA DEPRESS
Siwa Oasis

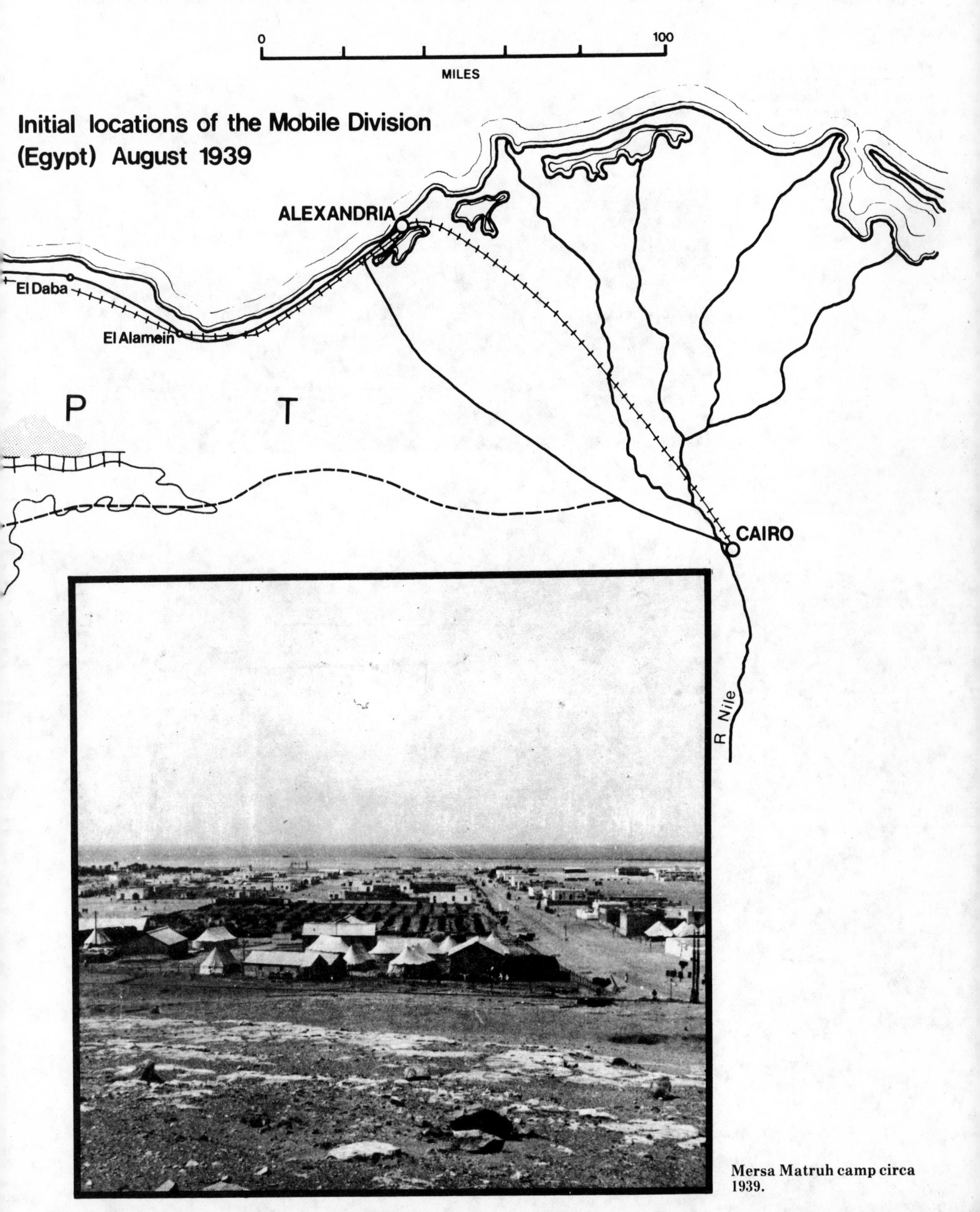

Mersa Matruh camp circa 1939.

Right: Sollum.

Below: Fort Capuzzo.

Far right: The Frontier Wire which ran along the Cyrenaican border and was known by all simply as "The Wire".

Above: Gate of Upper Bardia taken April 1942.

Above right: Eros statue at Piccadilly Circus.

Right: Siwa Oasis.

Far right: Sgm Jeff Orchard at a border post near Bir Sherferzen.

PICCADILLY
MR 610339
LIBIA
ليبيا
Nº 54

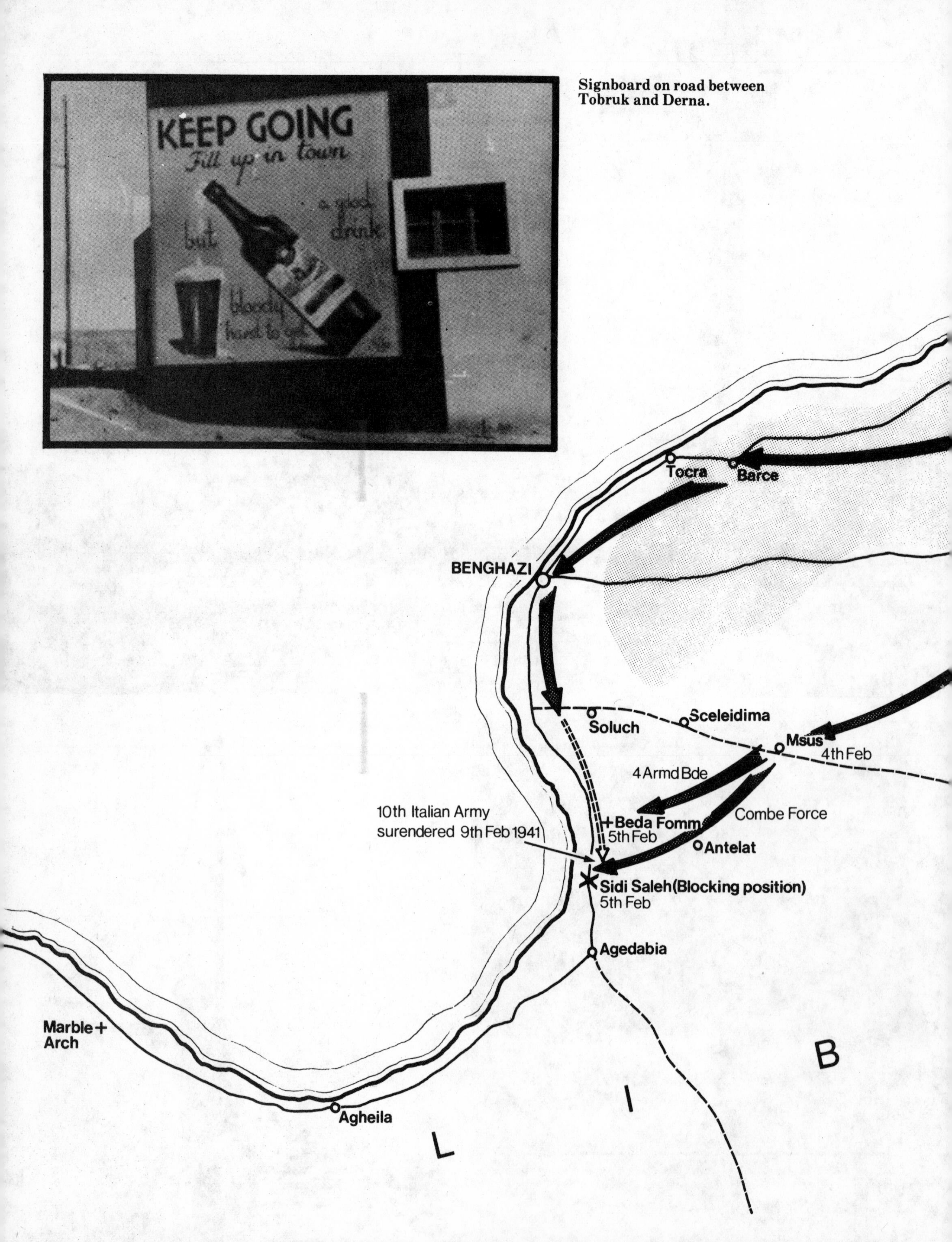

Signboard on road between Tobruk and Derna.

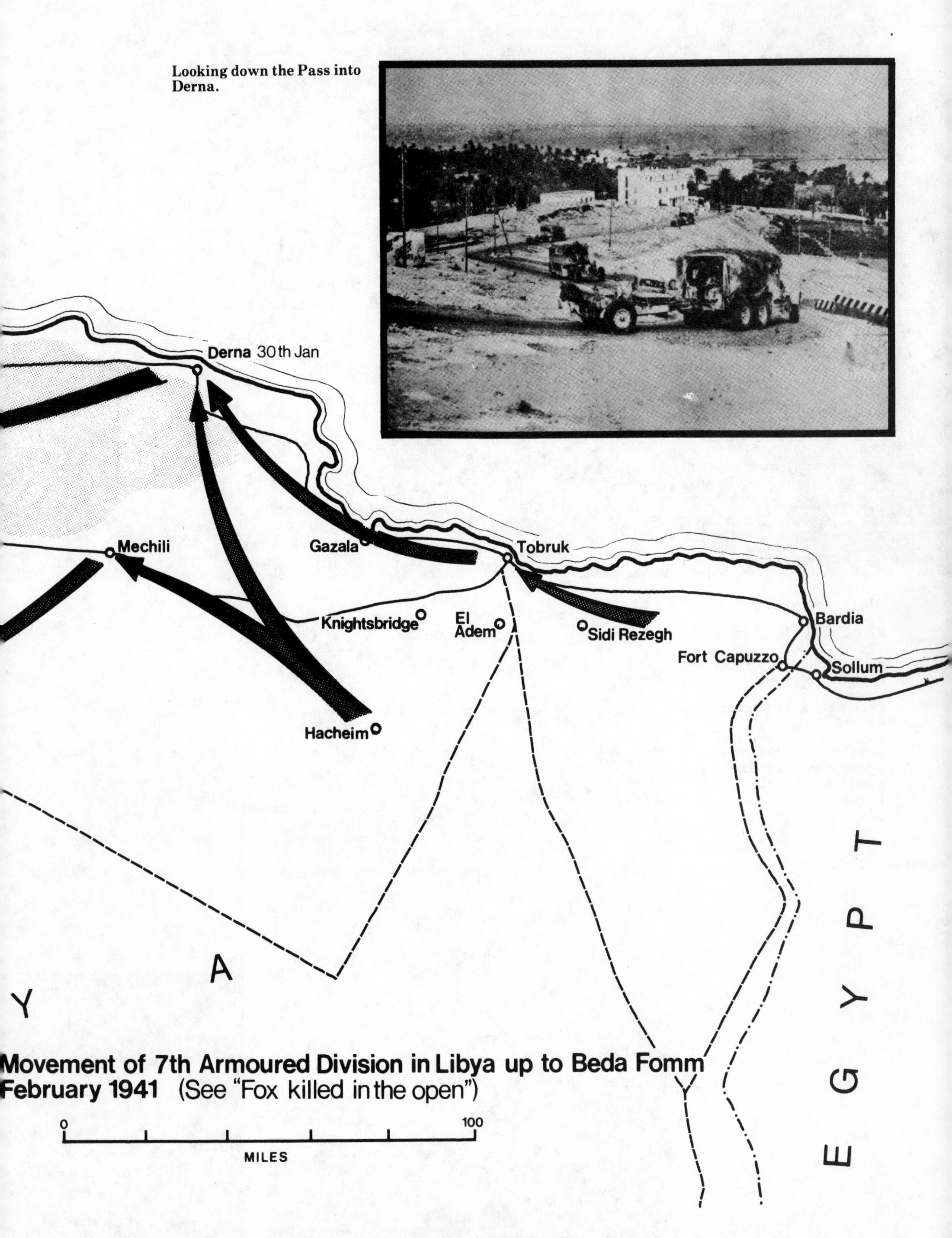

Looking down the Pass into Derna.

Movement of 7th Armoured Division in Libya up to Beda Fomm February 1941 (See "Fox killed in the open")

Above: Tocra Fort.

Above right: Benghazi.

Right: Wind pump at Beda Fomm.

Centre right: Dust storm approaching.

Far right: Marble Arch — which marked the halfway point between Tripoli and Egypt.

War imminent! 1 RTR crews being briefed, August 24th, 1939.

Prologue (The Mobile Division)

In 1938, the year of the Munich crisis, an officer was flown from England to Egypt on an important mission. "Create an Armoured Division" . . . those were his orders.*

In the Middle East at that time was the Cairo Cavalry Brigade, whose equipment by present standards would be considered prehistoric. There was a limited number of light tanks with worn-out tracks, and precious few replacements; an RASC Company scratched together from the Canal Area; and Blenheims from Iraq, 'the first we had ever had in Egypt'.

Such was the humble beginning. For it is not possible to write of the Seventh Armoured Division as we know it, and the Germans fear it, today without praising the name of the man whose enthusiasm and inspiration made it possible in the dark and dangerous pre-war months.

Major General P. C. S. Hobart was that man. He started from scratch. He had to create a new organisation and a new administration and he succeeded. He left behind him a Division fit to take the field in spite of limited equipment. It was ready, even before the start of the Wavell Campaign, to launch upon its magnificent fighting history.

*Extract from the *Egyptian Mail*, Wednesday 10th February 1943.

Below: The Mobile Division on parade near Mersa Matruh in 1939.

Bottom: Could this have been the original "Immobile Farce"?

The Cairo Cavalry Brigade, mentioned in the newspaper report above, was sent hurriedly to Mersa Matruh to form the Matruh Mobile Force, under the command of Brigadier H. E. Russell, on 17th September 1938. This Force initially comprised:

HQ Cairo Cavalry Brigade & Signals.
3rd Regiment, RHA, equipped with 3·7 inch Howitzers, towed by Dragons.
7th Queen's Own Hussars, with two squadrons of light tanks varying in Marks from III to VIB, but with no 5in ammunition for their guns.
8th King's Royal Irish Hussars, with Ford 15cwt pick-up trucks mounting Vickers-Berthier guns.
11th Hussars (Prince Albert's Own), with Rolls-Royce armoured cars and a few Morrises.
1st Royal Tank Regiment, newly arrived from England complete with 58 light tanks, but with little track mileage left and few new tracks available.
5 Company Royal Army Service Corps.
2/3 Field Ambulance, RAMC.
6th Royal Tank Regiment, equipped with old medium and light tanks, had been left behind in Cairo for internal security duties.
Air support for this motley collection of outdated vehicles and weaponry was equally prehistoric: 108 (AC) Squadron RAF, equipped with Audaxes, 80 (F) Squadron with Gladiators, and 45 (B) Squadron with Harts. A flight of Blenheims from Iraq also arrived, causing great excitement, as can be gathered from the newspaper report above!

This was the Mobile Force, known somewhat unkindly as the "Immobile Farce", which General Hobart came out from England to command. He was at the time working in the War Office, after having commanded the first (and only) Tank Brigade from 1931-35.

After a few exercises in the desert around Matruh the Force returned to Cairo, where they were joined by their first infantry element, the 1st Battalion, the King's Royal Rifle Corps, who had just arrived from Burma.

Hobo then set about the difficult task of organising from scratch the formation, train-

1 RTR leaving Cairo for Mersa Matruh during the war scare of 1938.

ing, equipment and administration of the Mobile Division (Egypt) and Abbassia District, as the Force was now called. He wrote: *

"I decided to concentrate on dispersion, flexibility and mobility . . . to try to get the Division and formations well extended, really handy and under quick control. To units unused to the speed and wide frontages made possible by mechanisation these matters presented considerable difficulties".

He had to fight against a great deal of obstruction, ignorance and even idleness, but his enthusiasm and determination never flagged. The difference between the Mobile Division of August 1939 and the "Immobile Farce" of only a year earlier was truly remarkable.

In addition to gaining much-needed expertise in the art of mobile armoured warfare, the Division also received some new equipment. 7th Hussars were now complete with three squadrons of light tanks; 8th Hussars had begun to receive light tanks from 7th Hussars and 6 RTR to replace their Ford 15cwt pick-ups; 3 RHA now had half 37mm anti-tank guns and half 25 pounders, and a 25 pounder battery of 4 RHA had been attached to the Division to provide extra gunner support; 11th Hussars had received more Morris armoured cars and 6 RTR their first ten A9 Cruiser tanks.

After war with Germany had broken out the Division went out on another series of exercises under Hobo's watchful eye, returning to Cairo once again in November 1939. It was then that Hobo left, his place being taken by Major-General Michael O'Moore Creagh. General Hobart's spirit was to remain with the Division long after his departure, and many times his views were quoted: "Hobo always used to say . . .". The Division would later prove what a truly magnificent job he had done.

More changes followed his departure; the Heavy Brigade became 4th Armoured Brigade, and the Light Brigade the 7th Armoured Brigade; the Pivot Group became officially known as the Support Group and was enlarged by the arrival of the 2nd Battalion, the Rifle Brigade, from Palestine. 3 RHA was converted into an anti-tank regiment and 4 RHA complete joined the Division, plus 2 RTR and various other units from U.K. The Mobile Division was officially redesignated the 7th Armoured Division on 16th February 1940.

War with Italy now became a distinct

* *Armoured Crusader* by Kenneth Macksey.

24

possibility and the Division moved light forces up to the frontier wire. On the night of 10 June 1940 war was officially declared against Italy and the complete Division moved up to the frontier area the following day.

Tanks of 1 RTR passing through an Egyptian town on their way to the desert, May 30th, 1940.

Divisional Order of Battle in November 1940
At the start of the desert campaigns 7th Armoured Division was organised as follows:

4th Armoured Brigade (Brigadier J. R. L. Caunter)
7H
2 RTR (less one sqn plus one sqn 3 H)
6 RTR
Bty 3 RHA
7th Armoured Brigade (Brigadier H. E. Russell)
3 H (less one sqn plus one sqn 2 RTR)
8 H
1 RTR
Bty 3 RHA
Support Group (Brigadier W. H. E. Gott)
4 RHA
1 KRRC
2 RB
Divisional Troops
11 H
3 RHA (less two btys)
106 RHA
2 (Cheshire) Fd Sqn, RE
141 Fd Pk Tp, RE
5, 58, 65 and 550 Coys RASC
2/3 and 3/3 Cavalry Field Ambulances, RAMC
7 Armoured Division Workshops and Recovery Section and 1, 2 and 3 Light Repair Sections, RAOC.

At this time one company 1 KRRC with a troop of D Bty 3 RHA formed the garrison at Siwa Oasis, and the Première Compagnie d'Infanterie de Marine, the vanguard of the Free French Forces of the Western Desert, was serving with the Support Group.

The magnificent reputation for fighting and for administrative efficiency which the Division gained later was based, to a large degree, upon the lessons they had to learn the hard way in those early days. They were short of everything from desert-worthy vehicles to radio sets and compasses, in fact everything necessary to fight effectively in desert conditions. There were however two commodities which they had in abundance. These were a unique talent for improvisation and a fine Divisional spirit; with these, as you will read later, they were able to take on and to defeat an entire Army.

Far top left: Light tanks of the 8th Hussars in their tank park at Helmiya, June 5th, 1940.

Above left: The original type of Armoured Command Vehicle used by Division Headquarters.

Above: 1 RTR on manoeuvres during the spring of 1939

Far centre left: A 2 pdr anti tank gun at Matruh.

Far bottom left: A crew of a 7H light tank washing cooking pots in the sea near Mersa Matruh

Left: Troops lined up on the quayside after disembarking, August 27th, 1940.

Divisional HQ

In the early days Divisional Headquarters was divided into two main groups or echelons — Advanced and Rear. Advanced HQ, later known as Main HQ, contained only those staff who were absolutely necessary for the control and command of the Division during operations; in other words, the GOC, his 'G' and 'I' staffs, artillery and engineer advisers, together with the crews of the communications and protection vehicles. Before the Command vehicles were armoured, two armoured cars were also included in this group, so that a Battle HQ (later called Tactical HQ) could be formed and all unarmoured vehicles withdrawn when action was imminent. The bodies of the original command vehicles were made of 5-ply wood with a zinc covering. When they were sent back to Cairo to be armoured, the wood was taken off, angle iron was clamped on to the chassis and South African boiler plate then bolted on with thousands of 3/16" bolts. Consequently there were myriad bolt ends sticking through the armour — a most uncomfortable arrangement for those inside!

Rear Division contained the rest of Divisional HQ, that is to say everything that was not required for immediate operational control. The Heads of the Services (CRASC, ADMS, SOME, etc) worked here under the AA & QMG. Their duties were mainly concerned with the control and direction of the administration of the Division. Rear HQ was usually located some distance behind Advanced HQ, where they could work free from risk of enemy ground interference.

When on the move Advanced HQ moved in groups, viz:
Three Cruiser Tanks — Protective Detachment.
Armoured Car — Navigator.

Group 'A'
ACV 1 — Command ACV
DR
ACV 2 — Intelligence ACV
ACV 3 — Rear Link
Scout Car

Group 'B' (160 yards behind)
Cruiser Tank — GOC's Charger
DR
Cruiser Tank — 'G' Charger
Armoured Car — 'Q' Charger
Scout Car

Group 'C' (160 yards behind)
ACV 4 — Spare ACV
Scout Car
Three Ford PUs — Liaison Officers

Group 'D' (160 yards behind)
Office Truck — G Office
Office Truck — Signals Office
DR
Ford PU — Frontier Force

When stationary they formed a scattered leaguer, closing into a tight box formation by night.

Naturally the organisation and size of Div HQ altered as the war progressed, and there is little point in explaining the various changes which took place. Suffice it to say that ACV1 remained the nerve centre of Div HQ and that the split between operations and administration continued to be the main dividing line between Main and Rear. The collection of photographs on these pages show examples of the vehicles and staff of Tactical, Main and Rear Div HQ taken during the desert battles from 1939 to 1943.

A typical Rear Div "brew up".

Far left: ACV 1 — Nerve centre of Div HQ.

Left: Col (later Maj Gen) G. W. Richards, GSO1 of the Division, outside ACV1 on Christmas Day 1941.

Far centre left: Part of Div HQ staff in early 1941 — L to R — Michael Creighton (IO), Brig Williams (CRA), Peter Hordern (G3 Int), Gerald Grosvenor (LO), Charles Gairdner (GSO1) and Guy Peyton (GSO2).

Far bottom left: The crew of one of the Div HQ protection tanks.

Below centre left: Crew of ACV 2 (Int) taken on Christmas Day 1941 outside Benghazi. L to R — Driver, Williams, Ashworth, Marshall, Paxton and Lynch.

Below bottom left: Members of Rear Div HQ in various desert wear — January 1943.

Below: "Tac Uncle", the Col AQ (later Brig) Charles Turner on top of his "charger".

Above: Major General Sir Percy Hobart, KBE, CB, DSO, MC, late Royal Tank Regiment, (Commanded, September 3rd-November 16th, 1939) Hobo was responsible for the initial training of the Mobile Division and was thus the architect of much of the Dert Rat's greatness. He was later to do the same for both 11th and 79th Armoured Divisions. As Liddell Hart said in his history of the RTR in his book *(The Tanks* page 347) "To have moulded the two best British armoured divisions of the war was an outstanding achievement, but Hobart made it a 'hat trick' by his subsequent training of the specialised 79th Armoured Division, the decisive factor on D-Day".

Above right: Major General Sir Michael O'More Creagh, KBE, MC, late 15th/19th The King's Royal Hussars. (Commanded November 16th, 1939-September 3rd, 1941). General Dickie Creagh led the Division throughout its earliest triumphs against the Italians, including the Desert Rats first major battle at Sidi Barrani in 1940 and his tenure of command was the longest during the war. It was he who took the bold decision to send a 'Flying Column' (Combe Force) south west across the virtually unmapped Libyan desert in order to cut off the Italians at Sidi Saleh. This daring and imaginative stroke resulted in the surrender of the entire 10th Italian Army.

Below right: Lt-General W. H. E. Gott, CB, DSO, MC, late The King's Royal Rifle Corps (Commanded September 3rd, 1941-February 6th, 1942). One of the greatest Divisional Commanders, 'Strafer' Gott began his career with the Division as its first wartime GS01, later he commanded the Support Group. After commanding the Division, he went on to become Commander 13 Corps and, in August 1942, was appointed to command the Eighth Army. Tragically, whilst flying back to Cairo from the forward area a few days later, his aircraft was attacked by a German fighter and shot down. General Gott survived the crash, but was killed by machine gun fire whilst rescuing others from the wreckage.

Below right: Major General J. C. Campbell, VC, DSO, MC, late Royal Horse Artillery (commanded February 6th-February 23rd). Jock Campbell was perhaps the most famous of all the Desert Rats. His name was a byword for courage throughout the Division. He was awarded the Victoria Cross at Sidi Rezegh whilst commanding the Support Group. It was he who conceived the idea of forming Mobile Columns to harass the Italians, which were called 'Jock Columns' after him. He was killed in February 1942 when his staff car skidded and overturned on a clay road near Halfaya Pass. He is seen here chatting to the C in C after being presented with his VC. For the period immediately following General Campbell's death, Brigadier A. H. Gatehouse commanded the division until March, 1942.

Bottom right: Lt-General Sir Frank Messervy, CB, DSO, late Indian Army, (commanded March 9th,-June 19th 1942). He took over the Division after commanding 4th Indian Division 1941/42. A great character, he tended not to shave in battles, growing on occasions a sizeable beard. This led to the Division being known on the radio as 'The Bearded Men'. Another of his idiosyncrasies was the insistence on cleaning his teeth after breakfast, whatever the circumstances. Peter Vaux recalls—"Early one morning I was out on a reconnaissance with him and we stopped for breakfast. Before we had finished we were alarmed by the approach of a troop of Germany armoured cars which opened fire. However, we had to wait with bullets spattering round us while the General finished cleaning his teeth before we were allowed to beat a retreat. He had a

name for rather reckless courage and was always in the thick of things himself". He went on to command IV Corps in Burma. For the period June 19th-September 14th, 1942 Major General J. M. L. Renton, CB, DSO, OBE, late the Rifle Brigade, took command. Callum Renton, known affectionately as 'Wingy' due to the loss of an arm was commanding 2RB in the Division during the battle of Sidi Saleh in 1941 and later commanded the Support Group 7th Motor Brigade, during the Gazala battles. In spite of his varied and distinguished career his love of soldiering with the Regiment was paramount. One of his contemporaries wrote in his obituary, published by kind permission of RHQ, The Royal Green Jackets, "He taught me a lot; how to look at life and the world as though it was a pastime, but one that should be pursued to a certain level of excellence."

Right: Field Marshal The Lord Harding of Petherton, GCB, CBE, DSO, MC, late Somerset Light Infantry (commanded September 14th, 1942-January 19th, 1943.). Field Marshal Harding took over command of the Division after serving as Chief of Staff to General O'Connor and his successors in the earliest days in the desert. He was a fearless and brilliant commander, responsible for the Division's breakout at El Alamein. On the escarpment near Tarhuna he was sitting on top of Brigadier Custance's tank discussing the situation when a salvo of shells landed nearby and he was badly wounded. Fortunately he recovered and continued a distinguished career, both during the war and afterwards, becoming C in C Far East 1949/51, C in C BAOR 1951/52, CIGS 1952/53 and Governor and C in C Cyrus 1955/57. John Harding possessed great physical and intellectual courage, was strong willed and persistent. Montgomery called him 'that little tiger'. For the period following General Harding's wounding, Brigadier G. P. B. Roberts commanded the Division until January 24th, 1943.

Above: General Sir George Erskine, GCB, KBE, DSO, late The King's Royal Rifle Corps (Commanded January 24th, 1943-August 4th, 1944). 'Bobbie' Erskine commanded the Division during its memorable advance from Tripoli to Tunis, throughout their short campaign in Italy and launched them into North West Europe. He was a man of integrity and great determination, with considerable physical and moral courage. Later on in his service he was appointed C in C East Africa during the Mau Mau rebellion and, on his retirement, became Lieutenant Governor and C in C Jersey.

The Bearded Man Escapes

There can have been few, if any, other Divisional Commanders in the last war who, together with most of their operational staff, were captured, escaped, walked through enemy-dominated territory and were in command again, with their headquarters functioning efficiently enough for "business as usual", all in the space of less than forty-eight hours! That is what happened to General Messervy during the Gazala battle in May 1942. The story of this dramatic event is told here by Brigadier Peter Vaux and Major Donald Reid, who were at the time both members of Main HQ 7th Armoured Division. Peter Vaux, the GSO3 (Intelligence) on Armoured Command Vehicle 2, begins the story:

"During April and for most of May 1942 the Division had been training quite intensively with some of the new equipment — such as Grant tanks — and developing numerous improved command techniques. Despite our proximity to the enemy this was a very quiet and peaceful period, enhanced by a carpet of wild flowers which flourished for a few days in the puddles left by the winter rains, before withering in the hot springtime winds which began in May. Nevertheless, for a week or two one drove about the desert in a scent of wild thyme as the wheels crushed these little plants. We received many visitors — the Duke of Gloucester went round the Division and even Cecil Beaton (disguised as a Flight Lieutenant) came out to take some PR photos of us. The French at Bir Hacheim found a means of cooking the desert snails, and in 4th Armoured Brigade some of the crews found that the CO_2 fire extinguishers in the Grant would ice the remaining beer which we had brought up from Delta.

As May advanced however, tension increased daily. The railway was being pushed forward to Tobruk, as was a water pipeline intended to provide almost unlimited water into the middle of the Corps area. Every few miles cement-filled barrels were put up in the desert, painted with a number and the map reference, and new maps were produced on which were marked these barrels. On every side it appeared that we were preparing for an attack.

For us in the 'I' Staff, whose map showed the enemy positions and strength in detail and our own troops in outline only, the signs all pointed to a similar state of preparation on the Axis side. They too were receiving new tanks and carrying out training, and their reconnaissance aircraft were overhead daily. We were able to predict that they had two possible lines of attack: a drive through the centre of the minefield, with the hard slogging that this would entail, or a sweep round the south of Hacheim and into our left flank. The operational staff were inclined to favour the former, on the grounds that a wide sweep would entail the enemy stopping to refuel south of Hacheim, but the 'I' Staff preferred the latter, based on Rommel's known preference for the indirect approach. In the event the 'I' Staff were proved right, but Div HQ prepared for both. A notable item in these preparations was the digging of a vast sloping hole, into which Armoured Command Vehicle 1 (the nerve centre of the Division) was driven and covered with camouflage nets so that it entirely disappeared. At about the same time all the ACVs had welded to their very distinctive roof a metal superstructure covered with hessian which, even at a close distance, transformed them into ten-ton lorries. There is no doubt that when later the headquarters was over-run the Germans, because of this disguise, did not realise the importance of the vehicles they had captured. Indeed, after his capture Donald Reid, the GSO3, overheard a German officer say, "This man was in one of those cargo lorries which was burnt out". Those of us who escaped owed the fact that we were not more actively pursued to this simple conjuring trick — which had in fact been devised by Major Jasper Maskelyne, the noted former peacetime illusionist and wartime camouflage officer. For the time being however, we were delighted that the modification made our vehicles cooler and provided extra storage space for our kit.

About 25 May the Free French picked up on the southern flank an Arab and his wife, the former riding a donkey and the woman walking behind; the French were suspicious, on the truly Gallic grounds that the woman was ill-favoured and much older than her alleged husband. Suspicious ourselves, we interrogated this man for some hours in both Arabic and Italian, of which he seemed to know a few words, but he stuck firmly to his story that he and his wife had been ill-treated

2nd Battalion The Rifle Brigade at Sidi Saleh in February 1941. The picture depicts the surrender of the 10th Italian Army soon after dawn on 9th February 1941./*Reproduced by kind permission of the Managing Trustees of the Royal Green Jackets from the original oil painting by Terence Cuneo RGI.*

by the Italians and were moving to the more friendly British sector. The more we talked to him the more doubtful we became of his tale, but were quite unable to break it. I felt sure that he was an Italian in disguise and was just about to strip him naked to check whether he was brown all over when a noted Arabist, Major Jarvis, chanced to drop in. On being told what was afoot, he laughed and said, "Go ahead, but I am quite sure he will turn out to be brown from head to foot". And so it proved, but then Jarvis turned to me and said, "Well, you've got him now, haven't you?". I couldn't see this at all, so Jarvis turned to the man and asked him in rapid Arabic, "You and your wife have been travelling on foot and by donkey from well to well, all the way from Benghazi, and have been in the desert for a month? Then how come your underclothes have been freshly laundered in the last 24 hours?" With that the man broke down and confessed to being a half caste Italian-Arab spy who had only met his "wife" the night before, when they were both set down in the desert from trucks. He had come to spy on the positions of our tanks, and we might well have shot him for it, but instead we sent him back to Army Headquarters where they used him for a long time as a source of information.

On 26 May there was a tremendous sandstorm, which approached us very slowly in the form of a 500-foot wall several miles long and then engulfed us for several hours. It was awe-inspiring and sinister — but how sinister we did not realise, for it was almost certainly formed from dust raised by the Axis tanks as they deployed for their imminent attack. I viewed it with particular distaste, for we were now entering the period of maximum probability — based on the state of the moon — for this attack, and I had on 27 May the two previous years lost all my possessions — first at Dunkirk and then when my tank was burnt out at Halfaya Pass. I wondered what was to happen on 27 May 1942, but would never really have believed that I was destined to lose all I had for the third successive time on the same date — as was indeed the case.

Donald Reid and I shared a peculiar edifice we had erected from Italian groundsheets and wireless aerials which we called "The Chateau", where we slept and kept our personal belongings; to this I retired at about 4am on the 27th, after doing duty for the first half of the night on the main positional control on ACV 1. Donald took over for the rest of the night. Although it had become plain from engine noises and floating flares that the enemy was on the move, nothing had been seen by our patrols and there was no scent that he was making anything more than a feint. In any case, something went very wrong with our wireless that night and no information at all reached either of us or 4th Armoured Brigade from the armoured car screen — who, we were to learn later, had been repeatedly reporting a large enemy force refuelling south of Bir Hacheim.

About 8am Donald came running to the Chateau calling out, "Wake up, the RAF report 300 tanks and 1,000 vehicles south of Bir Hacheim and we are moving in ten minutes." There was no time to pack up the Chateau, as I had to run to my own ACV 2, where my crew were already tightening the camouflage and the big aerial. This steel monster contained all our intelligence paraphernalia, including the maps and charts of the enemy and two large No 9 radios with separate receivers and transmitters. All around us was a sense of orderly confusion as some forty or fifty vehicles prepared to move.

ACV 1 had the blue flag up for an immediate move but was quite unable to do so itself, as the wheels churned uselessly trying to heave its 14 tons out of the hole which had been dug for it. Only when another ACV gave it a tow did it become mobile. By that time, and as we moved off to the west, shells were falling amongst us and Grant tanks of 4th Armoured Brigade were withdrawing through our column. Our own protective troop of light tanks had been sent off to the south and was in action many miles away. As we steamed away at best speed the northerly breeze sent a wall of dust from our wheels billowing out to the right. I was sitting on the roof of the ACV while the others were below sorting our maps and radio headsets, when suddenly there was a rattling of machine guns and thudding of 20mm cannon and a column of German armoured cars and half-tracks dashed through the concealing dust and were amongst us, firing in all directions. A number of vehicles stopped, clearly hit, and amongst these was ACV 1, from which I saw some figures jump a moment before it burst into flames. It seemed that the General and all the 'G' staff were being captured. An armoured car drove alongside and the commander shouted to me, "Put your hands up and stop!" I dived inside and slammed the hatch, calling for the Bren gun to be disinterred

'Pte' Messervy with his GSO1 and GSO2 shortly after reaching our lines following his dramatic escape.

from the heap of bedding, just as a hail of machine gun bullets bounced off our steel sides — deceived by our appearance, the Germans had not used their armour-piercing cannon. When the clamour stopped I climbed out again with the Bren, but we seemed to have driven clear of the battle, for behind us I could see a lot of smoke and shooting. There were with us a number of vehicles, some not our own, and it suddenly dawned on me that if anyone was commanding the 7th Armoured Division at that moment it must be me, so I hoisted the blue flag and the other vehicles converged on my own. We drove on a few miles, and then began a nightmare struggle to establish communications with the brigades — all of whom were heavily engaged with the enemy and had no time for us — and with Corps Headquarters. The latter seemed to us in our distraught state to be maddeningly obtuse in understanding our veiled language, for we dared not use the codes which we felt sure the Germans must have captured with the Command Vehicle. In fact, as I have said, they never realised that they had overrun a Divisional Headquarters and so did not search the captured vehicles as they should have done. Eventually Corps

Headquarters grasped the situation and we successfully passed the command of our various brigades direct to them. Next day some of us went into the storage depots at Tobruk and succeeded in obtaining enough vehicles and men to put the headquarters into working order again, pending the arrival of a new General and staff. No sooner had we completed this apparently academic task when to our astonishment we were rejoined by General Messervy and his 'G' staff — and at once were in business again as a Division. How this came about is best told by Donald Reid".

Donald Reid continues the story:

"At first light the Indian Motor Brigade reported that they had been overrun by tanks, then silence. Shortly afterwards loud gunfire was heard, and the ACV was hit, the driver sitting behind me being killed, and myself slightly wounded, by flying metal. I opened the door and told the General that vehicles all round were in flames, and that a German tank had its guns trained on us some 100 yards away. We quickly piled out on to the ground and set light to our codes and any other documents we could lay our hands on. Meanwhile the battle swept on and over us, and we saw that our small protective unit of armoured cars had been wiped out.

We then cut off the General's badges and when the Germans came up I was attended to by one of their doctors, who remarked that the man next door to me looked rather old for war. I replied that he was my batman — but it was of course the General minus his badges of rank. We were then told to pile into captured British vehicles with other prisoners, and instead of going back westwards, we joined the German columns moving east. Our truck was driven by a young German, and we discussed the possibility of knocking him on the head at an appropriate moment, taking over the vehicle and attempting to escape. At this point the whole column came under heavy artillery fire, and in the smoke and confusion we stopped and the driver flung himself flat on the ground. This was our chance, and we scattered. The last time I saw the General he was running hard, weaving all the time, whilst a German fired at him with a Schmeisser. My driver/batman and I leapt into a handy slit trench and feigned dead to passing enemy troops.

Night fell and the battle had moved on east, so we decided to walk in the same direction and to hide up later. We found a jerrycan, filled it with water from the radiator of a destroyed vehicle, and walked for several hours by the stars. Before dawn came we stumbled on an old well, and decided to make it our hiding place for the next few hours, until we could see the state of play. Soon after first light we saw some vehicles a mile or so away, approaching in our direction. They turned out to be a troop of the Royals, and on learning who we were, they sent us back, where we shortly joined up with the rest of the Headquarters staff and learned of their story since leaving us the day before".

Reconnaissance

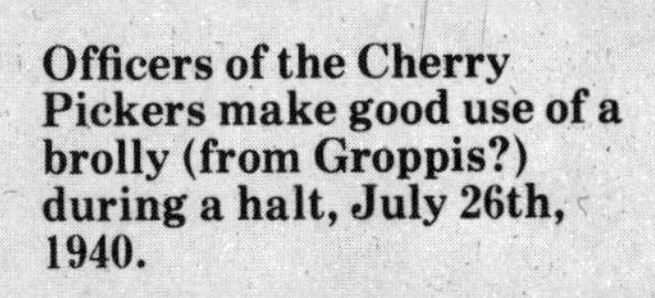

Officers of the Cherry Pickers make good use of a brolly (from Groppis?) during a halt, July 26th, 1940.

The main role of the Divisional armoured car regiment in the desert was to provide distant reconnaissance, anything up to fifty miles from the main body of the division. This difficult and dangerous work had to be undertaken in any direction — to the front, flanks and on some occasions even to the rear. There could never be any gaps of time or space in the reconnaissance screen, as a constant flow of information was essential. To meet this continuing requirement, the regiment was split into a large number of small, independent and widely dispersed patrols, each capable of operating on its own for extended periods. A proportion of each squadron was however not initially deployed, but held centrally as a reserve to meet unexpected situations and to allow time, in theory anyway, for much needed vehicle maintanance.

Initially armoured car regiments consisted of three reconnaissance squadrons, each of five troops of three armoured cars, although on occasions a fourth recce squadron was added. The armoured car troops acted as the eyes and ears of the recce screen whilst the rest of the regiment had control and supporting roles. Radio communications were its life blood, so that the unceasing flow of vital information could be passed back quickly to higher formation commanders. At the beginning of hostilities the armoured car regiment was equipped with a mixture of Rolls Royce and Morris armoured cars. Later the Marmon-Herrington, a South African-built armoured car, was issued.

Early in 1942 armoured car regiments were again re-equipped, this time with Humber armoured cars. The Humber was a vast improvement on the Marmon-Herrington, whose coffin-shaped body had given many an armoured car crew uneasy thoughts. It had better armour, and there was a neat turret with two useful guns, a 7·92mm and a 15mm Besa. The main drawback was an underpowered engine with a life of only 3,000 miles. Each car was manned by a crew of three and three Humbers made up a troop. Later one of the Humbers was replaced by a Daimler armoured car, mounting a 2 pdr quick-firing gun, probably the best armoured car of those so far issued.

Whatever the type of vehicle and equipment, the task of providing a full-time reconnaissance screen was an onerous one. With two squadrons manning a line of observation there would be six troops forward, spread across the desert some two or three miles apart, according to ground and visibility. Troops of three cars thus operated in small isolated units, separated by miles of desert from their neighbours and from squadron headquarters. Each car was self-contained, with its own ammunition, rations, water and bedding etc., and each crew had to work as a team. The regimental frontage was therefore about 15 to 20 miles. Squadron headquarters and reserve troops might be some 5 miles

Below: The Eyes of the Division — Cherry Pickers stand to at dawn in the desert.

Below right: A Marmon-Herrington of B Squadron, the Royals. These cars, built in South Africa, had only light armour and mounted a Boyes Anti-tank rifle and a Vickers ·303 machine gun. Although not ideal this armoured car was fast, reliable and comparatively roomy.

behind this forward line. 10 miles further back would be Regimental headquarters, with the reserve squadron in the same area. Another 10 to 15 miles back again was the Regimental Echelon leaguer, well spread out. Here lived the Supply Echelons, together with the Regimental fitters, ambulances and other vehicles carrying spare kit and equipment.

The Supply Echelons were divided into two parts and while one part was going back anything up to 20 miles to replenish at an RASC Supply Point, the other moved up to Regimental headquarters and to the forward squadrons to deliver petrol, ammunition and rations. Ideally these moves took place by night, with both elements returning to their own leaguer area before first light whenever possible. As it was normal practice to draw two days' rations at a time, both echelons would then get a day for the maintenance of their vehicles. The following day their tasks would be reversed and they would go out to replenish or deliver their loads.

Not only did the echelons have to cover great distances, often over very bad going which could reduce vehicle speeds to 2-3 miles an hour, but they also had to find their way alone across uncharted deserts with poor maps and cope with the problems of casualties from breakdowns and enemy action. Echelon commaders had a difficult and responsible task at all times, but it was particularly hard when the battle was fluid, with meeting points for replenishment and regimental positions changing constantly. During such phases the day for maintenance was seldom possible and echelons were often still trying to contact the Regiment far into the night, with the aid of tracer ammunition and sometimes Verey lights. Vehicle lights could seldom be used and it can easily be imagined how a clear moonlight night was welcomed for those.long journeys.

As has been explained, the job of the armoured car regiment was to reconnoitre ahead and to the flanks, fulfilling the historic role of light cavalry. Its speed and ability to operate over a far greater radius of action than anything else in the Division made it the ideal unit to give early warning of the strength and direction of any advancing enemy columns. But when war was declared General Creagh wanted the Division's single armoured car regiment to do more than just act as an early warning screen. "You are to dominate the frontier between Fort Capuzzo and Fort Maddalena", he told Colonel John Combe, Commanding Officer of the 11th Hussars, "and delay any Italian advance to the East". The armoured cars were to destroy the frontier wire wherever they could, penetrate into Italian territory, and if possible harass enemy communications along the Fort Capuzzo-Bardia-Tobruk road.

So it was that the Cherry Pickers were the first troops of the Division into action, on the night of June 11th 1940. A Squadron, operating between Maddalena and Sidi Omar, crossed the frontier at three points, cut enemy telephone lines and put out ambushes on the main tracks. B Squadron, with half its strength already committed to the protection of the most forward British supply dump at Hamra, had been allotted similar tasks on the smaller frontage between Sidi Omar and Fort Capuzzo. There was a series of brisk little actions that first night, the most spectacular being at Fort Capuzzo where the garrison of two officers and fifty others ranks surrendered to a Cherry Picker patrol of B Squadron.

By morning all patrols were safely back across the frontier, having suffered no casualties. No less than seventy bewildred Italians were on their way back to POW cages in Egypt, protesting sadly that Mussolini had forgotten to tell them that war had been declared!

That first night set the pattern for the type of active patrolling which the Eleventh carried out over the next few months. But all patrols did not have the dash and excitement of these first encounters. Here is a description of life behind the lines in Cyrenaica, written by one of the officers of A Squadron 11th Hussars:

"The days passed slowly. Patrols went out at dawn. Then we settled down to cook and eat our breakfast. We all lived with our crews. After breakfast I usually erected a bivouac in the rear of the armoured car. This consisted of an Italian cape, which we had found in Maddalena, tied to the car and pegged to the ground. It served to protect one from the sun during the heat of the day. After that I usually went to the Humber touring car, which was always parked about 100 yards away, and there attended to any correspondence which had been brought up by the echelon the night before. I sometimes walked round the one or two troops which I had with me in reserve, but one did not like to go too far from one's guns and armoured cars in case the horns sounded, to indicate that aircraft had been seen or heard. Any movement or running about to get back to one's car was liable to be seen. The cars were so well covered with camel thorn that, provided there was no movement, aircraft could pass quite close without spotting our position. Soon after 9am most days we had a visit from "Big Barney", a three-engined Italian bomber. He usually flew along the Trigh el Abd and sometimes returned a few miles south of it.

Patrols reported on the wireless at half-past every clock hour. 'Vic Ack' means nothing to report. 'Hello, Johnny three — Johnny calling — report. Johnny to Johnny three, over'. 'Hello Johnny — Johnny three answering. Vick Ack. Johnny three to Johnny over'. 'Johnny O.K., Off'.

At about 12·45pm we usually ate a cold midday meal of onions, cheese, army biscuits and tea, or else of bully and army biscuits. After lunch we usually slept or read till about 4pm and then I stripped and washed and probably also washed my shirt, trousers and socks. The evening meal consisted of bully

An 11th Hussars armoured car towing a captured Italian CV35 carrier.

stew and tinned fruit, or pancake and sausages with army biscuits, or sometimes just bread and tea.

As soon as that was over, we usually arranged to get one of the operators of the reserve Troop to tune in to the overseas service of the BBC. There was then just time for a whisky and water before starting, at about 8pm, to return some five miles to our refilling station, where we slept the night.

I usually tried to reach the night leaguer position just as the sun was dropping below the horizon. This gave just sufficient time before dark to get the bedding unrolled and to get as many Troops as we had with us filled up with petrol and water from B1 Echelon.

The evenings were very pleasant and cool. Moving to night leaguer, we kept a very sharp look-out in case anyone was waiting for us. Sometimes after we had arrived a light was reported in a direction from which we did not expect our cars or transport. Then I usually sent a car or Troop round the leaguer position to see if anyone was about. We were about forty miles into enemy territory and about forty miles from any of our own troops, so one could never relax vigilance.

It was maddening having to wait for the arrival of the echelon. Sometimes they arrived by 10·15pm, and sometimes they did not get in till 3am. I usually went to bed and woke up when they arrived, to deal with correspondence and the orders which they brought.

Reveille was at 5·30am, and we started to move to a new bit of desert at around 6·15am; so started another long and monotonous day".*

The success of these early operations can be clearly seen from a despatch written at that time by General Wavell to the Secretary of State for War:

"The Eleventh Hussars, the armoured car regiment, was continuously in the front line, and usually behind that of the enemy, during the whole period; its tireless and daring search for information and constant harassing of the enemy showed a spirit and efficiency worthy of the best traditions of this fine regiment."

This constant patrolling produced a strain not only on the Italians (who complained that they "couldn't move anywhere because of these 11th Hussars"!), but also on the regiment's elderly Rolls and Morris armoured cars, and before long there was a serious shortage of "runners". The situation was greatly improved by enlisting the help of No 2 RAF Armoured Car Company, old friends of the Eleventh from Palestine. Until then the airmen's own Rolls-Royces had been pottering up and down the Iraq pipeline and the Saudi-Arabian frontier. In October 1941 ten of them, under the command of Flight Lieutenant (later Squadron Leader) Casano, joined the 11th Hussars, complete with their own crews and transport vehicles. They became a temporary 'D' Squadron and for many weeks fought side by side with the Cherry Pickers. Here is the account of one patrol action carried out by these RAF armoured cars, as told by Victor Overfield, driver of "Sollum Sally":

Dawn, November 19th 1941: Yes, that horrible half-dead feeling we wake with, to prepare

*The Eleventh at War pages 108-109.

for three days' patrol. Half dead, half alive, from lack of a good meal. *If only* we had enough rations but we hadn't, for some Jerry pilot had riddled our ration locker on the previous day, during one of the strafing raids which had become so frequent in those days.

Our Commanding Officer, Squadron Leader Casano, MC, commonly known throughout the Middle East as "That man Cass", briefed my car commander for the job we were to do. Our position was 90 miles west of the Italian fort Jerabub and well behind enemy lines. We were to proceed north 90 miles without being discovered and effect a protective screen around a landing ground which was to be used by those gallant boys 'Our Fighter Pilots.' In the short time we kept that landing ground free of enemy interference those chaps must have given Jerry merry hell, for we certainly suffered for it on this patrol.

The crew was Car Commander Sgt Drabble, Gunner Micky Durell my devoted pal, Wireless Operator Jimmy Braddoch and myself, Vic Overfield, Driver of armoured car No 101, later nicknamed "Sollum Sally" in memory of the days at Hell Fire Pass.

At Zero Hour, 05·00 hours, we proceeded north over rough sandy ground for a trip we well knew would not be uneventful. It was cold and misty, rather suggesting a hot day ahead. By now we were beginning to feel more lively and started to sing and whistle in our turn. This always seemed to relieve the excitement that comes before action. As the car drove on, somehow we scented trouble, and soon Drab's (as we called Sgt Drabble) voice came into the turret: "Car OK, Vic?" — "Yes, Sarg"; "Guns OK, Mick?" — "Yes, Sarg"; "Wireless OK, Jimmy?" — "OK, Sarg", from Jimmy's farmer's boy voice. All ready, prepare action stations. Guns were set to fire, and battle shutters closed to protect the engine from stray bullets; they were not straying so darned far to the enemy's way of thinking.

Five miles, ten miles and nothing yet — what suspense, every minute a living age. This was far too good to be true. Then suddenly out of the rising, glaring sun came hell let loose; 14 Me110s swept down upon us, bent on death and destruction. Bullets slammed the armoured plating around us, then a bomb blast too close to be healthy. Steady now — one turn in the wrong direction would be fatal and the crew would be lost. Everything depended on our reaction to his first assault. Just await orders — when were they coming? — those horrible seconds of suspense that seemed like years. Had Drab been killed by that first volley? What was wrong with everybody, why doesn't someone shout or scream? — anything to break this waiting agony.

Thank God! there was Jim's voice coming to me at last; but what was he rambling about? Drab and Mick were lying on the ground behind us, with an Me110 just about to dive on them. I wheeled round as fast as possible, only to see them lying there looking like a couple of stiffs. I raced to them, putting the car between the diving 'Jerry' and the boys. The coast is clear for a split second, and they are on their feet and clambering into the turret — once more we made it, thank God.

Not too soon, for as we pulled away from that never-to-be-forgotten spot, so a sweet little 250-pounder dropped dead centre of the place we had just vacated. Nice people, these Nazi pilots.

Drab's voice soon came down to us, "All right, boys?" "Nice and comfy, thank you" was Mick's humorous reply. We laughed then, not because the crack seemed funny, but because the relief of being together again was so great. Together — what a feeling of security it was, that old feeling of knowing that we all depended on each other, that we found safety in the presence of a comrade. We were all steady now and ready, come what may. No thoughts of fear; there was no time for that. Just listen to Drab's instructions: 90° port, now starboard, now port — stop! Carry on, to port, steady on that. Every time missing a falling bomb or a spray of machine-gun fire. By this time the turret was full or swirling, choking sand and the smoke of our own guns, as we pelted back with everything we had, which wasn't very much in those ill-equipped days. On we went, swerving and dodging the death that was ours if we were to make the wrong move.

"Sollum Sally" and crew, Victor Overfield is on the left of the picture.

Twelve cars set out on that fateful morning across the barren waste, which was nothing but stony and sandy ground for miles. No cover here, no protection from those devils of the sky. Just keep moving, living on borrowed time. The attack lasted for an hour, in which time four of our cars had gone to Jerry's credit. They still burned, the black smoke of oil and petrol rising through the now still, warm air of that scorching noonday sun. The enemy had gone, so we carefully and speedily checked our petrol, ammunition and losses. Ready, always we must be ready, for more may be on their way soon. But none came, and we were to have peace until at least the following day. Dusk fell on this scene of blood and sweat as the cars moved into close rendezvous, as was the practice every night. Only eight cars remained now, and we knew only too well where the others were. All but one of the crews of the missing cars had made their getaway from those burning sacrifices of war.

He had been riddled with bullets while making his escape, but escape was not to be his. He died of wounds that evening. He died so that you may live in peace, died loving everything in life, just as others have done, but in the machine of war he was a mere nothing. We buried him by the side of his car, as was the tradition of the Desert Rats.

Sleep came easy that night, an exhausted sleep. Wrapped in a couple of blankets we slept until dawn spread her silver wings over "these battle-weary boys."

I have given pride of place to the 11th Hussars as they were the first armoured car regiment in the Division. However, other famous regiments joined the Division later on, the longest serving being the Royals (1st The Royal Dragoons), the King's Dragoon Guards and the 4th South African Armoured Car Regiment.

The Royals moved from Palestine to Egypt early in 1941 and by May of that year one squadron had joined the 11th Hussars "on the Blue". The complete regiment was due to relieve the 11th later that year, but in June was sent to Syria. They did not return to Egypt until the end of 1941, carrying out a forced march of some 700 miles in three days. At Tel-el Kebir they were issued with new Marmon-Herringtons and then moved up to the Egyptian frontier, where they joined 30 Corps on 7 December 1941. They were to work on and off with the Division for the remainder of the desert campaign.

The original pennant flown by "Sollum Sally" (Yes, the holes were made by bullets!)

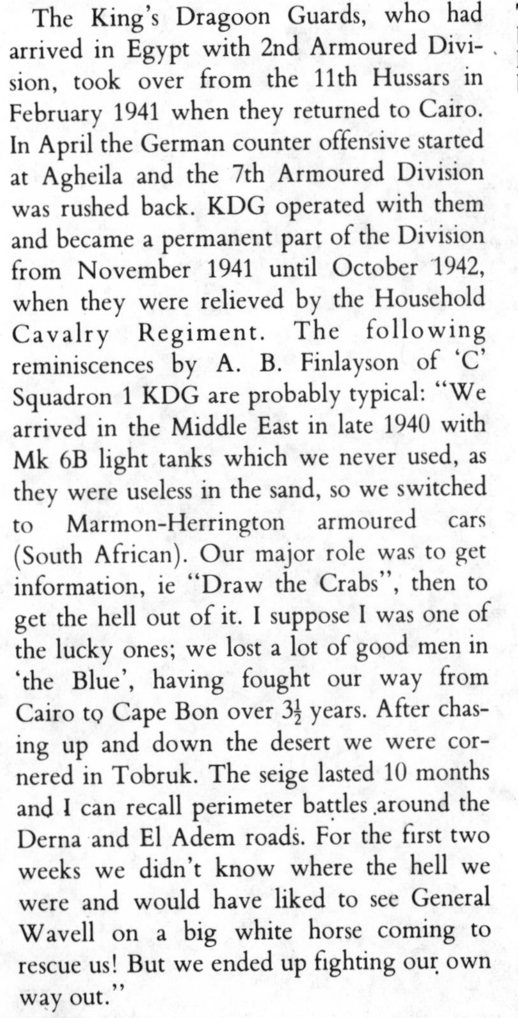

The King's Dragoon Guards, who had arrived in Egypt with 2nd Armoured Division, took over from the 11th Hussars in February 1941 when they returned to Cairo. In April the German counter offensive started at Agheila and the 7th Armoured Division was rushed back. KDG operated with them and became a permanent part of the Division from November 1941 until October 1942, when they were relieved by the Household Cavalry Regiment. The following reminiscences by A. B. Finlayson of 'C' Squadron 1 KDG are probably typical: "We arrived in the Middle East in late 1940 with Mk 6B light tanks which we never used, as they were useless in the sand, so we switched to Marmon-Herrington armoured cars (South African). Our major role was to get information, ie "Draw the Crabs", then to get the hell out of it. I suppose I was one of the lucky ones; we lost a lot of good men in 'the Blue', having fought our way from Cairo to Cape Bon over 3½ years. After chasing up and down the desert we were cornered in Tobruk. The seige lasted 10 months and I can recall perimeter battles around the Derna and El Adem roads. For the first two weeks we didn't know where the hell we were and would have liked to see General Wavell on a big white horse coming to rescue us! But we ended up fighting our own way out."

The 4th South African Armoured Car Regiment joined the Division at the end of July 1941, remaining under command until September 1942. The prowess of these salty fighting men from South Africa soon became well known throughout the Division. They were, for example, the first armoured cars to force a German tank (a new Mk 3 mounting a 75mm gun) to surrender.

Left: RHQ of the Royals on the Gazala Line. Lt Col R. C. Joy and Capt J. H. Russell with their Marmon-Herrington.

Below: A KDG armoured car moving south down the Tripoli road through the wreckage at Beda Fomm, February 1941.

Right: Men of the 4th South African Armoured Car Regiment having their Christmas dinner near Benghazi Cathedral.

The Tanks

Crew of a Sherman tank belonging to B Squadron 5 RTR.

The most powerful tactical unit in the Division was the Armoured Regiment. The numbers and types of tanks in regiments varied considerably over the years, but by way of example here is the organisation which applied in 1942:

Regimental Headquarters
4 tanks, for command and executive functions, also a 4-seater Staff car

Headquarters Squadron
HQ of a car and a wireless truck.
2 Anti Aircraft (AA) Tanks.
Reconnaissance Troop of 10 Scout Cars.
Intercommunication Troop of 8 Scout Cars.
Administrative Troop of transport, including an armoured ambulance and 10 motor-cycles.

3 Armoured Squadrons (each)
HQ of 2 tanks, 2 Close Support (CS) Tanks, 2 AA tanks, 1 Staff car and transport vehicles, 5 Troops each of 3 tanks.

Thus the tank strength of the regiment was 69 (45 gun tanks, 10 Command/executive, 6 CS and 8 AA). All carried wireless sets, with a second set in each HQ tank, so that Squadrons could be put on to separate frequencies, the second set providing a link back to RHQ. Each Squadron had 5 troops, enabling it to hit hard and yet keep an adequate reserve.

The photographs which follow give a good idea of how the size of both the tank and its gun power increased from the early days of the Mk VI light tanks, through the A9-A10-A13 range and on to the re-equipment with American tanks, Honeys, Grants and finally the Sherman with its 75mm gun.

After their initial successes against the Italians, British tank crews found themselves constantly out-gunned by the more powerfully armed tanks of Rommel's Afrika Korps. The balance was, however, partly restored by the arrival in the Middle East of American tanks on lend-lease.

I have already given at the end of the Prologue details of the armoured regiments which made up 4th and 7th Armoured Brigades in November 1940. A year later the Division had expanded to take in another armoured brigade (22nd), the three brigades comprising:

4th Armoured
8th Hussars
3 RTR
5 RTR

7th Armoured
7th Hussars
2 RTR
6 RTR

22nd Armoured
2nd Royal Gloucestershire Hussars
3rd County of London Yeomanry
4th County of London Yeomanry

By April 1942 however, only one armoured brigade (4th) still remained. Finally, before Alamein the Division once again had two armoured brigades under command.

Below: A. Vickers Mk VI light tank belonging to Lt Col W. G. Petherick, CO 3rd Hussars, taken December 11th, 1940. Capable of 30mph on roads, with a radius of action of 150 miles, the Mk VI was armed only with two machine guns. The Mk VI was the last of a series of "tankettes" which dated back more than a decade. Its armour was under ½in thick.

Below right: An A9 of 2 RTR. Designed by Sir John Carden in 1936, the A9 was a lightly armoured cruiser tank with a speed of 25mph. It mounted a 2 pounder high velocity anti-tank gun and was the first British tank with powered traverse.

4th Light Armoured
Royal Scots Greys
4th Hussars (plus a sqn of 8H)
2nd Derbyshire Yeomanry

22nd Armoured
1 RTR
5 RTR
4 CLY

Other armoured regiments, such as 4 RTR, 7 RTR and the Sherwood Rangers, to name but three, came under command of 7th Armoured at various times, particularly during the Crusader and Battleaxe operations.

What was it like to serve in a tank regiment? This account, written by Major Cyril Joly, tells of when he first joined his regiment (2 RTR) in the Middle East and gives a good indication of what being a member of a tank crew was all about:

"I was made particularly conscious of the feeling that I was a member of a good team when I was put in command of one of the tanks which had been overhauled and which we were to take up to join the forward squadron. I worked each day with my crew at the many tasks. We cleaned and greased the tank, checking the engine, the transmission, the suspension and the tracks. We cleaned the guns, fired them and adjusted the telescopic sights to coincide with the actual strike of the shots. We tested and fitted the wireless. Finally we stowed the tank with the ammunition for the two-pounder gun, the machine-gun and the light machine-gun, with cartridges for the Verey light pistol, with food, water and our kit. My crew were all old soldiers with a keenness and sense of humour which amused and encouraged me.

Orders were never necessary. A daily cataloguing of the tasks to be done was sufficient to ensure that each would be done during the day. So it was with my crew, and I welcomed the chance that had given me such men, as I was reluctant at that time to wield authority too obviously. Not that the use of naked authority was ever the best way to control a tank crew. Nowhere else did such a small body of men with such diverse backgrounds, interests and education live so much together for so long in such close contact with the enemy. In such conditions no man could hide his fears and weaknesses for long. As I had learnt in the fighting in France, in moments of stress in battle, in the periods of release from tension, something of the fundamental qualities of each member of the crew was revealed to the others. No shield of rank or education was of any avail behind which to hide any faults. Each drew some strength and courage from the qualities of the others. Each gave something of himself to build the spirit of the whole crew. Where there was a man who could not or would not adjust himself to these conditions, the whole crew suffered as a result. Among the crews with whom I was to serve in the years to come there were men of all races, religions and ranks. We each had our moments of

An A13 of 2 RTR. The A13 also had a 2 pounder gun as its main armament, but used the Christie suspension which gave it a much better cross country performance than the A9.

despair and distress, but nearly always some chance remark, some spark of humour, some small thoughtful act by one of the others, revived and restored our spirits.

The tanks we had at that time were the A9 cruiser tank, the first of the new range of tanks developed in peace time and just beginning to come off the production lines at the outbreak of war. It was armed with a high-velocity armour-piercing gun, firing a two-pound solid-steel shot, with a Vickers machine-gun mounted coaxially with the two-pounder, and with two further Vickers guns in two sub-turrets, one on each side of the driver, who was located forward and below the centre of the main turret. These latter sub-turrets were cramped and of only limited value. Due to a shortage of crews, they were seldom manned, the space thus freed being used to stow extra ammunition and the hundred and one other things needed on a tank. The armour thickness, though not great, was proof against any other tank-mounted guns at that time, though not against some of the higher velocity ground-mounted anti-tank guns. The main fault of these tanks, and of the A10, which gradually replaced them, was that their transmissions and tracks were unreliable. The engine, being similar to those of the London buses, was admirable, but the final drives from the engine to the sprockets, which transferred the power to the tracks, were weak. The tracks themselves, and particularly the pins joining the track-plates, were also not robust enough for the hard, stony ground normally met in the desert. The A10 was basically the same vehicle, but with a Besa machine-gun in place of the Vickers, and only one of these mounted next to the driver, instead of the two sub-turrets in the A9. It entailed hard work and not a little expert knowledge to keep these tanks running for months on end and over long distances.

On the day before we were due to move forward I gave my tanks a final inspection. I inspected the outside first. I walked slowly round, checking the tracks and road-wheels. I opened the bins which were fixed on the track-guards and made sure that the spares, the tools and the food were stowed neatly and correctly. Grasping the track-guards at the front of the tank, I climbed on to the frontal armour plate and so on to the hull above the driver's compartment. I opened the driver's hatch and looked down on to the seat, the gear lever and the steering levers, and beyond these, on the forward bulkhead,

to the mass of dials — the speedometer, the revolution counter, the pressure-gauges. All seemed to be in order. I opened the hatch to the cupola and climbed down into the turret and sat on the small, hard leather seat provided for the commander. From here, on the right of the turret, I could survey all I wanted to see. Immediately in front of me was the gunner's seat, so close that when the gunner was there my knees would be pressing against his back. In front of the gunner, at head height, was the rubber pad guarding the eyepiece of the telescope, flanked on one side by the brass quadrant of the range-drum. On the turret wall, at the gunner's right hand, was the hand-wheel for the mechanical traverse of the turret, and next to it the lever for the hydraulic power traverse. On his left were the firing triggers for the two pounder and the machine gun on the elevating handle for the mounting.

Behind me, in the bulge at the back of the turret, was the wireless set, flanked on one side by a fixed bin in which I kept my headphones and wireless microphone and the

Tannoy microphone with which I gave orders to the crew. On the far side of the wireless set was another bin in which the operator kept his spares and tools and where we also kept the Verey pistol and cartridges.

In the centre of the turret, jutting back from the gun trunnions on the inside of the frontal armour-plate, was the main mass of the two-pounder gun, the buffers, the breech-block and, behind that, stretching almost to the back of the turret ring, the metal deflector guard, to protect the crew from the recoil of the gun, and from which hung the large canvas bag into which the empty cartridge cases were automatically ejected from the breech which opened when the gun ran out again after recoil. Beyond the gun, on the left side of the turret, was the position for the gun-loader, who was also the wireless operator. Hinged from the turret ring was the small seat which had to be fixed back out of the way when the gun was firing so that the operator could have all the space possible in which to handle the ammunition and load the gun. Under the revolving floor of the turret, round the edge of this floor and beyond it on the inside surfaces of the walls of the tank hull, were clipped and stacked the two-pounder rounds and the boxes containing the machine-gun ammunition.

I sat in silent contemplation of all I saw, my mind only partly occupied by the inspection. Mainly I was thinking of all that a return to battle meant to me — preparing myself to meet the exhaustion and the fear."*

Powell Jones of 4 CLY recalls his first tank action:

"My first tank battle was in this Honey and it was like something out of a Bob Hope film. We'd finished recce'ing for the day and were moving towards leaguer for the night when we spotted some other tanks quite near which we assumed were ours. The Germans thought so also, and it wasn't until both sides were on top of each other that both realized the other were enemy tanks — instant pandemonium! Tanks milling about and firing wildly away

Take These Men by Cyril Joly Pages 11 to 15.

Above left: An American tank instructor explains the mysteries of the Grant tank.

Top: An M3 General Grant of 5 RTR. The first American medium tank used by the British. Its 76mm gun, (mounted rather unfortunately in a side turret which cut down its arc of fire) and heavier armour at last meant that British tank crews were on equal terms with the Germans. It also mounted a useful 37mm gun in the main turret and no less than four ·30 machine guns.

Above: Shermans of 3rd Hussars. The Sherman was probably one of the most widely used and best known tanks of World War II — the Americans produced nearly 50,000 of them! Armed with a 75mm gun, 300 new Shermans were diverted to the 8th Army in June 1942 and performed invaluable service from El Alamein onwards.

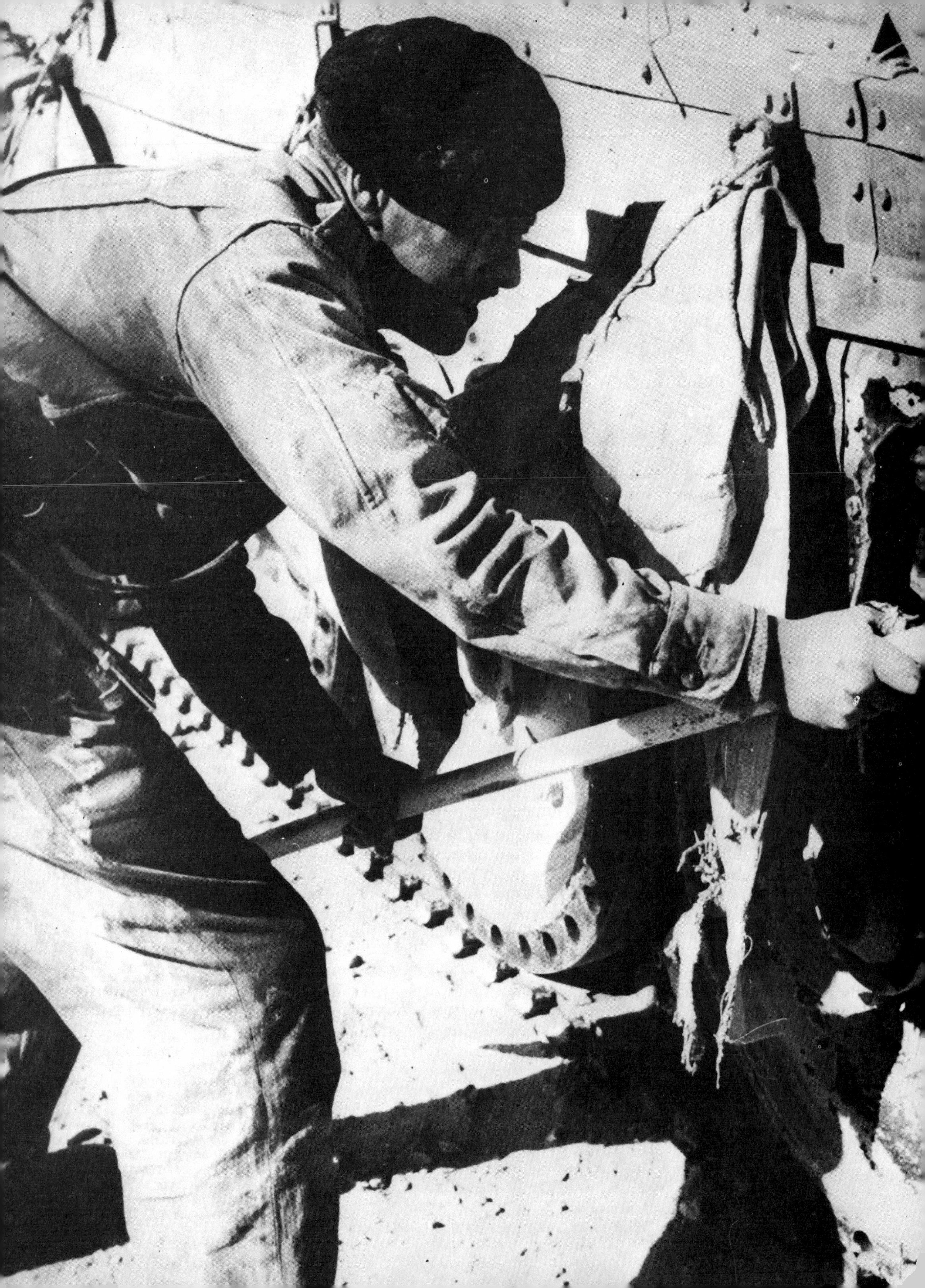

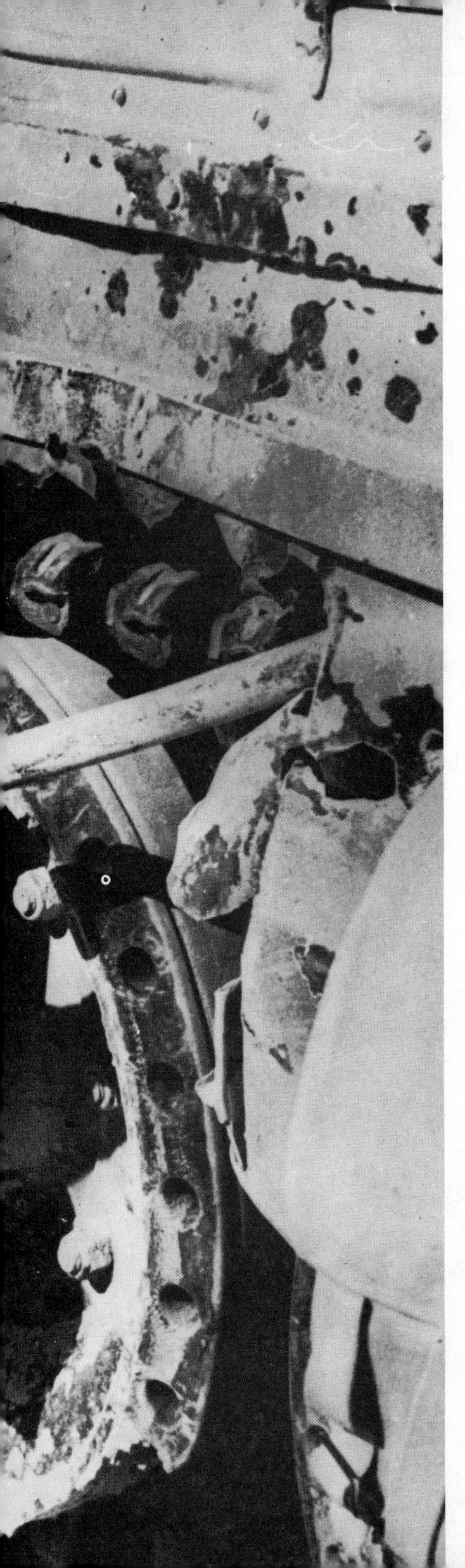

at other tanks and knocking out their own side's tanks — all this had started at dusk and it was rapidly getting darker — yelling and screaming in both English and German on the wireless, each being so near to each other. It was my commander's first tank battle as commander and I don't think he really knew what to do, because I got no instructions at all from him over the air, so I did what we'd been told to do in the Training Regiment — make the tank as difficult a target as possible by keeping moving, turning, going fast, braking hard, etc. I know now it was the correct action to take because our tank wasn't hit at all and I'm still here! However, I think our Squadron Leader assumed when he saw the weird antics of my tank that I, the driver, was panicking, and he came up on the air and told me to get hold of myself. I didn't realise that he was talking to me at first, but when he repeated himself I thought he must be and I said "Yes, sir". I was tensed up all right but I wasn't panicking, and I thought I'd tell him this afterwards, but the chance never came, so I just let it go. As I said, it was getting dark, and almost impossible to see anything through the closed-down visor, so I said to myself, "Sod this, I can't see a thing", opened up my driving hatch and carried on driving with my head stuck out the top. I was one of the lucky ones out there, anyway; the worst I ever got was the blast of a rocket bomb on my arm from a German fighter plane in France, and although very painful at the time it cleared up OK in a couple of days."

Eric Thompson of 5 RTR tells of his experiences in his first tank attack:

"I had seen action before, in the battle of France in 1940 as an infantryman, and at Alam Halfa in a scratch but highly successful tank crew. Both these actions were defensive and Alamein was my first attack in tanks. I was a very green soldier, who had been reluctantly accepted into a crew of veterans in the humble position of loader for the 75mm gun, and it was made quite plain that if I did not measure up I would be returned to the spare crews. The first impression I gained on the approach march to the Start Line was that everywhere vehicles were on the move, and this sight inspired me with the greatest confidence. The second impression was of course the barrage, which until I realised that it was ours frightened me to death! By now of course the enemy was reacting, and I received dire warnings that if I kept putting my head above the open hatch I would very

Another constant chore was "track bashing", ie adjusting the tension of the track to ensure that it did not slip off when turning or negotiating steep slopes. If the tension was too tight then the track would snap. This driver is straightening twisted metal away from his tank tracks. A heavy piece of shrapnel caused the damage.

likely get it blown off. Being a curious person, I could not resist having a look as we advanced through the minefields, and I could see the green tracer of an anti-tank gun firing from the right across our line of advance; he appeared to be firing high and was probably shooting on fixed lines. On the ground I could see two of our infantry with a Vickers machine gun belting fire at his flashes. Immediately after this I was ordered to close the hatches and in one sense this was fortunate, for a few minutes later the anti tank gun hit us; I can't really describe what this was like for I was disorientated, until a calm voice on the intercom said, "Everyone all right below, driver. If she will move, advance." Fortunately she would move, but slowly, and with the most unbelievable groans from the suspension. We later discovered that we had been hit on the front right sprocket, almost half of which had been torn away, but strangely the track was not damaged. I estimate that we were hit by a 50mm, or it could have been a 75, but I am sure it was not an 88. I have never been able to understand why, having found our range, he did not hit us again in a more vital spot. My pet theory is that the two boys on the Vickers made it too hot for him, but in truth I will never know.

When daylight came we engaged and were engaged by the enemy, and the day became one of fire and movement. This was a most frustrating time for me. I was of course busy loading, but I couldn't see a damn thing; every other member of the crew had his visor, gunsight or periscope, but the 75 loader had nothing, and this drove me to look up the gun barrel when the breech was open. The driver saw me doing this and warned me that splinters had been known to travel down gun barrels and if this should happen I would be minus one head.

During the day the atmosphere inside became quite acrid with the firing, and when the driver announced that he must answer an urgent call of nature, there were some groans of protest. As we were being shelled at the time and as we were liable to be ordered to move at any time, to get out to perform this function was unthinkable; the only receptacles we had inside were empty 75mm cases, so grabbing one of these the driver proceeded to use it with vigour and the atmosphere soon became indescribable. The enemy hit us at Alamein, and he didn't kill us, but the stench from the guns and the stench from the driver damn near did!"

Above left: A tank crew "bombing up" — ie loading ammunition into their tank before going into action.

Top: Without constant replenishment of ammunition, petrol and supplies armoured formations soon ground to a halt. So echelon vehicles like this one of 2 RTR were vital.

Above: A group of tank crewmen belonging to C Sqn 5 RTR are typical of the tough, seasoned "tankies" which made up the armoured regiments of the Division.

Left: Tanks normally formed in a tight leaguer by night to replenish, repair and rest. During daylight it was of course dangerous to stay in a close leaguer for long because of the risk of air attack.

When is a tank not a tank?

It is interesting to see the various methods used to disguise the true locations of our tanks. The photographs here show two types of deceptive device used, the first to make a dummy tank out of a truck and the second to disguise a tank as a truck. The latter consisted of a framework of tubing attached to the sides of the tank. The two halves were held by a catch above the turret attached to a string. When the string was pulled the catch was released and the two halves fell outwards. The framework was covered with suitably painted and shaped hessian so that it looked just like a truck from all directions. It was extremely effective.

Far left: This very lifelike cruiser tank was mounted on a small lorry as can be seen in the photograph below. Some dummies were not so well constructed, however, and blew over whenever there was a strong wind!

Left: When fitted with "sunshades" as they were called, a tank looked very like a heavy lorry; indeed one pilot of the RAAF who knew 7 RTR once queried the new large trucks appearing for the first time, not realising they were really camouflaged tanks!

"Fox Killed in the Open"

"Fox killed in the open" was the message sent by General O'Connor, Commander Western Desert Force, to his C in C, General Wavell, on 7 February 1941, following the defeat of the Italian 10th Army at Beda Fomm/Sidi Saleh.

There can have been few other battles in the last war where victory was so complete as at Beda Fomm/Sidi Saleh. Certainly, neither side ever achieved such a spectacular success again during the remaining two and a half years of fighting in North Africa, involving as it did the complete destruction of an entire army of ten divisions. And yet this victory was only achieved by taking a tremendous gamble, what Liddell Hart described as "one of the most daring ventures and breathless races in the annals of the British Army".*

In December 1940 the Western Desert Force began its offensive against the Italians who, some three months previously, had advanced cautiously into Egypt as far as Sidi Barrani. In a series of well-executed encircling manoeuvres O'Connor's forces pursued the enemy relentlessly westwards, cap-

* *The Tanks* page 57.

Left: Sidi Saleh — photograph shows the Italian tank which reached Bn HQ 2 RB and was knocked out near the Officers' Mess (in background). Lt Col (later Maj Gen) Callum Renton is in the foreground.

Left: A general view of the Italian Columns near Sidi Saleh after the surrender.

Below: Arabs looting the Italian Column soon after the battle. Orders were given to stop this looting which seemed incomprehensible to the Arabs!

turing the coastal strongholds of Sidi Barrani, Bardia and Tobruk. By early February 1941 it became clear that the Italians were going to pull out of Cyrenaica completely and, unless something could be done to prevent their flight westwards, the bulk of the Italian Army would escape. To achieve this interception in time meant leaving the good going of the coastal plain and sending forces due west across uncharted desert. Wavell flew up to the forward area for consultations with Generals Wilson, O'Connor and Creagh (Comd 7th Armd Div), and the bold decision was taken to send elements of 7th Armoured Division across the desert to try to cut off the enemy well to the south of Benghazi.

Early in the morning of 4 February the Division, with 11th Hussars leading, began to advance to Msus. Their orders were to strike due west after leaving Msus, but on learning that the Italians had already started to withdraw from Benghazi, Gen Creagh decided to aim south-west, in order to try to cut off as many enemy as possible. A flying column, known as "Combe Force", under CO 11th Hussars was despatched, and despite the terrible going and several enemy air attacks en route, they reached the coast near Sidi Saleh the following morning. "Combe Force" consisted of less than 2,000 men, with some artillery but no tanks.

Meanwhile 4th Armoured Brigade, with only 20 cruisers and 36 light tanks still motoring, was pushing on as hard as they could go for Beda Fomm. The leading elements of 7th Hussars and 2 RTR arrived there late on the afternoon of the 5th.

Earlier that same afternoon the head of the leading Italian column (some 20,000 men with many tanks and guns) had reached "Combe Force", who had established a block across the coast road. The appearance of British forces in front of them, when they thought that the nearest enemy were still several hundred miles away, had a paralysing effect upon the Italians. Instead of trying to outflank the tiny British force, they launched a series of unco-ordinated frontal attacks which were all beaten off.

The battle lasted until the early hours of 9 February, when the Italians finally surrendered. What took place I will leave to be told in two ways; first of all, an account of the actions of "Combe Force" as described by General Jumbo Wilson in a letter to His Royal Highness The Duke of Connaught; secondly, an eye-witness account by Topper Brown, who was a tank gunner in 2 RTR, and knocked out 20 enemy tanks in the battle at Beda Fomm. General Wilson wrote:

"It was apparent that the enemy intended to evacuate Cyrenaica on the evening of February 4th, when the RAF reported long columns of transport on the coastal road round the Gulf of Sirte. The 7th Armoured Division was sent to head them off and started from Mechili on a 150-mile advance across the Desert to cut off the retreating Italian Division and Tank Group. The first day's advance, February 6th, was difficult owing to bad going, with the result that it was decided to send on a wheeled fast-moving column to cut the coast road, while the tanks followed at the best pace after the column. The fast column consisted of Lt-Colonel Combe, 11th Hussars, in Command, 2nd Squadron, 11th Hussars, 1st RHA Battery (25-pr), 1 RHA Battery Anti-tank, and the 2nd Battalion. They were successful in reaching the coast road by the night Feb 7/8 and were hardly in position before the retreating enemy columns appeared. The 2nd Battalion took up a position on some sand hills and during Feb 8th and up to early Feb 9th resisted repeated attacks by enemy tanks to break through and open the road. Lt-General O'Connor said that the battalion did magnificently and specially mentioned the fact in his final situation report. The tanks frequently reached the position held by the forward companies, and in the final attack on the morning of Feb 9th 60 tanks attacked. They were dealt with by the anti-tank guns and the riflemen. The latter took toll of them by rifle fire from the Service as well as the anti-tank rifle and in some cases attacked the tanks on foot and shot through the apertures. One tank reached Battalion Headquarters and was brought to a halt alongside the Officers' Mess Lorry.

That this action will be considered an epic in the history of the Regiment, I am sure your Royal Highness will agree and that Renton and his Battalion are to be congratulated on their performance. While the attacks on the 2nd Battalion were taking place the 4th Armoured Brigade came up and attacked the enemy flank and a heavy tank battle ensued in which our tanks showed their superiority in manoeuvre and gunnery. The RAC certainly deserved great credit as well. The approach march was 150 miles and the action at the end of it decisive, to say the least of it. It is incredible that the Italian Army of Libya should have been wiped out in two months exactly from the date of the attack on Sidi Barrani."*

Topper Brown writes:

"My recollections of Beda Fomm start with the thirty-six hour run across the desert to the area. The day before a Hurricane fighter had dropped a message (lead-weighted) slap on the back of our tank. Apparently it was information that the Italians had left Benghazi. I can't remember the exact date; I only know that it was February 1941, and that I had been on patrol and on guard every night since December 8th 1940. I had also been "Up the Blue" since September and had knocked out three or four M13s at Mechili some time previously. My feelings were ones of complete indifference. I was just utterly fed up, absolutely filthy and badly underfed. The terrain we crossed to cut off the Italians was terribly rocky. As we approached Beda Fomm my commander brought me to my senses by telling me to shoot up an enemy staff car, but the range was too great and the tank was bouncing all over the place — whether I hit it or not I don't know, but some of my tracer certainly surrounded it. We then joined the rest of the squadron.

It was now quite dark, and after some time my commander told me that we had to go out to spike some deserted enemy guns; this was going to be my job. We mounted and advanced along the convoy of enemy trucks. When we got to the end we saw two Italian M13 tanks stationary, and we approached them from the side until we were about fifteen yards away. The operator, Taff Hughes, was then ordered to get the crews out. I offered to get them out with my 2 pounder, but Lt Plough rejected this, because the flash would have shown up our position.

Taff got out, went over to the tanks and knocked on the outside with his pistol. Seven enemy got out, Hughes took them prisoner and began to walk down the convoy with them. I told my commander that there should be eight and that if he would let me put a shell in the tank where the other man was, he would either get out or stay there permanently, but he again refused my offer. We then followed Hughes and the prisoners down the convoy. As we passed one large truck the driver, who was still in the cab with two others, switched his headlights on us. Lt Plough shouted to me to put the lights out, but I had already started firing; the three of them must have been dead within two seconds of the lights going on. We then returned to the squadron with Hughes, who was later awarded the DCM for this exploit.

It rained very heavily for most of that night — my duty was the second half of the guard and I was soaked, even wearing my great coat. We were hull down on a low rise and just as it began to get light, Lt Plough suddenly said, "They're here, reverse!" Whilst the driver (Cpl "Barney" Barnes) was reversing, I managed to get into my gunner's seat and the next thing I saw as I looked through my sights was an M13 about thirty yards away, coming straight towards us. Without thinking I pulled the trigger of the 2 pounder, but as I didn't see any tracer I thought, "Oh my God, I've missed". I gave it another one, but just then one of the crew climbed out of the top, so I shot him. Daylight shone through the hole made by my first shot — was I relieved! We were so close that the tracer hadn't time to light up. Another M13 came up almost alongside it so I hit that as well; knocking both out took less than a minute.

Practically all morning we never stopped firing, at wagonloads of infantry or tanks. I haven't a clue how many enemy I killed, but it must have run into hundreds. We definitely had a score of twenty M13s at the end of the day. On one occasion, when I had knocked a tank out on the road one of the crew stepped

Below: 2Lt (later Major) Norman Plough's tank and crew after the battle at Beda Fomm.

Bottom: Two of the Italian tanks knocked out by Topper Brown during the battle.

* Published by kind permission of RHQ The Royal Green Jackets.

out on to a knoll alongside his knocked-out tank; just previously my Besa had had a stoppage, so I asked Hughes to clear it. Whilst he was doing this I was looking at the Italian crew members through my telescope, when suddenly my Besa fired the jammed round and the Italian died. I told Hughes that he had killed a man. He didn't believe me.

At times we were getting overwhelmed and had to keep withdrawing to the Pimple. One time we came around the right of the Pimple and stopped. My orders were to traverse left and I then saw at about 600 yards an M13 coming towards me on absolutely flat ground. Just as I was about to fire Taff said, "There are only two rounds left". I cursed him soundly, but fortunately hit the tank with both. Taff and I immediately had a good fall-out. We had started out with 112 rounds of 2 pounder, 97 in the racks and 15 extra. Hughes had let us get down to the last two. If I had not been so well trained (I mean this), we could have died. We then went back for more ammo — I was also nearly out of ·30, so you can understand the amount of firing that I had done.

Next thing, we were in the thick of it again. I can honestly say that I didn't at any time feel scared; this I attribute to being so busy, also to the calm commands of my commander. We literally didn't have a quiet moment all day. If we weren't firing at guns or tanks, we would pull up behind a wagon full of infantry and just pour dozens of Besa into the packed wagon. They simply hadn't any idea, or maybe they were petrified. I can recollect each tank I knocked out quite vividly, also several of the infantry wagons. When we pulled back after dark it was sheer relief. My right eye was aching with the strain of looking through the telescope for about thirteen hours with hardly a break."

The Surrender

This is how Cyril Joly, who was also serving with 2 RTR, described the scene: *

"Before first light the leaguers were astir, and as the dawn reddened the eastern sky behind us, it lit the long, straggling, inert mass of the Italian column where it lay, still in its positions of the previous day. The Italians had been harassed throughout the night by our guns and a number of roving infantry fighting patrols, which had kept them on the alert and deprived them of rest and any chance to reorganise. From my position on the dune I watched an attack which was launched soon after dawn by about thirty Italian tanks against the position on the road. This was beaten off quickly and with little difficulty.

For a time there was silence on both sides. For all the efforts of the previous day, the Italian column still looked huge and threatening. I watched with apprehension the movements of the mass of vehicles before me. On either side of me, hidden behind the crests of other dunes and ridges, I knew that there were other eyes just as anxious as mine, surveying the scene before them. In the mind of each one of us was the sure knowledge that we were well outnumbered. Each of us knew by what slim margin we still held dominance over the battlefield. Our threat was but a facade — behind us there were no reserves of further troops. Even the supplies of the very sinews which could keep us going had almost run out. If we lost now we were faced with

* *Take these Men* pages 86 to 88.

Below: Victory at Beda Fomm. A light tank of the 3rd Hussars flying a captured Italian flag after the battle.

Below right: Italian medium guns on the "Pimple" at Beda Fomm which tried to cover the retreating Column down the Benghazi-Tobruk road.

capture or a hopeless retreat into the empty distances of the inner desert. It was a sobering thought. I felt that the day, with all its black, wet dullness, was heavy with ominous foreboding. The scene before me was made gloomy enough to match my mood by the black clouds of acrid smoke which shrouded the battlefield like a brooding pall.

Gradually I became aware of a startling change. First one and then another white flag appeared in the host of vehicles. More and more became visible, until the whole column was a forest of waving white banners. Small groups of Italians started to move out hesitantly towards where they knew we lay watching them. Larger groups appeared, some on foot, some in vehicles. Still not able to believe the evidence of his own eyes, the Colonel warned, "... Don't make a move. This may be a trap. Wait and see what happens. Off".

But it was no trap. Italians of all shapes and sizes, all ranks, all regiments and all services swarmed out to be taken prisoner. I felt that nothing would ever surprise me again after my loader suddenly shouted: "Look sir, there's a couple of bints there coming towards us. Can I go and grab 'em, sir? I could do with a bit of home comforts." We took the two girls captive, installed them in a vehicle of their own and kept them for a few days to do our cooking and washing. I refrained from asking what other duties were required of the women, but noted that they remained contented and cheerful.

The battlefield was an amazing sight. It was strewn with broken and abandoned equipment, tattered uniforms, piles of empty shells and cartridge cases. It was littered with paper, rifles and bedding. Here and there small groups of men tended the wounded who had been gathered together. Others were collecting and burying the dead. Still others, less eager to surrender than the majority, stood or lay waiting to be captured. Some equipment was still burning furiously, more was smouldering. There were many oil and petrol fires emitting clouds of black smoke.

There were few incidents. Soon the generals and the high-ranking officers had been discovered and taken away. The remaining officers were piled unceremoniously into Italian lorries and driven off. The thousands of men were formed into long columns guarded at head and tail by only one or two of our impassive, imperturbable and perpetually cheerful soldiers, who shouldered the unaccustomed new duties with the same confident assurance with which they had met and mastered all the other trials of the campaign."

Fox Killed

In conclusion, here is how General Verney sums up the battle in his history of the Division: *

"Later victories on a greater scale have eclipsed the Battle of Beda Fomm, and unhappily the territory it gained, the great Italian colony of Cyrenaica, was soon to be lost again.

Nothing, however, could alter the material fruits of the victory, the complete destruction of the Italian Army with a total of prisoners at Sidi Saleh of over 20,000, with six Generals, 216 guns, 112 tanks, 1,500 lorries and an immense quantity of arms, equipment and stores of all kinds, not to mention the toll of dead. All this was gained at a cost to the 7th Armoured Division of nine killed and fifteen wounded.

Despite almost incredible difficulties of terrain and supply, the Division had advanced in thirty hours across 150 miles of almost un-mapped Desert, without the benefits of air support — indeed, in the face of a much more powerful airforce than their own — at high speed into what was literally the unknown. There, outnumbered, short of water, food, ammunition and petrol, with no prospect of support or reinforcement, they had out-fought and conquered an Army more than ten times their strength trying desperately to escape from the trap in which they were caught. Small wonder that they felt pride in their achievement."

* *The Desert Rats* page 47.

The Infantry

The job of the infantryman
is to close with the enemy.

The infantry are a vital component of any properly balanced fighting force and this was certainly the case in 7th Armoured Division, because although the tanks could capture and dominate ground for limited periods, they could not hold it for long or sustain their attacks without infantry support.

Initially the infantry battalions (1 KRRC and 2 RB) were organised, together with the Gunners, into a Support Group. Early in 1942 however, this was enlarged to become 7th Motor Brigade (9 KRRC, 2 RB and 9 RB) and finally, before the El Alamein battle, 7th Motor Brigade was replaced by 131 (Queen's) Brigade (1st/5th, 1st/6th and 1st/7th Queens), whilst each of the two Armoured Brigades was given a Motor battalion (1 KRRC in 4 Light Armoured Brigade and 1 RB In 22 Armoured Brigade). Other infantry battalions, including 1 Scots Guards and 2 KRRC, also served with the Division and at one time both Free French and Indian Infantry brigades were under command.

The infantry brigade, unlike normal infantry, were termed "mounted infantry" and were carried in lorries. Their speed on roads and good tracks was considerable — even faster than the armour. However, they were not tactically mounted, that is to say their vehicles did not have the ability to manoeuvre in the face of the enemy, so care had to be taken not to expose their lorries to direct enemy fire. The ability to dismount and come into action quickly was a fundamental part of their training.

The motor battalion, on the other hand, contained a high proportion of armoured scout carriers, scout cars and anti-tank guns, so that they could provide the tanks with immediate infantry support.

Some of the basic infantry weapons are shown below, and whether they were riflemen of the motor battalions or members of the lorried infantry brigade, their ultimate job was to close with the enemy and to kill him with their short range weapons.

The tasks carried out by the infantry were many and various and I will merely highlight three examples — the 'Jock Columns' which

Jack of All Trades (reproduced from the Illustrated London News.

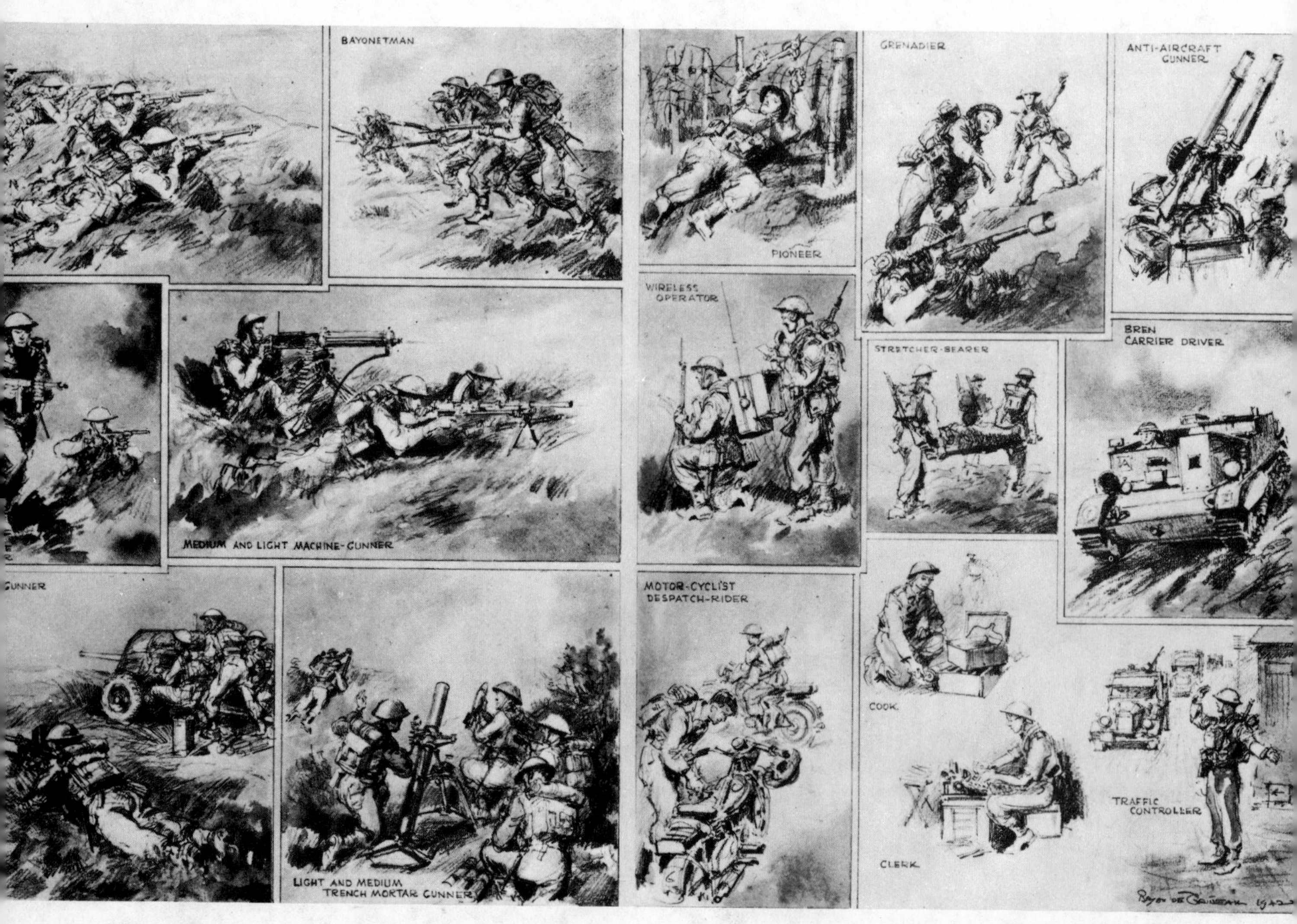

were used to harass the enemy, particularly during the earlier campaigns; secondly, a typical patrol action; and last, a stubborn infantry defence of a "Box" at the time of Rommel's attack on the Gazala line in May/June 1942.

Before doing so however, an anecdote on life in the infantry battalions of the Desert Rats, written by a member of the original contingent of "The Ceylon Planters' Rifle Corps" who served with the Rifle Brigade in the desert.

Robert Jacob, tea planter, writes:
"We numbered 50 NCOs and ORs, all volunteers and single men under 30 years of age. This represented a cross-section of the British community then resident in Ceylon. Most of us were either up-country tea planters or low-country rubber planters, but there were other men, from banks, engineering, business and mercantile firms. The selection was made from 350 applicants — which shows how high the feeling ran in July 1940. Due to some oversight we had been allocated numbers from 1-50 and not the usual British Army reference of seven figures, ie Rifleman Bolt, number 1754321.

Eventually we joined the Rifle Brigade at Bug Bug on 3rd September 1940. The RB's, as part of the 7th Armoured Division, were acting in their usual role with the King's Royal Rifle Corps, as a screen between the British and Italian armies. The latter were making their way forward by slow ponderous stages towards the conquest of Egypt, assisted from Rome by bombastic utterances from their small-bore dictator, Musso.

Now prior to coming to Egypt the RB's had been in India for 15 years. Their conversation as a result was spiced with (apart from the usual repetitive oaths and expletives, dear to Thomas Atkins) Hindustani words that with usage had become so mutilated as to be unrecognisable:

"Give the bobagy a bolo, for ——'s sake. Conor up pechi!"

Translated, it reads:

"Give the cook a call, we want our food quickly!"

So we took it as a compliment to be nicknamed "Those ——ing Char Wallahs", char being Hindi for tea.

Shortly after our arrival the RSM marched over to shed light on the efforts of an ex-tea planter digging a slit trench on rough ground:

"What is your name and number?"

"Rifleman Sword, No 6, Sir!"

Without a moment's hesitation the great man replied:

"Where is your bow and arrow?"

Our next move was on to the escarpment to a fresh position. We drove by night through the ruins of Sollum, over the battered road of the Hell Fire Pass. Now we were subjected to more frequent attacks by the Italian Air Force. Raids were sudden, heralded by the sound of approaching planes, the ack ack sentry's imperative shrill whistle and, as often as not, our Adjutant and Company CO, Captain Darling, sounding his hunting horn. This added tone and style as well as sending us to earth, as men sprinted for weapon pits and slit trenches; nobody noticeably hung about!

The Iti Macchi fighters came at us out of the sun, hip high, strafing the position with their machine guns. The noise of their engines and the firing rose to a crescendo as they hurtled overhead. To be caught out in the open, with neither cover nor a slit trench

Below: Infantrymen advancing under shellfire.

Bottom: Each infantry section consisted of a number of riflemen armed with ·303 Lee Enfields and a Light Machine Gun group — the Bren (also ·303) which had a rate of fire of 500 rpm, was fitted with a 30 round magazine and had an effective range of 800 yards.

nearby, with a shattering experience. Fear could be held in check if you had something to *do.* An altered verse by Dorothy Parker (with apology) explains it:

Your spirits go dim,
Your fears go black,
If they shot at you, and
You can't shoot back.

We did shoot back with brens and rifles, the red hot tracer curving up as the gunners endeavoured to hose a plane down.

By now dirt and dust swirled about, to mingle with the oily black smoke of burning vehicles; narrow tongues of flame licked out, before engulfing an entire truck. It stopped as soon as it had started. Sometimes we were lucky and downed an enemy plane, but usually they had the advantage of surprise and did not linger once the hornet's nest had been disturbed. We were left to lick our wounds. The tumult subsided and it was very still, except for the crackle of the fires. The surprise was that more men were not killed".

Communiques talked of "Mobile Columns" being active, the BBC called them "Flying Columns", but to the troops they were known by their original name of "Jock Columns", after the great Jock Campbell, VC, himself.

The columns' main job was to harass the enemy and to jab hard at his supply lines, playing havoc in his rear areas. However, this didn't stop columns from engaging enemy armour; indeed, a party from one once bagged a German Mk 3 tank by firing through the visor slits with a Bren gun at close range!

Columns usually comprised two troops of 25 pounders—their main hitting power—one or two motor companies of mobile infantry, anti tank and anti-aircraft artillery, a sapper detachment and, for protection, armoured cars and tanks. The column commander had his own adjutant, signals and intelligence officers and the column was supported by a specially designed 'B' Echelon.

As most of the administrative chores had to be performed after going into night leaguer, and because the column was usually on the move before first light, there was little chance to rest, but following Jock Campbell's precept of "First into battle, last out", this was nothing new to the men of the Support Group from whom the bulk of the columns were made up.

Here are some typical reminiscences by Philip Gibbs, of 2 KRRC, when he was a member of a Jock Column:

Left: The 3in Mortar was used with considerable success in the desert and was frequently carried over bullet-swept ground in a carrier. The 10lb HE bomb was better than the German equivalent, but the mortar initially suffered from the disadvantage of a shorter range (1600 yards). An experienced crew could keep up a sustained rate of fire of between 20-30 rds per minute.

Below left: The 2pdr Anti-Tank Gun. A 40mm anti-tank gun firing a 2pdr shell (hence its name) was the standard anti-tank gun for the first two years of the desert war. Although it was an excellent weapon it was short in both range and hitting power.

Above: Rhodesians with 1st Bn KRRC manning a 2in Mortar. Not nearly as effective as the 3in mortar, this smaller weapon came into its own in close quarter jungle fighting in the Far East. However, it was useful in the desert to produce smoke screens.

Below: A Vickers Machine Gun team of Z Company, 1st Battalion Royal Northumberland Fusiliers. The Vickers was the standard heavy machine gun in the British Army in both World Wars. It was renowned for its reliability and had a rate of fire of 450-550rpm. In an experiment one was fired non-stop for seven days!

The Column Moves Off. The Navigating Officer waves his blue flag to start the Column moving, July 1942.

Above right: Cheery Sappers. Life with a Jock Column seemed to agree with these sappers, to say nothing of their mascot, a little terrier pup called "Lady".

"The Column's role was harassing, leaving the RV at Division usually around dusk and making as much ground to the South and West as possible during the first night to get well under and to the rear of the enemy lines. During the day, while in action, the column dispersed and camouflaged up in depressions or wadis. Movement was very limited, due to tracks, footprints etc. Fires were lit during the day under cover and smoke kept down to a minimum.

As I have said, our role was to harass the enemy no matter where he was, including his tank formations, road blocks and airfields, or just by lying in wait at strategic cross tracks for enemy supply columns. When a target presented itself the column struck hard and fast, causing as much damage as possible, and then melting away in the desert. In fact we had a litle motto, which was "Whack whack and away!"

In one instance patrols from our column infiltrated an Italian leaguer and, hands in pockets, strolled round attaching sticky bombs to tanks, guns, petrol bowsers and water trucks, casually withdrawing to the RV point to watch the fireworks, then tearing off to rejoin the Column. The main object seemed to be harassing, making a nuisance of ourselves, so that the enemy did not know where the column were going to strike next."

As well as providing escorts for the guns of the Jock Columns, the infantry also carried out many night patrols. These patrols demanded a very high standard of map reading, compass work and leadership, if good results were to be obtained. The following extract from a light-hearted account written during the Wavell offensive gives a good idea of the general pattern followed by motor platoon patrols during the desert war:

"We received our orders in the morning, so the afternoon was spent studying the map, choosing the route and making up our plans. Maps of the desert areas which were patrolled nightly gave one little more than a very general idea of the country. There were few landmarks in the desert, such as houses, trees, gateways etc., which one would find in civilised parts of the world, and consequently navigation becomes of primary importance.

On this particular night our orders were to visit the neighbourhood of a certain enemy camp, report on their outer defences and, if a favourable opportunity occurred, to lay an ambush.

Ambush "parties" were not often on the programme, but in this case our armoured

car patrols had for several days been anxiously watching the vegetables ripening in a certain marrow bed. A party of Libyans were also in the habit of paying regular visits to this same marrow bed, and one day our friends were dismayed to see the Libyans come out complete with gardening baskets and solemnly take away the marrows.

We gratefully accepted what seemed to be an excellent opportunity to grab one of the "gardeners".

Accordingly, at 5·30 that evening, after a ten-mile run in the trucks, we "leaguered" for the night some three miles from the enemy camp. From here in the twilight we made a quick reconnaissance from a nearby hill of the area which the patrol had to cover during the night. We could just make out in the gathering darkness a prominent fig tree near which we had been told was the area of the marrow bed. We fixed that fig tree firmly in our minds.

The patrol involved covering a route of approximately six miles, and we calculated "Rouse" at 2am would give us ample time to seek out the outer defences of the enemy and choose our ambush area.

Leaving a small guard and the anti-tank rifles with the trucks, we set off with three strong sections at 2am. The formation adopted that night was the following: Two scouts fifteen yards out in front, a connecting file (who was the platoon sergeant) close behind the scouts, and then ten yards in the rear. the commander, with an oil compass and a pace-counter (an esential man in desert patrols), two sections in arrow-head just out to the flanks, and a rear guard. In this formation all keep station on the commander, who has adequate control and is also able to maintain visual communication with the scouts.

By 4am a march of three miles due west and one mile north-east brought us to within a short distance of the perimeter of the enemy camp. Until now we had neither seen nor found any signs of the enemy, and we sat down and established a listening post. An occasional cough was all that told us the camp was not far away, and we had frequent scares caused by tall, thin bushes waving in the night breeze, appearing like figures advancing out of the darkness.

We spent rather an anxious three quarters of an hour before dawn searching for the fig tree we all remembered; it seemed at one moment that we would still be caught in open ground when first light came, but by real good luck we suddenly hit the fig tree just as dawn was breaking.

A quick look round showed that here was

Top: Action! Having spotted the enemy, a 25 pounder gets to work.

Above: Getting down to some kip. There was little chance to sleep during Column work, so whenever there was an opportunity the column made the most of it.

an excellent position to lie up behind cover, but a much more important question to us was the exact whereabouts of the marrow bed.

We just had time to make a dash over to a nearby blockhouse which overlooked our position, found it unoccupied and settled down behind our little sand-ridge. We had no time to dig in.

It was now a quarter to seven, and sure enough from out of the centre of the camp appeared eleven Libyans, carrying baskets in addition to their arms. They came straight for our position, halting a few moments to post a sentry, and then continued on in a bunch across the remaining three hundred yards of flat ground in front of us. We had seen a little piece of dead ground fifty yards away, and here they apparently halted again to post a sentry. On they came, and in two minutes the heads of the gardening party reappeared out of the dead ground. Forty yards away they halted again, downed baskets — and then it suddenly dawned on us that we must be lying almost on top of the marrow bed!

With fixed swords the right section scrambled up and made off for their position. The big fat NCO let off a hurried shot with his rifle and ran for it. However, he didn't run very far before he was shot. At this moment the alarm signal of one red Verey light went up from the centre of the camp and the enemy seemed to open fire with every available weapon they had. Two 75mm guns opened up on to the high ground south of us; two heavy machine guns from the main road; rifle fire from the sentries on the road, and worst of all, "Mahomed the Mortar", whom the gardeners must have posted in the dead ground in front. Two sections were out of cover, so they were withdrawn back under control, and before we crept back with the high ground to our south we let them have it with the Bren guns. Three of the retreating gardeners offered their back views as an excellent target and they fell wounded about 300 yards away. We now quickly withdrew under cover into the broken ground behind. The enemy had as usual the line but not the range, and we were able to avoid their bursting shells by an easy detour. Only "Mahomed" gave us a moment of anxiety when he dropped one or two of his mortar bombs unpleasantly close: he must have been well sited. In ten minutes all firing ceased and we made straight back to the trucks and to breakfast in camp, where we were greeted with the words, "Glad to see you back, and what was all the AA fire an hour ago?" *

Below: French Light anti-aircraft gunners manning a Bofors gun at Bir Hacheim.

Right: Rommel's Message.

Below right: General de Gaulle decorates General Koenig after the battle.

Bir Hachiem

In late May 1942, with Rommel striking for Suez, the Division was occupying the southern portion of the Gazala line — a long, deep belt of wire and minefields interspersed with a number of fortified localities known as "Boxes", which were generally held in brigade strength. The Division had no less than five brigades under command at that time, 4th Armoured, 7th Motor, 29th Indian Infantry, 3rd Indian Motor and 1st Free French. The latter were occupying the Bir Hacheim box, the vital southern pivot against which Rommel launched a series of blistering attacks. For fourteen days and nights the French garrison, under General Koenig, withstood attack after attack both from the ground and air. News of their epic defence resounded around the world and was a tonic to French morale everywhere.

In the middle of the battle Rommel tried to get the garrison to surrender, sending them the following message:

"*To the troops at Bir Hacheim:* Further resistance will only lead to unnecessary bloodshed. You will have the same fate as the two English Brigades which were wiped out two days ago at Got Ualeb. We will stop firing as soon as you hoist the white flag and come out to us unarmed.

Rommel General"

General Koenig' answer was just three words,

**The Annals of the King's Royal Rifle Corps, Vol VI* pages 102-104.

"Allez au diable!", and the French batteries opened up heavy fire on all enemy vehicles within range. At the same time he sent an order to every man under his command. The order read:

"*1.* Very soon we must expect a heavy attack by all combined means (tactical air, tanks, artillery and infantry). It will be powerful.
2. I re-affirm my orders and my belief that everyone will do his duty, in his position, be he alone or with others, without flagging.
3. Our Mission is to hold out whatever the cost until final victory.
4. Make that clear to everyone, officers, NCOs and men.
5. Good luck to you all.

3 June 1942, 0930 hours
Koenig".

For the next seven days the garrison continued to fight on, although they were almost completely surrounded by two enemy divisions and continually straffed from the air by wave after wave of Stuka dive bombers. On 10th June, with increased enemy pressure and over one hundred aircraft attacking Bir Hacheim, it became apparent that the heroic resistance could not continue indefinitely, so the decision to evacuate the Box was taken. That night D Company 2 KRRC brought in sixty-nine 3 ton lorries and 33 ambulances, their movement being covered by a Jock Column under Lt Col J. C. Christopher RHA. First the ambulances brought out the wounded, then two convoys of lorr rescued all the other men who could be found. It was misty on the morning of the 11th and the carriers of the Rifle Brigade were able to sweep through the Box picking up stragglers. When they eventually withdrew, over 3,000 men, nearly three quarters of the garrison, had been successfully evacuated.

During their epic defence the 1st Free French Brigade destroyed over 50 enemy tanks, 30 Stukas and many enemy vehicles.

The Prime Minister, speaking in the House of Commons later and describing the background before the withdrawal to El Alamein, said: "After the 4th June the battle centered on Bir Hacheim, where the Free French resisted with the utmost gallantry. Around this place the struggle surged for 8-9 days. Here, no doubt, was a turning point in the battle". Truly the defence of the Bir Hacheim Box will live forever as a shining example of French courage.

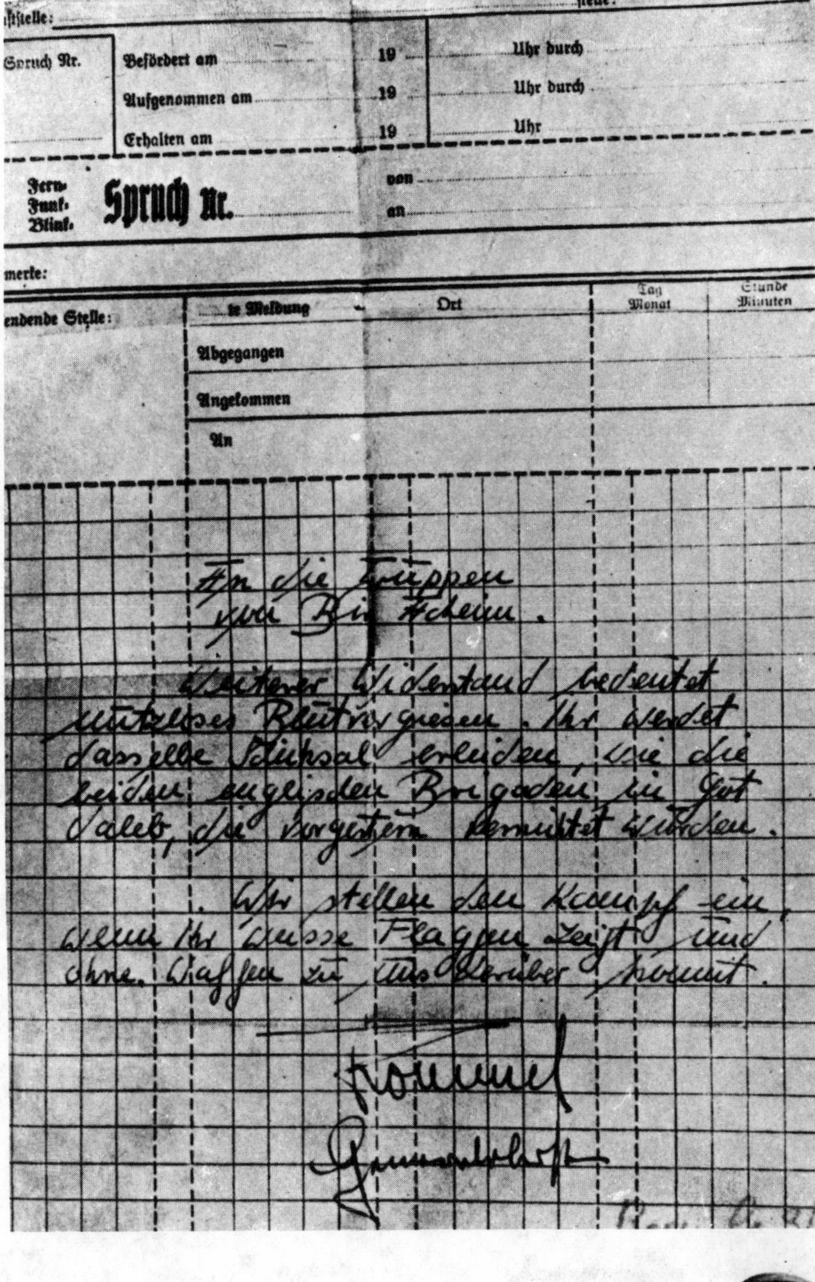

stelle:

Spruch Nr. | Befördert am ... 19 ... Uhr durch
Aufgenommen am ... 19 ... Uhr durch
Erhalten am ... 19 ... Uhr

Fern-
Funk-
Blink-
Spruch Nr.
von
an

merke:

endende Stelle: | te Meldung | Ort | Tag Monat | Stunde Minuten
Abgegangen
Angekommen
An

An die Truppen
von Bir Hacheim.

Weiterer Widerstand bedeutet nutzloses Blutvergiessen. Ihr werdet dasselbe Schicksal erleiden, wie die beiden englischen Brigaden in Got Ualeb, die vorgestern vernichtet wurden.

Wir stellen den Kampf ein, wenn Ihr weisse Flaggen zeigt und ohne Waffen zu uns herüber kommt.

Rommel
Generaloberst

The Gunners

25 pounders in action. Their primary task was the destruction or neutralisation of enemy weapons, in particular anti tank guns and field artillery. A secondary task was the disintegration of hostile tank concentrations by massed artillery fire. These tasks were best carried out in concealed positions from which the guns could effectively maintain their fire without the risk of direct enemy interference.

It would be impossible in a book of this size to cover every action fought by a Regiment whose motto "Ubique" speaks for itself. Suffice it to say that the Desert Gunners earned themselves a reputation for courage, resourcefulness and endurance which has never been surpassed.

The successful outcome of all operations was largely dependent upon the co-operation of the divisional artillery. In attack the guns provided the fire support without which victory was impossible to achieve. The Observation Post Officers directed this fire, usually moving with the leading troops. They were thus able to bring down effective fire on any target very quickly. During consolidation after an attack, or in defence, the guns formed the framework of the divisional layout.

There were normally three branches of artillery within the division — field, anti-tank and light anti-aircraft — and they could of course call on the fire of heavier guns from outside the division, such as medium artillery and heavy anti-aircraft. Some of those guns and their crews are pictured below.

Field Artillery (including the Royal Horse Artillery)

As has been explained, it was the job of the OP officer to direct the fire of the artillery guns. This task was both difficult and extremely dangerous.

The following account, written by Kenneth Watt of 3 RHA, recalls vividly what it was like to be an OP officer, spotting for the guns, in July 1942 on the El Alamein Line:

"*Monday 7th July:* It seems ages since we came out. Have had three days of Observation Post work, firing 25 pounders "in anger" for the first time. We are holding the enemy OK so far. The battle is centred round some ridges running east and west about ten miles inland from the El Alamein railway halt. Got some good shooting yesterday when I was observing from two ridges to the south. Have had a lot of shelling, but no tank attacks. The tanks mostly sit and look at each other from hull down positions along one of the ridges, although there have been two small tank battles that I have seen. It's a question of which side gets reinforcements first now. Wish we could attack.

The "Auk" (General, later Field Marshal, Sir Claude Auchinleck) is up here and passed my troop during the final approach on Thursday; I was greeted by a friendly and confident "Good morning". There is no special panic, but one feels that everyone, the "Auk" included, is on their toes.

A thick mist came down about 0530 this morning, just as I was starting out to a new Observation Post area. The mist gave us time to have some breakfast — a tin of bacon, which was super, and a marvellous mug of tea. It cleared at 0815, and now I am sitting on my armoured car in the middle of the desert, shooting now and again at distant MET (Mixed Enemy Transport).

Got chased off a better vantage point on a hillock this morning by three very close mortar bombs and two rounds from a hidden 88mm which whooshed very low overhead.

Went forward again at 1400 hours and was able to observe more to the west. Stayed out till 2015 hours — a fifteen-hour day out.

Tuesday July 8th: Tried the ridge to the north-east this morning. Higher ground but further back than my OP of yesterday.

The early hours are all-important, as that is the best time for observation — with the sun low behind. After about 10 or 11am the heat makes observation very difficult. Also one wants to get into one's OP area before it is light enough to be seen moving by the enemy.

The main enemy positions must all be beyond a low ridge about seven miles to the west. Very occasionally one engages black dots on the ridge — presumably enemy fixed OP's. There are, however, plenty of hidden enemy pockets in the intervening low ground, and it was to try to get a better idea of where these were that I came back a bit on to higher ground. It's a question of continuous and patient observation with the glasses for the least sign of movement.

As we weren't in any danger back there, I

An OP officer at work in the desert.

Lieutenant (later Captain) Douglas Boggie of the Norfolk Yeomanry is pictured here with one of his gun crews in a front line position. The gun is the 2pdr anti tank gun with which the British had to fight for the first two years of the war.

made sure that we had a good breakfast (not always possible!). Then the BC (Battery Commander) came up, and we went down on to the low ground to the north of where I was yesterday; I had been shot at from more or less this area. It had been so plastered however, by my own guns and some South African 25 pounders, that I thought they must have withdrawn.

Yesterday, too, the area had been attacked in a dashing raid by South African armoured cars, but I could not see what they were firing their machine guns at. This had all taken place very suddenly about 400 yards in front of me, and I thought at first that an enemy infantry attack was on.

The BC and I crept forward cautiously this morning, stopping every so often and having a good look at everything with the glasses, and eventually at one of these halts we saw enemy walking about two thousand yards ahead, and another lot closer to the left. By observing where they walked to and from, one got on to a couple of possible gun positions and I brought down fire on three "targets" here.

Then three of our tanks crept forward on my left, with a view to inspecting a group of derelict vehicles and mopping up the area. However, the same heavy mortar as I had had came down all around them and they withdrew. The mortar came from my right front over a crest. I searched a bit over there, and then after a spell of concentrated watching in the shimmering haze, I got out and did a recce on foot. Was just moving the OP into the next depression to the right front when Charles Aitchison came on the air and said he was on his way out to relieve me.

This was a pre-ordained half day for me and it was grand to get in at 1500 hours and have a tin of grapefruit from the mess, a wash in a mess-tin of water and a change. OP work is very good fun but a continual strain, and one afternoon off in four is a good idea.

Parsons of 'M' was wounded yesterday — five officer casualties, two of whom were killed, in five days.

Anti-tank Artillery

Here is an account of the work of an anti-tank regiment — 102nd (Northumberland Hussars Yeomanry), RHA — written by Major Leslie Hill, MC:

"I spent most of my time in the desert either right up on the wire, protecting the armoured cars against German tanks and armoured cars when they were on patrol, or a bit further back, digging gun positions from which my guns could catch any German attack in the flank.

Our day when supporting the armoured cars started with a stand-to before dawn, in case of a German attack, then usually an early morning patrol with a troop of armoured cars, flanked by my four guns and my own 8cwt command truck. We used to go through the wire at one of the points we had cut, after having made sure that it had not been mined. (Once the Germans mined one of the points during the night and then rolled a British tyre over it to give the impression that one of our vehicles had already passed over the spot. The result was a knocked out armoured car and several dead.) We would then make a sweep in No-Man's land, always hoping to catch a German six-wheeler armoured car, which would have been a big prize, as our side had not managed to get close to one yet.

We occasionally saw a German patrol, which quickly vanished, and as our armoured cars were not fast enough to catch them, pursuit was hopeless. At other times we spotted an LRDG patrol on its way back from a deep raid into enemy-held country and had a few words with them, after they had circled us warily to make sure who we were.

When we were in reserve, a few miles back from the wire, we had to dig gun positions in the sides of the small hills which rose out of the desert here and there. Often the hills were made of solid rock and sometimes we had the help of the Indian Army (4th Indian Div) sappers to blast for us. Most of my troop were Northumerbland or Durham miners — reinforced with Welsh miners after the debacle in Crete, when half the regiment was lost — so they were handy with a pick and shovel, but they strongly objected to having to use them

The 2pdr was normally carried "portee" in the back of a lorry and could be fired from this platform if necessary.

on solid rock in the heat of an Egyptian autumn on a meagre water ration.

I was mostly attached to the King's Dragoon Guards, who had Marmon Harrington armoured cars, but was also with the 11th Hussars (the Cherry Pickers) and the South African armoured cars for periods. The 11th were really old hands in the Desert, with more modern armoured cars, and tended to scorn anti-tank support; the South Africans were very welcome because they got a coffee ration instead of a tea ration, and as we got our rations through them, we had coffee too while we were with them.

For a young Second Lieutenant (I was 23 at the time), command of an anti-tank troop on "The Wire" was wonderful. Most of the time I was many miles from any senior officer. We spent most of the day on our own, several miles from the armoured cars, keeping a watch on gaps in the wire (patrols were usually early in the morning and late in the evening), and went into night leaguer alone too, so I was my own master most of the time.

At first I found desert navigation very confusing, because of the lack of geographical features, the heat haze which made bushes look like moving vehicles, the poor performance of magnetic compasses in our metal vehicles, and the inadequacy of the maps we had. The sun compass proved a great help once I had mastered its intricacies.

Then came "Crusader", the attempt to relieve Tobruk. I was attached to a squadron of the KDGs to provide them with anti-tank cover while they reconnoitred ahead of the main thrust. Whenever we ran into heavy opposition, the armoured cars withdrew behind our tanks and 25 pounders, and my troop stayed between the two (behind the tanks, but in front of the field guns), to catch any German tanks that broke through our tanks and threatened the artillery guns.

My troop took part in several big battles in this way, with the tanks making great clouds of dust in front of us, so that we could not really see what was happening, the German guns firing over them and trying to hit us and the 25 pounders, and our own 25 pounders replying over our heads. I was very surprised to discover that the Germans were using a lot of shrapnel. I had gathered, during my training on 25 pounders, that shrapnel had gone out after the First World War, and that now everyone used HE. By moving our position

The 6pdr replaced the 2pdr and was a much better gun, more mobile and with a higher rate of fire.

frequently to confuse the German artillery spotters, my troop managed to escape injury during these battles.

As we approached Sidi Rezegh, on the 21st November, we came across the HQ of 4th Armoured Brigade, to which my CO, Lt-Colonel Rob Waller, was attached as anti-tank adviser.
He told me to stay with the HQ to provide them with anti-tank protection. It was getting towards evening and we were still talking when the Second in Command of the Brigade, who had been left in charge while the Brigadier had gone off with the tanks to fight a big battle, called him urgently: "Rob, Rob!" My CO ran to him, and a few moments later came back to me and said, "There's a large body of tanks and soft-skinned vehicles coming in behind us. Get between them and our HQ and keep them off. But be careful, they may be the South Africans — we're expecting them from that direction."

I at once ran to my truck, jumped in, and raised my blue flag for the troop to go into action. We raced out towards the mass of approaching vehicles, then stopped and spread out as we always did when manoeuvring. My binoculars had been damaged so that I could see only out of one half, and there was such a shortage of equipment that I had not managed to get them replaced. I tried to see whether I could recognise the approaching tanks, but before I could be sure, they started firing at us. As our portees were unmistakable I took it as certain that the approaching vehicles were enemy, so I raised my flag for firing to begin. (We had no wirelesses in our anti-tank troops, as these were reserved for tanks and armoured cars. We communicated by flag semaphore when necessary.) The enemy had stopped and were firing heavily, the tracer making beautiful and intricate patterns. The water container on the portee I was on was hit and smashed into small pieces.

Our three guns were firing rapidly and I could see that we were scoring hits. My MC citation later credited us with three tanks destroyed in a very short time, which was not bad, as our little two pounder shells bounced off German tanks at any range over 800 yards, while their guns could blow us to smithereens at a much greater range than that. However, as the tanks were relatively blind when closed down, and we had a wonderful view from the decks of our portees six feet above the flat surface of a featureless desert, we found the German tanks had a healthy respect for us, especially as we had the reputation of using dashing cavalry tactics — rushing in, firing a few shots, then rushing out again.

After a minute or two there was a flash of flame from my left, and the crew of one of my guns came running over. "We're on fire, sir", they shouted, "and Bombardier Tinling (he was the commander of that gun) has been hit right through the chest". A minute after that, my other gun pulled out and began to withdraw fast. The enemy shells were getting uncomfortably close, so I gave the order to the driver of the gun I was on to move too. "Jink about as you go", I said. The driver set off, changing direction frequently to throw the enemy gunners off. After a short time we passed some of our light Honey tanks, also going the same way as us, firing, moving, firing again, and so on. I ordered our driver to stop too, but he was not keen to do so and I had to bang him several times over the helmet before he obeyed. "Go on firing,,' I said. The gun-layer and bombardier fired off some more shots, to discourage pursuit, and then we moved on again. We did this several times till we reached Brigade HQ, which had retired to a point where a desert track began to thread its way over the Escarpement."

Light Anti-Aircraft Artillery

LAA guns were used for both their conventional anti-aircraft role and against enemy tanks. Here is an account of the work of an LAA unit by Major A. L. King-Harman: *

"One of the convoys leaving England in January 1941 carried the 1st LAA Regiment under command of Lt-Col B L de Robeck. This was the first LAA regiment to be sent out to the Middle East and was in fact the only regiment of LAA in the Regular Army order of battle.

After nearly 12 weeks at sea, with a break of only four days on shore at Capetown, the Regiment disembarked in April at Port Said. Ten days later the leading battery moved down the Bir Enba track to join one of the two brigades holding the bare wastes of desert running south from Sollum. Although it was a regular regiment many of the officers and men were Territorials, and because of the shortage of equipment in England few had had more than a few hours' training on a Bofors 40mm gun, and even fewer had any real experience of operating with a field formation. No amount of bluff could hide the inexperience of both officers and men, and Colonel de Robeck set about teaching his regiment desert warfare from scratch. It was a hard school, with Stukas and Me109s the only aircraft in the skies, and our meagre ground forces, organised into Jock Columns, playing tip-and-run with the enemy.

Weeks passed, Stukas began to fall, Me's stopped flying at nought feet. Drill became perfect. The desert became a friend and not an enemy. Gradually these anti-aircraft gunners became accepted as desert soldiers, and bit by bit they earned their keep. Weeks turned into months, but still the autumn offensive dallied. The gunners led a lonely and solitary life, a life that many men in many regiments were to experience before Agedabia was passed for the last time. Life in those days was reduced to the basic necessities of sleeping and eating. Often enough, nothing else helped to pass the day. No radios, no books, no papers, no news, no tents or cover from the sun. But the men had beer — lots of it. And with beer they kept going.

Day after day of this monotony and then suddenly 'Action'. Down out of the sun came the Stukas. On their tails came the Me's. Gunners stripped to the waist man their guns and the staccato bursts of the Bofors mingle with the roar of bursting bombs. Suddenly all is quiet and the aircraft climb away. Flames lick round a burning petrol lorry. An ambulance tears up to one of the Bofors — one man is killed and two wounded. In the midst of all this the armoured car patrol calls up to report a Stuka crashed and burnt out. The gunners chalk one up.

This picture of the 1st LAA Regiment is typical of many units in the desert at that time. Conditions were harder than at home. Officers and men were separated from their wives and sweethearts, and the repatriation scheme stood at seven years! But the war was young and despite shortage of equipment and transport, Colonel de Robeck had his men at the peak of their training when the curtain lifted on November 18th.

Gone were the boredom and monotony. Into the even tempo of their desert life came Sidi Rezegh—Mechili—the Cauldron—Tobruk — Alamein. These fine gunners fought the 15th and 20th German Panzer Divisions at all these places, treating the

* Reproduced from the *Royal Artillery Commemoration Book 1939-45* by kind permissioin of the Royal Artillery Institution.

Luftwaffe as a spare-time job. Time and time again they stood in the open unprotected by any armour and fought the German tanks to a standstill. From dawn to dusk their tracer shells burst against the thick German armour. But gallantry was not enough; numbers and superior equipment were needed too, and these our men did not have, so when the 2nd, 3rd and 4th LAA Batteries totalled their losses at Alamein in 1942, it was found that 27 guns had been destroyed by German tanks, one gun by the Luftwaffe, and in addition 90 vehicles had been knocked out. Eight officers and 392 other ranks were missing, killed or wounded. But figures give little idea of what armoured war meant to an anti-aircraft unit. Typical of the many gallant actions fought by this regiment was that of A Troop under Lieutenant McSwiney (later J. M. McSwiney, DSO, MC), as described in the following extract from his diary:

"*November* **1st 1941.** (Still with 7th Support Group and operating with a Jock Column) "6am. Moved out of leaguer with 2nd RB and 60th Field Regiment. This is the third day of our unopposed advance across "The Wire" into Libya and we looked out this morning over Sidi Rezegh. The night had been spent uneasily, for the Boche had a good concentration of force to the north of the valley and we feared a night attack. As usual our main commitment was the protection of the 25 pounders and they had formed leaguer with us, as the Rifle Brigade were employed elsewhere. At 9·30am "Tank Alert" was given and my troop was ordered to protect a south eastern flank in an anti-tank role. There was a troop of 2 pounder ATk guns just in front of us, but otherwise we were very much on our own.

At 1100 hours some 50 Mk III tanks and a few Mk IVs approached from the east in an attempt to outflank us. They entered the valley where the 60th Field Regiment had deployed and promptly withdrew as soon as the 25 pounders opened up over open sights.

At 1130 hours the enemy came on again and were engaged by the anti-tank guns in front of my troop and were halted after six tanks had been put out of action. The Troop Commander (Captain Gunn) was killed, but was given a posthumous VC. The action eliminated our anti-tank protection, as only one member of the troop survived.

A few minutes earlier Colonel de Robeck had appeared and found me lying full length on the ground whilst moving between my guns. He was standing in front of his truck waving his fly whisk — presumably at the bullets which were flying thick and fast from the machine guns of the leading enemy tanks! We passed the time of day from our respective positions and I asked for permission to withdraw. I was informed that this was a case for no withdrawal! We opened fire at 600 yards range with a mixture of HE and AP.

The guns were in a triangle some 50-60 yards apart — I was with the leading gun and had organised a system of flag communication with the other two. Finding the enemy tanks less than 300 yards away and seeing that we had very few rounds left I decided to risk court martial and signalled the two rear guns to withdraw, I remained with the leading gun to give covering fire. The two guns got safely away and we were endeavouring to do the same when our tractor was hit and blew up in a cloud of smoke. A second later and the gun received a direct hit. Four men were badly wounded and somehow I got my truck across the 150 yard interval that separated it from the gun and all were lifted inside. This was mainly due to the 25 pounders, who had spotted our predicament and opened up on the tanks, which were now nosing around about 50 yards away. We only stayed to see one burst of 25 pounder shells, which was more than sufficient to speed us on our way. We claimed four tanks, and although we could not stop them, I think we held them up during a critical period until the 25 pounders could do their stuff.

On linking up with my remaining guns I found that we had lost three men killed and eight wounded. We were brewing up in the B echelon when enemy tanks came into view

The 40mm Bofors gun was probably one of the most widely used weapons of World War II. This one was photographed at Bir Hacheim in 1942. The Bofors had a rate of fire of 120 rounds per minute and a reasonable performance against tanks as well as aircraft.

again and we took up a rearguard position while the soft skinned vehicles cleared off. The tanks sheered away, but soon afterwards 30 Stukas attacked us, with no damage to either side. The rest of the day was spent skirting the edge of the armoured battle and at dusk we joined B echelon again.

Dawn the next day found us on the edge of the Sidi Rezegh valley close to the scene of our battle of the previous day. Seeing a battery of 25 pounders, I decided to link up with them, as the best part of an enemy panzer brigade was showing up over the horizon. We were shelled steadily for five hours and after two Stuka raids the Boche tanks came in again . . ."

While Lieutenant McSwiney was engaged in the series of actions that earned him an MC, the rest of his battery was taking on other sections of the German armour. Lieutenant I. N. Brettell engaged a German armoured brigade until all his guns were put out of action, his position overrun and he himself captured. He was awarded an immediate MC when two days later he escaped, walked back to our positions and recounted his story.

In further months of bitter fighting Lt-Col de Robeck's Regiment was credited with this remarkable score:

Aircraft destroyed	*Aircraft probably destroyed*	*Aircraft damaged*	*Tanks destroyed*
117	61	53	18

Medium and Heavy Artillery

Pictured below are some of the heavier guns used to support the Divisional Artillery.

Left: A 3·7in Heavy Anti Aircraft gun and crew belonging to 88 Regt RA just after getting out of the Knightsbridge Box.

Below: The 5·5in field gun, seen in action here near Derna, was one of the best guns used by the British Army. It could fire an 82lb HE shell over 18,000 yards.

Sidi Rezegh

Of all the major battles fought by the Desert Rats, Sidi Rezegh must feature as their most glorious. It was a not a great victory like Beda Fomm/Sidi Saleh, but rather a hard and bloody encounter in which the Division lost many tanks and suffered many casualities. It was, however, their "finest hour" and resulted in the award of no less than three Victoria Crosses to men of the Division.

The battle itself is well documented elsewhere, so I intend merely to use two eye-witness accounts of what took place. I have chosen two men in quite different places on the battlefield — Joe Lee, a Cherry Picker, who was driving the Brigade Major's tank in HQ 7th Armoured Brigade and Charles Bingham, the Adjutant of 60 Field Regiment, RA, who were part of the Support Group. One name features in both accounts, that of Brigadier Jock Campbell, then commanding the Support Group, who was a continual inspiration to all ranks throughout the battle.

Before these eye-witness accounts let us first read a Battle Memorandum written by Brigadier George Davy, CB, CBE, DSO, on 16th November 1941. He was then commanding the 7th Armoured Brigade, who were to play a vital part in the battle, and had based his memorandum on Nelson's famous Trafalgar Memoradum:

The brigade is expected, in the near future, to meet the German and Italian armoured fomations, and their destruction is to be the primary and constant aim of all commanders.

We shall meet the usual Italian and German tanks, and perhaps half a dozen captured British 'I' tanks and A.15 Cruisers. All these are penetrated by the 2-pounder at our usual ranges except some parts of the front and turret of the 'I' tank. The enemy's armoured cars include a few Marmon Harringtons.

The enemy can often be deceived and surprised by the skilful use of turret-down positions, giving complete concealement until he is within effective range, or by frequent changing of fire positions. Once fire is opened surprise is lost; the first round from every tank must be a hit and kill. The accuracy of your gun has been proved by you against targets only 2½ feet high and 5 feet wide. Your targets next time will be three times higher and often three times wider, and you can choose the point on the target where your first shot is to strike.

Whenever possible, commanders will concentrate superior tank forces against the enemy so that as many guns as possible may be brought to bear on him at effective range at the same time. But there will be many single combats and some against superior numbers. No tank can be considered out of

A wrecked Italian fighter on the airfield at Sidi Rezegh.

action as long as its gun can fire, even though it may be unable to move.

Commanders must guard against using too great force against small objectives, to the detriment of the main battle. This applies both to the handling of units and to the choice of weapons. The 2 pounder and its ammunition must be reserved for penetrating armour.

Vigilance must be constant, all round and upwards. Glasses must be freely used. All armoured vehicles which have wireless masts will be wearing pennants in the position of the day. Tanks wear the red and white sign, but newly arrived tanks may not have had it painted on. Armoured cars have no colour sign, but they show they are friendly by holding a flag out to their right. All these are only indications, and all commanders must take special care not to fire on a friend.

Our superior mobility will often allow commanders so to manoeuvre in the presence of the enemy that some tanks can shoot into his flank and rear while others engage him in front, and it should be possible to prevent any enemy escaping destruction. When manoeuvring in the presence of the enemy, movement should be at the greatest speed the ground permits. In a moving attack all tanks in a wave should be in such formation that they are able to open fire together, and come under enemy fire together.

Senior commanders will often be unable to know what is going on except in their immediate neighbourhood, and will themselves be engaged with the enemy. Orders may be few and far between and shortage of wireless sets will make control less easy. Much will depend on the co-operation and initiative of junior commanders and the enterprise and determination of tank commanders.

This will be a tank commanders' battle. No tank commander will go far wrong if he places his tank within killing range of an enemy.

16 Nov 41

George Davy
Brigadier
Commander

Eye Witness Account of the Battle by Joe Lee:

"It was common knowledge that something was going to happen before long; new tanks, equipment, reinforcements, conferences and a new 2 IC, all those things which go to make a "push" were beginning. Plenty of light aircraft — all ours now — in evidence lately We had never known the like of it. Instead of going in with bits and pieces and having the bitter and frustrating feeling of always being on the receiving end, we were at last going in with at least as much as Rommel had, if not more. Morale was high. Why, on our tank we had even stocked up with tinned sausages and milk, fruit, etc, which we had bought from the Canteen Wagon in the anticipation of another trek like our previous one — "Wavell's push". We'd thought of everything this time.

At last the day arrived — a long approach march south-west to a few miles from "The Wire". We were to leaguer there for the night, and off at first light on the morrow. Just before dusk the cookhouse wagon came up with a hot meal. There we all were, sprawled all over the place in various stages of eating our meal, when there came the sound of aircraft, the alarm was given and what a scramble! Everybody trying to put as much distance as possible between himself and the cookhouse. (Cookhouses were notorious for the way enemy aircraft seemed to be attracted to them, so they were given a wide berth by one and all). Then the aircraft came into view, flying low; it was a German 'plane all right, but it just flew straight on without any deviation from its route. Whether the occupants saw us or the surrounding units I will never know. However, it certainly left a lot of nerves behind its passing visit. After all, it could have seriously jeopardised the plans for the next day.

Up early and everything stowed away, then over to the cookhouse for the typical breakfast the British soldier thrives on. Tinned bacon, with the paper still all chewed up in it; a real hit and miss effort. The usual remarks to the cooks, hoping they would enjoy their breakfast of egg, sausage and beans etc. later on, and of course, the Soldier's Farewell.

At last the B.M (Major Noel Wall) came aboard, stowed his maps etc, and we were ready. The Brigadier went on his tank and in a few minutes we were off. I was driving, and the B.M told me to follow the Brigadier. We moved off at a good pace, straight up and through the gap in the wire made by the REs. All around there seemed to be a veritable armada of armoured vehicles. We couldn't go wrong! The day passed quietly enough. One little niggling thing was my tank tracks; as we moved along I could hear the occasional thump, thump of a track pin coming loose. The only thing to do was to stop, get out and

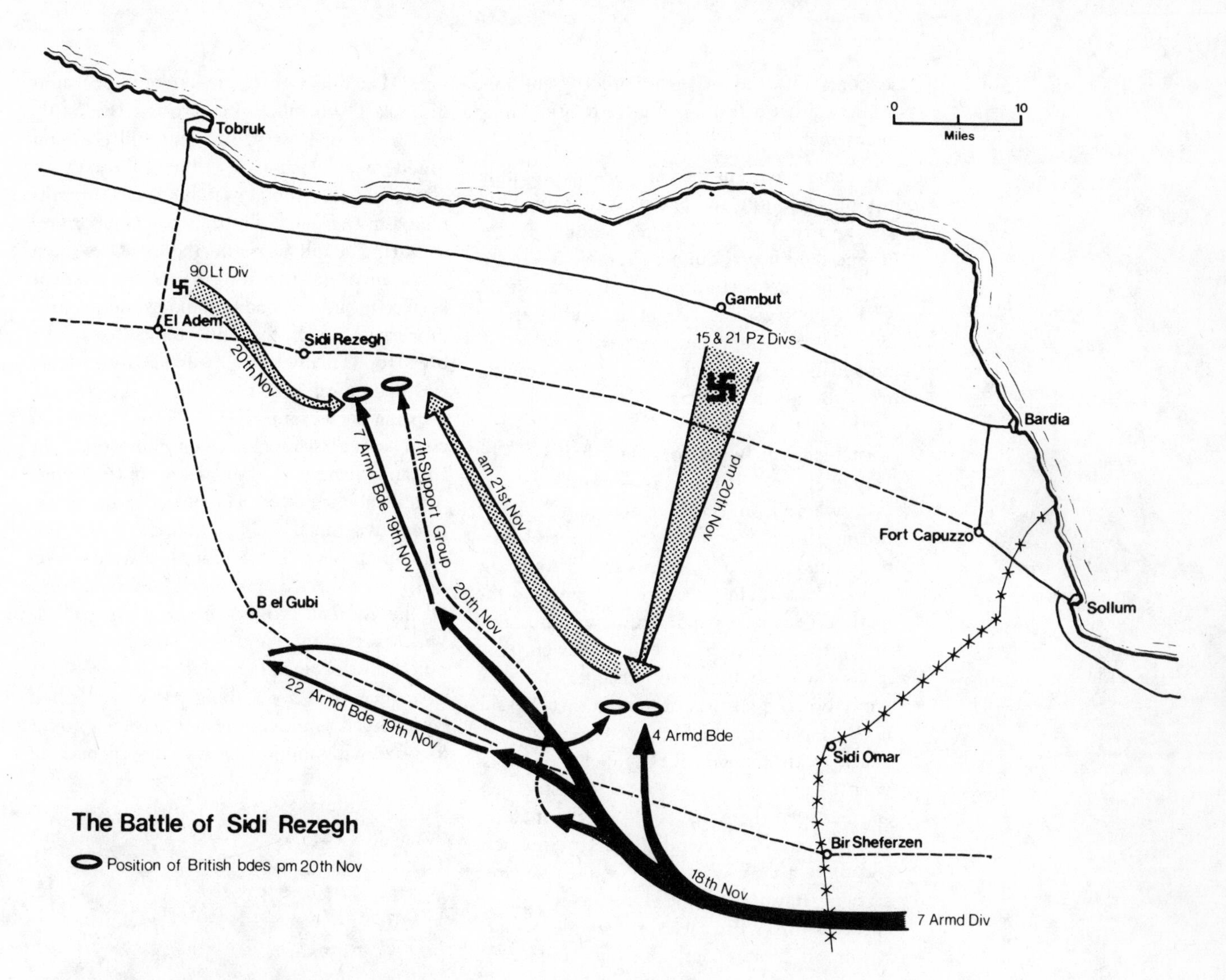

knock it back in — in case the pin came out and the track came off. We leaguered that night some ten miles from Sidi Rezegh. There was one incident; German prisoners were taken and brought back to Brigade for questioning. They looked very frightened men. I think the shock of seeing so many enemy tanks right on their own doorstep, so to speak, scared them.

The next day things started to move, and more reports about Divisional activities began to come in. During the afternoon we were on the move and the Brigade swept down on to the enemy aerodrome at Sidi Rezegh. It was a wonderful sight to see a whole cavalcade of tanks in full cry spread right out across the whole valley, going flat out. A few enemy planes were landing and taking off at the time and some tanks opened up on them. One or two planes circled and came in strafing the tanks, but to no avail. The 'drome was ours, complete with aircraft. Well, the morale of the troops was sky-high and it boded well for the morrow. Dusk was not far off and we moved back down to the bottom of the Southern Escarpment to leaguer for the night. Out came the petrol cookers, for a brew-up while the light was still good. On the flanks the regiments were doing the same and we were all quite happy, when out of the blue came the voice of Gabriel the Archangel: "Put those fires out, put them out!" At first no one took much notice; I think that enraged the speaker somewhat, since it was only the Divisional Commander! As it was, the order made the men do things that they would not normally do — in one sense of the word it sent them underground — tea was brewed up inside vehicles and in tanks, so everyone still had their brew. But if anything had gone wrong and a vehicle had perhaps caught fire, well, that could have had serious consequences. I think a lot of men felt cheated, and there is nothing worse to a British soldier than to be cheated, it makes him mad. The Army still hadn't reached the stage where the rank and file were told much about the operation they were taking part in, and to be forced to do something when there seemed no logical reason, plus the way the order went out, caused rather a feeling of uncertainty among many men.

During the night the Germans had brought up guns and dug in. The next morning, just before first light, they opened up into the leaguer and it was quite a scramble to get the 'thinskins' up to the top of the escarpment. One vehicle was hit, caught fire and lit up the whole surrounding desert. Eventually we all moved up. The sound of firing was coming from the north of the aerodrome and things really started to happen. That day became a veritable whirlwind of tank battles. The Brigadier and B.M. was here, there and everywhere from action to action. The desert became littered with knocked-out and burning tanks, and full of smoke and dust; the brigade was taking a severe battering. So the battle raged; parry and thrust, with no hope of reinforcements, as each unit was engaged in its own life-and-death struggle and they were too far apart to assist each other. To the north, I watched the Support Group go into attack with the 6th RTR. Shellfire caused what I can only describe as huge dust spouts, and between them one could see the infantry going forward in extended order, while here and there a tank was visible and a few Bren carriers. It wan't long before the weight of enemy artillery fire caused the whole scene to be almost blotted out, and one could only wonder whether anyone could come out of such an inferno alive. But we had the first taste of success that day when several hundred prisoners were taken; it put good heart in one to see the long column of prisoners under escort wind its way across the valley and off to captivity. That day left several vivid impressions on my mind: during one tank action I caught the sound of music across the desert and there amid the noise of gunfire, came the strains of the 'Bolero'. A Bren carrier came up from the action of the KRRC and 6 RTR just about crammed full of badly wounded men lying at all angles. The driver asked for the nearest First Aid Post, and it was pointed out to him, some 250 yards away. He just looked at it, then at us — no more no less — then turned round and went straight down into the battle area again. There were many unsung heroes at Sidi Rezegh.

I remember watching our own artillery knock out three German field guns. It was like a skittle match, but they started from right to left. I could feel myself willing the shells to fall straight on the right-hand gun, and as the next salvo went I remember saying, "This time, go on, this time". The sight of Jock Campbell flying around the battle area in his open staff car. The dull clanging sound of solid shot as it hit steel, and the queer whirring sound as richochets went sailing past. The smell of burning oil and cordite.

During a lull in battle there was a small conference on the top of the escarpment between the Brigadier and some senior officers. We took this opportunity to make a brew for as many as we could. Tea was made and poured out when there came the crash of bursting shells some 100 yards away; the second salvo was clonk on position, but amazingly the only casualties were two mugs of tea knocked over. The next one hit an artillery wagon. Then I saw just what a real downpour of shells could do. In a wadi to our right our wheeled transport was resting, and all the German artillery in range opened up with everything they had. There were airbursts and normal HE, and in a very short time there was not a thing left there. It had been forced to move. I saw two lorries going forward with ammo. The two drivers had the

shellfire off to a T; they rushed on, stopped, jumped out, ran a few yards off and dropped flat — down came the German shellfire — then back into the trucks and off again, followed by a repeat performance, and so on up to the unit requiring replenishment. At the back of my mind was the worry over my gearbox lever; the links had stretched and it was a devil of a task to get a gear, but it was a workshop job.

Later that afternoon we were halted among the wheeled transport, and the Brigadier and BM were in the ACV, when without warning a vehicle burst into flames 100 yards or so away, and vehicles started to scatter in all directions. On came a German tank column with guns blazing. What a scramble! We had the ACV with the Brigadier and his staff on board to look after, and it was quite a job to keep between that and the enemy tanks. Taffy the Lap Gunner had to come up and fire the main armament, while Corporal Bill Rawlings (killed two days later) commanded. Utter chaos for a while, with vehicles going all ways, gunfire, smoke and dust. Remnants of the 2nd RTR were well into action, but I think it was just a matter of time before they and the 7th Hussars were virtually wiped out. The Brigadier and B.M. piled into their tanks and off we went towards a cloud of dust and tanks moving in the distance. It was the 22nd Armoured Brigade and we steamed flat out to them, the Brigadier waving a small white handkerchief. Stop!

During the night we could see burning tanks, some glowing red, and the occasional spout of flame and sparks as ammunition caught fire, while the stench of burning oil and smoke wafted across the desert.

The next day we saw the South Africans moving up, who were to have such a terrible pounding down in the valley which came to be known as the Valley of Death. Later that day we were withdrawing and my tank was towing the Brig's tank, which had engine trouble. We were moving slowly along, when vehicles started to go past us at a terrific pace, and then came the sound of gunfire. Immediate thoughts: what now? We stopped, the Brigadier surveyed the situation and

A general view of the battlefield at Sidi Rezegh.

deducted rightly that a German tank column had broken right through the 'B' Echelons and was creating havoc everywhere. We towed the Brigadier's tank into a hull down position and the Brigadier took over command of my tank. He gathered the few remaining tanks and led them into the attack. Commanding and directing the gunner himself, he hit and stopped the nearest German tank, and its crew jumped out. I remember asking the Brigadier whether we should use the co-ax machine gun, but the reply came, "Concentrate on the tanks". There was a flurry of dust as a German shot landed some 30 yards in front of us and seemed to zoom slowly over the tank. I can remember thinking, "Blimey, that must have just about whipped his head off" — meaning of course the Brigadier. After firing so many rounds the two pounder jammed solid and we could not move it anyhow. There was one tank with its gun out of action, but whose engine was mechanically all right towing another whose engine was u/s but whose gun was working; the crews of knocked-out tanks had formed a chain and were transferring ammo from one tank to the other as they moved along. It was quite an inspiration to all. When we found we could do nothing about the gun, it was decided to try and tow another tank and perhaps use its gun, but this did not materialise; as we came round to get alongside we crashed straight into it, and that was that. We were trapped and things looked hopeless. But all was not lost, for just at that moment a lot of Stuart tanks (the protection squadron of HQ 30 Corps) came up and into the fray. We were told to bale out, so we ran across the desert and one of these tanks picked us up. There we all were, hanging on to the front of the tank — at least, some were hanging on and they were holding the others on — there were six or seven of us altogether. The gun was in action and firing over the back as the tank drove straight out of the immediate line of fire, dropped us off and returned into action. A scout car picked us up and took us further on, to where a few armoured cars and a couple of lorries stood. These turned out to be from the 4th South African Armoured Car Company. The Brigadier himself had jumped up on to the back of a tank and the last I saw of him that day he was directing and encouraging the tanks in action. It was a running battle which gradually moved away from us.

A knocked out German Mk 3 tank.

A little later we were told to pile aboard the trucks. Richy, our wireless operator, and myself got on one and the rest on the other. I remember thinking at the time, "We've picked a right one here!" — it was a petrol truck, full of cans of petrol! However, when we stopped later that night, we found we had split up. The next morning found us with just two armoured cars and a couple of lorries. The rest of the desert was ours. Richy and I had just what we stood up in. Later on we saw a scout car coming across the desert. The S.A.'s were dubious who it might be, friend or foe, and they took up defensive positions. When I saw who it was I had quite a shock — it was Brigadier Jock Campbell. The S.A.'s were not quite sure what to think. When he saw my beret (11th Hussars) Campbell asked me if I knew who he was, and I then told the South Africans. He then asked me what I was doing there. After hearing my story, he said, "Good, you can drive tanks. There are a lot on the way back, so we'll see if we can get any to go". We went over to the scout car — there were six of us in it — and made our way across the desert, passing burnt-out and derelict tanks and vehicles. The first one we looked at seemed all right from one side, but we found it had received a hit underneath the turret ring, which was jammed and lifted. So we went on — some tanks were burnt out, some needed major workshop attention, some were in a very bad state where there had been wounded personnel — none were moveable without attention of some description.

Then we arrived back at Brigade Headquarters. It was like a missing persons bureau, everybody enquiring about everyone else. I was pleased to see the Brig and the B.M. still there. And the luck of the draw? What about the rest of the chaps who had got on to the other wagon? Their column ran into a German column during the night and they were all either wounded or killed."

Charles Bingham (extract from a letter to Brig Hallifax):
"We crossed "The Wire" well south on day 1, immediately after the armoured brigades, and turning north west reached the approaches to Sidi Rezegh without opposition. Our tanks had been on the landing ground and smashed 22 Axis planes, and when we arrived they were covering it from the south from hull down positions; the Boche and Italians were dug in on the north side and occupied the valley and next crest to the north of that. We deployed in the valley to the south of the drome, trying to establish an all-round defensive position. Our positions were covered, but as soon as they were occupied the Boche searched the whole valley with airburst HE, fortunately doing little damage. The following morning we tried to link-up with the Tobruk garrison.

Our task was a fire plan to support the KRRC, whose objective was the northern side of the aerodrome. We then lifted to concentrations on the far ridge. Registration was done by Majors Peel and Sugg in Marmon Harringtons and by Garth in a carrier, and O.P's where then to to go forward with the infantry for observed shooting; the KRRC were using their carriers. The fire plan was a brilliant success, and perhaps the best proof of this is that now we are back, the KRRC rifleman cannot do too much for the 60 Field gunner. Observed shooting afterwards was very difficult; targets were completely obscured by smoke and dust, and all O.P's were using concentrated salvoes to find their own bursts. Major Peel was wounded fairly early on. Using an armoured car in support of carriers was a mistake, since it was of course picked out as a target.

After the attack the Brigadier moved one troop on to the SE corner of the aerodrome, while the other three remained to establish an all-round position in the valley. Meanwhile the echelons of both sides were being chopped up by the tanks.

In the next 48 hours we fired continually from O.Ps on the north of aerodrome ridge, mainly at MET and tanks. Results were difficult to determine, as observation was bad, but we certainly had successes. Three times tanks (40-50) came in to within 2000-2500 yards of the eastern position (F Troop) and shelled us heavily for about 2 hours each time; we had two guns knocked out, some M.T and several casualties, but nothing as bad as one might have feared. They used 75mm and six pounders. Our tanks attacked several times using Cruisers (A.15) and Honeys, but I am afraid they were out-gunned and took some bad punishment — the A.15 seemed to burn too easily.

The following day the Boche counter-attacked heavily; his tanks attacked from the west and south west and his infantry from the north. I was with Brigadier Campbell and Major James Galloway when the attack started, and we each took a gun and fought it for about 1½ hours. Again they stood off and shelled us; observation and correction was the most difficult as there were several tanks and planes on fire and everything was obscured by a pall of smoke and dust. Then our Honeys attacked and the Brigadier left, but they were beaten off and the whole thing started again. Meanwhile our infantry and O.Ps had been overcome to the north and hostile infantry appeared on the west, to our right flank, and machine-gunned us down the line of guns. At the same time the rest of the regiment had been withdrawn from the valley, leaving us isolated. Again Brigadier Campbell rushed on to the position, but fell wounded as he stepped out of his car. Major James piled him into a tank, and saying to the tank officer, "Why don't you attack, you are killing all my boys?" he (ie Brig Campbell) passed out; fortunately the wound proved to be slight. Meanwhile our position was getting pretty bad. Desperately we pulled some guns round against the infantry, but it was really only a gesture, as our ammo was almost exhausted — attempts to get ammo to us had failed.

Casualties were now getting bad, so we tried to get the tractors onto the position. Two were knocked out 50 yards from the position; my own and another got hooked in but an incendiary entered the petrol tank and it burst into flames. Major James got hooked in but a solid shot smashed the back axle, and two got away. The whole place was now swept with fire, so we went to ground. Fortunately the infantry couldn't advance, as our Honeys covered the intervening ground from a hull down position.

We tried to filter those who could crawl away, then Major James and I agreed to toss for who stayed with the badly wounded. Unfortunately, as it happened, every movement and attempt to get sights etc brought down such a hail of fire that we had to abandon the attempt. About 16·30 a smoke screen was put down and practically everyone was got away, when suddenly the screen lifted and down we went again. Those who were left managed to get away at dusk with sights, firing mechanisms etc.

Meanwhile the other three troops were attacked again; this time tanks came right into the positions. Infantry of both sides, tanks, guns and carriers were all mixed up, and at dusk the regiment was ordered out. Colonel Hely, who was marvellous throughout, had one truck shot from under him trying to get some guns out, but managed to get another. Slinky was last seen taking his troop out, holding a blue flag up as though it was a drill order. Brig. Campbell was kind enough to say to Col Hely afterwards that "The 60th Field were the talk not only of the Division but of the Corps".

For Valour

Here below are inscribed the names of those of the 7th Armoured Division who in the performance of their duty at Sidi Rezegh displayed such conspicuous bravery as to merit the supreme reward of the soldier, the Victoria Cross.

Brigadier (Acting) John Charles Campbell, DSO, MC, Royal Horse Artillery

On November 21st 1941, Brigadier Campbell was commanding the troops, including one regiment of tanks, in the area of Sidi Rezegh ridge and the aerodrome. His small force holding this important ground was repeatedly attacked by large numbers of tanks and infantry. Wherever the stuation was most difficult and the fighting hardest he was to be seen with his forward troops, either on his feet or in his open car. In this car he carried out general reconnaissance for counter-attacks by his tanks, whose senior officers had all become casualties early in the day. Standing in his car with a blue flag, this officer personally formed up tanks under close and intense fire from all natures of enemy weapons.

On the following day the enemy attacks were intensified and again Brigadier Campbell was always in the forefront of the heaviest fighting, encouraging his troops, staging counter-attacks with his remaining tanks and personally controlling the fire of his guns. On two occasions he himself manned a gun to replace casualties. During the final enemy attack on November 22nd he was wounded, but continued most actively in the foremost positions, controlling the fire of batteries which inflicted heavy losses on enemy tanks at point-blank range, and finally acted as loader to one of the guns himself.

Throughout these two days his magnificent example and his utter disregard of personal danger were an inspiration to his men and to all who saw him. His brilliant leadership was the direct cause of the very heavy casualties inflicted on the enemy. In spite of his wound he refused to be evacuated and remained with his command, where his outstanding bravery and consistent determination had a marked effect in maintaining the splendid fighting spirit of those under him.

2nd Lieutenant George Ward Gunn, MC, Royal Horse Artillery

On November 21st 1941, at Sidi Rezegh, 2nd Lt Gunn was in command of a troop of four anti tank guns which was part of a battery of 12 guns attached to the Rifle Brigade Column. At ten o'clock a covering force of enemy tanks was engaged and driven off, but an hour later the main attack by about 60 enemy tanks developed. 2nd Lieutenant Gunn drove from gun to gun during this period in an unarmoured vehicle encouraging his men and reorganising his dispositions as first one gun and then another were knocked out. Finally, only two guns remained in action

Far left: **Brigadier (later Maj Gen) Jock Campbell, VC, DSO, MC.**

Centre left: Lieutenant George Ward Gunn, VC, MC.

Left: Rifleman John Beeley, VC.

and were subjected to very heavy fire. Immediately afterwards one of these guns was destroyed and the portee of the other was set on fire and all the crew killed or wounded except the sergeant, though the gun itself remained undamaged. The battery commander then arrived and started to fight the flames. When he saw this, 2nd Lieutenant Gunn ran to his aid through intense fire and immediately got the one remaining anti tank gun into action on the burning portee, himself sighting it while the sergeant acted as loader. He continued to fight the gun, firing between 40 and 50 rounds regardless alike of the enemy fire which was by then concentrated on this one vehicle, and on the flames which might at at any moment have reached the ammunition with which the portee was loaded. In spite of this, 2nd Lt Gunn's shooting was so accurate at a range of about 800 yards that at least two enemy tanks were hit and set on fire and others were damaged before he fell dead, having been shot through the forehead.

2nd Lt Gunn showed the most conspicuous courage in attacking this large number of enemy tanks with a single unarmoured gun, and his utter disregard of extreme danger was an example which inspired all who saw it. He remained undismayed by intense fire and overwhelming odds, and his gallant resistance only ceased with his death. But for this very gallant action the enemy tanks would undoubtedly have overrun our position.

Rifleman John Beeley, 1st Battalion The King's Royal Rifle Corps.

On the 21st November 1941, during the attack at Sidi Rezegh, against a strong enemy position, the company to which Rifleman Beeley belonged was pinned down by heavy fire at point-blank range from the front and flank on the flat, open ground of the aerodrome. All the officers but one of the company and many of the other ranks had been either killed or wounded. On his own initiative, and when there was no sort of cover, Rifleman Beeley got to his feet carrying a Bren gun and ran forward towards a strong enemy post containing an anti tank gun. He ran thirty yards and discharged a complete magazine at the post from a range of twenty yards, killing or wounding the entire crew of the anti tank gun. The post was silenced and Rifleman Beeley's platoon was enabled to advance, but Rifleman Beeley fell dead across his gun, hit in at least four places.

Rifleman Beeley went to certain death in a gallant and successful attempt to carry the day. His courage and self-sacrifice were a glorious example to his comrades and inspired them to further efforts to reach their objective, which was eventually captured by them, together with 700 prisoners.

The Sappers

Mobility

The work of the Royal Engineers within the armoured division was of the greatest importance. Whether in the advance, attack, defence or withdrawal, the Sappers were constantly needed, primarily to assist the Division in maintaining its mobility. To achieve this they had to cope with a wide variety of natural obstacles, as well as with enemy demolitions, booby traps and minefields — in fact anything which hampered the Division's progress. In addition, they were responsible for many other engineering tasks, the main one being the supply of water — vital in the desert — and the destruction of equipment, both our own and that of the enemy; the destruction of abandoned AFVs was particularly important. All these different activities required great skill, as well as personal initiative, because they often had to be done by small, scattered detachments, led by a young NCO who had to make decisions on his own and then get on with the job.

Sappers clearing a minefield.

The key to all engineer work is timely information, so RE reconnaissance parties were always found with the leading troops in any advance, providing technical assistance to the commander. They were also responsible for carrying out technical recces, so that no time need be lost on the arrival of the Sapper squadron which would actually carry out the work.

In the advance most of the Sappers' work consisted of bridging, preparing diversions around obstacles, removing booby traps and clearing safe lanes through enemy minefields. These tasks often had to be carried out under fire, so although the Sappers were, like any other troops, primarily responsible for their own protection, when they were fully employed on technical tasks they had to be covered by protective troops.

In defence their main role was to carry out specialist engineer tasks such as laying and recording minefields, and they also gave advice to other arms on the construction of defences and strong points.

The first engineer units in the Division were 2 Field Squadron and 141 Field Park Troop, both mainly composed of Cheshire Territorials. Later these units were replaced by 4 Fd Sqn and 143 Fd Pk Sqn, who remained with 7th Armoured Division for the rest of the war. Just before El Alamein, they were joined by 21 Fd Sqn.

A scout car belonging to 4 Fd Sqn, with Sapper Harry Green manning the LMG, which was used for long distance patrols into enemy held territory. Patrols would go out for a week or more to gather information and data on enemy patrols, routes, minefields etc.

Here are some recollections of life in the desert by men who served with the field squadrons.

Major J. S. Revers writes:

"I was posted as a troop leader to the 2nd Cheshire Field Squadron, RE. Now here was a funny thing. Years before I had been PSI of this Territorial Army unit, based in Birkenhead, and yet I had no idea that they were in the Desert.

My first incident of note happened just before Tobruk was captured. My OC sent me and the troop off to some salt flats about 5 or 6 kms west of Tobruk and near the coast. He gave me a map reference just south of Tobruk and said I would find a line of telephone poles there that would lead me to the coast road. Off we went, but ran into a sand storm and when I found the line of poles, they were running in all directions! I followed the line which I thought to be the right one, but when we came into a clear space — no sand storm — the Iti's opened up on us; we had run into their defences from the south. We were sitting targets, but luckily had no casualties, except for our compressor truck which would not start and had to be left behind. We all got out, followed the right line of poles and got to our salt flats, where we had to drill for water and take salinity tests.

The next day after arriving at the salt flats, a Bedouin boy wandered up and tried to explain that a plane had come down near us, but I could not make out if it was British or not. I took a Sergeant and one man and we followed the boy to where the plane — a Heinkel — was sitting on the ground some distance away. There was not another soul about and the plane seemed to be undamaged. As we approached, three immaculately-uniformed Germans jumped out, yelling at us in English to lie down. I was not going to do that, but they did. Suddenly the plane blew up, but there was no fire.

Anyway, we disarmed them, as they carried pistols. We had no transport, but eventually we got to the coast, and luckily a 15cwt truck came along and we took the prisoners to Brigade HQ. I found out later that their plane had been on a bombing mission around Malta, had got lost and they thought they were near Benghazi!"

In the early days Brig Eddie Myers was commanding 2nd (Cheshire) Field Squadron, RE: "The Advanced Headquarters of the 7th Armoured Division, together with my own field squadron headquarters, was then at Buq Buq, a fly-infested bit of scrub-covered desert adjoining the coastal sand dunes, about half way between Sidi Barrani and Sollum. Each of my field troops was affiliated to a brigade, and I had detachments with each of the armoured brigades along the Libyan frontier, mostly employed on destroying enemy tanks after forays into Libya, finding and developing sources of water, laying and clearing minefields, and also on track marking, which was particularly important for B Echelon supply vehicles.

Shortly after the Italian build-up had forced us to withdraw from the frontier, I was called upon to assist battleships of the Royal Navy in bombarding Fort Capuzzo. At the appointed dawn we had to help identify its whereabouts with a column of smoke over the high coastal headland a mile or so west of Sollum. This was achieved by unobtrusively building a rough vehicle track along the shore to the foot of the headland in No Man's Land, sheltered only the steep cliffs from the Italian forward positions. We brought up several drums of diesel oil, which when set alight produced a thick, tall column of black smoke. It was quite an experience to hear 15 inch shells hurtling overhead like air-cushioned express trains, and to wonder whether our headland perch would be molested by any enterprising Italians before we could withdraw to the safety of Sollum, which was occupied by the Support Group.

Throughout the coastal belt in the Western Desert, in addition to some cleverly-sited underground aqueducts in the porous limestone alongside the actual coast, the Romans had constructed numerous rain-water catchment cisterns, carved out of the solid rock. Because of the Italian build-up and the possibility of a further British withdrawal, it was decided to deny the use of these cisterns to the enemy, without actually contravening the Hague Convention by poisoning them. Some clever chap decided that an adequate concentration of bone oil, which has the smell and taste of very rotten eggs, would make the water in these cisterns undrinkable.

For a couple of weeks or more, RE detachments roamed the desert, often only a Lance Corporal's command in a couple of 15cwt trucks, map reading by sun compass, and pouring this stinking fluid into all known cisterns. A few months later, during our subsequent advance to Bardia, Tobruk and beyond, we badly needed these valuable sources of water once again for ourselves. Greatly to our relief, most of the horrible smell and taste had gone!

Shortly before the Italians, now heavily outnumbering us, decided to advance further into Egypt, they started dropping from aircraft clusters of a lethal type of anti-personnel bomb entirely new to us. Shaped like a thermos, they soon became known as "Thermos" bombs. A jolt on landing automatically armed them; thereafter the slightest movement tripped the detonating device. Within twenty-four hours of the first arrival of these bombs one of my Troop Leaders, Captain Cartmel, had succeeded in safely dismantling one of them, as a result of which we were able to report to all units of the Division and to Corps Headquarters, exactly how they worked and the best way of dealing with them; this was by moving them with rifle fire from a safe distance behind cover. Over the next few months they caused a number of casualties and proved to be of considerable nuisance value.

A 15cwt Bedford of 4 Fd Sqn pictured here at their base camp. These Bedfords formed the main means of transport carrying a section of 8 men plus mine detectors, explosives, shovels and other Sapper kit.

Any withdrawal tends to be demoralising. When eventually the gallant Italian hordes advanced further and we withdrew in front of them — not without giving them a few hard punches on the nose — what worried me most was the poor communications with my widely-scattered squadron and the lack of accurate information as people became tired and harassed. I still had "bone oiling" detachments out on distant missions. With not one of my many detachments had I any wireless contact; there were no R.T. sets for Sappers in those days. To establish communication with these scattered field troops I eventually relied upon liaison NCOs, mostly hand-picked Lance Corporals, who travelled to and fro in single 8cwt trucks, fore-runners of the Land Rover, carrying orders and reports, and filling in the picture at both ends verbally.

When the Italian advance started, Advanced Headquarters 7th Armoured Division was withdrawn to a position well south of Mersa Matruh. I remained with my Squadron headquarters some forty or more miles further forward, in a comparatively pleasant but isolated spot on the coast about ten miles west of Sidi Barrani, just off the Sidi Barrani-Sollum road. I had been advised by my Chief Engineer that we would probably be wanted to destroy the Mersa Matruh-Sidi Barrani road. This was apprently on the personal instructions of Winston Churchill, who had noted on his map the solitary and important-looking coastal road, not realising that it was possible to motor on either side of the road at a slower pace, except across the occasional steep — but at that time of the year, dry — wadi bed.

When most of the lorry-borne infantry and gunners of the Support Group had withdrawn past my headquarters, leaving between us and the advancing enemy only a thin observer screen of 11th Hussars' armoured cars, I decided to withdraw my Squadron HQ, and the field troops which had fallen back on me, to a previously reconnoitred position just east of a fairly tank-proof wadi bed astride the Sidi Barrani road at Kilo 44 (44 kilometres out from Mersa Matruh). Here we took up an all-round defensive position and waited hopefully for the fog of war to lift a bit.

I had hardly slept for the past two days and nights but a few hours after our arrival at Kilo 44 I was woken up from an incredibly deep sleep by the arrival of one of the Chief Engineer's Staff Officers with a truckload of demolition devices to sow into the Sidi Barrani road, and the promise the next day of a large bulldozer with a rooter attachment to break up the surface of the road.

And so it came about that we "destroyed" the Sidi Barrani road, gradually working our way westwards towards the enemy, who had not ventured east of Sidi Barrani in any strength, sowing all sorts of contact mines, demolition charges and booby trapped devices into and under the rooted-up road surface and placing demolition charges under such wadi bridges and culverts as there were. After much bleating I was eventually given a company of the 60th Rifles to protect my Squadron position at Kilo 44, so that my sappers could get some sleep at night after working forward all day. Our bulldozer, affectionately christened Cynthia — I don't

Sappers clearing anti tank mines on the Tobruk-Derna road, early on in the campaign.

remember why! — was too slow a mover to be withdrawn at night into our Squadron leaguer. So we used to booby-trap the robust lady and leaver her out alone at night. She was never molested."

As I have explained, one of the most hazardous tasks for the Engineers was the breaching of enemy minefields. At Alamein, for example, the entire operation depended upon this breaching being carried out successfully. Sapper Sydney Morgan, who was in those days a member of 4 Fd Sqn, is now Brother Bernard, a monk at Pluscarden Abbey in Scotland. He recalls the breaching operations in which he took part:

"The Sappers' operational task was to make traffic lanes through Allied and German minefields. An officer, two NCOs and about twelve men, a wireless crew and a Flail formed a Lane Group. The Flail, a tank with a roller in front with lengths of steel cable attached, was to advance along a predetermined route exploding mines with the 'flails'. The men were to follow with white tapes to make the traffic path. If the Flail broke down (ours did) then Sappers with mine detectors would continue the work.

Shortly before the attack Montgomery gave us a 'pep' talk. The details have gone, but memories of the general informality and relaxed atmosphere remain. He spoke to us as he might have done at an officers' briefing session: he gave an assessment of the enemy strength and quoted figures of our own resources. One got the impression that he had calculated everything, including the inevitable losses. Monty stood on top of a tank (I think) to reach his hearers, who leaned against vehicles or sat on the ground. There was nothing of a 'Parade' about it.

I was only indirectly involved with the Lane work, being in charge of the radio along with another Sapper. Wireless sets had been in normal use until about 24 hours before Zero Hour, when a complete ban was imposed. There was in fact considerable silence everywhere and this was most impressive, even for one who had spent a long time in the desert. I went over to the water wagon to fill my bottle, singing softly a piece of Gregorian Chant. As my voice trailed off someone continued the music. I wonder who he was?

Was I afraid of death? I think not. When one is faced with so much slaughter it is a question that is bound to arise. A convert to Catholicism, I had thought much about the existence of God and of man's immortality about a year previously, but I felt the fear that uncertainty creates.

A Bren carrier had been issued for the wireless crew (a driver and two wireless operators) and shortly before 10pm I was ready, watch and set checked, code and message pad to hand. ZERO HOUR! The control set called for signals, in rapid succession we answered and then we were deafened by the barrage. Somehow I felt detached from it all and was fascinated by the slowness of the shells as they seemed to crawl through the sky. Early in the morning, before dawn, a shell or a mortar crashed down just outside the Bren carrier. We all went up in the air. When calm was restored I was able to take stock. There was shrapnel in my back and arm — small pieces — but the Bren carrier had saved us. What happened to the infantrymen nearby I do not know. I remained there until the morning, when my officer sent me off to the CCS. The chaos, now visibile, unnerved me a bit and I was glad to depart, supporting a complete stranger injured in the leg. To get along he grabbed my injured arm; there was nothing to do but keep my mouth shut and hope that he had not noticed.

En route I joked with some men trying to dig in. It would have needed a pneumatic drill to get anywhere to make the shallowest of trenches — but they were managing!"

Communications

Left: An operator manning a WS No 11 — note that he is wearing "Bombay Bloomers"!

Below: Land line being laid near Agedabia.

Lifeblood of the Division

Communications are the lifeblood of any mobile armoured force and it is no exaggeration to say that the successful operation of an armoured division in the desert depended largely upon the reliability of its communications system. The system had to be flexible enough to meet any situation which arose, since in a mobile battle covering vast areas of trackless desert, events were constantly changing, producing new problems hourly.

The Royal Corps of Signals personnel of the division were responsible for communications at Divisional HQ, Brigade HQs and down to the units. Within units it became the responsibility of the regimental signallers.

Three types of communications were available — wireless, message carriers and land line. Wireless of course provided the fastest and most flexible means up to the range of the sets, but was dependent both upon the skill of the operators and on the amount of outside interference. It also lacked security, as the enemy could easily listen in. This led to the use of codes and ciphers by both sides.

Message-carrying agencies, such as Liaison Officers (LO) and Despatch Riders (DR), were ideal for carrying maps and documents, but could be wasteful both in men and vehicles if used to excess. To make their difficult job a little easier, all headquarters had to be clearly signed both day and night. There was of course an element of risk in using LOs and DRs in forward areas, due to the possibility of capture. Here are some reminiscences by an LO and a DR which explain the type of task they had to perform.

Major Chris Milner, MC, was then a Liaison Officer with an Armoured Brigade HQ and wrote in a letter home:

"Your mount may be an American Jeep, a British armoured scout car (known as a dingo), an 8 or 15cwt truck, or in certain circumstances a tank. The base for operations may be with the Brigadier's party up with the tanks, or with Main Bde HQ working either way — forward or rear. There is usually an LO from each of the tank and infantry regiments in the brigade, of which the tank wallahs are most likely to go forward and the infantry rep, as I was, to stay at main HQ and work either way. And so it was. One covered quantities of miles. When on a job it meant tearing around, smothered in dust very often, taking a ration lorry up forward, guiding a recovery tractor to one of our tanks which had gone up on a minefield, trying to find a unit which has gone astray, taking written operation orders round to several regiments — "You do 1, 2, 3 and 8. You 4, 5, 6, 7, 9 and 10, as they're all close together". Navigating the Brigadier or someone else around, and probably most unpleasant of all, setting out at about ten o'clock

Below: An armoured command vehicle with large radio mast erected near Mersa Matruh, 1940.

Below right: Signalman Jeff Orchard on his beloved Norton.

at night on a bearing to find night leaguers and deliver instructions to perhaps three different colonels — all of whom have to move somewhere at first light and have to receive sufficient warning from your early arrival to be able to implement the orders. When none of these things are happening you sleep, eat, write letters or help the Intelligence Officer."

Jeff Orchard was a Despatch Rider in the Royal Corps of Signals:
"World War II broke out on 3rd September 1939, and on the 4th I went to join the Navy, full of romantic ideas about destroyers etc. On arrival at the Naval Recruiting Office in Plymouth I was told "Welcome, sir — regular engagement?" I asked what that was. They said it entailed signing on for 12 years!! I said, "It's going to be a long war, but not *that* long", so that was that!

I then tried to join the Royal Armoured Corps, but they said, "Stay at home and wait", so I became a "Graham Walker Boy", ie joining the Royal Signals as a DR because of my experience as a motorcyclist. Eventually six DRs arrived in Command Signals Egypt and the three lucky ones joined the 7th Armoured Division. We were posted to the Support Group and after approximately a week Mussolini obligingly declared war on us. We immediately proceeded "up the Blue" and I really was one of the first few folk in Sidi Barrani.

In the early days the British forces were ludicrously small and there was little action. We carried out the usual DR duties on motorcycles which, although we loved 'em, were unpractical in the desert. Eventually we lost them and were very cut up about it. Sporadic action between light armoured columns took place for some months, until our successful push against the Itis. I of course missed this completely, being in hospital with jaundice, as were a goodly proportion of MEF at one time or another. The desert rations were really diabolical during this period, being comprised largely of greasy bacon and more greasy bacon! I returned to my unit just in time for the intervention of Rommel (really the desert war looked up from then on!), and was transferred to the 4th RHA Signal troop, where I had a marvellous time, but not a great deal of plain DR work.

There was a fair amount of action, a wonderful sense of companionship and no civilian intervention, refugees or suffering. Played like chess, it was really war at its best, if there is such a thing. Unfortunately the famous 'Jock' Columns were made up of such sparse weaponry that a serious armoured force was non-existent for long periods and real 'pushes' featured augmented casts, so to speak. As time went on material became more abundant and we used to pursue the Hun with added mechanical vigour. Eventually I went through "The Wire" once too often and that was that".

Typical storm dress for a message carrier.

The Services (A&Q)

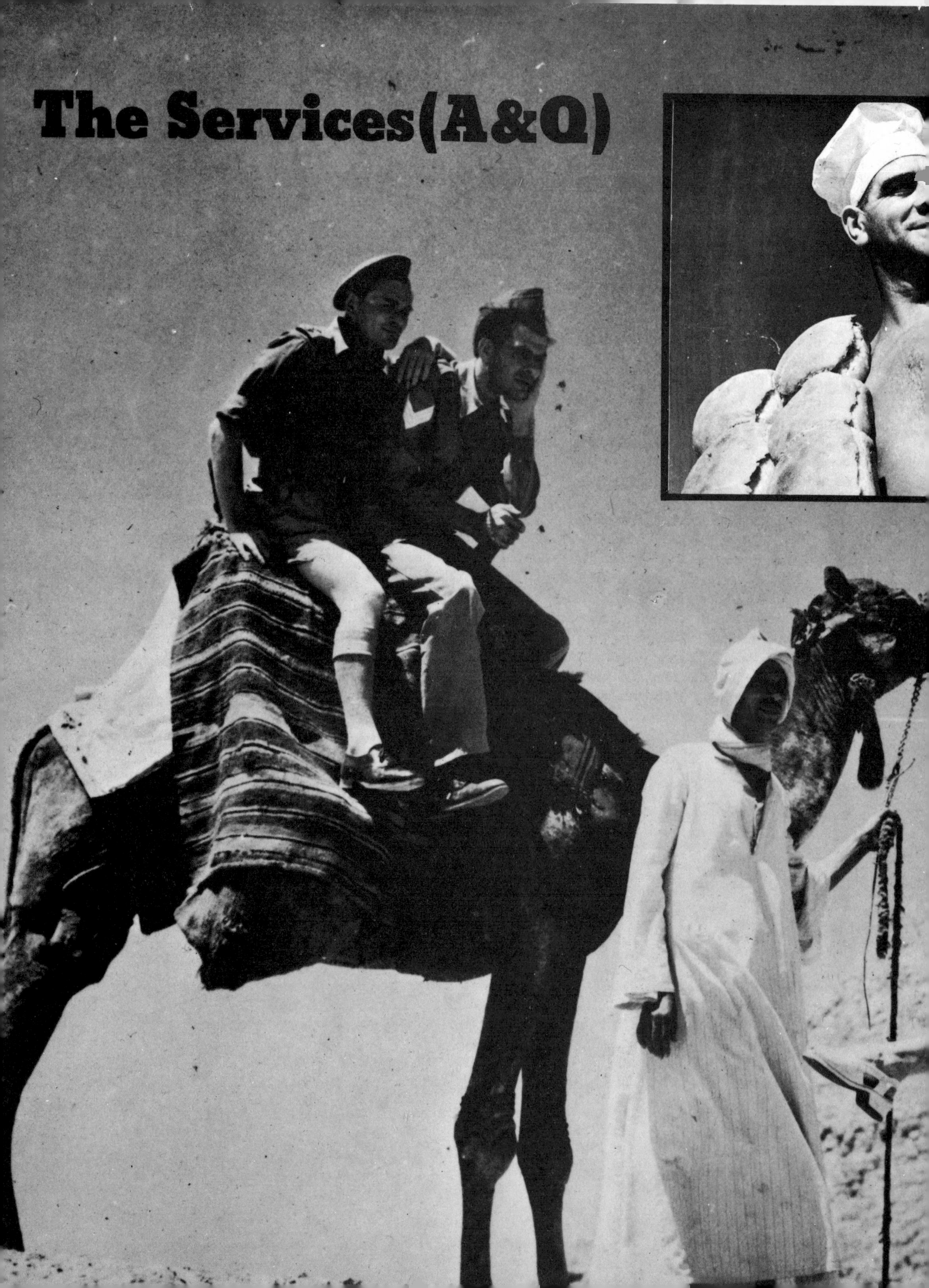

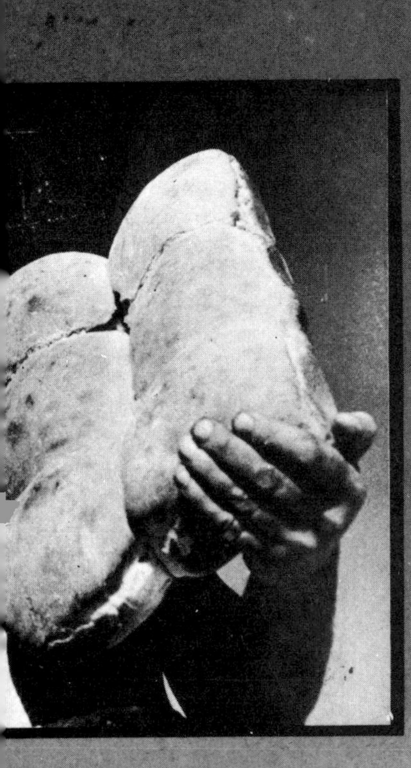

Left: A very satisfactory loaf was produced by the Field Bakeries in Libya, using a 4 double decker oil fired oven, designed (appropriately enough!) by Messrs Baker Perkins.

Below: The Naafi Entertainment Branch sometimes even provided an ENSA chorus line-up to rival the Tiller Girls.

In the introduction to this book I stressed the fact that the Division was a formation of all arms, in which the administrative services played no less vital and dangerous a role than that of the "teeth" arms. In this section I would like to illustrate the work of the administrative services. In doing so I am aware that I cannot hope to tell the complete story of the thousands of brave men who served the Division with courage and devotion to duty in a whole host of seemingly mundane jobs. However, I hope that the few examples I have included will suffice to explain their work, without which the Division would surely never have achieved greatness.

I have divided the administrative services under the general headings of 'A' and 'Q'. The 'A' services are those which deal primarily with the soldier himself, so include medical, dental, provost, pay, welfare and the like, whereas the 'Q' services are more concerned with material and thus include supplies, transport, repair and recovery. The overall control of both A & Q rested in Rear Divisional HQ, where the Colonel AQ and his staff, together with the heads of the services, worked out the administrative plans for the support of operations.

The following extract from a contemporary *Egyptian Mail* uses the term 'Q' Branch loosely to cover both 'A' and 'Q'. It is also not strictly accurate, as ACV 1 at Main HQ was normally some miles ahead of ACV7 at Rear. Nevertheless, the spirit of the report is correct and it serves to maintain the "on the spot" atmosphere of this section.

"Men of the Echelons Desert Heroes Too"

The Army's 'Q' Branch, on which the fighting troops depend for ammunition, petrol, food, water and clothing supplies, is playing a vital role in the present pursuit of Rommel across the desert. Possibly never before in its history has 'Q' been faced with keeping up supplies over such a long distance covered at such great speed.

The men of the supply echelons have done magnificent work. The work of the 'Q' services is not spectacular. It is unostentatious, arduous and often monotonous. It is sometimes more dangerous that that of the fighting troops. And it is so vital that serious interference with it could paralyse the Army.

Within a stone's throw of each other at the main HQ of an armoured division are two ACVs (armoured command vehicles). When circumstances permit — as by night — they always travel in company.

In one the talk is all of flanks and enemy dispositions, of concentrations of MT and movements of armour. Several officers are talking over the radio and all the talk is of the battle proper. This is the 'Ops' (operations) ACV.

In the other ACV the scene appears much the same. The mood of urgency is just as marked as in the 'Ops' branch. But the orders going over the wireless deal with food, clothes, blankets, water. There is little or no mention of the battle.

This is the 'Q' ACV. It is the nerve centre on which the division depends tonight for the safe and sure delivery of those necessities without which an armoured force would be quite ineffective. With other supplies it sends up letters, the daily *Egyptian Mail* and other comforts and extras which help to make life a little more tolerable.

All of these 'commodities' are brought up to the fighting men at the battle stations by a little-known band of men, who in their own quiet way are heroes everyone of them — the men of the echelons.

The echelons are the first-line 'soft skinned' vehicles of the fighting units. Their drivers bring them right up to the tanks or other fighting troops wherever they may be. Often they arrive in the middle of a battle. And the enemy always makes a dead 'set' at them.

Not once in the recent fighting has any unit in the 7th Armoured Division, which advanced 100 miles in two days, suffered from shortages of any of the essentials without which men cannot fight. Even such luxuries as letters, parcels, newspapers and chocolate reached the combatants in the heat of battle.

In addition to essential food and water supplies, also 'Q' administers the medical side of the division. For the ambulances which come back so slowly so that the wounded they carry will be jolted as little as possible, special 'tea-posts' are arranged at intervals of an hour's journey on the routes to the rear."

THE 'A' SERVICES

Medical

The desert imposed special problems for the Royal Army Medical Corps because of the great distances which had to be covered and the lack of roads and tracks over which to evacuate casualties by ambulance car. Casualty evacuation by air, which has become such an essential feature of modern war, was still in its infancy in those early days and, when available, was reserved for the very seriously wounded.

In the Division each vehicle carried its own first aid kit and all crews were trained in the rudiments of first aid. The focal point for casualty evacuation within the unit was the Regimental Aid Post (RAP) and there were also sections of Field Ambulances with each column, working back to the main body of the Field Ambulance located well forward. Some miles further back, usually in the general area of Brigade HQ, were the Casualty Collecting Stations (CCS) and in the difficult desert conditions it could take anything up to two or even three days for a wounded man to reach a CCS. For example, in the winter of 1941-42, a soldier who was wounded at Agheila had to travel 125 miles before he reached a CCS at Tobruk. Two Light Field Ambulances, with two Field Surgical Teams, formed a Medical Centre at Msus, and when a wounded man was fit to travel he was evacuated across the desert by ambulance car via Mechili to the road at Gazala.

Here is how one Colonel AQ of the Division, Colonel (later Brigadier) C. E. F. Turner, described a Light Field Ambulance in a letter to his young daughter:

"We saw a Light Field Ambulance today, where the wounded are brought to in ambulance cars from the Regimental Aid Posts and Advanced Dressing Stations further forward.

The RAMC had put up a sort of circus tent called a "Shelter" around three sides of a 3 ton lorry. The patients lie on stretchers, either on the ground or propped up on empty petrol tins. There they have their wounds dressed and are given a cup of tea and a packet of cigarettes. In busy times they are sent further back as soon as possible to a Casualty Clearing Station (CCS).

Sometimes there are lady nurses as far forward as the CCS, but generally not. At the Field Ambulances all the nursing is done by soldiers.

At the CCS they have an operating threatre inside a specially fitted lorry, or in a tent or a shelter. It is wonderful how clean everything is kept, in spite of the dust."

The job of the RAMC and RADC. (Reproduced from the Illustrated London News.)

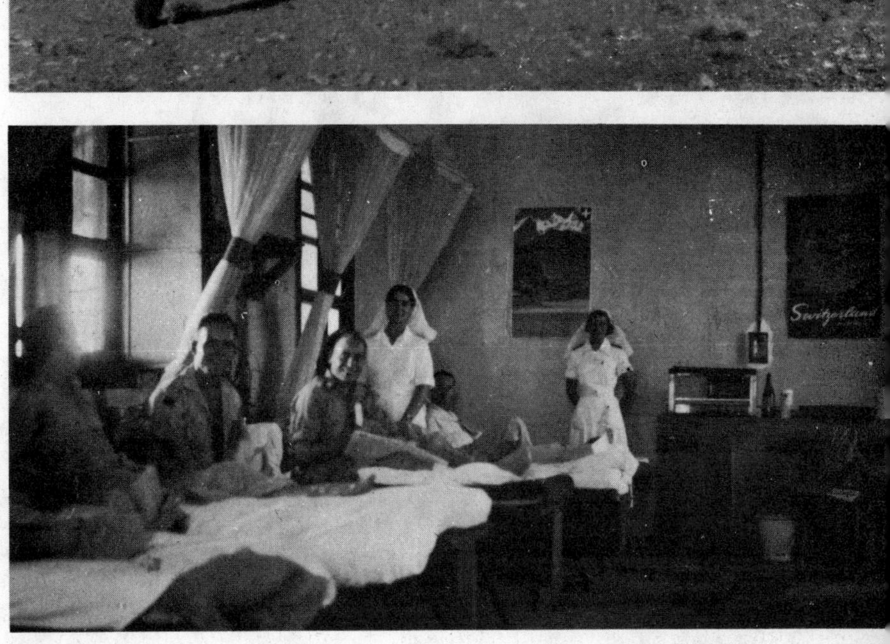

The RAMC in the desert were superb, but the same devotion to duty was displayed by the nursing staff of the larger hospitals farther back in the rear areas and in the base hospitals around Cairo and Alexandria.

Field Security

In battle the main job of the Field Security Sections (FSS) was to assist the intelligence staffs to interrogate prisoners who had just been captured. Captain (now Brigadier) Peter Vaux, then the GSO3 (Int) of the Division, recalls the kind of hurried interrogation which took place: "To assist in these we had an excellent interpreter in Corporal Kenneth Paxton, who had attended university in Berlin and Padua and was fluent in German, Italian and Arabic. Of course, we had very little time available as we were constantly on the move and had nowhere to guard prisoners properly, so no interrogation in depth was possible. Nevertheless, it was surprising how much information could be gleaned from a man still suffering the shock of capture, especially by a sympathetic approach and a cup of tea and a cigarette. The easiest to question were, surprisingly enough, the officers, some of whom were arrogant and thought themselves clever enough to fool us. Typical was one major who was captured just before the Gazala battle started. He was an artillery expert and it only needed a taunt that the Germans did not know how to handle their self-propelled guns (which in fact they certainly did) for him to give us a complete rundown on the organisation, distribution, strength and method of using these weapons which was to prove invaluable to us. At Alamein, a captured battalion commander talked so far into the night that we had to question him in relays. Conversely, the most impossible and maddening subject to interrogate was the officer or man who simply said, "I am a German (or Italian) soldier and I know the rules. You may only have my name, my rank and my number".

During operations FSS were also needed right forward with the leading troops; immediately a town had been occupied, they had to locate all the enemy headquarters, including those of both the military and civil police, prevent sabotage and arson by enemy troops and civilians who had not been rounded up, and also collect documents and maps to be sent back with all speed to Corps HQ.

FSS were in addition responsible for the security of our own side — men, information, materials, operations, even training, all

Far top left: Casualties on stretchers in the vicinity of an RAP.

Centre top: The MOs of 7 Motor Brigade.

Centre: The Advanced Dressing Station, 7 Motor Brigade.

Top: The more seriously wounded on both sides were sometimes evacuated by air — photograph shows a de Havilland DH86B of the RAAF used for casualty evacuation.

Above: A ward in No 2 British general Hospital Quasasin, August 1942.

Left: Medical officers at work.

came under their watchful eye and they would test the security-mindedness of individuals and units, look for weaknesses and advise accordingly.

The Red Caps

The duties of 7th Armoured Division Provost were extremely important, involving such essentials as route signing and traffic control in all parts of the divisional area. As Eric Thompson of 5 RTR recalls, this was often a difficult and dangerous job:

"When we were ordered to advance I saw members of the RMP, whom I had long believed were misbegotten sons whose sole reason for existence was the persecution of the poor innocent soldiery, calmly directing us through the swept lanes in the minefields, one of them not even wearing a steel helmet — he had his red cap on. After this I had to revise my opinion of the RMP".

Captain R. F. Wood recalls his early days with the RMP:

"Our first assignment in the desert was the setting up of a police post at the 180 kilometre mark on the Mersa Matruh-Sidi Barrani road. This was some two miles from Sidi Barrani and about three or four from Sollum.

As the police post was situated on the only road leading to the front line, it must have been of great assistance to all those coming out or going up to the battle area. We were an information — staging cum canteen for those who drifted in. It was also from this post that policemen went to route the tracks to and from the various units in the area.

We were well dug in, some fifty to a hundred yards into the desert off the tarmac road. The cookhouse came in very useful — for example, I remember once cooking sausage and mash for a complete Guards battalion who arrived in the area during the night!"

Postal

Letters from home were of course one of the most important features of life for everyone in the desert. Separated as they were by hundreds of miles of land and sea from their loved ones, all looked forward to receiving news from home. It was undoubtedly a very important factor in sustaining the morale of the Division, and the Sappers who have traditionally run by Army Postal Service did their best to keep mail flowing as smoothly as possible. Censorship was of course imposed on outgoing mail and unit officers had the unenviable task of censoring their soldiers'

Far top left: A member of 270 Field Security Section checks the documents of recently captured prisoners.

Far centre left: Members of 270 FSS in March 1942.

Left: An RMP checks a vehicle work ticket.

Below left: Pay parade for men of the Royal Tank Regiment somewhere near the Libyan Border in late 1940.

Below: The Postal Staff at Rear Div.

Top: A typical Unit Padre. Geoffrey Warner, chaplain of 5 RTR pictured here in his 'Kumangetit'' wagon.

Above: Outside the gates of the Jerboa Club, Tunis, May 10th, 1943.

letters. On the whole the system worked well.

The Chaplains

It is impossible to speak too highly of the work of the Royal Army Chaplain's Department in the desert war. Their selfless devotion to duty was an inspiration to all. They brought comfort to the wounded and dying, assisted medical officers and stretcher bearers, and performed myriad non-combatant duties.

In battle the best place for the Chaplain was found to be at the Advanced Dressing Station (ADS) or the Regimental Aid Post (RAP). From there he was best able to find out where his services were most needed. His truck might on occasions be used for carrying sitting wounded, and a good knowledge of First Aid was obviously desirable for both the Chaplain and his driver. Whilst he had to spend as much time as possible up with the units in action, he could not neglect the other parts of his "parish" — for example 'B' Echelons and workshops — so the ability to navigate in the desert was also essential.

Except when the Division was static, which was very rare, religious services were difficult to arrange and chaplains had to take any chance they could to hold them. For example, Canon Kenneth Meiklejohn, who was SCF (Senior Chaplain to the Forces) 7th Armoured Division in the desert, told me that on Christmas Day 1942 in the Agheila area his programme went something like this: "I took Services at Main HQ, Rear HQ and the next morning at 143 Field Park Squadron, RE. 2 KRRC had no chaplain and had asked if I could give them Holy Communion; the rest of Boxing Day I spent travelling with them, and I succeeded in holding a Holy Communion in the dark. Two days later I did the same for 11th Hussars. After the campaign was over, one 11H officer told me that this was about the only Service they had had, but that he had managed to keep in touch with God each day by himself. In mobile operations therefore the Chaplain could do little more than encourage such men and help any who needed help (home worries, the death of a friend etc). The Chaplain just had to be available to members of his unit".

Burial services were naturally performed as and when required. The Chaplain had to keep a record of all burials, with a map reference and full details as per the burial form, and when possible write to the next of

kin of the deceased. They were also able to assist the seriously wounded by attaching a note on to the patient's label addressed to the Chaplain at the CCS (Casualty Clearing Station) so that he could know if the man had received the Sacrament or had any special requirements.

The Jerboa Club was started after the fall of Tripoli. Kenneth Meiklejohn recalls: "In Cairo I extracted from the Kumangetit 1½ tons of comforts. These were sent by rail to Alex, where I took four days repacking them and persuading the OC of a hospital ship to take them to Tripoli; there I had to persuade the RASC to provide two 3-tonners to take them up to Medenine, where the Jerboa Club was installed in a former French officer's bungalow. The comforts included cigarettes but no pipe tobacco, which I eventually got by post and gave to the military police who had the especially nasty duty of directing traffic under sporadic gunfire.

The Club produced cups of tea and anything else it could lay its hands on (at Medenine the milk curdled owing to salts in the water). It had a stock of old easy chairs etc picked up from time to time. It was closed for two days at Medenine, owing to heavier shelling than usual, but otherwise was open there for over a month. We re-opened at Sfax (one full day only), at the German legation in Tunis (2½ days — odd to be the only British troops in there at night), and at Homs (Leptis Magna Hotel) from May 22 until the Division left Homs. To get it there we needed two 3 tonners, owing to our accumulation of furniture. An officer of another division was astounded to find that the Hotel was not an Officers' Club but was open to all ranks. Needless to say, it made a very useful centre for the Chaplain. As at Medenine, the 3 ORs who ran the Club and I were the only people who slept there. The difference was that we each had our own bedroom and I had a separate office."

Fighting Fit and Fit to Fight

To survive the rigours of the desert war soldiers had to be fighting fit, tough and aggressive. This meant designing and putting into effect special fitness training known as "Tough Tactics Training". The leading lights in formulating this and putting it across to units were the stalwart members of the Army Physical Training Corps. After Alamein, Tough Tactics Mobile Teams were

Above left: Tough Tactics — This photo appeared on the front of the Tough Tactics pamphlet.

Above: Major (later Lt Col) Jerry Hedley with one of his Tough Tactics Teams, led by Capt Vaughan. Jerry Hedley was largely responsible in starting this training.

formed. Each team was self-contained, with its own transport and apparatus, and they visited all 8th Army Units to give demonstrations of Tough Tactics.

THE 'Q' SERVICES

Supply and Transport

A fighting Division, particularly one containing such a high proportion of armoured fighting vehicles and lorries, needed an enormous amount of fuel, spares and other supplies to keep it going. The overall logistic requirements of the Eighth Army in the race for Tunis were, for example, 2,400 tons of supplies every day. Most of this went forward by lorry, some 120,000 of which were in constant use. The main commodities were ammunition, petrol, water and food, but of course there were in addition a wide variety of other items to be carried. The majority of these supplies were brought forward to the fighting troops by the men of the Royal Army Service Corps, whose job was of vital importance and whose casualty rate was as high, if not higher, than that of most "teeth" arms.

The drawings on the opening pages of this section show the many and varied jobs carried out by the RASC. Within the Division this work was done by RASC companies, which included at one time both 4th New Zealand (Reserve) MT Company and the 1st Supply Issue Section of the Royal Indian ASC.

Here are two accounts written by RASC drivers which describe vividly what life was like as an MT driver in the desert:

"We ran into El Adem after a nine days' run from the Nile Valley. During this time we had not washed or shaved. Our water ration was one pint per man per day. Thirst was very bad during the first few days, but the iron discipline with which we controlled the water supply soon hardened us. We had not yet even scratched the surface of the desert cruelties, although we really did feel we were now veterans.

How we were to be disillusioned!

At El Adem we tasted our first salt water. The water supply there came by pipe line from Tobruk and was distilled sea water. When we first used it to make tea the milk curdled and fell in great lumps to the bottom of the dixies. In our ignorance, we threw this tea away and then made fresh. When the same thing happened again we realised it was the water. After a few days we learnt to drink this tea and like it. So much so that when we went on our first leave to Cairo it took us two or three days to get used again to tea made with ordinary water.

From El Adem we were directed to unload our 70,000 gallons of petrol at the Acroma Petrol Dump. When we reached there, the 70,000 gallons had been reduced to 30,000 gallons during the desert journey. Much to our surprise, we were told this was a good effort. This wastage was because of the "flimsy" petrol containers which leaked badly, a state of affairs not eradicated until the introduction of the "Jerrican", copied from the Germans.

Back to El Adem again, and there we reloaded with petrol, ammunition and food. We were ordered to take these to the Armoured Division at Msus, some 300 miles away. At Msus our armoured forces had thrown a cordon across Rommel's retreat. It was a great thrill to be heading for the scene of battle.

Imagine our disappointment when we made three trips, each two and a half day's run each way, without as much as a shot being fired. But on the fourth trip we got a rude surprise. Rommel, instead of retreating further, had turned about. He flung the whole of his weight against our "screen" outside Msus. When we arrived at the Msus aerodrome with our usual load, the aerodrome was under shell fire. We were greeted with a salvo of shells which fell clean across the aerodrome. Nevertheless, we were told to unload. While we were doing this a despatch rider came through and said that three German Armoured columns had broken through our centre, and two of these were heading in the direction of Msus.

He had no sooner left than two Stukas screamed down and dropped a stick of bombs across the lorries. We went to ground but three men were killed. Six lorries packed in a tight circle finished as a heap of metal.

When the excitement had died down, we carried on with the unloading". *

Arthur Knight was an RASC driver attached to a Light Field Ambulance, and this extract from his diary tells of his journey going back to rejoin his unit:

"Back to Unit — 12.2.42 — Thank God!

Leaving 9·30 on back of gas-wagon, ADS, carrying 12 passengers; not much wind, thank goodness. Approximate distance to travel 750 to 850 miles: roll on! Slow travel first day,

* *I was an Eighth Army Soldier,* by R. J. Crawford

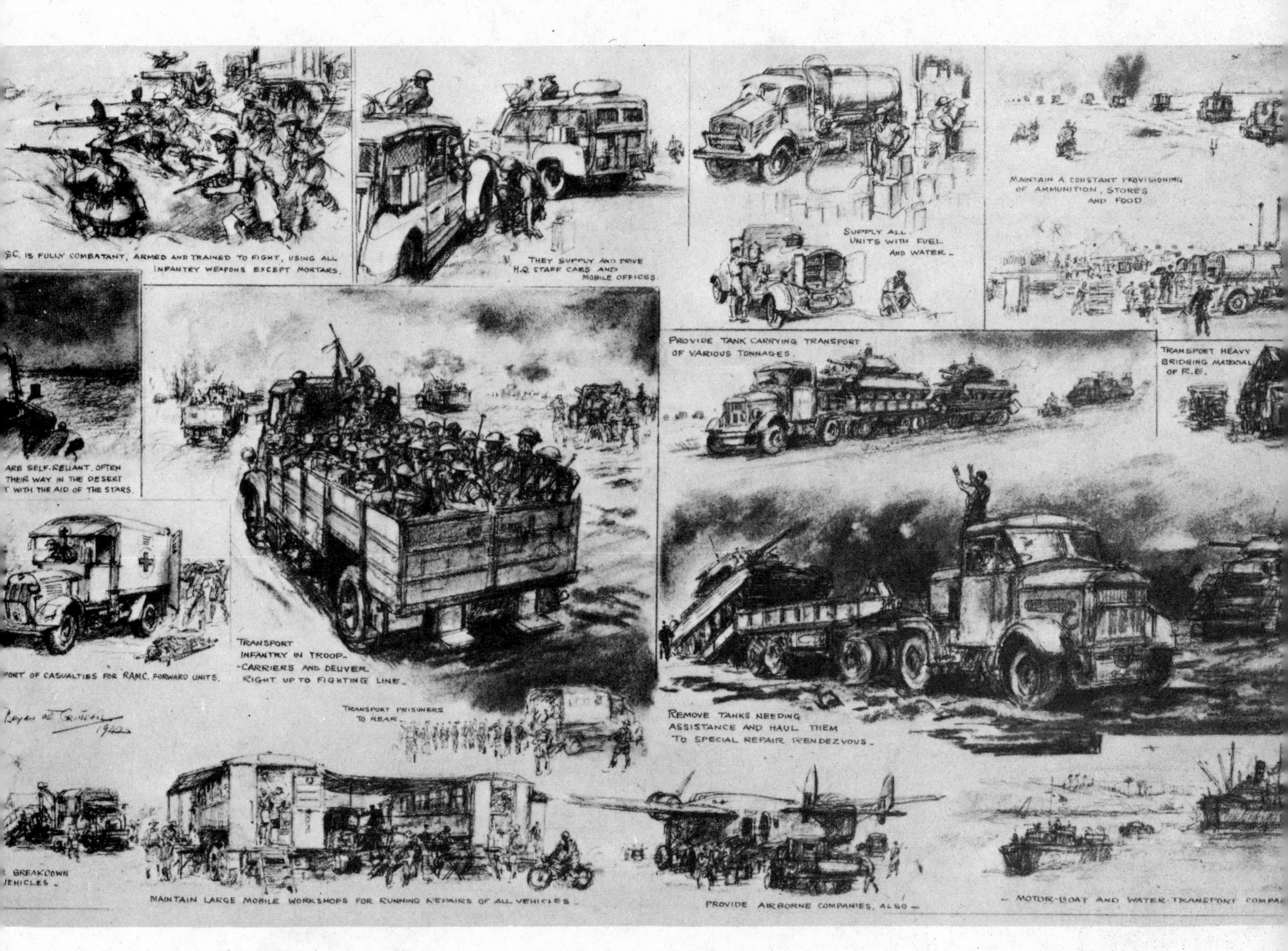

The Job of the RASC (reproduced from Illustrated London News.)

about 80 miles; ruddy war will be over before we get back. Put up bivvy, lit fire and had some biscuit duff, not bad, bed early, lit fire; had a tom-tit, first for two days — great!

2nd Day. Over the hills to Derna, up and down, almost sea sick, but no dust, lost convoy just before coming to metalled road, to Derna, pulled up in valley, marshland, waiting for Column Commander. Going to stop soon, although it's very early yet, so will get a hot meal. Italian fort on top of hill, had a look round, not been used for some time evidently, dugouts full of water, warned not to enter fort by Column Commander.

Anglo/Indian wants me to go duck shooting, O.K., bullfrogs kicking up an awful noise. Indian shot duck, water-cart bloke fell into water up to waist, back just in ime for grub, got a piece of duck, lovely. Some of the boys had bath in hot spring in side of cliff. Italian tank workshops here, liable to floods. Most of pits useless. Frogs a nuisance with their croaking. Now started raining and our 'bivvy' in bed of a stream! Had a fair night though expecting to be washed away, only a couple of wet blankets.

QM Stores will change all wet ones at dinner time, but don't want to lose my own blankets, so put them through canopy rails to dry on the move. Gone about 300 yards, been here nearly two hours now, what the hell are the officers doing, probably having a shot at those ducks themselves, heard a couple of shots.

Off again, passed farm house used by the medics about 100 yards from Barce/Derna road, great going on this stretch, batting along, some big stuff from t'other way.

Pulled off road for grub, this is just heaven to us, deeeply green, wooded country on either side of road, dark brown earth, grass, searched proximity for souvenirs, few letters strewn about, trenches are a masterpiece, but bloody wet in winter.

Got bully stew with *spuds* in it, somebody must have lost 'em! First for months, plenty of posey. Off again, nobody wants to loiter now and it's toe down.

Driver got shits (can't spell diarhea) kept getting at rear of convoy, jeers from wagons passing at bare-arsed driver. Can't be far off Derna now".

A very important part of the RASC's work in an armoured division was to provide tank transporters to move tanks over long distances by road. This was usually faster and caused less wear and tear to the AFVs than moving them on their tracks.

RAOC at the Start of the War

At the outbreak of the war Middle East Ordnance units were both sparse and understrength. There was a Command Ordance Depot and Workshops at Abbassia, plus a small ammunition depot; a tiny clothing and mobilisation sub-depot at Kasr el Nil, and some forward dumps of tentage, accommodation stores and ammunition at El Daba and Mersa Matruh. Indeed, one can gather how seriously the Middle East was considered as a potential theatre of war by the fact that the War Office ruled that peacetime accounting should continue!

Naturally, once the fighting began in earnest much had to be done. The following are examples of the technical problems which Ordnance had to tackle in those early days:

a. All tanks arriving from UK had to be modified for desert warfare. This included fitting locally manufactured air-cleaners, and racks to carry extra food and water.
b. Suitable tank recovery vehicles had to be purchased locally and modified, to fit with winches, cranes and desert equipment.
c. The production of a local pattern of 160 gallon water tanks for fitting to 15cwt trucks, in order to make up for the very large deficiency of water carts in units. For example, 7 Armoured Division war establishment allowed for only 20 water trucks for the entire Division. This had to be increased to 35 and later to 64.
d. 3,000 sun compasses were made and issued.
e. Thousands of mines were designed, manufactured and filled by the RAOC.

It would be wrong, even in a book which deals with one single Division, to forget the men of the base workshops and base ordnance installations, who put in many a twenty-four hour day on behalf of those "Up the Blue". The Division could not have functioned without them.

Forward of the Second Line and Base

Left: A resupply column on the move on the coast road.

Far bottom left: Enemy action was of course the major hazard — photo taken during the withdrawal from Benghazi.

Below centre left: CRASC (now Brigadier) Jimmy Gilman standing in Div HQ leaguer about 0600 hours one day early in August 1942. Note the wide dispersal of vehicles which was normal practice in daylight hours.

Below: Loading up a tank transporter.

Workshops were the First Line, units such as the Light Repair Sections, RAOC, which supported brigades. Here is a poem written by a member of the Light Repair Section, 7th Support Group, (Motto: U BUSTEM — WE MENDUM) taken from the menu of a Christmas 1941 Dinner Dance which took place at the Slade Club, Abbassia, on 5th March 1942.

SERVICES RENDERED

Sing a song of grease and oil,
Of piston rings and spanners,
Of men who toil, and muck and moil,
And engineering manners.

This is the tale of an L.R.S., Of men not looking for glory,
Their exploits never appear in the press,
But they make a worthwhile story.

While others defend, its their's to mend,
Repairing damaged M.T
Whether it's done by the road or the Hun,
Or the Wop — from Italy.

So if there's a truck on the road that's stuck,
Or a cruiser tank that falters,
It's up to the L.R.S to pluck
These wrecks from troubled waters.

It's the L.R.S., both night and day
When trouble spells disaster,
Get on to the job, and there they stay
'Till the crock becomes a fighter.

So here's to the chap in the L.R.S.,
Who fights with his monkey wrench.
Success depends on him — no less
Than the man who fights in a trench!

The Formation of REME

Operations in the Middle East revealed that a major reorganisation was necessary in order to cope with the growing importance of electrical and mechanical engineering and that a Corps of trained engineers should be formed to carry out this work.

Army Order 70 of May 1942 authorised the formation of the Royal Electrical and Mechanical Engineers as a regular and permanent Corps of the Army and the necessary transfers of men to the new Corps were completed by 1st October 1942. All RAOC units with a workshop role were transferred. The RASC were also affected, in fact they provided the first Director of Mechanical Engineering. Many RASC officers and men with the appropriate qualifications and some RASC workshop units were also transferred.

The REME units now formed carried on with the vital work of repair and recovery all over the battlefield. Here are two accounts of the type of work in which they were involved. The first is by Norman Hall, who was at the time a fitter with the Light Aid Detachment of the 1st Royal Tank Regiment in Tobruk in 1941. He remembers how, during the day, the LAD would work under cover at Spanish Farm near the harbour, but by night the fitters would go out to work on the perimeter.

"I was duty fitter one particular day and at five minutes to midnight I was called out to go to repair one of the tanks, stuck in a perimeter minefield with a track blown off. As it was nearly midnight I took the next for duty fitter along with me as well, a young chap called Ginger. We got to the minefield OK and to start off with everything went well, we got the mine out from under the tank and repaired the track. The tank then pulled away, but the track broke again and had to be repaired a second time. After completing our repairs and testing for mines, the tank was just driving off when it hit another mine. The explosion caught Ginger right in the face — he lost an eye as far as I remember.

Next morning I went down to see him in the Hospital near the harbour. I managed to

Below: The Heavy MT Repair Shop in a second Line RAOC Workshops.

Bottom: AFV Repairs at a Main Workshop. Matildas in the Paint Shop.

Right: The many and varied jobs of the Royal Army Ordnance Corps. (Reproduced from the Illustrated London News.)

Below right: 2nd line Workshops, Alexandria 'Tank Park'.

.A.O.C. CENTRAL DEPOT TRANSPORTATION SHEDS
. WAR MATERIAL FOR THE VARIOUS FRONTS ARE
.ND DESPATCHED BY DAY AND NIGHT FOR MONTHS PRIOR
DURING OPERATIONS.
2/ EVERY TYPE OF ENGINE AND EQUIPMENT HAS SPECIALLY DESIGNED CRATES FOR TRANSPORT.
.O.C. TRAINS RUN THROUGHOUT THE DAY AND NIGHT
.HE PORTS OF EMBARKATION.
5/ AN R.A.O.C. FIELD PARK DEPOT AT WORK IN THE REAR OF THE 8TH ARMY.
4/ "DESERTISING AND ARCTICISING" — ORDNANCE PERSONNEL
HERMETICALLY SEALING TANKS FOR OVERSEAS RANGING FROM TROPICAL HEAT TO 40° BELOW ZERO.
BRYAN DE GRINEAU
'ORDNANCE'
6/ ANOTHER BRANCH OF THE ORDNANCE CORPS - SPECIAL
BEACH DETACHMENTS ACCOMPANY LANDING OPERATIO
7/ R.A.O.C. UNITS STATIONED IN
RUSSIAS ARCTIC PORTS UNSHIP AND DELIVER TANKS,
GUNS AND STORES TO OUR SOVIET ALLIES.

30

find him OK; he was lying on the floor waiting to be evacuated when the boat came in — we never quite knew when one would arrive. Ginger was under shock and just then we had an air raid. It was one of those things that I shall never forget as long as I live, Ginger holding my hand as we listened to the bombs coming down. . ."

Next an account by Major Alan Barnes of the work of a recovery officer in the desert:
"The day started like hundreds of others in a Western Desert year, with a fine clear blue sky and the sun up and already warm at 0645 hours.

The last man coming off guard is noisily clearing up the night's brew can and enamel cups, determined that everyone else should be as awake as he is; the Signals Corporal is heard calling up HQ CREME and chats in clear with his friends, "Saida wogs, what's for breakfast? We've got eggs and bacon! Over". "It's all right for you squaddies out in the bluey, with your expert Clifti Wizzicks swapping eggis for chai with the Arabs. Us poor base wallahs have to put up with soya links and char". This friendly banter is finished and CREME's instructions come over in code, giving the instructions for the day's jobs.

The Unit being highly mobile everyone except HQ staff is on individual rations, and very soon the whole camp is awake. The vehicle crews' cook of the day is busily frying up his own idea of Australian tinned bacon, biscuits, onions and eggs (if he has been lucky enough to scrounge some), whilst the remainder of the crew are washing and shaving (if there is enough water), and finally rolling up bedding rolls. After breakfast there is just time to wash up the dishes in the washing water saved for the occasion and then out into the blue for "spade drill".

The vehicle commanders chase their crews into a quick Diesel, Oil and Water check and top up where necessary from the supply truck.

During this check-over the 'Q' has reported to the Captain O.C the Unit, who has decoded CREME's instructions during his breakfast and together they work out the day's work schedules. 8th Armoured Brigade,

Below: A novel type of crane!

Bottom: 4th Armoured Brigade Recovery Section, Timimi Pass, Gazala.

Below right: An RAOC Fitter at work.

along with 22nd Armd, have had a night march with their tank units to take up new positions and several of the 1st/2nd Tanks have ended up in a deep uncharted wadi, some on their sides and most bogged down in the natural tank trap and unable to extract themselves. They are urgently required for an expected enemy counter-attack, so the Scammels and Diamond T's, along with their crews, are despatched flat out — at 18mph — to get the tanks mobile again.

The lighter recovery section vehicles are despatched to 131 Inf Brigade's workshops to clear several vehicles BLR'd (Beyond Local Repair) back to Corps' workshops somewhere in the rear. They also have a drop off a couple of 15cwts, written off in a minefield, at the "help yourself dump" just off the main track. These vehicles will be picked clean by the unit fitters, who are all born scroungers and take pride in keeping their unit's vehicles running. You have to be very careful where you park your own jeep when you are "helping yourself" or you may find all the wheels missing when you return for it.

The O.C makes a quick check with his HQ Sergeant, Cook, Rations Corporal and finally with the water man, who can sometimes be the most important man in the unit, and then sets off with his jeep and driver to check on how the tank recovery is going.

The Recovery Sgt has gone ahead in his jeep to have a quick "shufti". He finds the wadi and then goes back to guide the cumbersome but highly mobile Scammells down into the wadi floor. Using their powerful winches and snatch blocks, and each other's vehicles as anchors, they start to get the tanks back on their tracks. After four hours hard work five of the tanks are mobile again and they set off for their own Regimental HQs. Two young German soldiers who have been hiding for two days to get away from their units give themselves up, with their hands in the air. After a quick frisk over by the Recovery crews they are fed with bully and biscuits, given a long drink of sweet tea and, after it is seen that they are harmless, they are only too willing to give a hand in righting the tanks. One of the Germans had been a tram driver in Hamburg who had

Near Bir Hacheim, one month before the German attack.

been unlucky enough to clout Hermann Goering's Mercedes, and for his sins had been shipped out to the Afrika Korps; his opinions of Hitler, Goering and Co., were far from polite and he was quite a comedian in his antics.

After a few more hours the final tanks are back on their tracks and the non-runners are winched up behind the Diamond T's on to their multi-wheeled trailers. It is rapidly getting dark and the final tanks and recovery crews decide to drive for a couple of hours into more friendly territory, where they settle down for the night before moving on to Brigade workshops in the morning.

The OC and his driver have not brought their bedding with them, so they set out for their camp in the dark, driving by the stars, instinct and some lucky compass work.

On his arrival, the OC's batman prepares an evening meal for his officer and driver and after the meal some good Italian coffee is brewed and the driver sits down for a smoke and chat with HQ staff and returned crews. The driver had a good tale to tell about the two young German soldiers and there is some laughter over the German's description of Goering etc. Someone has a 'liberated' Jerry tank radio, and a very good German forces radio station is pounding out some excellent dance music followed by the inevitable strains of "Lili Marlene". The whole camp joins in and sings the verses, as it was a very popular tune with the soldiers; it is nearly always followed by the news and propaganda in English, which is greeted with jeers and laughter but does also provide some food for thought.

The radio is switched off, cigarettes put out and the lucky ones that are not on guard roll themselves up in their blankets and with the soft sand as a mattress and the sky for a roof, drop off to a wonderful sleep that only those who have slept in the Western Desert know.

So ends another day in the Desert."

SERVICE TO THE SERVICES

The Job of Naafi

Naafi followed the troops with essential supplies (tinned food, soap, tooth and shaving gear, cigarettes, matches, biscuits, chocolate and beer), which often had to be dumped on the bare sand with only a barbed wire fence to deter looters and a tarpaulin to keep off the sun. In circumstances of sudden retreat and shortage of transport the dumps often had to be blown up and a fresh start made elsewhere.

Below: Fitters of LAD, 2 RTR at work on a lorry.

Right: Members of LAD, 1 RTR repairing an engine.

Far centre right: Sgts' Mess 22 Armd Bde Workshops at lunch.

Far top right: Crew of S.V.I. at Berg-el-Arab.

Below right: Lt Col John Berryman, a well known CREME of the Division, surrounded by an admiring crowd at Djerba March 1st, 1943.

Below: A Naafi mobile canteen somewhere "Up the Blue"

Right: Naafi girls try their hand at riding camels in the shadow of the Pyramids.

Below right: The Naafi Entertainment Branch organised shows for the troops.

Naafi people hated to waste good food. During one North African retreat a Naafi manager, reluctant to let the enemy enjoy his store of eggs, slung a tin bath full of water between two posts, lit a fire underneath, and handed hard-boiled eggs to the troops.

In the towns, Mersa Matruh, Tobruk and Benghazi, Naafi requisitioned buildings and established breweries and bakeries. As the military position became more stable, tented supplies in the remote locations were replaced with more substantial premises. The necessary labour emerged from the desert by what seemed like spontaneous generation. An army unit would encamp in a stretch of sand without any sign of other life or human habitation. Suddenly, like a mirage but without the illusion, a band of as many as 100 Bedouin would appear, willing to act as bearers in return for standard rations and pay, which they carried around in tobacco boxes. They would help to collect wood and corrugated iron and load it on lorries to provide a solid structure for the Naafi oasis. Later, when the desert war had turned in Britain's favour, Italian prisoners undertook these labours. They shared the life of their captors and were allowed to move about freely. Unlike the Bedouin, they had nowhere else to go.

The troops were much more dependent upon Naafi in the desert than in populous Europe, and some of the permanent roadhouses, such as the Ship Inn at Mersa Matruh, the Two Bees at Buq Buq, and the Noah's Ark at El Daba, were widely known and appreciated. The managers were ingenious in finding ways of making them attractive. One lined the walls of the Ship Inn with wicker work taken from German shell containers, cut out the porthole glasses from wrecks in the harbour to adorn his windows, and enhanced the nautical effect with festoons of white rope; made tables out of barrels and ashtrays from shell cases which were screwed to the tables to save them from marauders.

The appreciation of the customers, including well known generals, ENSA celebrities and visiting journalists, was recorded in hundreds of entries in the roadhouse logbooks; formal and slangy, humorous and stilted, in verse and prose, and in a dozen languages including Maori. Some of the simplest were the most revealing: 'Tea always hot', 'Even flowers on the table', 'I do hope this Naafi never moves while I have to travel this ruddy road'. Naturally, there were a few complaints, the most frequent being lack of 'alk', ie alcohol. *

* *The story of Naafi,* by Harry Miller.

NAAFI

Officer's Mess Truck. This well equipped mess truck belonging to the Rifle Brigade was capable of producing many a good brew.

Desert Life

Left: Members of 31st Field Hygience Section at Kilometre 38.

Below left: 31st FHS showers.

Introduction

The harsh, inhospitable desert presented a unique challenge to the soldiers who fought there. Not only had they to combat the enemy on the battlefield, but also nature itself in order to survive. The simple, everyday business of living took on an entirely new dimension and it is interesting to see how each nation set about overcoming the problems which the desert produced.

"The Italians tried to transform this alien land in their image, instead of learning to live with it. They built marble monuments. They had the luxury of fine sheets, grandiose uniforms, good food and drink, ice cream, even mobile brothels. It was preposterous; a recipe for defeat.

The Germans were more realistic. They were good desert soldiers: excellent at fast movement, map-reading and navigation. They had palatable food and fine equipment — from guns and tanks to pills, purifiers and goggles. But they loathed the desert and it was unkind to them.

The British were by contrast, perky as fleas in the desert. The Allied army was one of the fittest in history; bronzed and tough. May be this was because the colonising British had had centuries of experience in tropical medicines". *

As well as describing the battles, therefore, it is only right and proper to devote part of this book to living in the desert and in this section we shall examine photographically how the Desert Rats used to the full that sometimes maligned British flair for improvisation.

Desirable Residences

In the desert some form of shelter was essential to ward off the intense heat of the sun by day and the bitter cold of the nights. As the majority of the Division led a mobile existence, never static for more than a few days at a time, their main dwelling places, like those of the nomadic Bedouin, were various kinds of tent. The WD issue models were seldom entirely suitable on their own, and also clearly lacked character. Consequently,

* *Alamein and the Desert War,* edited by Derek Jewell pages 7–8.

Below: Tank Bivouac. Tank crews were perhaps the most fortunate as they had plenty of space to carry their kit. The tank 'bivvy' consisted of a large tarpaulin sheet which was attached to the side of the tank and then pegged out to form a useful sized tent.

Bottom: A Palace? Some desirable residences almost defied description like this "Palace" occupied by Norman Harper of the Field Hygiene Section!

Above: Vehicle Bivouac. Even with a smaller vehicle it was still possible to rig up a satisfactory shelter using a bit of ingenuity.

Left: Dug in Tent. In the echelons, workshops and semi static areas, shelters could be a little more permanent, but had to be dug in and camouflaged in order to provide protection from air attack.

as you will see from the photographs, imagination was allowed to run riot. Most vehicles bearing the Desert Rat emblem looked more like gipsy caravans or tinkers' carts than military war machines. However, do not run away with the idea that this prevented these desert warriors from fighting properly. Far from it — by applying the British soldier's usual adage that "any fool can be uncomfortable", the Desert Rats provided themselves with anything that would make their spartan life more agreeable.

Water

The most precious single commodity in the desert was water, without which no one could survive for long. It was invariably in short supply and for much of the time the troops had to exist on less than one gallon per man per day for *all* purposes. So they used petrol to wash clothes, hoarded dirty water in spare water bottles and filtered it for use in vehicle radiators. The flimsy nature of the original British water and petrol cans did not help and many precious gallons were lost in transit. The German $4\frac{1}{2}$ gallon "Jerrican" was far better and the Allies were not slow in adopting it.

Cooking

Not all attempts at cooking, however, produced such appetising results, as is witnessed by this anecdote from Rfn Noel Cleave of 2 RB: "I was appointed section cook with a larder of corned beef, marmalade, Army biscuits, tea and milk. One morning I was delighted to be able to vary our breakfast with a tin of oatmeal that had lost its label but was a welcome find. Alas! this treasure turned out to be camouflage paint, and from then on a new cook took over!"

Personal Hygiene

"Cleanliness is next to Godliness" and in the desert it was essential, not only from the morale aspect, but also to prevent cuts from going septic or scratches turning into wicked desert sores.

Sand

Unlike water there was of course no shortage of sand!

It was very easy to get 'lost' on one's own in the desert, for example through a vehicle breaking down, as Alfred Barnes recalls:

"I was driving a 15cwt "vintage" open vehicle in a column heading for the relief of Tobruk when it broke down. The LAD came to my aïd and after inspection said they could not do much at the time, as a small part needed repairing, and told me they would come back later as they had to keep up with the column. That was the last I saw of them and the regiment for quite a while. The incident happened about 4 o'clock in the afternoon so I could do nothing but settle down. Came the nightfall and not a thing for miles. The next day I looked all around and as far as the eye could see there was nothing but undulating sand and the tracks where the columns of guns, vehicles etc had gone.

Altogether I was there for three days and nights, and was getting a little desperate for food and especially water. I drained the radiator of the vehicle, and although rusty, "how sweet" it tasted! In the morning of the fourth day I heard the sound of a plane and saw one in the distance heading my way. I stood on the vehicle and waved a once-white towel like mad, not caring really if it was friend or foe. It turned out to be an RAF plane which flew overhead, "waggled" its wings and was off. Saved at last, I thought. About half an hour later I saw a plume of dust heading towards me, out of which appeared a South African vehicle. It pulled up and out jumped a SAF officer. He wanted to know what was wrong and, after my explaining, remarked I didn't know how lucky I was. Apparently he had been scanning the desert through his glasses, saw me waving my towel and had come to investigate. Of course by the time he arrived the plane had long since departed. He told me to jump in his vehicle, and said, "We have no time to lose. Do you see those dust clouds on the horizon? Those are German tanks, so let's get out of here" which we did pretty quick, after I had destroyed my vehicle."

Dress

Dress in the desert was informal yet eminently practical. It varied from greatcoats or shaggy sheepskin coats against the cold, to simply boots and shorts for working during the heat of the day. Suede desert boots, coloured neck scarves and fly whisks looked somewhat bizarre but in fact all served a useful purpose.

Perhaps Jon's "Two Types" should be allowed the last word on dress.

Entertainment

V Cigarettes and Stella Beer will be remembered by all!

A Desert Rat's vocabulary *
(Taken from The Victory Number of the Eleventh Hussar Journal).

It would be impossible to print (at least in a polite journal) a complete vocabulary of expressions in use in the Regiment, which vary even between squadrons. But our next-of-kin should know the following terms of Basic English if they are not to be quite clueless when we get our tickets and go home to talk to them. We have adopted a mahleesh attitude to spelling, going rather for the sound than for the correct native way of writing the words.

Aiwah Yes

Alles Everything OK

Alles kaput Everything hopeless or broken up

Alles plunders No cameras or binoculars or shot guns in the village: 'D' Squadron has already been there.

Alakeefek With a mahleesh attitude.

Akker A piastre; any small piece of money; a mark; a franc; a sixpence, etc.

Akkers The Field Cashier.

Bint A female

Bint kwoyees A good female; a honey; an amorous objective.

Bella Seenyoreena Bint kwoyees (Italian version)

Bono Kwoyees = goot = good. Niente bono = mush kwoyees = no good. Molto bono = kwoyees kater, or kwoyees ouwie = very good.

Blue, The Ghot, The = the original haunts of the Rats, Desert.

Brew-up Afire; to cook shai; to destroy by fire; to burn down

Charlie Love, Charlie Harry, Charlie Iffter Centre line; main axis of divisional or brigade advance; haunt at times of oozlebarts, q.v.

Clueless Out of the picture; with no idea of what is going on.

Creased Wounded, not however "toppled off one's perch", which implies that the person toppled is alles kaput.

Dove sono ee (tedesci, canonee, seenyoreenee)? Where are the (Germans, guns, girls)?

Dolce fare niente It's nice to do nothing; be on B3.

Feloos Money, akkers.

Frat Fraternization with Moffer bints. A nice bit of frat = ditto skirt.

Gyppo See Wog.

Goot shlaapen Sleep well

Hooch RSM's milk (See Zbib).

Imshi See Yallah

Kutch Niente; nothing

Kit Anything from a bomb to a bint; "good kit" or its opposite "ropey kit" may refer to an armoured car, a shirt, or a peroxide blonde in Oudenbosch.

Kaput Destroyed, hopeless, dead.

Liberation Complete destruction by bombing or shelling, as at Hamburg or Caen. Also verb "to liberate" = to plunder, sack.

Mahleesh It doesn't matter, couldn't care less, not interested.

Moffer Tedeskee, German, Boche; Mofferland = Germany.

Mongerear Food, scoff.

Moya Water, pahni.

Mushti A Chap, fellow.

Niente See Kutch, also Bono.

Nigger A Wog; a person not of British birth, a person not in the Conservative Party.

Oozlebart A guerrilla, a sniper, an enemy; a Socialist candidate in a Tory constituency.

Sugar Sugar SS Nazi type of Moffer. Always have bazooka, definitely mush kwoyees.

Shai A sticky, sweet drink made by stewing tea, sugar and tinned milk with moya to taste.

Shufti Observe! or observation; Shufti bint! = a long low whistle; Shufti patrol = a patrol to observe something.

Sarkam What time? (If in doubt, brew up).

Shwaya Small.

Shlaapen To kip; yoch; sleep; honk.

Shlaak Vehter Dirty weather; Dutch greeting on rainy mornings.

Squaddy Soldier; trooper; soldaten-mushti

Tamam Just the job.

Tala hinnah Come here.

Vino Wine; intoxicating drink, occasionally mixed with 45% gin and 5% peach juice in "C" Squadron Officers' and Sergeants' Messes. This produces Stromboli, a non-inflammable beverage with many of the properties of Zbib (qv).

Wallad Boy; shwaya mushti.

Yallah Imshi! Scram!

Zift Useless

Zbib A lethal, volatile, inflammable, persistent, corrosive and explosive beverage popular in Sergeants' Messes. Consists of 95% wood alcohol and burns with a fierce blue flame.

* *Reprinted by the kind permission of Home Headquarters, The Royal Hussars.*

Top: Desert Well — Bir El Naqua. Native wells were to be found in widely scattered places across the otherwise dry desert. Some were deliberately salted by the enemy which, although not injurious to health, curdled the milk in tea making it virtually undrinkable.

Above: Water Cart. A welcome sight in any leaguer was the arrival of the water cart from which to fill individual water bottles.

Brewing Up. Alan Potter of 270 FSS enjoying a brew. The recognised way of making a quick "brew up" was by filling half a petrol tin with sand and pouring a little petrol on to it. If the sand was then stirred and lit, it burnt for a good thirty minutes, the sand of course being a good condutor of heat. Water could be boiled like this in under ten minutes. When boiling a dixie for tea on this type of fire, it was an almost universal practice to float a bit of twig in the water. The origin of this custom is obscure, but there may be something in the idea that it collected and disposed of any stray petrol fumes, on the whole however, it seems to have been more an inherited army superstition and would thus come more appropriately under the less scientific heading of folk lore!

Right: Good advice for any Desert Rat!

WHEN IN DOUBT.
BREW-UP.

M.433396

Far top left: Cooking Courses. The Army Catering Corps taught the rudiments of field cooking on special courses (I wonder if they ever got this oven to work!)

Far centre left: Homemade Oven. This photo was taken in honour of a new oven made by this tank crew of 5 RTR from empty petrol cans and mud.

Left: Petrol Tin Oven. Ovens came in all shapes and sizes — this one made by 3rd Hussars, looks large enough to roast an ox!

Far bottom left: Shaving. Even the simple act of washing and shaving was difficult with water at a premium. Photograph shows Col (later Maj General) Rickie Richards, GSO1 of the Division shaving at 0630 hours November 30th, 1941.

Below centre: Haircut. Someone who was handy with a pair of clippers was a godsend to any unit. This one learnt his hairdressing down a coal mine where he used to crop the miners' hair with horse clippers!

Below: Desert Sores. Cuts or grazes did not always heal and quickly became infected. The infection was liable to spread all over the body and could produce sores which were in some cases even more painful than wounds and usually resulted in the person concerned being evacuated for hospital treatment. (Hugh Hill of 2 KRRC told me that his remedy against desert sores was to drink daily some of the salt water in which the canned potatoes arrived—this he swears to this day prevented him from getting any desert sores).

Left: Digging In. Slit trenches had to be dug at most halts in order to provide some protection against being straffed by passing enemy aircraft.

Top right: Digging Out. Another regular occurrence in soft sand was the digging out of bogged vehicles.

Centre right: Desert Navigation. In many ways the desert was like a vast ocean without landmarks, so that even the simplest journey had to be plotted accurately. Units normally employed navigation officers to guide them about. (Note the sun compass at the top edge of this vehicle's cab).

Far right: Great coats, pullovers and the like were needed in the bitter cold winter nights.

Below: This Workshop group of HQ Sqn 44 RTR shows many different forms of working dress.

Below right: "Obviously a this year's model old man!" (Reproduced by kind permission of Jon).

"Obviously a this year's model, old man!"

Above: Bathing Beauties. When near enough the sparkling waters of the Mediterranean provided plenty of opportunity for relaxation. This virile group (taken in March 1942) were from 22 Armd Bde Workshops.

Above right: The Long Spit. Cambrai Day (November 21st) was celebrated whenever possible by all Royal Tank Regiment units — the photo shows the winner of the 5 RTR "Long Distance Spit" competition (Sgt "Wag" Fry) in action!

Below: Newspapers from home were very welcome. Sgt (later Captain) R. W. E. Smith of the Divisional Workshops reads his Poole & East Dorset Herald at Mersa Matruh in January 1941.

Right: V Cigarettes.

Far right: 'No grazie old chap we only smoke V's!' (Reproduced by kind permission of Jon).

"No grazie, old chap, we only smoke V's!"

Lucy

by Sydney Busby K BTY 5 RHA

I first made the acquaintance of Lucy at the Tunisian township of Ben Gardene. Night was closing in and we had leaguered just outside the town. Perhaps I should explain that we were part of a force engaged in the pursuit of the retreating German and Italian units, and were settling down for the night after a somewhat hectic day. Lucy's owner was a tall, dark Bedouin type Arab. His command of the English language was somewhat limited, being strictly confined to the repeated phrase "Eggis for chai Askari". He apparently desired that above anything else in the world, in exchange for which he was prepared to sacrifice Lucy. Let me explain, before you jump to the wrong conclusion, that Lucy was a chicken. I named her this after she passed into my ownership. The Arab had magically produced her from beneath his jellabiah (a kind of long voluminous shirt) after failing to impress me with his sales expertise with regard to eggs. He would, so I was made to understand, part with the very source of his merchandise for just a small amount of tea. I had no real desire to own Lucy and my stock of tea was very low. However, his persistence finally wore me down and I parted with about an ounce of my precious tea and a German tunic shirt which I had acquired during the mopping up operations after El Alamein. Thus did Lucy become my property and I incarcerated her in the cabin of M5, this being a 3 ton truck on which we carried some of the impedimenta required to wage war. The floor of the cabin was sandbagged against land mines so I was not unduly worried about any mess Lucy might make. A handful of rice, some water, and Lucy was bedded down for the night. In the morning, at first light, I went to the truck to see how she had fared. She made no attempt to leave when I opened the door, in fact she gave me welcoming cluck, and proceeded to perch on the driving wheel. She was pathetically thin so I decided to keep her for a few days in order to fatten her up in preparation for the day when there would be time to deal with her. It was my intention to supplement the rations with chicken a la Benghazi. Whenever we stopped I would let Lucy out to forage around for whatever she could find. On the morning of the second day I had owned her, she rewarded me by laying an egg on the sandbagged floor of M5. Soya links and a fried egg for breakfast — I was the envy of every man in Edward Freddy troop. That was when I decided that Lucy should not die. I have always been glad that I made this decision. We became quite attached to each other. I would release her whenever the troop went into action; she was utterly impervious to exploding shells and the bark of guns, and took them in her stride. During the period of time between engagements, when we were on the move, she would perch on the edge of the passenger seat, looking as regal as any dowager. Right up to the time that it took to reach Enfidaville, some four or five weeks later, Lucy invariably provided me with a breakfast egg. When the order "Halt—Action Front" was given and the convoy halted, Lucy would look expectantly at the door on her side of the cabin. "Prepare to Advance" brought her scuttling back to the truck; I always set her free to search for food whenever the troop stopped. I was never quite sure what it was she found but on one occasion I made her disgorge a chameleon which was stuck, tail first, down her throat. I only had to call her and she would show up immediately. No dog could possibly have been more faithful. She was also an air raid alarm extraordinary. She could hear the sound of aircraft long before we could and would alert us by the habit of cocking her head to one side and peering skywards making loud clucking noises, after which she would disappear beneath M5. Whether or not she could differentiate between ours and theirs is a matter for conjecture. Unlike us she took no chances. It was at Enfidaville that Lucy became broody. She failed to show up for her morning meal of rice and broken biscuit and I found her sitting on the floor of M5 looking very sorry for herself. I decided, although I had no way of knowing, that she was in fact broody. As we were static at the time, there were the inevitable 'Eggy for chai' wallahs roaming amongst us. We were supposed to chase them away, but we did occasionally buy or barter for whatever it was they were offering for sale, chiefly eggs. I exchanged some tea for four eggs. These I placed into an old ammunition box lined with mule fodder. Lucy took over immediately and for the next three weeks dutifully obeyed her maternal instincts. I had wedged her incubation box firmly between two boxes containing 25 pounder high explosive shells so that the swaying motion of the truck would not unduly disturb her. I fed her with whatever she would accept and let her exercise at suitable times. At about this time the Brigade was ordered to join up with the 1st Army for the final assault on Tunis. This move had to be carried out in secret. The Brigade travelled mostly at night, and were static, camouflaged, during daylight. The mountainous nature of the country and the rock strewn terrain over which we travelled was nightmarish. M5 was thrown on to its side on one occasion and had to be winched upright. The contents of the truck were thrown about but my foresight in wedging Lucy's box paid off. Although two of her eggs were broken, she herself was undamaged. This was a testing time for all concerned, but after three nights we joined forces with the 1st Army and were practically ready for the final act of the desert campaign. On the morning that the troop reached the outskirts of Tunis, Lucy proudly produced two chicks. These were promptly christened Tunis and Bizerte. On the completion of hostilities in North Africa, the regiment were ordered back to Homs, some sixty kilometres east of Tripoli. We were to rest, wash the sand out of our systems and generally smarten up ourselves and our equipment in preparation for the next operation. This was May 1943. Lucy and her progeny settled down well at Homs. Everyone in the troop knew Lucy and her chicks, and they lived like fighting cocks, if you'll forgive the term. However, towards the end of July I had to get rid of the chicks. Chicks did I say? By this time they were twice the size of Lucy.

Without wishing to appear to be oversentimental, I had no desire to destroy the two, or in fact make a meal of them. I therefore presented them to Abdul, a local boy with whom I had become friendly, and who on occasions had done my dhobi-ing. He was overjoyed and for the remainder of my stay at Homs I was overpowered by the boy's determination to keep me clean. At the end of August 1943 we were alerted for further active service. The honeymoon was over; we were to embark at Tripoli for a secret destination. Rumours and wild statements were rife, some of us even had it on good authority that we were bound for "Old England" On the day we left Homs we were informed that we were going to make a beach landing on the Italian mainland. We were to form part of the American 5th Army under General Mark Clark and were to be transported in American tank landing craft. Some days before we were due to leave Homs, a regimental order appeared to the effect that all pets, that is dogs, jerboas, gerbils, chameleons, and all livestock must be disposed of before embarking. What of Lucy? I simply could not bring myself to part from her. We were attached to each other. You may accuse me of being childishly sentimental, but I could not bear the thought of abandoning her. She had been my companion for mile after lonely mile, so I decided to take her with me. To do this I had to make sure that no one else found her en route. Underslung below M5 was a tool box that had a drop end door. I removed the tools and placed them elsewhere. The space inside the box was ample for the purpose needed and I drilled several holes to allow plenty of ventilation. On the day we departed from Homs I placed Lucy in the tool box together with an ample supply of rice, broken biscuit and water. I locked the door and bade her goodbye. I did not see her again for three days, by which time M5 had been loaded on board a tank landing craft. We were allowed below decks during the voyage to check loads and to start up engines. I was thus able to feed Lucy, but could not let her out for exercise for obvious reasons. Seven days after leaving the North African coast we reached our destination, the beaches of Salerno. The details of the landing have been recorded before by better writers than I. Let it suffice rhat within two hours of landing, M5, Lucy and I were safely hidden in a grove of walnut trees. After North Africa this was Utopia. Lucy was in her element. No longer for her the spartan diet of the Desert Rat, for life had taken on a completely new outlook. She would disappear into the masses of tomato plants, cauliflower beds, grape vines, whatever happened to be growing wherever we stopped, and it became increasingly difficult to get her to return. I finally lost her just outside a town named San Sebastian. We had halted by the wayside and the "Brew up" sign had been passed down the column, Lucy jumped down and disappeared among the trees. No sooner had she done this than the "Prepare to move" order came and the "Brew up" was cancelled. I knew it was hopeless to try to find her in the short time I had. I called her name but she failed to respond. As far as I was concerned Lucy had vanished. I fervently hope that she lived to a ripe old age; she certainly had everything she wanted to enable her to do so. She had been my companion for four thousand miles and nine calendar months.

The Pyramids.

Back from the Blue

After months of fighting and hard living in the desert the prospect of a few days leave in Cairo or Alexandria was something to look forward to, but of course it meant very different things to different soldiers. A chance to have a decent bath perhaps — this was universally top priority; to sleep in a bed, between clean sheets — sheer luxury! A chance to forget about the war for a while and to behave like a tourist, visiting the Pyramids or the old City, or wandering around the *suqs* (Arab shopping areas) buying souvenirs for the folks back home — and probably getting rooked in the bargain too! To sample the excitement of an evening "on the town", with as much wine, women and song as one could pay for. Yes, Cairo and Alex had much to offer. And after a long, bumpy, uncomfortable drive or an equally nightmarish ride in an iron cattle truck — described by someone as being as hot as the inside of the Great Pyramid — Desert Rats on leave deserved a few pleasures. Over the next few pages I have tried to illustrate some — what sort of memories will they evoke?

Of course some Desert Rats preferred their own transport, and I was told by Hugh Hill, of 2 KRRC, of one occasion when a battered Dodge truck pulled up in the centre of a busy square in Cairo and the crew solemnly got out their brewing kit and proceeded to make tea in the middle of all the traffic. Everyone but the local police were amused!

One of the favourite haunts of Desert Rats on leave in Cairo was the Sweet Melody Club, where they would go for an evening of drinking, dancing, singing (etc!), regularly "wrecking the joint" at closing time. In fact the proprietor was well prepared and provided the cheapest furniture he could find. The band was perched high up in one wall, protected from the patrons by barbed wire! The nightly carousel ended with the playing of first the British and then the Egyptian National Anthem. As the words of the troops' version of the latter were not particularly pleasing to the Egyptians present, it was usually the signal for all hell to breal loose! However, there was no real bad feel ing on either side; certainly the proprieto made enough money out of the troops not t have to worry about the nightly breakages.

There was much to see in Cairo and th surrounding area. Few who visited th Pyramids or the Citadel, for example, coulc fail to be impressed by the magnificence o Egypt's past.

Entertainments Various

As we appear to have reached the subject o girls, a few words from one who spent he war years in Cairo would not go amiss. Bery Morton writes:

"I wonder if there is ever any mention of tha small group of ATS, Nurses, WAAFs anc WRNS who have the right to wear th Africa Star. Myself and a small group o Signals ATS were posted to the Middle Eas in August 1942, bashed away at the antiquated teleprinters installed in HQ Cairo al through Alamein and the North Africar campaign, and followed the progress of th Eighth Army up Italy until VE Day. wonder if the now staid and middle-aged e Desert Rats remember the girls in uniforn who they escorted to Groppi's (remember th luscious cakes?), to picnics at the Barrag (green grass!!), to watch cricket matches a Gizera, and to the Garrison Theatre (first clas artists) and culture at the Cairo Opera Housc (gilded splendour). Shopping the Muski helping them choose presents to send home tc wives and children, and the showing o precious photographs of wives and gir friends. On the first meeting, always th question "Where are you from?" hoping tc meet somebody from our own part of Britain. Memories of so long ago, but ver vivid; I still remember the tall sun-tannec men in khaki, Stella beer and the uncomplicated comradeship of that now historic time".

Leave over, the road back "Up the Blue" stretched endlessly in to the distance.

Above: A ride in a horse drawn 'gharry' was a must, although how all these members of 5 RTR were able to squeeze into the one remains a mystery!

Right: Another popular means of transport — when you wanted to get off you merely pulled the rope attached to the top arm, much to the annoyance of the driver!

Far right: There were many bars such as the Cyprus Bar pictured here — note the 'In Bounds'' sign.

Below: Not the place for the type of goings on which took place at the Sweet Melody. Here, at Shepherds' Hotel, the officers drank in surroundings reminiscent of a staid London club.

Bottom: The Victory Hotel, Alexandria looking towards the sea from one of the hotel windows.

Below right: Don't drink the water!

Far bottom right: Presents for home? A shop in Cairo.

13
IN BOUNDS

Above: Sports enthusiasts might even play the occasional game of cricket at the leave centres. Picture shows Officers v. Sergeants at Ismalia leave camp.

Right: "Vive le Sport!"—Not quite cricket, but perhaps far more entertaining.

Centre right: Beryl Morton and friends of the ATS — who worked in Headquarters Cairo.

Far top right: Nurses at tea time in their ante room at No 2 General Hospital, Quassasin.

Far centre right: A party on a River Nile boating trip.

Below: Tickets etc.

Below right: "That bint from the Sweet Melody promised she'd write!" (Reproduced by kind permission of Jon)

"That bint from the Sweet Melody promised she'd write!"

Right: Monty's Message.

Far right: Monty.

Below: The Prime Minister visits the Division before the battle. Mr Churchill is seen here being greeted by Major Castle of 5 RTR, whilst Major Biddell talks to more VIPs in the other car. General Alexander is standing behind Mr Churchill.

EIGHTH ARMY

Personal Message from the ARMY COMMANDER

1—When I assumed command of the Eighth Army I said that the mandate was to destroy ROMMEL and his Army, and that it would be done as soon as we were ready.

2—We are ready NOW.

The battle which is now about to begin will be one of the decisive battles of history. It will be the turning point of the war. The eyes of the whole world will be on us, watching anxiously which way the battle will swing.

We can give them their answer at once, "It will swing our way."

3—We have first-class equipment; good tanks; good anti-tank guns; plenty of artillery and plenty of ammunition; and we are backed up by the finest air striking force in the world.

All that is necessary is that each one of us, every officer and man, should enter this battle with the determination to see it through — to fight and to kill — and finally, to win.

If we all do this there can be only one result — together we will hit the enemy for "six," right out of North Africa.

4—The sooner we win this battle, which will be the turning point of this war, the sooner we shall all get back home to our families.

5—Therefore, let every officer and man enter the battle with a stout heart, and with the determination to do his duty so long as he has breath in his body.

AND LET NO MAN SURRENDER SO LONG AS HE IS UNWOUNDED AND CAN FIGHT.

Let us all pray that "the Lord mighty in battle" will give us the victory.

B. L. MONTGOMERY,
Lieutenant-General, G.O.C.-in-C., Eighth Army.

MIDDLE EAST FORCES,
23-10-42.

El Alamein

Operation Lightfoot

In late October 1942 the Eighth Army fought its most famous battle and gained a remarkable victory. It was, as Field Marshal Montgomery had forecast in his personal message to his Army prior to the battle, a turning-point in the war. For some time things had not been going well for the Allies; the campaigns in Greece and Crete in 1941 had proved ghastly failures, and setbacks in the Western Desert had by June 1942 forced the British to withdraw to within a few miles of Cairo and Alexandria. The surrender of Singapore in February 1942, the loss of great warships such as the *Prince of Wales* and *Repulse,* the continued reverses suffered by the Russians, all these disasters did little to help Allied morale. In Africa they were now facing strong German and Italian forces under Rommel, who had already tried to break through the El Alamein line for a second time at the Battle of Alam Halfa in early September.

Now, at long last, they had received the much-needed reinforcements of both men and material, including American tanks such as Shermans, which went a long way to redressing the armoured balance in firepower and protection which had until then been so heavily weighted in the Germans favour. The Desert Army was now better equipped than ever before and ready for anything. However, the very nature of the terrain was against the classic "left hook" into the desert which had been a standard feature of all the previously successful campaigns. This was because the Quattara Depression, a vast area of salt marsh covered with soft sand and lying many feet below sea level, inhibited movement on the southern flank.

So Montgomery decided that it would have to be a frontal attack, supported by a

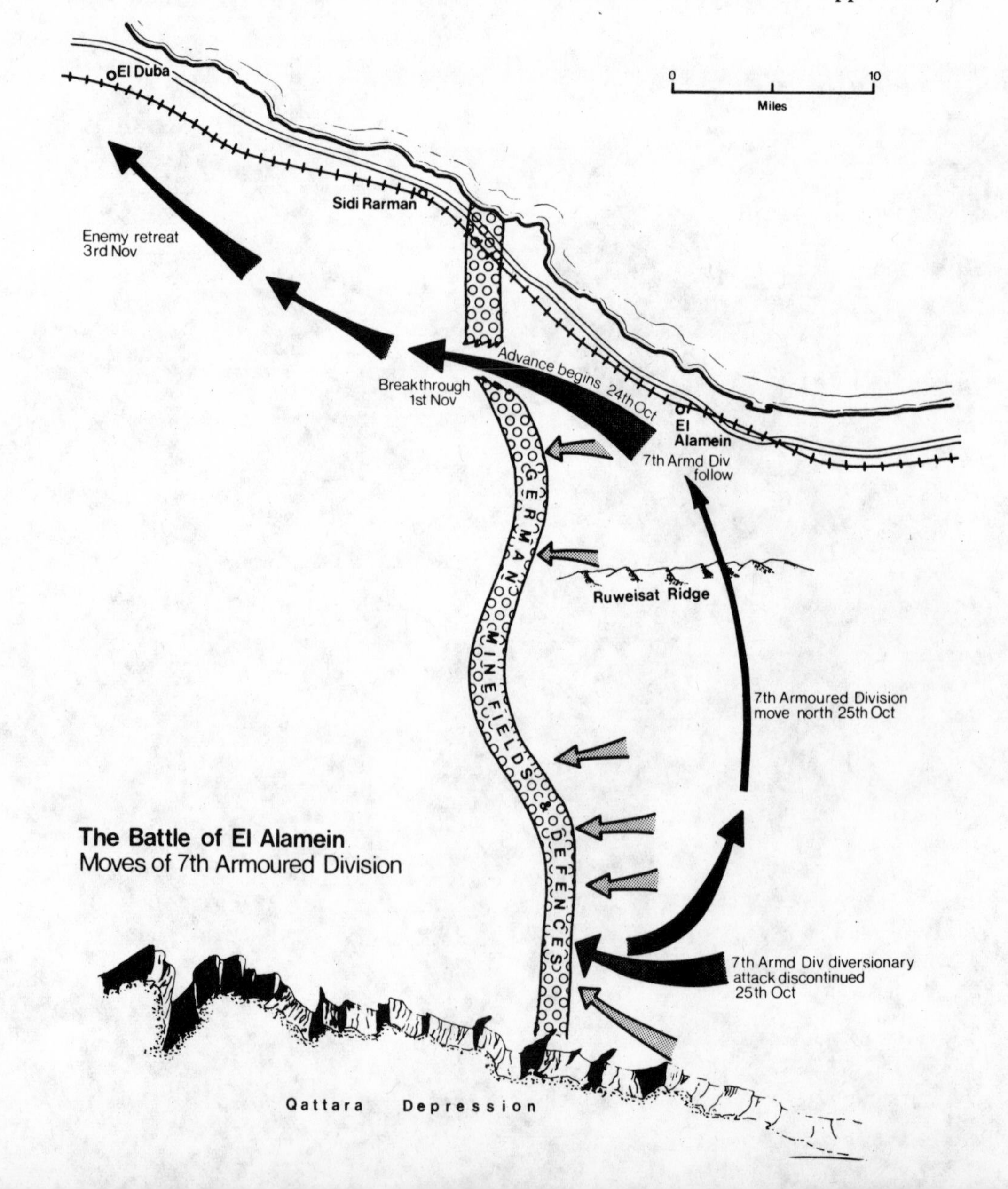

The Battle of El Alamein
Moves of 7th Armoured Division

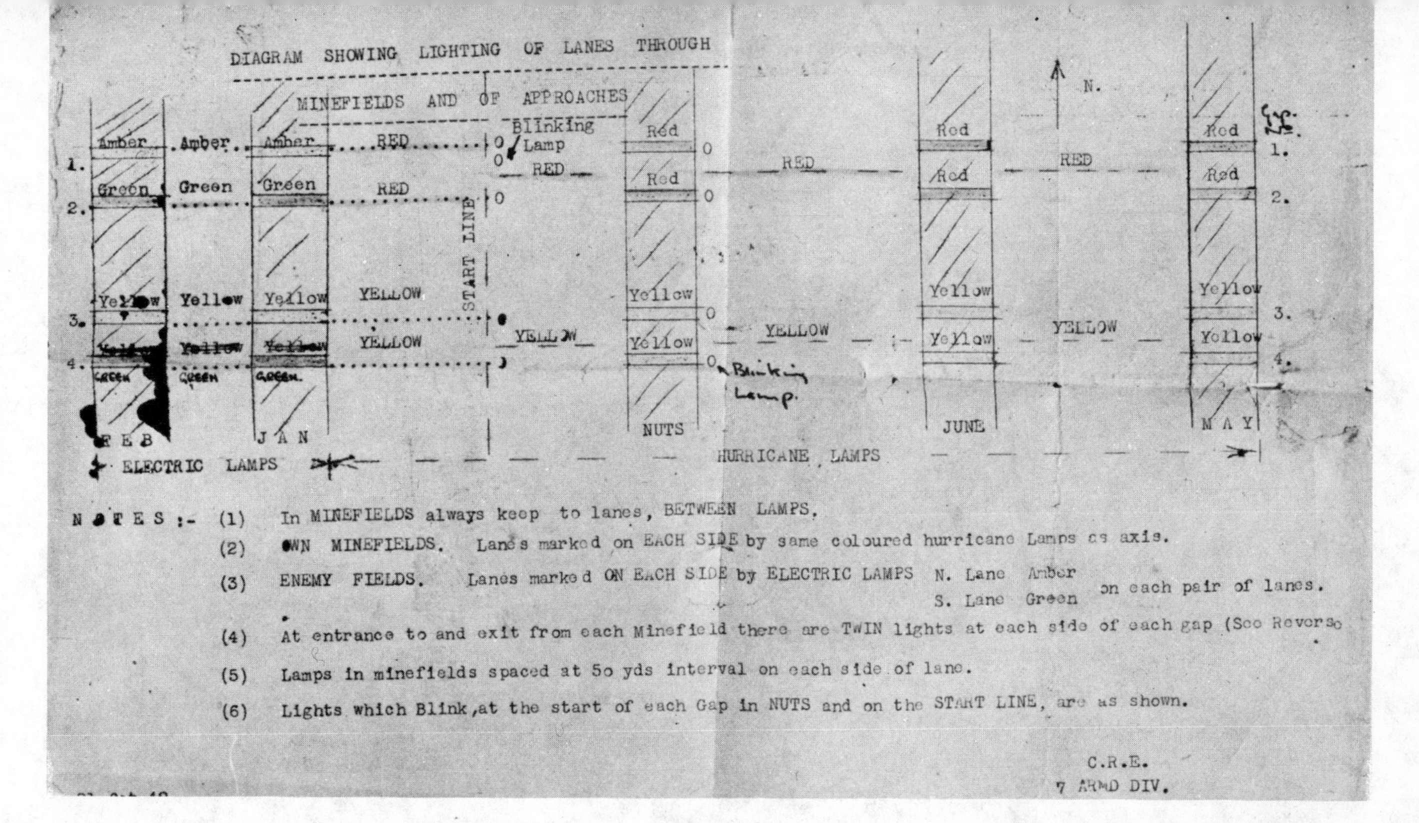

Photograph of the actual minefield lane diagram as issued by CRE 7th Armoured Division.

massive artillery bombardment, in order to break into and through Rommel's position. In essence his plan was to try to persuade Rommel into thinking that the attack was to come in the south, by the use of all manner of deceptions (such as the dummy tanks pictured in the "Tanks" section of this book). The main attack would actually take place in the north, and once the infantry had broken into the enemy defences and opened corridors through the massive defensive minefields (5 miles deep and containing over 5 million mines), then the armour would break out and destroy the main enemy forces.

7th Armoured Division had been placed originally in the south of the line, opposite two enemy armoured divisions, 21st Panzer and the Italian Ariete. Later, when 21st Pz was moved up to join 15th Pz in the north, Montgomery also moved the Division up north as Army reserve, to be allotted to 10 Corps in due course for the breakout, which in the event they spearheaded. However, before coming on to the breakout, which was naturally the main task of the Division, let us examine the breaching of the minefields, as this was such an important factor in the success of the plan. Here is an extract from a diary written at that time by Colonel Hugh Brassey, then commanding A Squadron of the Royal Scots Greys in 4th Light Armoured Brigade:

"As far as we were concerned we were to attack in the south. To do this we came under 7th Armoured Division, commanded by General Harding, but for the minefield "Lightfoot" operation we were loaned to the 44th Division, a comparatively new Division in the field, but one which had had a very good name during training days in England.

On the night of the 23rd the Recce Battalion of the 44th Division was to go through the May and Nuts minefields, which we held, and then to force the January minefield and the February minefield, held by the enemy. The Greys would follow close on their heels, and form a bridgehead at the February minefield, through which the 22nd Armoured Brigade would pass, followed by the 131st Lorried Inf Bde.

The Recce Battalion was to force four passages in two pairs — the pairs being 500 yards apart and the two passages in each pair 50 yards apart. Scorpions (I-Tanks with flails) were to be used for the mine sweeping, and also detectors. We were to supply 3 Honey Tanks to each pair of passages, to escort the I-Tank Sweepers. The January and February minefields were known to be very heavily sown with mines of all sorts, and were held by the Italian Folgore Division, the only first-class Italian division in the field. These were backed up by numerous guns — mostly German 105mm and 150mm, and many anti-tank guns of 88mm and 50mm calibre. The 21st Panzers, consisting of about 150 tanks, were also reported about 3 miles to the west.

On arrival at the Hun end of the February minefield we were to form a bridgehead in a half moon, and the anti tank guns were to dig in right behind the tanks to prevent being

A Scorpion Minesweeping Tank. Based upon the Matilda hull, with two additional engines to turn the revolving drum which carried the chains. The tank was driven into the minefield at about 2mph with the drum revolving, the chains detonating any mines they struck.

shelled to bits. All tanks were to have rear lights and all tank commanders were to wear tin hats. I should add that the ground over which we were operating was all dead flat. Distance from the May minefield to January was about 7 miles.

We had a dress rehearsal on the night of the 21st, and we got through the two fake minefields and formed our bridgehead without trouble. I discovered my obvious difficulty on "the night" was going to be seeing the light on the back of the Colonel's tank and keeping pace with it, but he promised to let me know on the air what he was doing. The lights marking the lanes through the minefields appeared to be very clear, but there again I was a bit dubious how clear they would be on "the night".

The 22nd passed without incident. No tanks appeared for us, and the Colonel told us that zero hour was the evening of the next day, the 23rd. It looked as though we were going to have to do it with five tanks only in each of the heavy Squadrons.

On the 23rd we moved up into assembly areas at about 10am. The Colonel came round at 12 noon and told all the chaps what was going to happen and gave them some figures. For instance, along the whole front we had 1,300 tanks as opposed to about 600 German and Italian. The air strength was considerable — a permanent 500-fighter umbrella and a shuttle service of Bostons, also Hurricane "tank-busters" which did good work.

During the afternoon we checked ammunition, wireless sets, engines — everything. 5pm came and still no tanks. We were due to move up by 7·30. . .

At 6pm we had just finished our tea when eleven Grants appeared as if by magic. Within about three-quarters of an hour 'A' Sqn had received six more tanks, which brought us up to full strength. At last we got the order to move up, and to tell the truth I was very glad. I had my old tank back and my old crew.

By 7·30 we were formed up; the KRRC Coy took up its position on A Sqn's left, with C Sqn headed by RHQ and the Colonel 500 yards on my right. We started to waddle forward in the evening light behind the 44 Recce Battalion, the rear vehicle of which was a whitish colour and fairly easy to see.

We went through May minefield and Nuts — both beautifully lighted — without any trouble. We went on for what seemed ages. Soon the sound of gunfire and shells landing came from in front. The night was a bit darker now and I could see no sign of the right columns. I rang up the Colonel on the air and we decided we were about level.

After a bit our column was halted and shells started to drop around us. Looking through glasses I could see the edge of the January minefield. I was told that Nos 1 and 2 gap were going very slowly, and Nos 3 and 4 gap were blocked.

Meanwhile, the Colonel's column appeared to have swung off right. I couldn't move to conform with him without losing direction, and I spent an agonising half hour on the air, trying to get a bearing on where we were. At last, when I was almost in despair, we moved forward about 300 yards and I could see the entrances of 3 and 4 gaps. At the same time the Colonel put up a burst of tracer from a Browning and said he was opposite No 2 gap. I breathed a sigh of thankfulness, which expired quickly when an 11th Hussar subaltern, acting as Traffic Controller, strolled up through a couple of shell bursts and informed me No. 3 gap was blocked by a blown-up Honey and a Carrier.

So we had to halt there for about 20 minutes until it was cleared. In No 3 gap, a squadron of 40 Carriers went in, and four got to the other side; there is no doubt that the Folgore fought very well indeed that night and the 44th Recce had a very bad time.

I held a wild and disjointed conversation with the 11th Hussar chap, who was on the air to the 44th Recce, fighting their way through, and also to the brigadier of some infantry brigade. Both said it was no good going through as 3 and 4 gaps were blocked. I told the Colonel this, and he replied *"You must get through"*. Back I went to the control and this time he said I could go. 'A' Sqn trundled down the slope and entered the No 3 gap nose to tail. No 4 column had to right wheel and come behind us.

We had gone about 200 yards when we came to the blown-up Honey and the carrier. I tried to lead past them, and was taking care to keep a foot inside the lane tape, when I struck a mine which blew my track off. I jumped down and looked at the damage and at that moment I really didn't know what the hell to do. There was 'A' Squadron, nose to tail, plumb in the middle of the minefield, unable to go back or forward, and offering a very nice target to the Hun when dawn came. Luckily, a little RE officer appeared — apparently from the ground — and said they

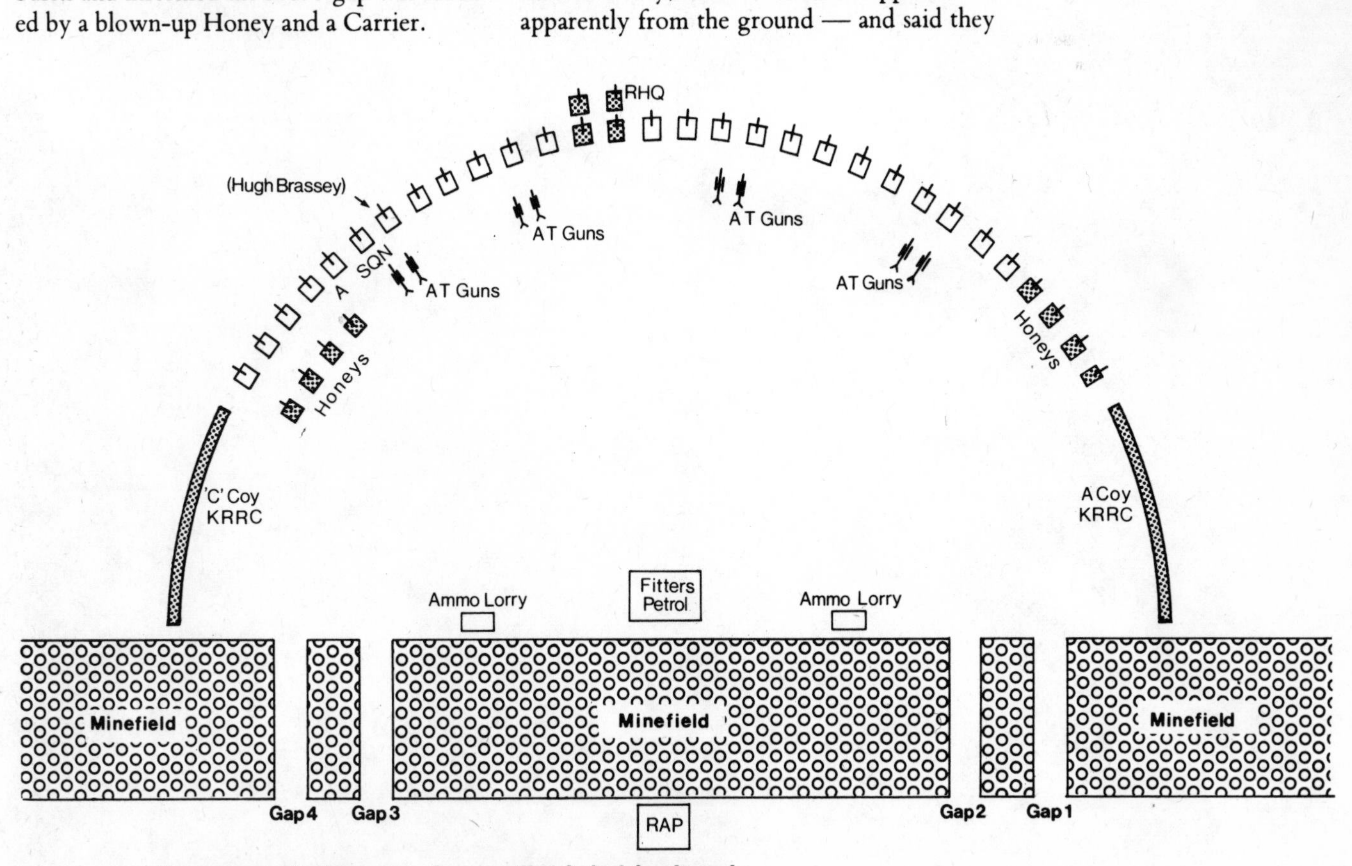

Diagramatic layout of minefield bridgehead

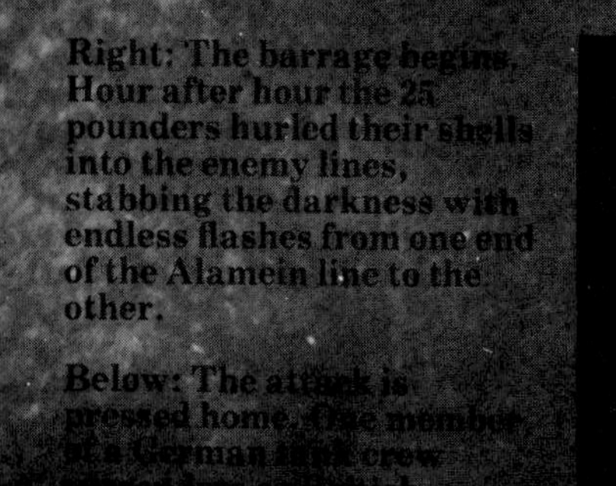

Right: The barrage begins. Hour after hour the 25 pounders hurled their shells into the enemy lines, stabbing the darkness with endless flashes from one end of the Alamein line to the other.

Below: The attack is pressed home. One member of a German tank crew surrenders as British infantry rush his tank...

would sweep a new passage round in fifteen minutes. This they did and I popped into the next tank and on we went.

As we came out of the minefield I could just pick out the light on the Colonel's tank and he ordered me to form the bridgehead there. It was obvious by then that we would not make February that night, and 'A' Sqn formed a line (as per the diagram) on the left of the Colonel's tank. The rest of the night we spent in our tanks trying to spot guns and keeping our heads well down. Gradually dawn broke and we looked around and started to square ourselves off.

October 24th. Directly in front of us, about 4,000 yards away, was the north side of Hemeimat, and to our right and right front was the February minefield, about 2,500 yards away. Between us and Hemeimat could be seen dug-in positions and one or two heads popping out. About 9am the Colonel ordered 'B' Sqn to push forward cautiously and see what these dugouts were. I was told to support with fire if necessary. Alwyn was having a little private war of his own against some Hun cars just right of Hemeimat, at about 3,500 yards range.

Frank took his Honey Squadron and ferretted out 150 Italians and 2 anti-tank guns with no trouble. His orders on the wireless were more reminiscent of cub-hunting or rabbiting than war. The rest of the day was spent making sure of our bridgeheead and keeping out of the way of HE and AP shells. Nothing could be done about the February minefield during the day, and anyhow the 44th Recce were very cut up. We could see vehicles, a gun or two, and some men behind the minefield, and duly shot them up whenever the opportunity occurred.

As the sun was going down 30 German tanks were reported behind February and looking as if they were going to counter-attack. An exchange of shots took place at about 2,000 yards. I was ordered to take three tanks forward on the left and create a diversion. I pushed off, but honestly had very little idea how far to go or quite what to do. However, this was decided for me by a wire

fence — obviously the offspring of February — pulling me up short. My tank's engine was shooting out flame and going very badly, so I changed into another. Darkness arrived and the Colonel told us all to rally. By one of those miracles which sometimes occur, we all found ourselves somehow and reformed our original bridgehead in front of the infantry of the KRRC.

The Colonel sent for squadron leaders and said they were going to have a shot at cracking February at 11·45pm that night, backed up by the 22nd Armoured Brigade. We sat in our tanks till 11·30 and then formed a closed-up double line ahead behind the Colonel. The 22nd Bde moved up, and this noise was the signal for a really good but erratic barrage from the Hun, which caught me with an armful of Tommy guns trying to make the tanks hear me above the din when the hatches were closed down. I think I came as near to losing my temper then as I ever did in that operation.

However, we formed up and waited, but soon we heard the attack was off. The Hun had got February pretty well taped by now, and we did not have the infantry there to really crack it enough. So we eventually retired to our old bridgehead area about 800 yards back, guided by the light of one of our ammunition trucks which had been hit and was going off in pops and bangs. We sat in our tanks all night from 3am onward and so ended Oct 24th with really not a lot done. The Free French had apparently got to Hemeimat, but the going was so bad they couldn't get their anti-tank guns up there and they had been driven off by about 10 Hun tanks (mostly captured Honeys).

October 25th. The 25th dawned very much as the 24th had, with a bit of shelling from the Hun which prevented any of us getting out of our tanks and caused some casualties amongst the infantry. During these two days there were vehicles about 20 yards apart in the area of the bridgehead and any shell landing was bound to hit something. The tanks got near misses once or twice, but we only had two badly damaged, and this was by 88mm AP which came very close at times. The whole of the bridgehead was of course under enemy observation from about 8000 yards.

At about 9am the Greys were withdrawn from the January minefield, leaving the 22nd Armd Bde forming the bridgehead. We went back through our gaps about a mile and had breakfast. At about 11·30am we received orders to move into the Munassib depression on the immediate right of the January minefield, to support a probe forward by the 4th/8th Hussars. We entered the depression in single file, owing to unlocated mines. I had grave misgivings as to whether the whole squadron was following me, as we went at quite a fast pace, and Munassib was nothing more than a succession of little sandy wadis which made it difficult to see your neighbour. However, they all came on all right and A Sqn took up a position to support the 4th/8th if necessary. Their composite Squadron move was not a howling success, as most of their tanks went up on the top instead of keeping in the wadis and ran on to wired mines and anti tank guns, losing 9 tanks — though they recovered most of them that night.

Dark came and we were preparing to move out of the Munassib again, when the order came to about turn. So back we went, and eventually joined leaguer in the Munassib next door to HQ 4th Lt Armd Bde.

As you can imagine, we were all pretty flogged by now. I went back and told the chaps to fill up with ammunition and petrol, get something to eat (cold of course) and then get to sleep. Rations would not be up till about 1am.

I had such bloody painful "tank legs" that I lay down in front of my tank with my legs on two sandbags to keep them above my head and was soon asleep. I was woken up by a runner who said the Colonel's order was

Above left: A Sherman tank hitting a mine.

Above: The Pursuit begins! A General Grant tank moves up at speed.

everyone into the tanks. I was very peevish and walked over to the Colonel to find out what was "on", only to discover that two shells had just fallen into the leaguer — one about 60-70 yards away from me, which had killed a man. I had slept peacefully through it all.

I went round and told everyone to get into the tanks, and at the same time the rations arrived. I then lay down in front of my tank again and went to sleep. I knew that if I went into the tank I would be unable to move the next morning — fortunately no other shell came near us the whole night.

October 26th. We took up the positions of the previous day. The Colonel was darting about in Astra (the cut-down Honey) and being much too pugnacious, but found nothing to attack except minefields. The 4th/8th took over from us at 12 noon and we pulled back about four miles to have a slight breather.

We arrived at a very nice secluded spot. I had a bath and started to walk round the tanks. About ten Hurricanes came over us, and then suddenly we heard a rush of air, meaning bombs. I fell flat on my face and the bombs landed about 200 yards away, near RHQ. Apparently some Me109s above the Hurricanes; the Colonel got a small bit in the leg, and two men were killed. In the evening we again moved up to Munassib to leaguer.

October 27th. Next day we moved back again and were told we would probably be there for about 3 or 4 days. Maintenance at last was carried out, and the three days passed very uneventfully, except for one day when they suddenly lobbed about 20 shells into our area; I sheltered firmly behind the engine of a Grant.

October 31st. We took part in a fake attack. It consisted of us all moving up in the evening, followed by the 4th/8th Hussars and two squadrons of dummy tanks. We moved up towards January and got nicely photographed by a Hun recce plane, and then at 9pm we moved into the January lanes, where we sat until 4am, with half the Squadron running engines at high speed, to lend "tone". Up ahead was an armoured car playing a record of tanks advancing on a loudspeaker. Rumour has it the chap put on the wrong side first, which was an artillery barrage, but this is not vouched for. We came back from this at 4am and went to sleep.

November 2nd. We moved up to Alamein via Beachy Head and came under command of 4th Lt Armd Bde. We arrived at Alamein Station full of rumours of following up the break-through by 10 Corps, but at the station the Colonel found the road so blocked with vehicles all moving west that he decided to stop where he was.

November 4th. We moved out at first light and started on the trek after Rommel which landed us at Acroma on November 15th.

The Race to Tunis

Tobruk recaptured. Men of the 1st/6th Queens enter Tobruk.

After more than two years fighting in the desert the Division had learned many lessons, which they put to good use in their long and speedy advance to Tunis. In his history of the Division General Verney described how they operated:

"The Division moved across the Desert always in fighting formation, covered by armoured car patrols of the 11th Hussars, experts at Desert reconnaissance, deployed on a wide front astride the Divisional axis. Following the armoured car patrols, with which were Engineer reconnaissance parties, came the Armoured Brigade moving deployed for battle in three Regimental groups, each with its supporting element of motor infantry, artillery, anti tank guns, etc well dispersed against air attack, but ready to fight in any direction. Following the Armoured Brigade came Divisional Tactical Headquarters, the Commander, ADC, one Staff Officer, the CRA and one RA Staff Officer. The Infantry Brigade followed in similar formation behind, or echeloned to a flank according to its task. The whole Division was controlled by the Divisional Commander personally by his wireless direct to subordinate commanders or through main Headquarters.

As the light began to fail each evening and the risk of air attack passed, Regimental groups closed, as they moved, into a single column in close formation, and then closed upon each other so that when darkness fell and the order was given to halt they formed one compact group, each vehicle and subunit in its appointed place. In the morning they moved on as soon as there was enough light to see to drive, opening out once more into battle formation as they advanced. This drill stood them in good stead, it saved time and avoided confusion, they were always ready for battle and everyone knew where he stood.

When the armoured car patrols encountered the enemy they probed his dispositions and reported them in detail as the armour moved forward to contact and the artillery came into action. The Armoured Regiments worked their way forward, supported by their artillery, to pin down or outflank the enemy under the wireless control of the Brigade Commander, using ground and fire to cover movement or to close the range. Infantry and anti-tank guns were disposed to cover the flanks, or held in reserve as the stituation required.

As the tanks moved forward the fire fight began, a grim struggle for supremacy between tank and tank or anti-tank gun, and between the opposing artillery, like a medieval battle on a widely extended front. The Germans were clever at disposing their tanks and guns and always fought stoutly. The skill of the troop leader and tank commander in the use of ground, the accuracy of the tank gunner and of the artillery Forward Observation Officers were the decisive factors. The evidence of success was the smoke pile from a brewed up tank, or the sight of remnants of a gun crew scuttling from their position when it was hit.

The aim was always first to pin down the

Below: British Infantry hot on the heels of retreating Germans. British infantry advance westwards through smoke and dust, passing one of the many knocked out enemy tanks which litter the desert.

Below right: Mersa Matruh is captured. Crusader and Sherman tanks entering Mersa Matruh after the town had fallen.

enemy and discover the flanks of his position, then to over-lap or outflank him on one flank or both, always taking the greatest care to keep all three Regimental groups within close supporting distance of each other so that the enemy had no chance of dealing with them individually. This, combined with the skill and experience of the commanders and crews, and sound team-work on the battlefield between tanks, guns and infantry, were the secrets of success, plus of course the fact that for the first time since the campaign against the Italians in 1940–41 the British tanks compared favourably with those of the enemy.

The Germans always fought hard to maintain their positions until dark and generally succeeded. Facing east with their backs to the sun, the light gave them a valuable advantage in the afternoon and evening. When the half-light came, the tanks moved into close range and the rattle of the Besas replaced the crack of the tank guns as "soft" targets presented themselves. At this stage the motor infantry were launched to complete the work of the tanks by attacking such enemy gun crews as remained in position, finishing off lame ducks, clearing the battlefield and pushing forward patrols to harass the enemy as he withdrew into the darkness.

Then the tanks and guns were concentrated, supply echelons called forward, fitters brought up to work on damaged tanks, and the whole arduous business of re-fuelling and re-arming was put in hand. In spite of the most careful foresight it was often far into the night before the supply echelons arrived. Replenishment was seldom fully completed before the early hours of the morning and the fitters were hard at work until their units moved off. These were the main reasons why it was seldom possible to follow up the enemy at night. Also great risks are involved in moving a mass of vehicles at night over unknown ground which may well be mined as well, in the face of an enemy who knows precisely where he is. It is one thing to withdraw armour at night over known ground and into areas already in your possession, quite another to advance into the unknown with no means of telling when or where you may run into an enemy position or minefield, even if you are fortunate enough to complete your replenishment and give your men the minimum of rest in time to resume your advance before daybreak. There are, of course, exceptional cases when the risk is fully justified, but as a general rule, it was thought that it would not pay a dividend and experienced commanders believed that was right". *

It would be impossible to cover in a few pages all that took place during the two thousand mile pursuit. Instead, I have chosen to describe one or two typical incidents that happened en route. I have deliberately mentioned 131 (Queen's) Lorried Infantry Brigade first, as they did not join the Division until Alamein, but were then to remain a vital part of it for the rest of the war.

By early January 1943 the Division was advancing, together with the New Zealand Division, inland across country, whilst 51st Highland Division moved along the coast road. On the 19th the 1st/6th Queens, commanded by Lt Col (later Colonel) Bill Kaulback, successfully occupied the small town of Tarhuna, which lay in front of the main enemy positions covering the Tripoli plain. During the night the Germans withdrew from these covering positions back to their main line, astride the pass through which the road from Tarhuna descended to the plain. Here they had excellent observation and concealment and successfully held up the 8th Armoured Brigade.

It was decided on 21st January that the Queen's Brigade would put in a night attack through the hills, with 1/5th south and 1/6th north of the road. Let us follow the fortunes of 1/6th Queen's in an extract from Col Bill Kaulback's diary:

"There is a rocky defile leading down

* *The Desert Rats* pages 139–141.

through the mountains from Tarhuna to the Tripoli plain. The Boche are holding this very cleverly with MMG covering the artillery OPs well forward astride the road and the guns well back. The road is mined and blown, so our tanks are stuck. The 1/5th were sent out early this morning to outflank to the right but no word has been heard of them since. I was watching progress from a hill-top when at 11·30 I got orders to prepare an outflanking night attack. This presented some dificulty as the maps are very inaccurate. Secondly, the total distance from where we must leave our vehicles is 15 miles through very broken hills and I have no mules to carry the heavy loads, wireless, mortars and ammunition. Finally, the divisional plan includes an intense artillery programme right down the valley from 2030 to 2100, so I must be careful not to get into its area before it starts, while at the same time I must be close enough to hop straight in behind it as soon as it lifts.

I decided to accept the map as it stood, and chose a forming-up position half way down the valley, just on the edge of the planned artillery target. To judge the distance accurately during the approach march at night I selected 5 officers who would pace in front of the battalion column and take the average every 1,000 yards. To carry the heavy equipment I took all the spare drivers, cooks and others that I could lay hands on and used them as porters. The map showed goat tracks and I decided to use them, leading the battalion along in single file. We would of course be very vulnerable if attacked en route, but I judged that the enemy had not enough strength to be far out in the hills and the risk was worth taking.

While we were planning this, press reporters, including one each from the *Times* and *Daily Telegraph,* turned up and I invited them to join us for the operation. They accepted gladly.

The plan went off well and strangely enough the primitive method of measuring distance worked excellently. Shortly afer we had turned north off the goat track we came under heavy mortar fire, but the light was fast fading and their aim was inaccurate, so we

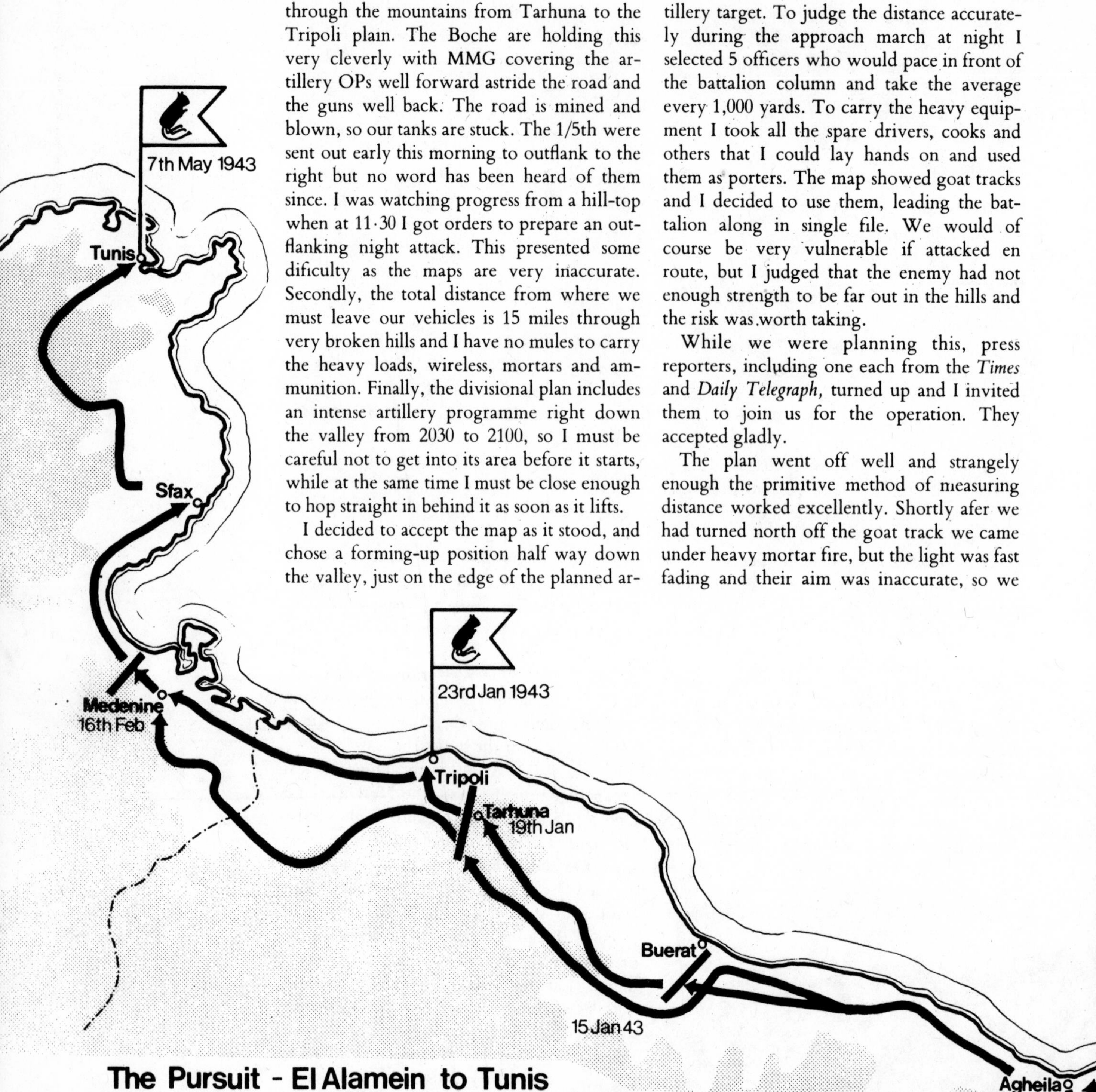

The Pursuit - El Alamein to Tunis
Showing route taken by 7th Armoured Division

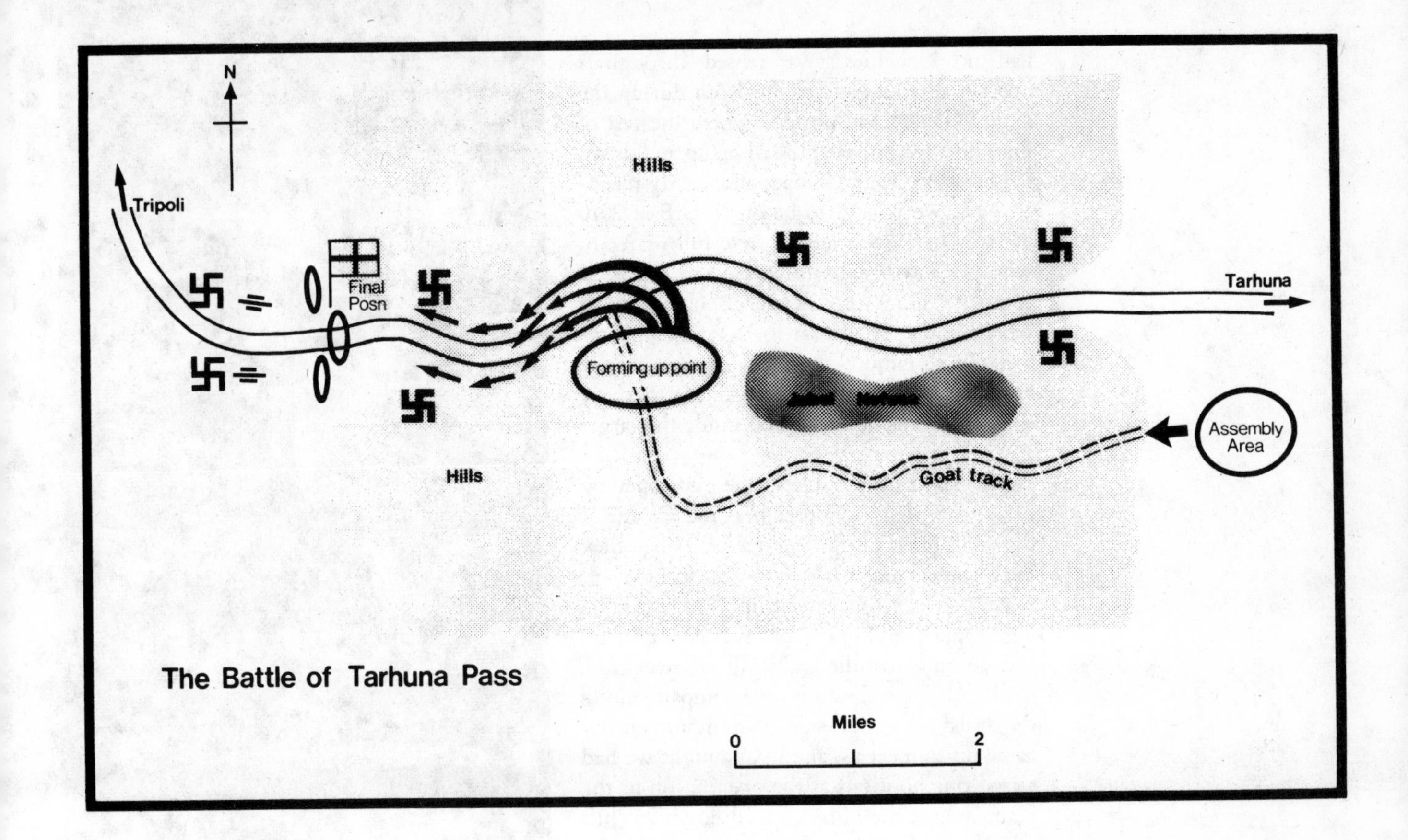

The Battle of Tarhuna Pass

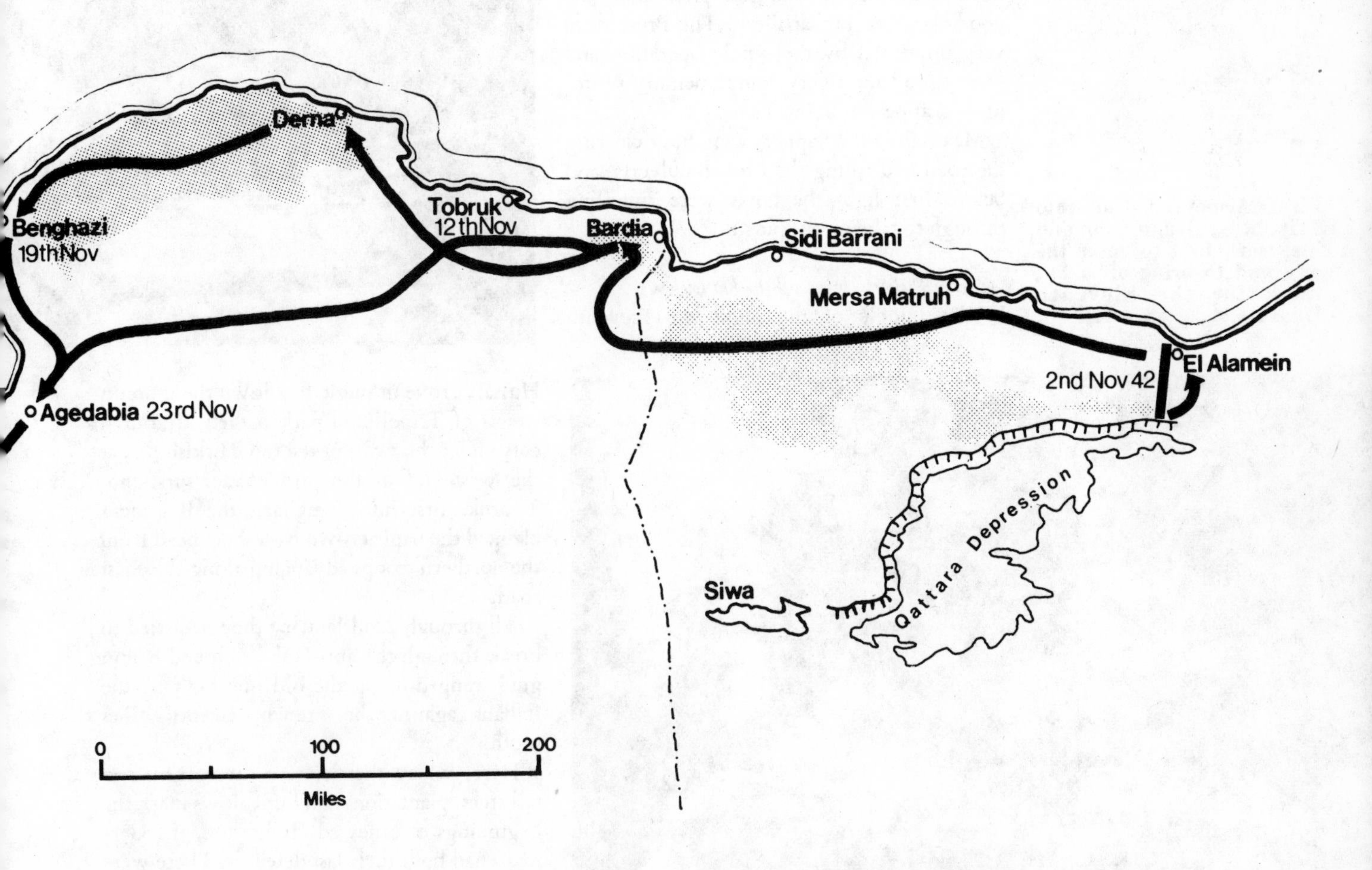

had no casualties. We passed through a number of stragglers of the 1/5th during the dark and they had no idea where the rest of their unit was, so we pressed on up and down the most precipitous slopes and finally reached what we judged to be our F.U.P at 2010 hours. There we found a cave full of Arabs who presented me with cheese and professed complete ignorance of the Boche and his whereabouts. So we sat for a rather uncomfortable 20 minutes, waiting for the artillery barrage and hoping to goodness that we weren't too far forward and inside the target area.

We heard the rumble of the guns opening fire and all held our breath as the scream of the shells grew nearer and nearer! When they burst some hundreds of yards in front of us, what a sigh of relief went up! When the firing stopped at 2100 hours we advanced up and down across the wadis till we struck the road and swept down it, one company along the hills on either side. No living enemy came up to meet us, and by midnight we had seized our positions at the opening on to the plain, where the hills dropped down in cliffs on either side for as far as the eye could see. There were several enemy dead here and a smashed 37mm anti tank gun, presumably the good work of our artillery. The Press were very impressed by the whole operation and some time later a very complimentary write-up of it appeared in the *Times.*

Meanwhile the Sappers were busy clearing the road and filling the broken culverts, and before first light the tanks were rumbling through to take up the pursuit."

"Cherry Pickers" bring off the hat trick

In the middle of the night the Eleventh Hussars drove in single file down the moonlit streets of Tripoli and parked their armoured cars under the walls of the old Turkish fort at the west end of the promenade. First into Tobruk, first into Benghazi, the Regiment claimed the triple crown by a short head from the northern troops advancing along the coast road.

First Armoured Car into Tripoli. Sgt Hugh Lyon and his crew, first to enter the city and to bring off a hat trick for the Eleventh Hussars.

All through 22nd January they had tried to break through the anti-tank ditch and 88mm guns, ranged along the old line built by the Italians against the French, twenty miles south.

Here, where the desert grows green, and tall trees, plantations and bungalows mark the beginnings of renewed civilisation, the Germans had built their last defences. There were

gun positions on mounds camouflaged with leaves, slit trenches in woods, mines flanking the roadway.

In the darkness the infantry went forward and the sappers set to work to make a track over the anti-tank ditch. Behind them the armoured cars formed up in single file waiting for the signal to advance on Tripoli. Six miles away in Castel Benito the infantry were to signal the town all clear by Verey lights.

Shortly after midnight the track was prepared and then in the distance the lights hung in the air. The Germans had gone, the road lay open. The armoured cars crept off, expecting ambush and a mined tarmac every yard of the journey. The cypress trees by the roadside were new and cast suspicious shadows to these men of the desert. Every fig tree was an anti-tank gun, every white cube-shaped villa an infantry stronghold.

In Castel Benito they passed a scrawled notice: "Tommy, we shall return". Already one of the infanteers had added a surprisingly restrained comment: "Yimkin" (perhaps). The kilo stone read "Tripoli 23". This was the stone every man in the Eighth Army had wanted to see since that day three months ago, when the final assault on the Afrika Korps began. The moon was full and the wind was cold.

Eighteen kilometres, fourteen kilometres. Ten . . . eight . . . six. It seemed too good to be true. They began to pinch themselves. After three thousand miles of being shot at,

Tanks of the 7th Armoured Division lined up in the main square of Tripoli.

mined, strafed, shelled and Stukaed, it couldn't be as easy as this. Occasionally the column halted. The leading car was investigating what might have been a German on a tall observation ladder. It was a wind-pump.

The first man to ride down the streets of the capital was Sergeant Hugh Playfair Lyon, MM, of Treegreeves Cottage, St Austels, Bristol, in armoured car No 118775. The fact is disputed by his driver, who maintains that by virtue of his position in the driving seat he was the first man in.

No one quite knew what sort of reception to expect. It was four-thirty in the morning and it was a dead town. They had expected bombs thrown from buildings and snipers on the rooftops. But there was not a soul stirring.

They begun to wonder if the entire population had vanished. Then, as they passed the hospital, they saw two lights burning. Still in single file, they drove down to the Lungo Mare Conte Volpi and looked across the harbour.

Several ships lay there, mast-deep in water. One ten-thousand tonner still rode on the surface, a gaping hole in her side.

A feeling of elation crept over the leading squadron. They were in. After a journey half across Africa they were in. The first British troops to enter Tripoli. In the dead of night one of the crew of a car let his spirits give rein. "Taxi", he yelled into the darkness, "Taxi"

But there was still work to be done. There might be some German forces east of the town, and down on the docks saboteurs might be trying a last-minute explosion. The wireless and power stations had to be visited. They went along the promenade eastwards to the docks and found the road completely blown. Ships filled the mouth of the harbour.

Under the mosque on high ground overlooking the docks they leaguered. And from the east a strange sound met their ears. A sound which gave them a sneaking satisfaction. It was six o'clock in the morning and along the coast road came the sound of bagpipes.

The Hussars had beaten the Highlanders by ninety minutes.

Perhaps awakened by the sound of the pipes, or maybe because he was an early riser, the first Tripolitanian prowled the streets. A solitary Arab came out of a doorway and looked at the armoured cars near the mosque. He looked and looked again. Quite sure the

Tripoli Victory Parade. The Prime Minister passing through the main street in Tripoli with the tanks of C Sqn, 4 CLY in rear.

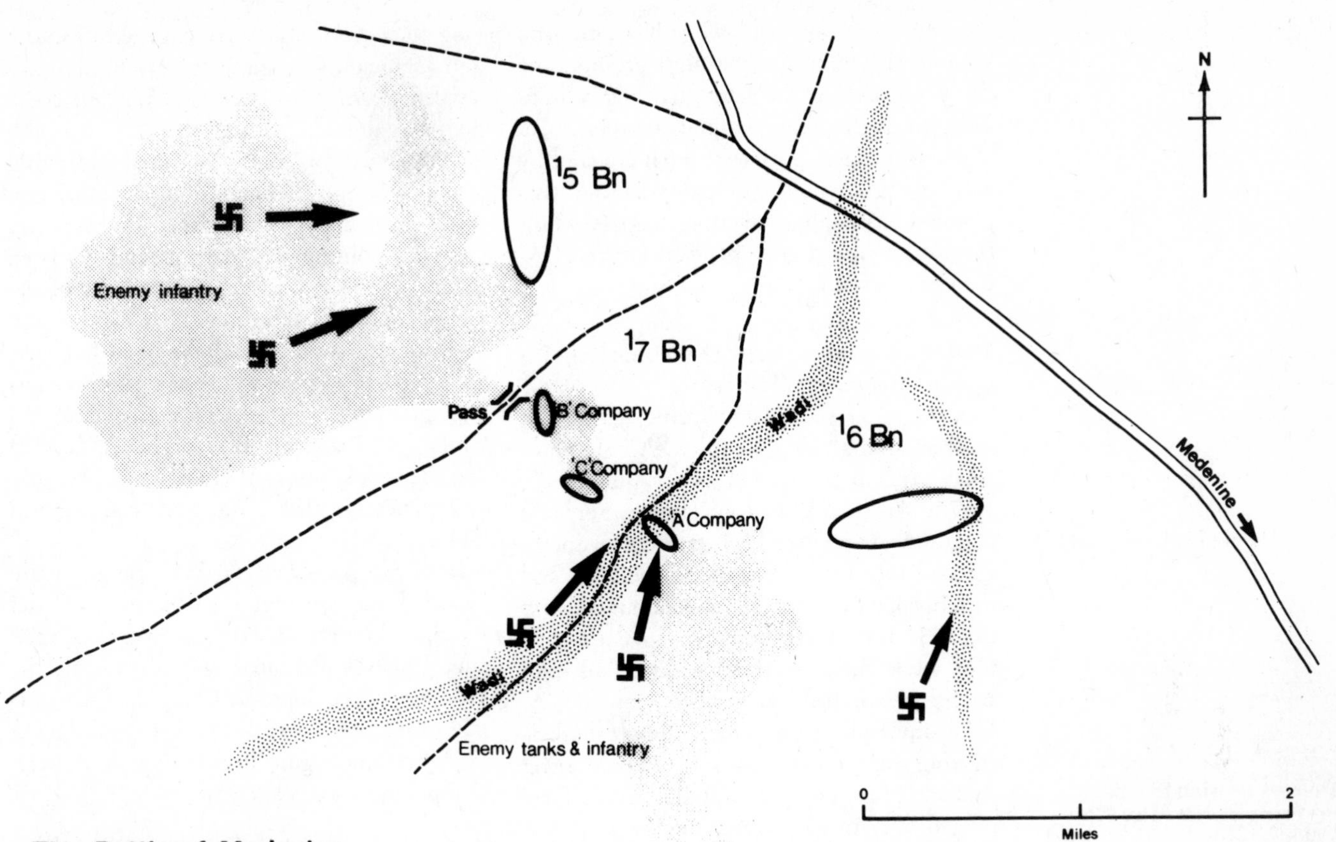

The Battle of Medenine
The first attack

Italians had not come back, and seeing a cherry-coloured beret that was new to Tripoli, he woke up the city like a town crier. Soon the Hussars were besieged. The inhabitants of the quarter came out in whatever clothes they could pull round them — pyjamas, shirts, trousers and sheets. The British were in. After years of Italian oppression they were glad to see them.

While the crews had breakfast the crowd grew and grew. You ate food with your elbows pinned to your sides. Seated in a chair, the Major of the leading squadron was surrounded like a monarch.

It was past the time when you could move in comfort. The throng was so large you could only hope to breathe.

In another part of the town another squadron was receiving a terrific reception from the natives. The sergeant-major had been kissed on both cheeks, to the terrific delight of his men, and had his hair cut by an Arab barber.

The natives had bowed, shaken hands, kissed the tip of their fingers to our men. Now British troops were crowding in from all sides. The tanks had lined up in file under the old fort. Along the promenade men were curling up in their blankets, worn out and too tired after two nights march to care whether it was Tripoli or the desert.

The unsolicited comment of the Eleventh Hussars was "We're glad we did it. But it's just another job." *

Shortly after the capture of the city the Prime Minister visited the victorious troops and took the salute at the Tripoli Victory Parade.

On 5th March 1943 Rommel, who was by then a very sick man, spoke to his troops in the mountains overlooking Medenine and told them that unless they could drive back the Eighth Army their days in Africa would be numbered. The following morning savage armoured and infantry attacks were launched by the Germans in a desperate attempt to save the Mareth Line and halt Allied progress. The 7th Armoured Division were in the Medenine area, and the main enemy pressure fell on the Queen's Brigade, with 1st/7th Queen's coming under particularly heavy tank attacks. 1st/7th was holding its sector (see diagram) with 'B' Company on the right, covering a pass through which a small

* Extract from the *Egyptian Mail* dated 29 June 42, which appeared in a wartime edition of the 11th Hussars Journal and is reproduced here by kind permission of Home HQ, The Royal Hussars.

road ran from the south west; 'C' Company were in the centre on the high ground, and 'A' Company on the left, guarding a wide wadi through which wound another road. The two danger spots were well covered by anti-tank guns, 'B' Company having two platoons of RA guns covering the pass, whilst the battalion anti-tank platoon covered 'A' Company's wadi.

Here is how the battle is recorded in the Queen's Regimental History:

"Enemy tanks and infantry came against this front as soon as the mist lifted. A column of tanks came into view of No 5 gun of the 1st/7th Anti-Tank Platoon under Sergeant Andrews. As he had been trained to do, he allowed four to proceed along the track and then opened fire on and knocked out the next two. He then successfully engaged the first four while the rest, about a dozen all told, swung into hull down positions on the 'A' Company front, from which, almost defiladed from the anti-tank guns, they could bring damaging fire across the battalion front. They offered very small targets, but Sergeant Andrews managed to engage them. The parapet of his gun position was smashed and he ordered the rest of the crew to take cover while he continued loading and firing the gun alone. Two more tanks were knocked out and the enemy prevented from entering the vital wadi. The remaining tanks had managed to work into a smaller wadi running to the east and were engaged by No 7 gun (Sergeant Crangles) and No 8 (Sergeant Vincent). One tank was disabled, but No 8 gun was put out of action. No 7 was also heavily fired on both by small arms and armour-piercing ammunition and the gun shield riddled in twenty places. But Sergeant Crangles continued to fire it, and his Bren gunner by his fire to deny the enemy observation, until at last a direct hit put No 7 gun also out of action. The crew fixed bayonets and prepared to resist to the last, but three undamaged tanks first overran the covering infantry (10 Platoon, 'B' Company, 1st/6th) and then took Sergeant Crangles and his party prisoners. In all No 7 gun claimed fourteen tanks." *

Both Sgt Andrews and Sgt Crangles were awarded the Distinguished Conduct Medal for their bravery. Later Sgt Andrews' anti-tank gun was presented with a plate, by the UK Inspection Board of Canada, in recognition of it having destroyed more enemy tanks tan any other gun in the North African Campaign.

Tunis was reached by the leading elements of the Division on 7th May 1943. Here is how George Stimpson of 5 RTR remembers that day:

"That morning the 5th were on the high ground overlooking Tunis and 1 RTR were

*The History of the Queen's Royal Regiment pages 193-194.

Below: British troops entering Tunis May 7th, 1943.

Top right: Enthusiastic crowds greet victorious British troops as they drive into Tunis.

Bottom right: Trust a Desert Rat to find two pretty girls to celebrate with!

more or less level with us, but on slightly lower ground. After a while — I think we had had breakfast — the order was given to charge down the valley and take the city, a mass of white buildings in the green valley below. About 100 tanks in line abreast charged flat out down the open slope, until the close country forced them to take to the roads. 5 RTR were first to do this and got to a junction just before the 1st, who then had to wait until the 5th had passed. As 'B' Squadron, who were leading, got near to the outskirts of the town, armoured cars of the 11th Hussars tried to overtake them,but 'C' Squadron, who were behind 'B', deliberately blocked the way until we were well past the sign which said "Tunis".

I believe that the 11th Hussars and the Derbyshire Yeomanry agreed to call it a dead heat as to who entered Tunis first — but they didn't ask anyone else! They may have been the first into the centre of the town, but 5 RTR were first past the post and therefore first into Tunis. In fact I was standing by the sign, with one foot in Tunis, when the Cherry Pickers went in!"

So ended the campaign which had started six months before at El Alamein. The 7th Armoured Division had been continuously in action for almost the entire period. Two thousand miles were covered in those 180 days of chasing the Afrika Korps through such places as Mersa Matruh, Tobruk, Benghazi, Msus, Buerat, Wadi Akarit, Sfax and Enfidavile. Many battles had been fought and won and the Division could now prepare for their next major task of carrying the war on to the continent of Europe.

General Montgomery's message to the Eighth Army, published on 14th May 1943, read:
1. Now that the campaign in Africa is finished I want to tell you all, my soldiers, how intensely proud I am of what you have done.
2. Before we began the Battle of Egypt, last October, I said that together, you and I, we would hit Rommel and his Army "for six" right out of North Africa.

And it has now been done. All those well-known enemy Divisions that we have fought, and driven before us over hundred of miles of African soil. from Alamein to Tunis, have now surrendered.

There was no Dunkirk on the beaches of Tunisia; the Royal Navy and the RAF saw to it that the enemy should not get away, and so they were all forced to surrender.

The campaign has ended in a major disaster for the enemy.
3. Your contribution to the complete and final removal of the enemy from Africa has been beyond all praise.

As our Prime Minister said at Tripoli, in February last, it will be a great honour to be able to say in years to come:

I MARCHED AND FOUGHT WITH THE EIGHTH ARMY

4. And what of the future? Many of us are probably thinking of our families in the home country, and wondering when we shall be able to see them.

But I would say to you that we can have today only one thought, and that is to see this thing through to the end; and then we will be able to return to our families, honourable men.
5. Therefore, let us think of the future in this way.

And whatever it may bring to us, I wish each one of you the very best of luck, and good hunting in the battles that are yet to come and which we will fight together.
6. TOGETHER, YOU AND I, WE WILL SEE THIS THING THROUGH TO THE END.

BL MONTGOMERY
General, EIGHTH ARMY

TUNISIA
14th May 1943

Below: His Majesty King George VI visits the Division after the capture of Tunis. Also in the car are General Montgomery and General Erskine (GOC 7th Armoured Division).

Bottom: Spoils of War—ACV7 flying a captured Nazi flag.

Floreat Jerboa

The Division's Desert Rat emblem has undoubtedly made the Jerboa one of the most widely recognisable of animals, and its history deserves to be told. The emblem came into being early in 1940, soon after General O'More Creagh took command. Until then the Divisional emblem had consisted of a plain white circle on a scarlet ground, but the General decided that the circle should carry some symbol truly representative of the Division's desert background. He chose the Jerboa — or to be more accurate, the Greater Egyptian Jerboa (*Jaculus Orientalis*) — those hardy, highly mobile little denizens of "The Blue".

Having chosen an emblem, the next stage was to find a live Desert Rat to copy. After much searching, Mrs Creagh and Mrs Peyton (wife of General Creagh's GSO3) eventually located one in the Cairo Zoo, and the first "Desert Rat Rampant" was drawn on a sheet of hotel notepaper! This was transferred, in flaming scarlet, to the white circle of the Divisional Commander's flag and thence onto every vehicle and eventually evey topee flash.

At the end of 1941, 7th Armoured Brigade left the Division and went to Burma, but they were not to be parted from their beloved Jerboa. They simply changed its colour to green — presumably to blend with the jungle!

It was not until the Division was resting in the Homs-Tripoli area in the summer of 1943 that a shoulder patch was produced — this time with the original scarlet Jerboa on a

khaki square. When the Division left Italy at the end of 1943 General Erskine, then GOC, gave orders that shoulder patches for the whole Division should be ready for issue when the troops arrived back in the UK. Unfortunately, the clothing firm chosen by the War Office had their own ideas of what a Jerboa should look like, and the resulting animal was more akin to a kangaroo than a Desert Rat! To add insult to injury, the colour was changed to red-brown and the background to black. When General Erskine got back, all the patches had been produced and the War Office, in its infinite wisdom, refused to sanction a new and different issue, so the altered flashes had to be accepted.

Before this major change took place other Jerboas had in fact come into existence; for example, when 4th Armoured Brigade left the Division permanently after the capture of Tunis, they also did not part with their emblem, but instead changed its colour, to black this time, and put its tail up over its head. Not to be outdone, the Queen's Brigade for a long time carried a black Jerboa in a red oval background on their vehicles.

The red-brown Jerboa on its black background remained as the emblem for the rest of the Division's lifetime until final disbandment in 1958. However, even then the Jerboa refused to be demobilised and was once again proudly worn by the 7th Armoured Brigade.

Perhaps the last word on the subject should go to Major General G. L. Verney (GOC in 1944): "Whatever his shape, his colour or his attitude, the Jerboa remains the farthest-travelled animal with the longest fighting record. Long may he be honoured.
FLOREAT JERBOA" *

* *The History of the Desert Rats*

The Crouching Jerboa of DD (Jerboa) Battery, 4th Regiment, Royal Horse Artillery.

The Price

A litter of knocked out Shermans and Grants, giving a graphic impression of the ferocity of the tank battles.

AULD

The carnage of modern war left its mark upon the face of the desert. Twisted lumps of metal, which had once been death-dealing mechanical monsters, littered every battlefield. The material waste was enormous, but far more tragic was the waste of human life. By far the saddest reminders of those grim times are the graveyards — at Tobruk, El Alamein, Sollum and in many other places. The lucky ones, perhaps, were those who were captured; at least they would have a chance of living through their captivity, with the ever-present hope of escape to bolster their morale.

I leave the description of the horrors of desert war to two poems; the first was written by an acknowledged poet, Keith Douglas, who was later killed in Normandy.

Desert Flowers
Perched on a great fall of air
a pilot or angel looking down
on some eccentric chart, the plain
dotted with the useless furniture
discerns dying on the sand vehicles;
squashed dead or still entire, stunned
like beetles: scattered wingcases and
legs, heads, appear when the dust settles.
But you who like Thomas come
to poke fingers in the wounds
find monuments and metal posies.
On each disordered tomb
the steel is torn into fronds
by the lunatic explosive.

On sand and scrub the dead men wriggle
in their dowdy clothes. They are mimes
who express silence and futile aims
enacting this prone and motionless struggle
at a queer angle to the scenery,
crawling on the boards of the stage like walls,
deaf to the one who opens his mouth and calls
silently. The decor is a horrible tracery of iron. The
eye and mouth of each figure
bear the cosmetic blood and the hectic colours death
had the only list of.
A yard more, and my little finger
could trace the maquillage of these stony actors:
I am the figure writhing on the backcloth.

Living in a wide landscape are the flowers —
Rosenberg, I only repeat what you were saying —
the shell and the hawk every hour
are slaying men and jerboas, slaying
the mind. But the body can fill
the hungry flowers and the dogs who cry words
at nights, the most hostile things of all.
But that is not new. Each time the night discards
draperies on the eyes and leaves the mind awake
I look each side of the door of sleep
for the little coin it will take
to buy the secret I shall not keep

Here is a simple poem by ex Desert Rat Harry Perkins, who says he has not written a line of poetry before or since:

The Price of War
Day is fading o'er this wasted land,
The fiery ball of sun has fled,
The moon is throwing shadows on the powdered sand,
Shadows of the crosses, on little mounds they lie
Gallant men beneath.
A price to pay, they had to die —
Sollum, Tobruk, Benghazi, Allied gains today
But men that moved in life are stilled
Yes, we had a price to pay.

* *Reprinted by kind permission of Faber & Faber Ltd, from Collected Poems.*

Below: This French Lorraine armoured cargo carrier was transformed by the Germans into a formidable piece of self-propelled artillery by the addition of a 155mm gun.

Right: This M13 was probably one of the first Italian tanks to be knocked out by 7th Armoured Division in December 1940. Manufactured in Turin, the M13 had a top speed of 25 mph, a range of 125 miles and mounted a 47mm gun.

Far right: This German Pz KW Mk IV D2 was knocked out at Sidi Rezegh. It mounted a 75mm gun which was very effective against infantry in trenches or in the open and against anti tank gun positions. (Note the Afrika Korps insignia).

Below right: A Pz KW Mk III special, mounting a long barreled 50mm gun. The Mk III was an excellent tank and Rommel had about 70 of these "specials" at El Alamein.

Above left: Mobile, as accurate as a sniper's rifle, the 88 was probably the most effective anti tank gun of the war. It had been, of course, originally designed as an anti aircraft gun, but was used almost exclusively by Rommel in a tank killing role.

Above: The Sd Kfz 231 was a heavy German armoured car, mounting a 20mm cannon. The drive and steering were to all wheels and it had a top speed of over 50mph.

Far left: Renegade. This British Matilda had been captured and used by the Germans. It was eventually knocked out near Bardia and the shot holes can be plainly seen.

Left: An Italian 90mm anti aircraft gun captured at Sidi Omar. This fine gun was also mounted on the back of a Lancia truck and used in the anti tank role.

Below: The Volkswagen, or "People's Car", was as well known in the desert in its military form (known as Kdf 82) as its civilian equivalent is known all over the world today. The captured Volkswagen in the photograph was known affectionately as "Dogsbody" — an appropriate name for this ubiquitous little vehicle.

Top: An ME 109F captured at Fuka airfield.

Above: Fragments of aircraft of all three nations are seen here, symbolic of the carnage which took place in the sky as well as on the ground.

Above right: Very few British troops could be spared to guard the hordes of Italian prisoners taken during Wavell's initial offensive. This column, seen outside Tobruk, was typical of the enormous numbers which had to be looked after.

Below: Italian troops surrendering near Mersa Brega. For them the fighting is over.

Right: A group of German POW waiting to be moved back to the rear.

Far right: German and Italian troops pictured here driving in to surrender near Enfidaville.

UNKNOWN SOLDIER
1939
Generalmajor
Major
1939
Generalmajor

Far left: Tobruk Cemetery, one of many to be found in the battle area.

Centre left: The propeller of his crashed aircraft was used as a headstone for this pilot's grave.

Above left: German soldier's grave, location not known.

Left: British soldier's grave in Tobruk Cemetery — Lt Col Robbie Uniacke, CO 5 RTR, was killed on June 2, 1942 during the Gazala/Knightsbridge battles.

Below left: The grave of General Major Neuman-Silkow, GOC 15th Panzer Division, killed in action December 9th, 1941.

Below: The grave of Major General Jock Campbell, VC, DSO, MC, in the Protestant Cemetery, Cairo, taken shortly after his funeral March 24th, 1942.

Setting the Scene for Europe

In order to give the reader some idea of what it was like to be a member of the Division in action in Italy and North West Europe, I hope to highlight a few of the momentous events which took place in those countries. I hope those who fought so gallantly in other Divisions will excuse the favouritism I am showing towards the Desert Rats, but I am in good company for did not the late Sir Winston Churchill call them his 'Dear Desert Rats' and go on to say that he hoped that 'the fathers would long tell the children of this tale'. So I am after all only doing as he asked.

I have started in Homs, where the Division rested and re-fitted after the Allies' great victory in Tunisia. Then, leaving their natural habitat in September 1943, the Desert Rats sailed across the Mediterranean to Italy as part of the American Fifth Army under General Mark Clark, landing at Salerno in early September 1943 just as Italy signed the armistice. After a brief, but exceptionally hard-fought campaign, they re-embarked at Naples, reaching the United Kingdom early in January 1944. There followed a period of hectic preparations for D-Day during which time the Division had to master a completely new tank, the Cromwell. As you will read there were some misgivings over this tank which many considered to be inferior to the Sherman they knew so well. In addition, the Division lost a large number of experienced officers and soldiers, sent to bolster up other Divisions who lacked the Desert Rats' battle experience. This must have caused General Bobbie Erskine many sleepless nights, especially as once again his Division

Right: Christmas Broadcast, December 25th, 1944 – The Journey Back. Corporal Bob Pass of 1/5th Queens, one time Brixton window-cleaner, assisted by Frank Gillard, gets ready to deliver the Christmas Day message which was heard by the folks back home just before the King's address. It was entitled 'The Journey Back' and told the story of every soldier's hopes for the future. Afterwards Bob, who had served at Dunkirk, in Crete, Libya, Sicily and Italy, went on fighting with the Division deep into Germany. Surrender was near and the end of the war had become something one could think about in easy terms like days or weeks. Then on Sunday April 22nd, 1945, Corporal Bob Pass and a patrol flushed a group of Germans out of a wood. One raised a white flag and Bob went forward to meet him. As he did so the other Germans fired at him and he was mortally wounded. For Corporal Bob Pass there was alas no 'Journey Back'.

was to be in the spearhead of the assault, as the first armour ashore at Arromanches.

After the almost limitless space of the Desert, the Division had to learn many new skills and in particular had to become accustomed to fighting within the constraints of close country and built-up areas. Some of these skills could only be learnt the hard way, as is evidenced by the bitter and bloody fighting in the bocage of Normandy. From then onwards the Division was virtually never out of action, in the forefront of the advance across Europe, which for them included such high spots on the way as the relief of Ghent and the surrender of Hamburg. It was fitting, therefore, that as 'first in and last out of the battle' they should be chosen to go to Berlin and there to take part in the great Victory Parade held in July 1945. The story of the Desert Rat does not end there I'm glad to say, otherwise I might never have had the privilege of wearing one on my arm! And so I have tried to bring the story up to date, by including some brief reference to the post war years and to the Seventh Armoured Bridage, the natural successors of this great Division.

I must again thank Michael Haine for his excellent maps and diagrams, Mrs. Nancy Rogers for her ever-smiling countenance and ever-efficient typing; Jon for once again allowing me to include his 'Two Types' and Giles for his own inimitable rendering of 'Dear Desert Rats'. To them and to all the other kind people who have given me so much help and encouragement during the months of preparation I offer my sincere thanks.

May the spirit of this great Division live for ever.

Floreat Jerboa!

George Forty
January 1976
Lulworth Camp, Dorset

Left: Longest Serving Member of HQ Seventh Armoured Division. The photograph, taken in January 1957, shows the late Captain 'Richie' Richardson, BEM, RTR, shaking hands with the then GOC, Major General J W Hackett (now General Sir John Hackett, GCB, CBE, DSO, MC). 'Richie' Richardson had a record any Desert Rat could be proud of, having served with Headquarters Seventh Armoured Division continuously since its formation in August 1939. A sergeant at the outbreak of war, he was promoted WO2 and then WO1 with the Headquarters and was recommended for an immediate commission in August 1943. However, he chose to remain in his job with the Divisional HQ and consequently was not commissioned until September 1945. Captain Richardson served with no fewer than sixteen different GOCs, a record which to my knowledge is quite unique.

Homs~The Division Relaxes

Probably the most well-remembered concert party to perform in the Leptis Magna amphitheatre included Vivien Leigh, Bea Lillie and Leslie Henson, seen here on the stage in August 1943.

Leptis Magna – A concert party in progress in the Roman amphitheatre of Leptis Magna, close to Homs.

The North Pole?

'I suppose we could have been put in a worse place than Homs, those I can think of offhand – the North Pole, Devil's Island or the middle of the Amazon jungles. It was a place with a population of perhaps two hundred, one main street with some lemonade shops and a few quite nice villas down by the sea. We were camped about five miles to the east on the shore. On the north side of the road there was a cultivated patch of palm trees, water melons, limes and beans of different sorts, with some huts scattered about. There was a track leading through this patch and from the edge of it to the sea about three hundred yards away – that is the place we lay all summer. Between the camp and the village lay the ruins of Leptis Magna'. (*Wardrop of the Fifth, Ed Major J. Garnett, MC*).

Jake Wardrop was perhaps being a little hard on the choice of Homs as the place where the Division would spend the three months before going to Italy. It certainly was better than Bou Arada, the Division's first stop after the capture of Tunis which was a wilderness with no sign of life apart from the odd cactus. Homs was at least close to the sea, with all the unit camps within walking distance of the beach which made up for a lot. Almost everyone swam daily and by the time the Division left, there was hardly a non-swimmer to be found. Even Jake cheered up a bit and the next entry in his diary recalls: 'It was about the end of May and we were sitting at Homs. We still had our tanks, but had moved into Troop areas with tents, or if somebody had no tent he built a little shelter out of groundsheets and that kept the dew off at nights. I was in Headquarters Troop and we had four crews, less the officers, who all slept in an area together. Behind us was 11 Troop, Henry and Cliff; behind them was 9 with Snowy and Digger, and on the left were 10 with Joe and Ted and 12 with Jumbo and Bertie. In the middle was the cook-house and near it the Quartermaster's lorry. We ate together here as a squadron, sitting on the sand like wogs in the sun. Up on the edge of the cultivation, the fitters had built a hut of boards, galvanised iron and sheets. It was a great little shack, just like a beachcomber's hut on one of the islands. We did nothing for weeks but sit in the sun, swim, read and eat. At night we'd sit around listening to the wireless or go to Leptis to see a concert. There was some beer, most times two bottles per man, but there were always

A general view of Homs, taken from the roof of the Jerboa Club.

some who didn't want it and Stan, George and I did miles running round to see who didn't. The Sergeants had a bottle of whisky occasionally and I bought Ted's as he didn't drink it and it came in handy. The first excuse for a party was the return of Dixie from South Africa, he had gone away sometime before. By good luck he arrived on a beer day and we had a nice little session that night. One day somebody had a brainwave, to build a Mess Room, so that we could sit down to eat. We got a few lorries and scoured the countryside for weeks and it was surprising how much there was. There was enough to build a cookhouse, dining room and a little Officers' Mess, so now we had our meals from a table sitting on a form, all our own work. One day we built a raft, it wasn't a huge success, but we had a lot of fun making it.'

The Jerboa Club

One amenity which was established at Homs, thanks mainly to the hard work and perseverance of the Division's Senior Chaplain, Kenneth Meiklejohn, was the Jerboa Club. It had opened very briefly in Tunis in what had been the German Legation, but on May 17th the furniture was loaded onto lorries and driven to Homs, as Kenneth Meiklejohn recalls:

'The furniture and other belongings of the club were loaded on to two or three 3-tonners, and left Tunis at 1300 hours on Monday, May 17th, 1943. We stopped at El Djem the next morning to look at the Roman amphitheatre, and my driver and I found later that we were infested with fleas as some of the tunnels had been used by the Bedouin. We reached Tripoli on the 20th where Peter Ashton told me what he had arranged at Homs, which we reached on the 21st and took over the Leptis Magna Hotel, the only sizeable building in the village. It was quite empty except for some headed writing paper and the hotel rubber stamp, but we had enough chairs etc to furnish the large main hall. We did in fact, open that evening. All we could offer were cups of tea, such magazines and papers as we could get, and a few things, cigarettes etc., either from the NAAFI or from a YMCA or Church of Scotland van which called on its way to Tripoli. "We" were three or four men and myself. We alone slept in the hotel, where I turned one room into an office and another into a chapel. The Club was open to all ranks – to the surprise of some officers from other Divisions who assumed it would be an "Officers Only" club. Every Sunday we had an evening Service in the hall, which was quite well supported. We also had a weekly Bible study group, Confirmation classes, meetings for such ordinands as could be traced, and two Toc H meetings (no lamp!)'.

The walls of the club were soon adorned with frescoes of tanks and armoured cars and, more important, of English countryside scenes and Arab dancing girls. There was also a cinema set up nearby and a 'Music for All' club was well supported.

Leptis Magna

The spectacular ruined amphitheatre of the old Roman town of Leptis Magna made a marvellous open-air theatre and was used for concert parties, church Services and other gatherings. The Army produced a leaflet on Leptis Magna which ended with these words: 'A great deal of work and money has gone to unearthing these remains for you to see. Please treat them carefully, watch where you tread in your army boots and if you must write your name, keep it for somewhere else!'

The Homs St Leger

One of the highspots of the rest period was a race meeting organised by 8th Armoured Brigade. The local sheikhs, who had been invited to take part, were delighted with the handsome presentation plaques made for the occasion by 8th Armoured Brigade Workshops. A tote, side-shows and a Sudanese band completed the 'all the fun of the fair'

atmosphere and the meeting was a resounding success.

Leave Parties

Leave parties were organised to Tripoli and Tunis as Jake Wardrop recalls:

'In the middle of June we started to run eight-day trips to Tunis, this was inclusive of time for the journey, so whenever a party went, they hammered the whole way only stopping for petrol, punctures and food. As soon as one driver got tired, another would take over, they'd go all night and there was a record for the trip which everybody tried to break. The distance was about seven hundred miles and the record, never broken, was twenty five hours, which wasn't bad for a three-ton Ford with fifteen in the back and maybe a blow-out thrown in.'

Main Problems Facing the Division

But it was not all recreation as three main problems faced the Desert Rats. First was the fact that the Division had to be completely re-equipped during the three months out of action. Second, individual training and in particular weapon training, had been neglected during the last few months of strenuous operations and had to be brushed up. Finally, the Division had to be trained for a completely different type of warfare in close country and also had to practise for their coming seaborne landing. Jake Wardrop recalls:

'About the beginning of August we started to equip again, the campaign in Sicily was drawing to an end and we all had a pretty good idea where we would be going next. The Highland Division had taken part, also 30th Division and the 4th Armoured Brigade. The tanks with big mileages were taken away and we got new ones, tracks were renewed and things started to move. I got a Sherman and the crew were Stan – driver, Carlo – machine gunner, Jimmy – 75mm, and old Pathan Woody – operator. We did some shooting and "Sure-Shot" Jimmy blew the targets to pieces at any range. All the old hands were there again. The ones who had sworn that they were finished after Tunis, the bugle blew and they were off to war. Henry and Cliff, Snowy, Digger, Dixie, Ted, Joe, "Slap Happy" Joe, who went to Headquarters Squadron, and we had some pretty good officers. The Major, Captain Burt, Captain Boon and the commanders of 9, 10, 11 and 12, were Messrs. Heywood, Eckersley, Osborne and Daniels. My old commander from Mareth was back and he was second in command of the Battalion.

Two chaps came from the REME one day and gave a demonstration of how a Sherman could be waterproofed to drive in six feet of water. They fitted a cowling over the air intake, extended the exhausts to stick up in the air, plugged everything up with putty and pitch and sealed down the driver's and machine gunner's flaps. It was then possible to drive in right up to the turret which they did one Sunday morning. We all turned out to cheer or laugh, depending on whether it was a success or not, and just in case, a tow rope was shackled to the tank on the beach. It was a huge success, the tank reversed right in until the water almost went into the turret, then came out forward. They did it once more for good luck and the experiment was over. Within a week all the tanks in the Battalion had been treated for taking to the

Top left: Good Bathing. The best feature of Homs was the bathing and most of the Division swam every day.

Centre left: The Jerboa Club. The Divisional sign which hung over the club entrance. The club, like all those established by the Division, was open to all ranks.

Bottom left: The ruins of Leptis Magna. Tripolitania, the Land of Three Cities, takes its name from the cities of Oea (the modern Tripoli) Leptis Magna and Sabratha. They were founded as trading stations by the Phoenicians some time before 500 BC. The Roman city belongs to two periods, the earlier dating back to the first century BC – hence the notice!

Below: Cover of the race card for the Homs St Leger Meeting, 29th August 1943.

8th Armoured Brigade Group Race Club

HOMS ST LEGER MEETING

August 29th, 1943.

Patron

Maj. Gen. G.W.E.J. Erskine, D.S.O.

Stewards

Brig. C.B.C. Harvey, D.S.O. — Lt.-Col. D.A.H. Silvertop, M.C.
Brig. W.R.N. Hinde, D.S.O. — Lt.-Col. I.F.M. Spence.
Lt.-Col. J.A. Eadie, D.S.O. — Lt.-Col. H.W. Lloyd.
Lt.-Col. D. Darling, D.S.O., M.C.

Judge

Col. R.C.G. Joy, D.S.O.

Starter

Capt. W. Enderby

Clerks of the Course

Major Lord Glenarther
Capt. V. McCalmont

Secretary

Capt. L.H. Crossley

Medical Officer

Lt.-Col. T.M. Robb, R.A.M.C.

Tote Supervisors

Capt. J.F. White
Lieut. J.C. Cowley

After each race, if there is no objection, a BLUE flag will be hoisted and the Tote will pay out on the horse whose number is shown as the winner on the Result board.

If there is an objection a RED flag will be hoisted. If the objection is sustained a GREEN flag will be hoisted. If the objection is over-ruled a BLUE flag will be hoisted.

Left: Coming up the straight in the Homs St Leger. It was a five furlongs race for Arab ponies owned and ridden by local sheikhs.

Below: Homs St Leger – the Tote.

water except for some finishing touches which were to be done in the Tripoli area. We started to buy rations for the campaign, sausages, tins of steak and kidney, and all sorts of stuff like that. Below the turret the tool box was crammed full of tins, we hoped that at least we would get a chance to eat some. On August 27th the tanks were packed, the work was finished, we were ready to go. It was great, the lads were frisking around like dogs with two tails, our spirits had soared sky-high again. That day the canteen came again and by the old ruse Stan, George and I got five each of beer, which was better than nothing. We had a little party for a farewell to Homs, that delightful seaside resort.'

Visit of HM The King

Another of the highlights of the Division's rest period was a visit by His Majesty the King. Most troops had the opportunity of seeing him and the Eleventh Hussars, whose Colonel in Chief he was, had an informal visit all to themselves. Not long before *The Times* had described them as 'those incomparable paladins'.

Sicily

The Division was not used in Sicily although General Erskine, with a tactical headquarters, containing operations, intelligence, supply and medical representatives, did participate. The idea was that if there was a need to weld together the independent armoured brigades

Practising for the Invasion. A Sherman being backed onto a landing craft from a rocky North African beach.

in Sicily, then HQ 7th Armoured Division would assume control. As things turned out, however, this proved unnecessary and after about a fortnight the 'Tac' HQ became definitely and officially superfluous and had to return to Tripoli. The period had not been entirely wasted, however, some valuable lessons had been learned and to quote from the Division's official history: 'Sicily at that time of the year was not without its compensations, which included the sweetest and juiciest oranges known to man, sixteen varieties of Marsala and a gaggle of artistes from the Italian version of ENSA, one of whom had been endowed by Nature with scarlet hair and green eyes'.

Invasion of Italy

The main operation for which the Division was now preparing was of course the invasion of Italy. There were two schemes – one a landing down at the toe of Italy, the other, a bolder scheme, to land at Salerno with the object of capturing Naples. The Division first of all prepared to take part in the former – Operation 'Baytown' – the Eighth Army's landing in SW Italy, but was later switched to Operation 'Avalanche' – the Fifth Army's landing on the Gulf of Salerno. This meant that for the first time the Desert Rats were to come under command of an American Army, that of General Mark Clark. Planners soon found that they were grappling with 'bumf' on a lavish scale (known as 'Poop' by the Americans) and one staff officer was heard to enquire whether 'Avalanche' referred to the actual operation or the paper preceeding it!

Re-organisation and re-equipment

As well as taking every opportunity to enjoy themselves in the Homs area the Division, as has been explained, had much to do reorganising and re-equipping units. Every vehicle that could possibly be repaired was repaired, every wireless set was stripped, serviced and checked. Indeed the Workshops and Light Aid Detachments worked just as hard as they had done during the long months of desert operations. Most spares and new equipment had to come by road from the Delta, over 1 500 miles away, because all shipping was required for the invasion of Sicily.

There were no great changes in the equipment of units except in the case of the Divisional Armoured Car Regiment, the Eleventh Hussars, where each squadron was given an extra troop of White half-tracks in addition to their five armoured car troops. This troop combined the tasks of infantry and engineers to assist the Daimlers and Dingoes in their unceasing task of gathering information whilst following up the enemy as he withdrew. In addition, a formidable change had taken place to the Jeep Troop which had been replaced by a Gun Troop of two 75mm guns mounted on White half-tracks. Squadron Headquarters operated in three Humber armoured cars and a Dingo and an anti-aircraft gun section had been added to the B1 Echelon.

Order of Battle

For the invasion of Italy the Division was now organised into two brigades, one armoured and one infantry. It was to remain roughly in the same organisation for the rest of the war. The complete order of battle was:

22nd Armoured Brigade

1st Royal Tank Regiment (Equipped with Sherman Tanks)

Below: His Majesty, Colonel in Chief of the 11th Hussars inspects the regiment on June 21st 1943. (Left to right: Lt Col Smail, HM The King, General Erskine and General Montgomery).

5th Royal Tank Regiment (Equipped with Sherman tanks)
4th County of London Yeomanry – The Sharpshooters (Equipped with Sherman tanks)
1st Rifle Brigade (Motor Battalion)
131st (Queens) Brigade
1st/5th Queens Royal Regiment (Lorried Infantry Battalion)
1st/6th Queens Royal Regiment (Lorried Infantry Battalion)
1st/7th Queens Royal Regiment (Lorried Infantry Battalion)
'C' Company 1st Cheshire Regiment (Medium Machine Guns)
Divisional Troops
11th Hussars – Divisional Armoured Car Regiment
Divisional Signals
Royal Artillery
3rd Royal Horse Artillery
5th Royal Horse Artillery
15th Light Anti Aircraft Regiment, RA
24th Field Regiment, RA
65th (Norfolk Yeomanry) Anti Tank Regiment, RA
69th Medium Regiment, RA
146th Field Regiment, RA
Royal Engineers
4th and 621st Field Squadrons, RE
143rd Field Park Squadron , RE
Royal Army Service Corps
No 5, 58, 67, 287, 432 and 507 Companies, RASC
Royal Army Medical Corps
2nd Light Field Ambulance
131st Field Ambulance
70th Field Hygiene Section
21st Mobile Casualty Clearing Section
3rd Field Surgical Unit
7th Field Transfusion Unit
132nd and 135th Mobile Dental Units
Royal Army Ordnance Corps
Divisional Ordnance Field Park
Royal Electrical and Mechanical Engineers
22nd Armoured Brigade Workshops
131st Brigade Workshops
15th Light AA Workshops

Below: Gen Erskine, GOC 7th Armd Division, greets His Majesty, King George VI on his arrival to inspect the Division in June 1943.

Salerno

Salerno – View through the windscreen of a Divisional RASC vehicle soon after landing.

EIGHTH ARMY

PERSONAL MESSAGE FROM THE ARMY COMMANDER

To be read out to all Troops

1. The time has now come to carry the war into Italy, and into the Continent of Europe. The Italian Overseas Empire has been exterminated; we will now deal with the home country.

2. To the Eighth Army has been given the great honour of representing the British Empire in the Allied Force which is now to carry out this task. On our left will be our American allies. Together we will set about the Italians in their own country in no uncertain way; they came into this war to suit themselves and they must now take the consequences; they asked for it, and they will now get it.

3. On behalf of us all I want to give a very hearty welcome to the Canadian troops that are now joining the Eighth Army. I know well the fighting men of Canada; they are magnificent soldiers, and the long and careful training they have received in England will now be put to very good use—to the great benefit of the Eighth Army.

4. The task in front of us is not easy. But it is not so difficult as many we have had in the past, and have overcome successfully. In all our operations we have always had the close and intimate support of the Royal Navy and the R.A.F., and because of that support we have always succeeded. In this operation the combined effort of the three fighting services is being applied in tremendous strength, and nothing will be able to stand against it. The three of us together—Navy, Army and Air Force—will see the thing through. I want all of you, my soldiers, to know that I have complete confidence in the successful outcome of this operation.

5. Therefore, with faith in God and with enthusiasm for our cause and for the day of battle, let us all enter into this contest with stout hearts and with determination to conquer.

The eyes of our families, and in fact of the whole Empire, will be on us once the battle starts; we will see that they get good news and plenty of it.

6. To each one of you, whatever may be your rank or employment, I would say:

GOOD LUCK AND GOOD HUNTING IN THE HOME COUNTRY OF ITALY

B. L. Montgomery.

General,
Eighth Army.

July, 1943.

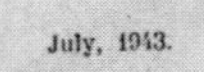

Salerno – Operation Avalanche

As I have explained, whilst Montgomery's Eighth Army was crossing the Straits of Messina to land on the toe of Italy, the men of the Seventh Armoured Division found themselves for the first time part of an American Army – the Fifth United States Army under General Mark Clark. The Fifth Army, which was to land higher up the Italian coast close to Naples in the Bay of Salerno, was composed of two Corps, one American (the 6th) and one British (the 10th). 10th Corps was commanded by General McCreery, who had recently taken over from General Horrocks when the latter was badly wounded in an air raid on Bizerta. He decided to use the two infantry divisions – the 46th and 56th (London) for the initial assault (see map), keeping 7th Armoured in reserve, ready to follow up and break out of the bridgehead once it was secured. Shortly before leaving North Africa General McCreery issued the following special order of the day:

SPECIAL ORDER

To be read to ALL Ranks of 10th Corps

We are now on our way to attack the Mainland of Italy. This decisive operation, in conjunction with the attack of Eighth Army in the toe of Italy, is the opening of the second front in Europe. Our landings will be a milestone in the downfall of Germany.

We form part of the American 5th Army. We shall be fighting and working alongside our American comrades, we must go all out to help each other. I have told General Clark how pleased all ranks of 10th Corps are to form part of an Allied force under his command.

We must expect hard fighting. Early success will depend largely on the speed of the initial landings and on the determination and dash shown by all ranks.

Throughout the world the British soldier has always been respected for his attitude to the civil population. We shall be in one of the most thickly populated districts of Europe. I rely on all ranks to make their conduct a model, and an example.

The 10th Corps forms the spearhead of the Army. I am very proud to be the Commander of such a splendid formation. Of the outcome I have no doubt. I wish you all good luck and God speed.

(Sgd) *R. L. McCreery*
Lt Gen
Commander 10th Corps

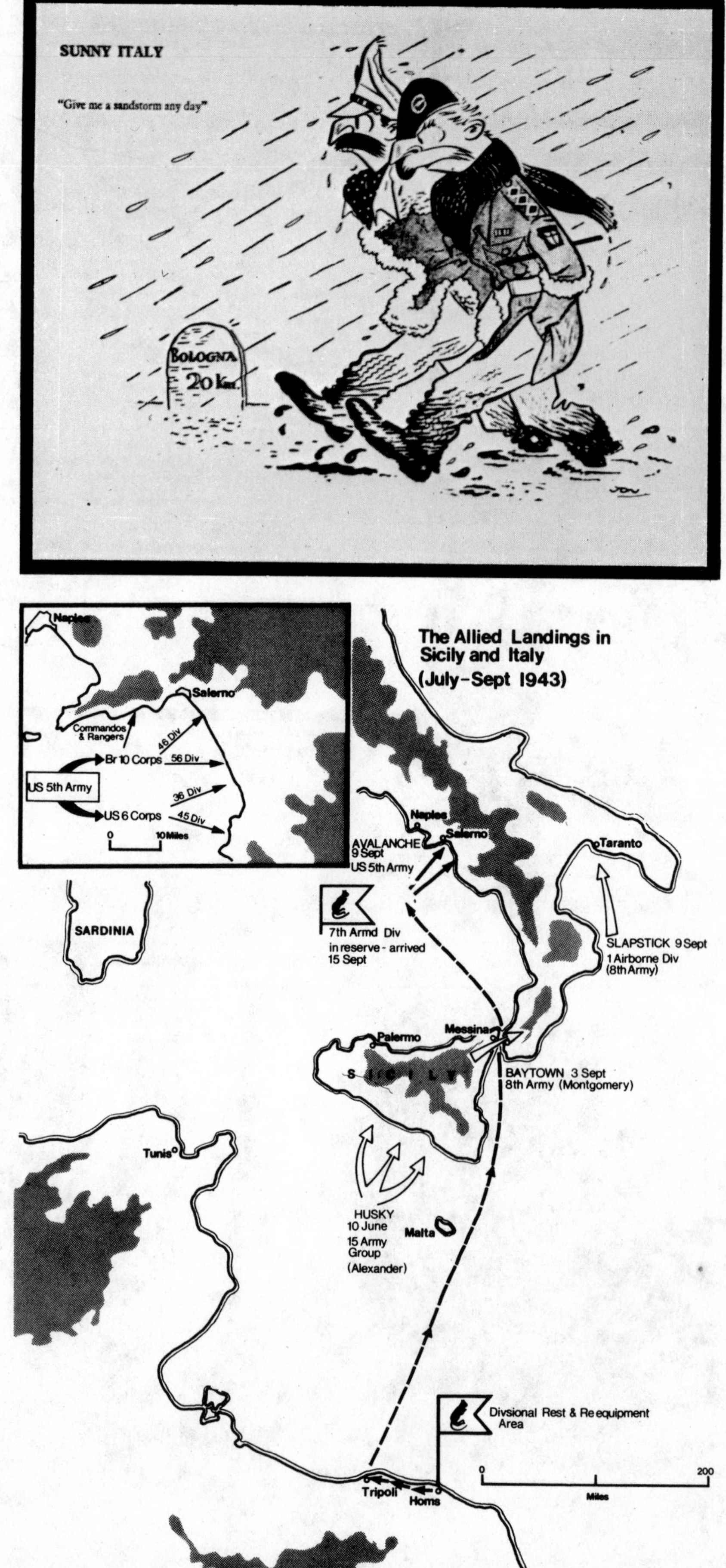

Far left, top: And so on to sunny Italy – but some Desert Rats preferred North Africa! (Reproduced by kind permission of Jon).

Left: Ready for Italy. Vehicles belonging to one of the brigade workshops lined up ready for loading at Tripoli docks.

Below: An Armoured Command Vehicle loading through the bow doors of a landing ship.

Left: Leaving North Africa. One of the landing ships passing wrecks in Tripoli harbour.

Right: Colonel (now Major General) Pat Hobart, the GSO1, briefs Divisional Headquarters personnel during the voyage to Italy.

Far right: The American captain of the landing ship which carried Divisional headquarters.

Below: Salerno, September 15th, 1943.

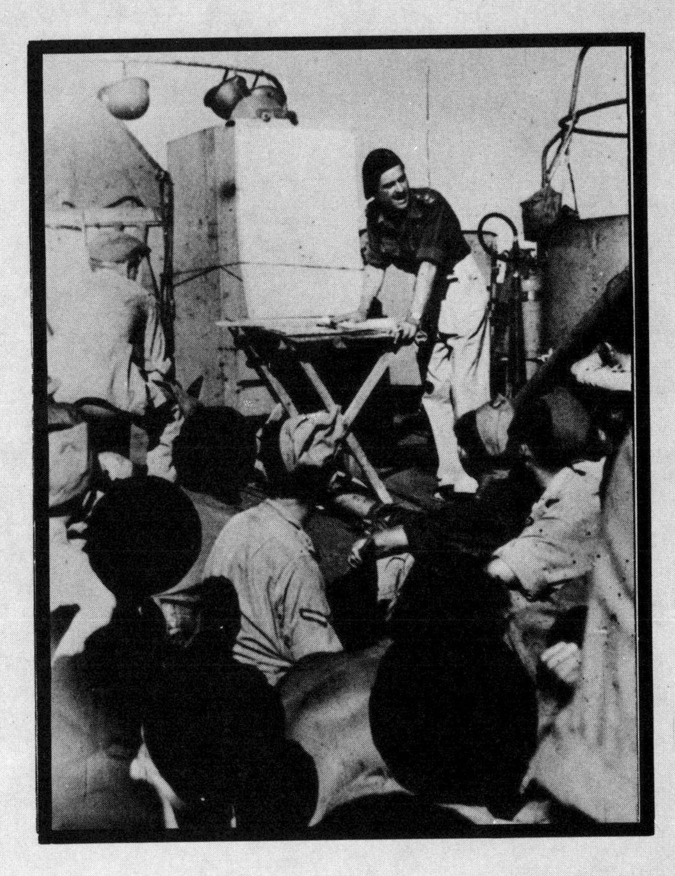

Salerno Beach. Generals Alexander, Mark Clark and McCreery survey the beachhead.

Final Preparation and Loading
Their final preparations made, the Division moved from Homs to Tripoli, where they boarded the landing ships which were to take them to Salerno.

First Desert Rats Ashore
Brigadier 'Bolo' Whistler, commanding 131 (Queens) Brigade, together with representatives of unit and brigade staffs, went ashore with the assault divisions, their task being to reconnoitre the proposed Divisional Concentration Area. They went in on September 9th, but surprisingly were not the first Desert Rats ashore as the following story from E. Mallas, a wartime member of 131st Field Ambulance explains:

'After the Division's great success in Tunisia, the 131st Field Ambulance were rested at Homs, east of Tripoli, near the ruins of Roman Leptis Magna. At the end of August 1943, ten volunteers were called for to take part in an "unknown" operation. I was one of those volunteers, who together with a "new to the unit" Medical Officer, set off along the coast road to Sfax, then on to Tunis and finally to Bizerta where we boarded an LCT (Landing Craft Tank) with our 15cwt Dodge truck and an ambulance, eventually reaching Sicily where we were attached to the 41st Royal Marine Commando. On the same evening as we arrived a hurried departure was made in the middle of our preparations for the first real meal (American rations) we had had for days! Embarkation was followed by a voyage to the Italian mainland in another LCT, during which we heard the announcement of the armistice with Italy at 1800hours, September 8th. Late that same night we landed on the beach below the village of Vietri, on the road north of Salerno. I have now no knowledge of the date when the main body of the Division landed on the Salerno beaches, but 1 officer, 1 sergeant, 2 lance corporals and 7 privates of the 7th Armoured Division were among the first troops to land at Vietri, and like Horatio, to hold the bridge. At the first opportunity a Divisional Sign was drawn, coloured and hung from the balcony of the building for all to see who passed that way that the 7th Armoured were there before them. Our little "jaunt" brought one MC and one MM to the eleven Desert Rats, and one MM to the RASC driver of the ambulance'.

The Main Body Arrives
The main body of the Division started to

A knocked out German StuG III assault gun near Salerno. This low compact, self propelled 75mm gun had a top speed of 25mph and a crew of 4.

arrive on the evening of the 15th. They were expecting a hot reception as the BBC communiques, heard at sea, had talked about the sky over the beach area being 'dark with planes locked in mortal combat'. However, things were not quite as bad as that, although the situation was far from easy, as both the 46th and 56th Divisions had had some very tough fighting and the bridgehead was small and thinly held. The harbour of Salerno could not be used, whilst the town itself, like most of the bridgehead area, was under continuous enemy shellfire. Enemy counter attacks were numerous, but fortunately not properly co-ordinated. General Erskine's own White half-track broke a spring on its way to the concentration area and had to spend the night in a ditch, only to be chased out at 0400 hours the following morning during a spirited counter attack by 67th Panzer Grenadier Regiment – it withdrew at full speed with the sagging chassis tearing strips of rubber off the tyres!

The Advance Begins

After some anxious days the assaulting troops gradually began to gain the upper hand, helped by the continual pressure which the Eighth Army managed to put on the enemy from the south – they covered over 300 miles in seventeen days against considerable opposition, a remarkable achievement. By the 27th the Division was almost complete and the time had come for them to break out of the bridgehead. The plan was for the 46th Division to clear the pass through the mountains north west of Salerno as far as Camarelle. There the American Rangers would form a bridgehead through which the Division would pass, with 23rd Armoured Brigade under command. 23rd Armoured Brigade consisted at that time of only the Royal Scots Greys in Shermans, the King's Dragoon Guards in armoured cars, 24th Field Regiment less one battery, and one field squadron of sappers. The first objective was to be Scafati on the River Sarno. From there 23rd Armoured Brigade would advance straight on to Naples along the coast road, whilst the rest of the Division went north of Vesuvius and made for Capua on the River Volturno. The Division was unable to concentrate forward due to the close nature of the country and had to form up in line ahead behind the 46th Division. Due to the possibility of air attack the density of vehicles per mile was reduced to forty and at that spacing the Division covered no less than fifty-five miles of road – the distance from London to Brighton!

Tanks of 22 Armd Brigade on the road to Naples. Whilst 23 Armd Brigade moved swiftly along the coastal route the rest of the Division swung east of Vesuvius in order to come upon Naples from the other flank.

The Desert Rats in Italy

Action at Cardito, October 3rd, 1943

Although the Desert Rats were only in Italy for about three months, the campaign in which they fought was never an easy one. Italy had surrendered even before they arrived, but the German Army was still full of fight and conducted a masterly delaying battle as it slowly withdrew northwards. Crack Hermann Goering units faced the Desert Rats, their rearguard parties usually consisting of one or two self-propelled guns, protected by dug-in machine gun and rifle positions. An armoured car some distance in front of the main position would give timely warning of approaching British forces, whilst roads were mined or blocked with felled trees, and booby traps abounded. Artillery guns or 'Moaning Minnies' (Nebelwerfers) in depth would bring down accurate fire on anyone who advanced without due caution. Typical of the small but bloody engagements fought by the Division was the

Far left, top: A Sherman tank of the 1st Royal Tank Regiment passing an Italian farmer with his ox-drawn farm cart on the road to Aversa.

Far left, centre: 1/6 Queens enter Scafati. The battalion under Lt Col M Forrester was leading the Division and made a lightning dash for the main bridge over the R Sarno. It had been prepared for demolition and was guarded by the 2nd Herman Goering Panzer Regiment. The 1/6 Queens managed to capture the bridge intact and beat off all counter attacks.

Far left, bottom: An 11th Hussars Armoured Car enters Pompeii. After Scafati the Division made slow progress against skilful and energetic German rear-guards. Roads were mined and blocked by felled trees then covered by self-propelled guns, machine guns and rifle positions. Towards the end of September opposition lessened and the main body of the Division pushed on, led as usual by 11th Hussars patrols.

Above left: HQ 7th Armoured Division in the main square of Pompeii, Div HQ was never far behind the leading troops throughout the advance.

Left: A self-propelled Priest in action near Torre Annunziata. The US M7 'Priest' was equipped with a 105mm howitzer which was mounted onto a Sherman hull. The Priest seen here was supporting 23rd Armd Brigade in their thrust along the coast to Naples.

battle of the 1st Battalion of the Rifle Brigade at Cardito, a small town surrounded by thick vineyards and woods. The enemy had a number of self propelled anti-tank guns in the vineyards, protected by machine gun posts on the outskirts of the town. After some of 1 RTR tanks had been destroyed by these guns, the motor company working with them, C Coy, 1 RB, put in a spirited attack, but this proved unsuccessful and so the whole of the battalion had to be used.

Here is an account of the action as told by Major General Sir Victor Paley KBE, CB, DSO, DL who was then commanding the battalion:

'At the beginning of October 1943 the Division was engaged in an outflanking movement which entailed passing east of Vesuvius to get round behind Naples. On October 2nd, 22nd Armoured Brigade passed through the lorried infantry brigade and spearheaded the advance on two roads. On the right, 1 RTR with its motor company (C Coy 1 RB) under command, had just about reached Afragola, but the next morning the tanks were held up south of Cardito by unlocated enemy anti-tank guns well concealed in vineyards and standing maize. An attempt by the motor company to dislodge the enemy proved abortive, as on their start line the two motor platoons came under heavy shell fire probably directed by a concealed OP close at hand, and lost one third of their strength in casualties.

The Brigade Commander, to whose tactical headquarters that of my own was attached, then told me to recover my other company and take on the task of clearing the town, as 1 RTR had lost tanks both to the left and to the right of Cardito and could not get on. Recovering this company ("I" Company) which was away behind with 5 RTR took some time, as the platoons had been dispersed on reconnaissance tasks. Brigade Tactical HQ was located in the northern end of Afragola some two hundred yards from the main road which rather avoided the centre of the village. Immediately in front was a wood, widish at our end but tapering to a point at Cardito. There was the occasional airburst shell probably unobserved, a bit short, far too high and quite harmless. It was quite obvious that there was no future in attacking across the open ground on either flank, and that the wood was the only sensible approach, even though no real

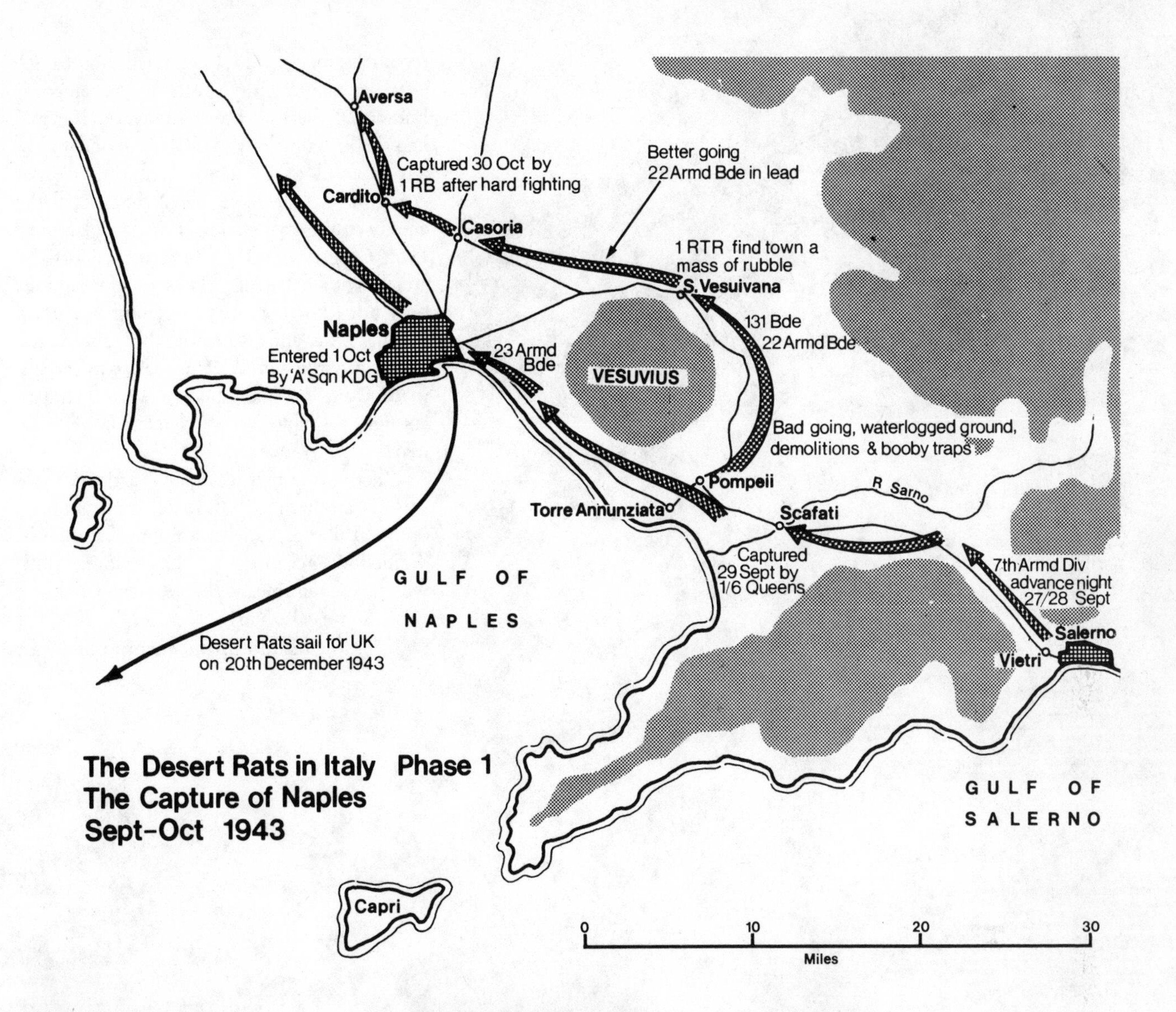

The Desert Rats in Italy Phase 1
The Capture of Naples
Sept–Oct 1943

Far left, top: Greys tanks carrying men of the 1/6 Queens into Torre Annunziata. A Sherman of the Royal Scots Greys loaded with men of 1/6 Queens, searching the streets of Torre Annunziata on the road to Naples.

Far left, centre: First KDG armoured car into Naples. At 0930 hours on October 1st, 1943, the leading armoured car of A Squadron of the King's Dragoon Guards triumphantly entered Naples.

Far left, bottom: 4 CLY in Casoria. The crew of a Sherman tank of the Sharpshooters carry out their morning toilet with an interested audience in the background!

Left: 5 RHA OP in Arzano. Captain Tacey of 5 RHA mans an observation post in a bell tower in Arzano, bringing down accurate fire on enemy positions.

reconnaissance could be carried out to see exactly what enemy posts it contained. I knew that the first 150 yards were clear as I had walked a little way into the wood and in any case all of us standing at the edge of Afragola would have been shot at if the enemy could have seen us. I made a plan with Peter Gregson (CO 5 RHA) to support the attack with a barrage. I forget the timings now but I know that the opening line got a double dose and was probably about 200 yards into the wood. The plan was largely made from the map and we were fortunate enough to have very accurate large scale maps.

When my other company arrived there was not all that much time left for giving out orders. Bill Apsey, who was commanding it, decided to go in on a one platoon front, which was sensible, as the wood tapered to a point. It was also fairly thick, so the riflemen were almost on top of the enemy posts (not

Right: GOC 7th Armoured Division, General Bobbie Erskine driving his jeep near Naples.

Below: A Divisional supply column moving towards Naples. Soon after Naples the network of roads increased so the armour could take the lead. Behind them the columns of supplies rolled on unceasingly.

Right: The GOC receives a bouquet from the orphans of Casaluce. The Desert Rats earned the undying gratitude of this small town by organising transport to collect their most prized statue – 'The Silver Virgin of Casaluce' from nearby Aversa. The Aversans had borrowed it just before the Allied invasion and then boasted that because of the war they would be able to keep it for ever. But thanks to the 'Generale Magnifico' and his 'Liberatori Arditi' honour was satisfied. By the time the orphans had sung a very long anthem composed specially for the occasion, the sun had melted most of the chocolate General Erskine was carrying for them.

Centre right: 1/5 Queens in Aversa. A patrol searches the wreckage of a bombed train for possible snipers.

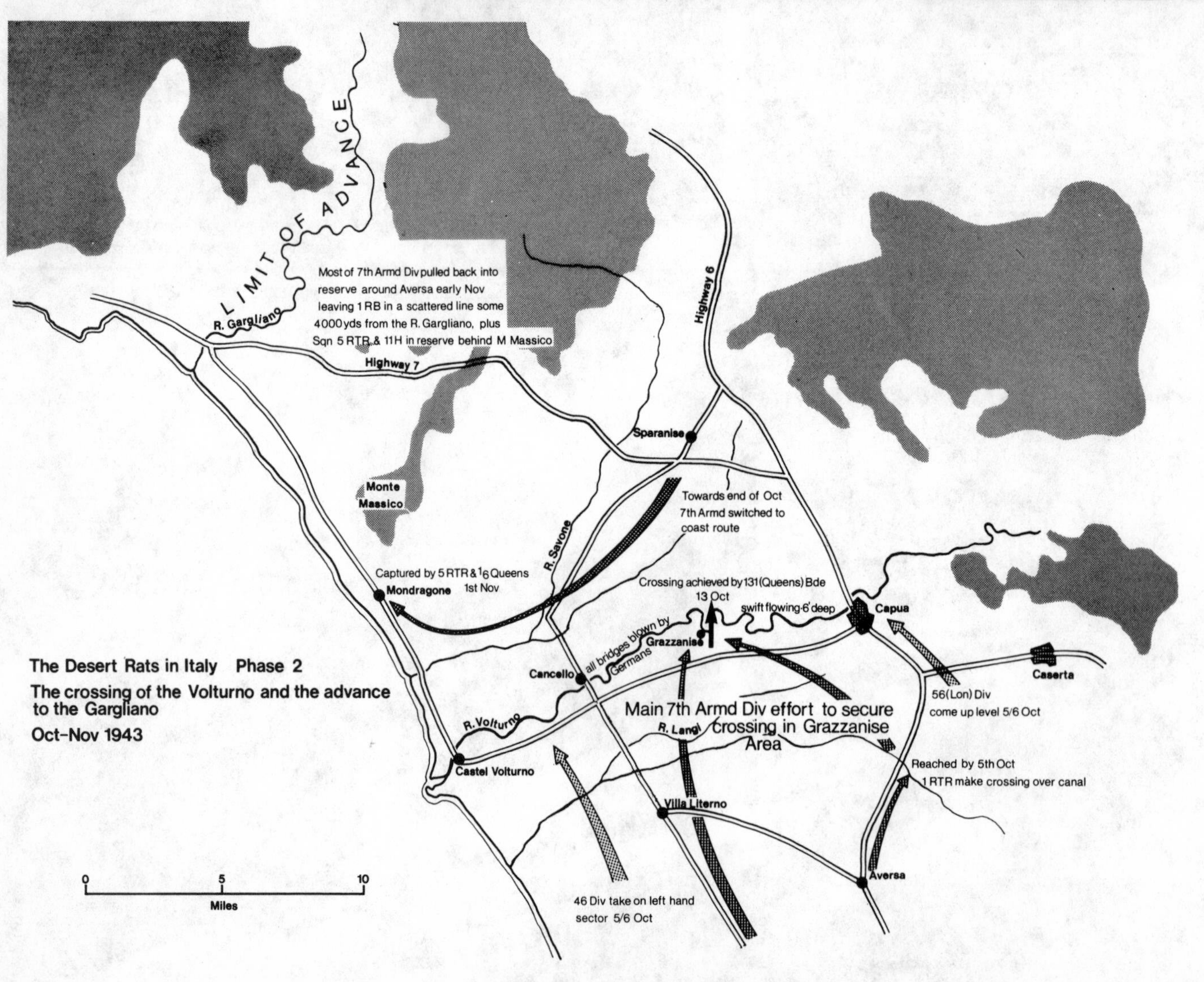

The Desert Rats in Italy Phase 2
The crossing of the Volturno and the advance to the Gargliano
Oct–Nov 1943

that there were many of them as it turned out) before their occupants could use their weapons. The southern tip of Cardito was thus reached without much difficulty. The company then had to clear the village, a straggling place some seven hundred yards long – quite a task for a motor company which only had two motor platoons and only assaulted about 40 strong. As it turned out the actual clearing of the village was not too difficult and it was during the consolidation at the northern end that we had most of our casualties, as the enemy brought down some very heavy concentrations of fire at hourly intervals. There is no doubt that they had intended to hold their positions for several hours at least until nightfall or possibly even for another day. And there was always the possibility of a counter attack. Things were not helped by electrical storms which put all our radios out of action for a period. It was impossible to locate the hostile guns until after dark when the medium regiment with the Division was able to silence the opposition and the Riflemen in Cardito got some relief. During the night the Germans broke contact and the advance was resumed the next day'.

Their Outstanding Feat in Italy

Thus, the attack and capture of Cardito was a complete success, indeed the Rifle Brigade considers it as their most successful engagement in Italy: As Major R. H. W. S. Hastings, DSO, OBE, MC says in his history:

'If Djebil Saikhra had been "I" Company's and possibly the Battalion's most successful battle in Tunisia, then the capture of Cardito was their outstanding feat in Italy. The company's attack on its narrow front was completely successful despite considerable opposition'.

Into Reserve

After reaching the River Garigliano in early November the Division was withdrawn into reserve behind the Massico feature, less 11th Hussars, 1st Rifle Brigade and a squadron of 5th Royal Tank Regiment, who took over a scattered line some four thousand yards

Above: 1/5 Queens practise for the crossing of the Volturno. By October 6th the country south of the R Volturno was clear of enemy. 46th and 56th Divisions had come up on the flanks of 7th Armoured and the stage was set for a crossing over the river. First, however, many preparations had to be made. The initial assault would be by infantry in small boats like these.

Left: A 2" mortar in action on the northern bank of the Volturno. After ceaseless patrolling a suitable crossing place was found near Grazzanise and on the night of October 12th, 1943 elements of 1/5 and 1/7 Queens managed to cross. In the course of the next two days each battalion established a company on the far side.

Top left: An MMG of the Cheshires in action at the Volturno crossing. The medium machine guns of C Coy 1st Cheshire Regiment provided wonderful support to the Queen's Brigade during the crossing.

Centre left: A Sherman of 4 CLY crossing the river. Having bulldozed a gap on the far bank the tanks could now get across the river. At dawn on October 16th, 1943 the 1/5 and 1/6 Queens set out to clear the bridgehead as far as the canal some 2 000 yards north. A torrential downpour meant that the tanks which had crossed could only support this operation from the roads, but by nightfall the area had been cleared.

Bottom left: Sign on a pontoon bridge over the Volturno at Cancello.

Right: Gen Eisenhower talks with the GOC. The bridge over the Volturno which 7th Armoured Division sappers built at Grazzanise was the first across that river, so Gen Erskine has every reason for looking pleased as he talks with Gen Eisenhower.

Below: 1 RB mop up in Sparanise. Having crossed the Volturno the Division pressed on towards the next line of enemy resistance around Francolise and Sparanise and in the hills to the north. 1st Rifle Brigade entered Sparanise on October 22nd, 1943.

from the Garigliano. By the 7th however, all were withdrawn to the area of Aversa where they handed over their vehicles to the 5th Canadian Armoured Division. The official history, (*A Short History of the Seventh Armoured Division June 1943-July 1945.*), relates that the Canadians were a little surprised by some of the vehicles which had been with the Division since the previous February when they had been obtained secondhand from the 4th Indian Division. 'Several thousand miles, mostly over open desert had not subsequently improved them. However, all that could be done was done, and it was a misfortune that the crews who had worked so hard to freshen up tanks and vehicles as much as possible, should have had to hand them over in a field several inches deep in mud'

The Division then moved to concentrate on the northern side of the Sorrento Peninsula. Billets were reasonably comfortable and life agreeable as Jake Wardrop recalls:

'A day or two later some of the crew moved off down the coast to Sorrento and Castellamare and shortly after we drove the rest of the tanks to a dump in Napoli. It was a good trip. We waved to the signorinas and laughed when the lads on the pavements shouted that we were going the wrong way. Wrong way, indeed! On December 2nd the rest of the unit moved to Castellamare and we sat there for two weeks.

'C' Squadron was camped in a red jam factory which had been blown up by the Bosches, and a very good job they had made of it. I don't suppose the place will operate for months to come. It was a good spot and I met some people, quite a number. The first was a Canadian who could play the guitar and sing just like Jimmy Rogers. I met him in a wine shop and saw him again by chance one day on the road. One day I bought a guitar in a little shop, the one from Tunis had become a bit worse for wear. The owner of the shop was a lad called Antonio and he was a wizard on the guitar and mandolin. He invited me to come to his house any night and we could have a little jam session. His father and two brothers also played the strings and he had three sisters. One was married and living in Rome and they used to worry about her a lot. They also had some smashing gramophone records and we used to hear them often. I got a lot of instruction from Tony on the guitar and in Italian, too. They called me Giovanni and I went to dinner with them a few times. The cooks in the Squadron were

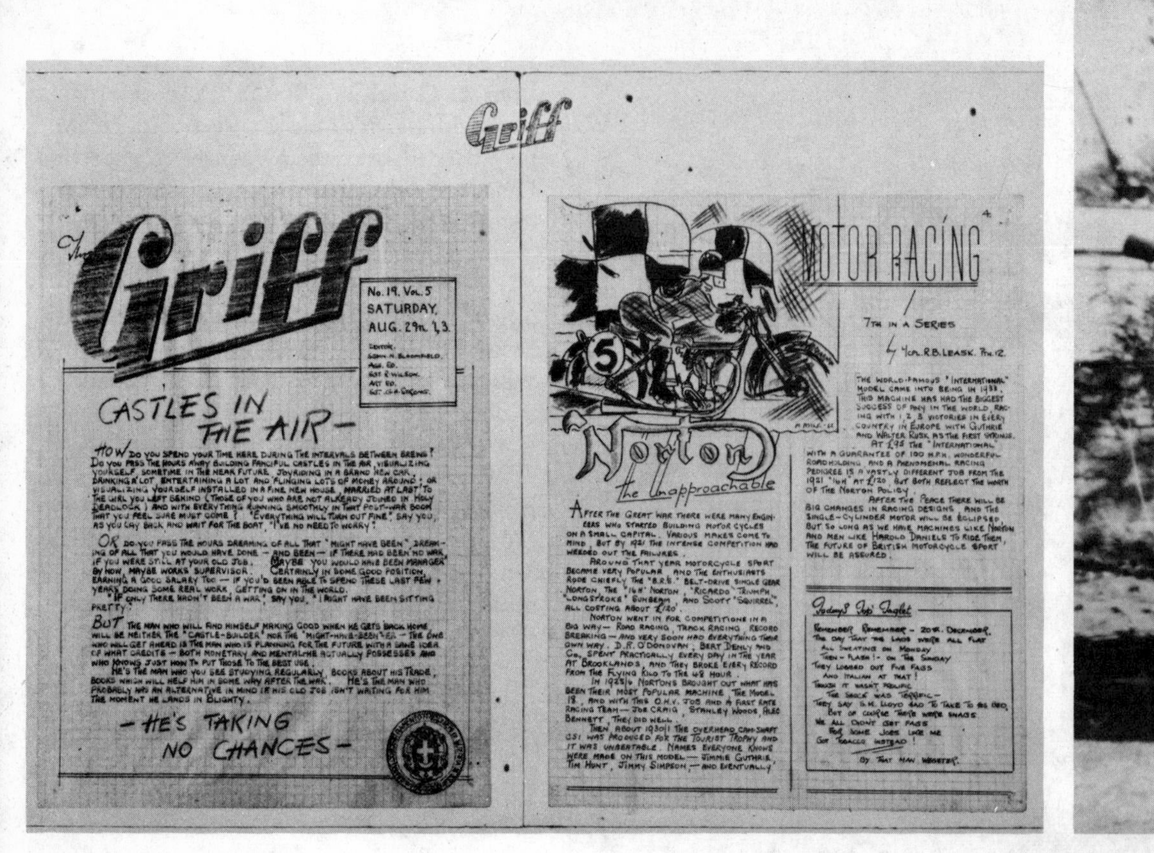

The Griff

No. 19. Vol. 5
SATURDAY,
AUG. 29th '43.

CASTLES IN THE AIR –

HOW do you spend your time here during the intervals between brews? Do you pass the hours away building fanciful castles in the air, visualizing yourself, sometime in the near future, joyriding in a brand new car, drinking a lot, entertaining a lot and flinging lots of money around; or visualizing yourself installed in a fine new house, married at last to the girl you left behind (those of you who are not already joined in holy deadlock) and with everything running smoothly in that post-war boom that you feel sure must come? "Everything will turn out fine," say you, as you lay back and wait for the boat, "I've no need to worry".

OR do you pass the hours dreaming of all that "might have been", dreaming of all that you would have done – and been – if there had been no war, if you were still at your old job. Maybe you would have been manager by now, maybe works supervisor. Certainly in some good position, earning a good salary too – if you'd been able to spend these last few years doing some real work, getting on in the world.
"If only there hadn't been a war," say you, "I might have been sitting pretty".

BUT the man who will find himself making good when he gets back home will be neither the "castle-builder" nor the "might-have-been"-er – the one who will get ahead is the man who is planning for the future with a sane idea of what credits – both monetary and mental he actually possesses and who knows just how to put those to the best use.
He's the man who you see studying regularly, books about his trade, books which will help him in some way after the war. He's the man who probably has an alternative in mind if his old job isn't waiting for him the moment he lands in Blighty.

– HE'S TAKING NO CHANCES –

Griff

MOTOR RACING

7th in a Series

by L/Cpl. R.B. Leask. Pn. 12.

Norton the Unapproachable

AFTER the Great War there were many engineers who started building motor cycles on a small capital. Various makes come to mind, but by 1921 the intense competition had weeded out the failures.
Around that year motorcycle sport became very popular and the enthusiasts rode chiefly the "B.R.S." belt-drive single gear Norton, the "16H" Norton, "Ricardo" Triumph, "Longstroke" Sunbeam, and Scott "Squirrel", all costing about £120.
Norton went in for competitions in a big way – road racing, track racing, record breaking – and very soon had everything their own way. D.R. O'Donovan, Bert Denly and Co. spent practically every day in the year at Brooklands, and they broke every record from the flying kilo to the 48 hour.
In 1925/6 Nortons brought out what has been their most popular machine, the Model 18, and with this O.H.V. job and a first rate racing team – Joe Craig, Stanley Woods, Alec Bennett, they did well.
Then about 1930/1 the overhead cam-shaft CS1 was produced for the Tourist Trophy and it was unbeatable. Names everyone knows were made on this model – Jimmie Guthrie, Tim Hunt, Jimmy Simpson, – and eventually

The world-famous "International" model came into being in 1933. This machine has had the biggest success of any in the world, racing with 1, 2, 3 victories in every country in Europe with Guthrie and Walter Rusk as the first strings.
At £95 the "International" with a guarantee of 100 m.p.h., wonderful roadholding, and a phenomenal racing pedigree is a vastly different job from the 1921 "16H" at £120, but both reflect the worth of the Norton policy.
After the peace there will be big changes in racing designs, and the single-cylinder motor will be eclipsed, but so long as we have machines like Norton and men like Harold Daniels to ride them, the future of British motorcycle sport will be assured.

Today's Jap Jinglet

Remember Remember – 20th December
The day that the lads were all flat
All sweating on Monday
Then – flash! – on the Sunday
They logged out five fags
And Italian at that!
Though it wasn't prolific
The shock was terrific –
They say G.H. Lloyd had to take to his bed,
But of course there were snags
We all didn't get fags
For some jobs like me
Got tobacco instead!

By That Man Webster.

Above: A page from *Griff*, a POW newspaper published by ex Desert Rats in Camp No. 53, Macerata, Italy. Begun soon after their arrival at this camp, the newspaper was entirely hand written and hand drawn, six pages daily, it was a valuable morale booster for the inmates of the camp. After 15 months captivity Signalman Norman Bloomfield, the Editor, escaped with his two assistants and spent some 9 months fighting as guerillas until they were able to get through to the Allied lines.

Right: A Sherman of 1RTR fording a river near Mondragone. At the end of October 1943 the Division was moved south east to take over the line of the Regi Agena near the sea. They then pushed on northwards clearing Mondragone and occupying the Massico Ridge. It was by then bitterly cold and with enemy resistance hardening the Division fought its last action in Italy – a sharp engagement at Cicola.

continually weeping about the bread and rations that were missing every morning. I used to cane them, but what did it matter, we didn't starve and these people were hungry. I have their address and when I learn some more Italian and it is possible, I shall write to them. Nearby the 1st Tanks were staying in a big house and we visited them, then sent invitations to them to visit us. Many good nights were enjoyed by all and a lot of vino was consumed. There were some hospitals in the area and the personality kids, I mean the officers of 'C' Squadron, soon got chasing the nurses. One night I was coming back from the 1st, hazed a bit, guitar at the slope, jacket over one arm and had reached the door when Jock came dashing out and led me away to one side. He said there were some sisters in the Mess, so watch the language and so on. He was in quite a state. I got organised a bit and went in and there they were. Five English Sisters, looking clean and slick, sitting at the table. We sent out for ten bottles of vino and had a sing-song, it was very good'.

Going Home

Early on 20th December the Division, after a short night's rest in a wet and uncomfortable transit camp at Casoria, moved down to the docks of Naples to embark. By four o'clock, after spending most of the day in an almost stationary queue, all were on board and the

convoy weighed anchor. The voyage home was uneventful. Christmas and New Year were both celebrated fairly quietly, although the ships could scarcely have been described as "dry" except from the official point of view. On the 7th of January 1944, the Division docked at Glasgow where trains were already waiting to take the Desert Rats to their new concentration area in Norfolk. The short Italian campaign had at least given them a foretaste of what lay ahead and formed a useful transitional period between the Desert and the highly cultivated and urbanised battleground of North West Europe which was still to come. Jake Wardrop wrote in his diary aboard the boat home:

'The big job was finished and another one would be starting soon. We had done well in Italy and had the valuable experience of operating in continental conditions. That was the reason we did not come home after Tunis, we had to be introduced to the conditions of the continent, so different from the desert. And we had done so. We had learned some new tricks and improved on the old ones and now we were going home. There had been a lot of speculation about where we would dock, but I knew. I knew that morning when we got to the quay and I saw the ship, the Cameronia, and why not. I had set off from Princes dock and I'd go back there. It turned out that I was wrong by about a penny-one by tram; we landed at Shieldhall'.

Above centre: Handing over to the Canadians. 22nd Armd Bde workshops hand over a Sherman to their Canadian counterparts of the 5th Canadian Armoured Division. Conditions during this particular handover were better than for most of the units who had to contend with a sea of mud!

Above: Transit barracks near Naples. The Division spent a short night's rest in a rather wet and uncomfortable camp at Casoria near Naples before embarking.

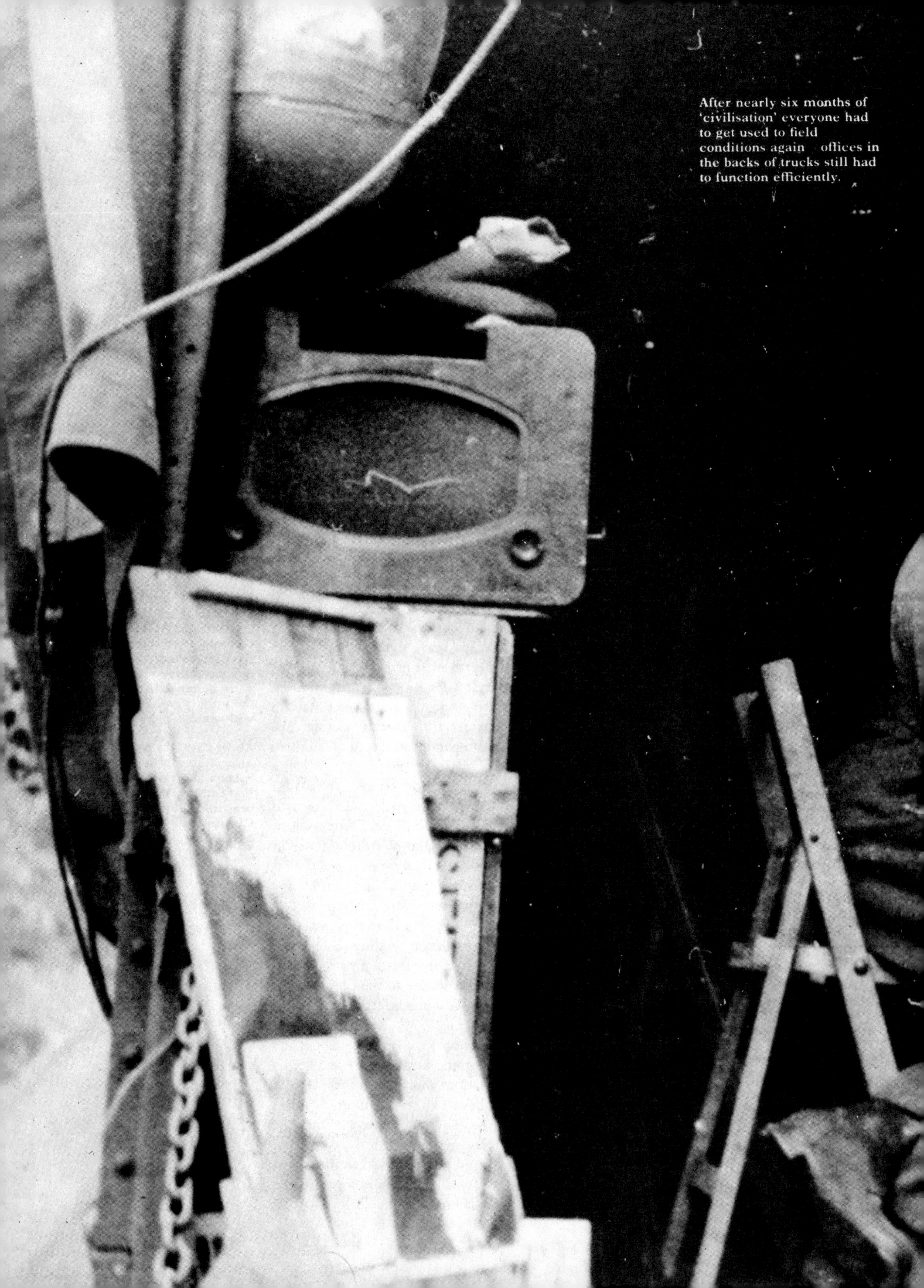

After nearly six months of 'civilisation' everyone had to get used to field conditions again offices in the backs of trucks still had to function efficiently.

Blighty~Preparation for 'D' Day

Above: Most of the AFV crews lived in their vehicles and fed themselves, but administrative units usually fed centrally – here cooks of the 7th Heavy Recovery Section put in some practice on their field cookers.

Norfolk
The concentration area allocated to the Division was in Norfolk. The Queen's Brigade got the better choice of billets, being mainly quartered in civilisation around King's Lynn, but 22nd Armoured Brigade were around Brandon – not a particularly attractive area as the Divisional history relates:

'The Armoured Brigade was perhaps less fortunate in the Brandon area. Our misgivings had already been aroused by the publication of an article in *Country Life* which, while attributing to the district considerable importance for both archaeology and ornithology, made it clear that it possessed few, if any, other amenities. *Country Life* was right. Eager watchers, at the windows of the long troop trains, saw flat black fenland give way to sandy heath; Brandon station gave a glimpse at least of houses, and a pub; but the troop carrying vehicles into which we were detrained carried us inexorably away from this brief vision of paradise, farther and farther into the waste, depositing us mercilessly into groups of decayed Nissen huts, clustered beneath the tall pines. The 4th County of London Yeomanry were perhaps the most unfortunate, the greater part of their camp having been constructed well below the water level for the district, and they glared enviously at their neighbours, perched on their sandy islands above the waste. NCOs complained of the inadequacy of one hut for their platoons or troops; colour-sergeants enquired bitterly how they were expected to put the stores into "that there 'ole there" and deep inroads were made into the coal stocks before it was discovered that this commodity was, in England, severely rationed'.

Preparations for Normandy
Of course few really had much time to worry about their surroundings for there was a great

deal to do. The GOC, General Erskine, later wrote of those busy days:

'When the Division arrived in early January they had to have their leave. We then had to draw complete new equipment for the entire Division as we had left all our own in Italy. This in itself is a fairly major undertaking. It did not make matters easier when we found that the Armoured Brigade was to be equipped with Cromwells which was an entirely new tank for us. We all knew the Sherman inside out, but none of us knew the Cromwell. This had various repercussions. The Armoured Regiments had to learn the gunnery and maintenance of a new tank which many of them judged inferior to the Sherman. Many of the Cromwells suffered from minor defects and the reputation of the tank did not improve as we had to repair the defects ourselves. The Armoured Regiments all had to go to Scotland (Kirkcudbright) to do their gunnery which was absolutely necessary, but took up much time on a form of training which could have been avoided if we had been given Shermans.

At this time we were also very busy "planning". The enormous amount of detail required in this planning involved most of my staff and the brigade staffs. For a period of several weeks the senior members of my staff lived in London with 30 Corps planning staff. Matters were not made easier for me by the removal of Brigadier Whistler, commander of 131 Brigade to a brigade in 3rd Division. My GSO1, Lieutenant Colonel Pat Hobart, was taken to boost the Guards Armoured Division and my OC Signals was also taken away. A number of other valuable officers were taken away to boost other armoured divisions and divisions for the assault.

Our role was the immediate follow up of the assault and we had to commence our landing on the evening of D-Day. Naturally we paid a good deal of attention to landing in face of opposition. We could not rely on the assault being entirely successful and we had to be prepared, as much as an assault division, for landing in the face of opposition over beach obstacles. This required careful rehearsals with the Navy both in the proper loading of the LSTs (Landing Ships Tank) and in their disembarkation either direct on to the beach or onto large rafts. The tanks and all other vehicles had to be carefully waterproofed as we had to anticipate a "wet" landing. A tremendous amount of hard work and training was involved in all this which other armoured divisions did not have to undertake as they came to Normandy much later and could assume a "dry" landing. Therefore much of the training time available was spent

Top left: Mon Repos. In May 1944 units were moved from their Norfolk concentration areas to complete waterproofing, 22 Armd Bde to Ipswich and 131 Bde, plus most of the supporting arms, to the London docks area. Camps were mainly tented, like this desirable residence belonging to Maj A H Barnes of 7th Heavy Recovery Section REME, near Southampton.

Above: General Montgomery inspects the Division. Monty visited every unit of the Division on February 16th and 17th, 1944. Here he inspects 3 RHA. Lt Col Norman (then CO 3 RHA) is standing next to him, Brig Mews (Commander, Royal Artillery) and Gen Erskine (GOC) are next behind.

Above: The GOC inspects 8th Hussars. General Bobbie Erskine inspected the 8th Hussars at West Tofts, Norfolk on May 11th, 1944. He is seen here being greeted by the CO, Lt Col Goulburn. 8H were equipped with Cromwell tanks – seen in the background. The Cromwell VII usually mounted a 75mm gun, but can you spot the short barrelled 95mm? Two of them were in each Squadron Headquarters.

in the technicalities of an assault landing.

The time available was extremely short. I have no access to dates, so I speak from memory. Working backwards we had to embark our tanks on June 2nd and 3rd in Force S at Harwich – this was my own HQ and the 22nd Armoured Brigade Group. We had to be in our concentration areas some ten days before this and again before that we had to have all our kit packed and vehicles loaded and waterproofed. There were thus no opportunities for training after the beginning of May. In the end it worked out that we had about two weeks in the Stanford battle area to train and that is a very small area to exercise an armoured division. At the same time we had come from Italy where we had plenty of experience in working in close country. I should of course have welcomed a longer time to train. I am sure we all felt we were rushed, but bearing in mind the number of different things we had to do we gave as much time as we possibly could to field training in close country. I never for one moment felt I was taking to Normandy an untrained Division. I had the greatest confidence in them.

Morale was as always a very important factor. The Division contained many people who had been in it since 1941, who had seen the North African campaign through and had done Salerno. There was undoubtedly a feeling amongst a few that it was time somebody else had a go. I had to pay considerable attention to this attitude and I am sure I did so successfully, but it meant several heart-to-heart talks with every unit. There was a fundamental difference between troops like 7th Armoured Division who had been fighting continuously and fresh troops who had never been in action. The latter wanted to "win their spurs" and were ready to take on anything without question – once or twice. With 7th Armoured Division it was no use trying to pull the wool over their eyes. They knew war too well to take it light heartedly or carelessly. We left for Normandy with a high state of morale, but it is no use concealing the fact that we felt we had been rushed. We were nothing like so well teamed up as we had been before Salerno'. (Taken from the private papers of the late General Sir George Erskine and published by kind permission of Major P. N. Erskine.)

New Recruits

The Division received their quota of new recruits to make units up to strength. Some of these had most interesting backgrounds as the following reminiscences from R. Parker of London recall:

'Let me first introduce myself. I was born a German Jew and came to this country as a refugee in March 1939, aged 24. When war broke out we – that is countless young German and Austrian Jewish refugees – volunteered at once to fight Nazi Germany, in any capacity. The British Government eventually agreed to let us serve in the Army, but only in the Pioneer Corps. Some of the "alien" pioneer companies went to France with the BEF – I went as well – and we were amongst the last evacuated back to Britain in June 1940. From then onwards the pressure, especially from the younger members of the "alien" pioneer companies, to join fighting units continued to no avail. The disinclination of the War Office to employ what were, after all on paper anyway, enemy nationals is understandable. Perhaps the significance of what it meant to be a Jew in Germany had not yet sunk home in this country. But as the war went on and application after application to fight went to the authorities, gradually the official attitude changed. I think that it was in some of the first Commando raids (St. Nazaire etc) that ex-Pioneers were fighting bravely and also some became casualties. Finally in 1943 there was a complete turn about by the War Office. Everybody who wanted to could apply for a transfer to a fighting unit. Some of the boys – but very few – went for the most glamorous undertakings – Commandos, Airborne, or were dropped as spies over occupied Europe. (In this last category, an old friend of mine in 93 Coy, Pioneer Corps even lived to tell the tale of a year as a wireless operator in wartime Southern Germany). The Infantry held little attraction, some went for the Gunners, but the bulk of transfers were to the Royal Armoured Corps. So it was that in the autumn of 1943 the RAC Training Regiments in Farnborough and Barnard Castle had for some weeks almost entirely ex-Pioneer Corps "aliens", as new intakes. By the time our training had finished, it was 1944 and it now so happened that 7th Armoured Division arrived in this country from Italy and its regiments were scattered over Norfolk, mainly in the Thetford area. The Division wanted reinforcements, and we had just finished our training, so the major part of the new RAC recruits, all alien ex-Pioneers, went to the armoured regiments of the Division in bulk. What the exact numbers were I don't of course know, but I estimate it was about 80 to 100. Most of them went to 8th Hussars and 1st RTR. Some to 5th RTR and some to HQ 22nd Armoured Brigade and HQ 7th Armoured Division. I myself was lucky enough to be posted to Divisional Headquarters, where I finished the war, without a scratch, in "Tac" – Divisional Tactical Headquarters Tank Troop (for the close protection of Tac HQ). Many of my former friends, however, were not so lucky. I personally know of Troopers Sandford, Richmond, Franklin and Jacobi in 1st RTR, who were killed in the first few weeks in Normandy. Others in 8th Hussars, including my good friend Tommy Halford, also fell in Normandy or were wounded. One Trooper Marshal, was wounded and then taken prisoner by the Waffen SS, and spent a year as a POW in Germany, without any of his British mates giving him away to his captors (and his English was strongly accented). You will notice that we all served as troopers only. It was hardly to be expected to get promoted in a division as battle-hardened as 7th Armd by the time we were allowed to join. Let me add that my relations with my British comrades were perfect. I have never heard of any of my foreign comrades who did not integrate completely with their crews, many of them regulars and veterans of all the Desert battles. The fact that so many "aliens" were in the Division at the time was not well known to everybody. I heard officers in Div HQ in Norfolk remark about the amazing fact that teutonic accents could be heard in the 8th Hussars lines! Colonel Carver, as he then was, took a mate of mine in his own jeep to say a Jewish prayer over the grave of a fallen trooper in a Recce tank of 1st RTR. When I got demobbed in February 1946 and found myself an alien again in Civvy Street, General Lyne personally intervened for me at the War Office and saw to it that I became a British naturalized national at once. Of course all our names are not the ones we were born with. The War Office changed all those in 1943, even our original army numbers were changed. It certainly was a help to Trooper Marshal when the SS took him prisoner'.

Top left: Three Cheers for Monty! Characteristically Gen Montgomery spoke to every unit he visited. He always considered it essential to let the troops under him know what was going on and what he expected of them. This he started as commander of the Eighth Army and continued to do as C-in-C 21st Army Group.

Above: General Erskine talks to the Signals Troop of the 8th Hussars. Every armoured regiment had specialist personnel attached to it from other Corps, such as these signallers. As well as the GOC, the C-in-C and His Majesty the King, the 8th were visited by General Skliaron the Russian Military Attaché. He noticed their battle honour for the Crimean War and remarked upon it – things could have been difficult, but when he discovered that the regiment celebrated the 'Charge of the Light Brigade' at Balaclava every year, he remarked that the Russians did likewise which caused much laughter!

Above: Leaving for the docks. Having completed their waterproofing and made all other preparations, units were moved down to the docks to embark – the armoured brigade in LCTs (Landing Craft Tank) the rest in LSTs (Landing Ship Tank) and Liberty Ships.

Bottom right: A line of tank transporters belonging to 7th Heavy Recovery Section look strangely out of place in a peaceful English country lane.

Visitors and Inspections

The Division was once again honoured by a visit from His Majesty on February 24th, 1944. An eyewitness of his arrival in one location was Mrs Jessie Jary of Attleborough, who happened to be near the station just as the Royal train arrived. She writes:

'His Majesty the King visited a small company of the 22nd Armoured Brigade who were stationed at Attleborough and were drawn up on the platform at Attleborough station early one morning, it was a very well kept secret. I was going shopping and walked through the gates just as the Royal train drew in. I watched the King speak to the troops and was so close I could have touched him when he came to the end of the platform. I will always remember the nice smile he gave me as he passed'.

General Montgomery was of course another visitor as the photographs in this section recall. General Erskine visited all his units on numerous occasions. Amongst them were some new arrivals, for example, the 8th Hussars who had replaced the 11th Hussars. The Eighth were an Armoured Reconnaissance Regiment which meant they were equipped very much like an Armoured Regiment, but without any heavy armament and with more than the normal complement of light reconnaissance vehicles. In fact the Eleventh rejoined the Division very soon after D-Day and the Eighth functioned as a fourth armoured regiment within 22nd Armoured Brigade rather than in a reconnaissance role.

Final Preparations

W. F. Halford of Norwich recalled the final period of preparation thus: 'A few weeks later we moved to High Ash, we were camped in the fir woods out of sight and spent most of the time waterproofing our vehicles. There was no leave, but I well remember on several occasions riding my motor-cycle between the trees, coming onto the road well away from the main guardroom and off home to Norwich for the night'.

All over Southern England the invasion forces readied themselves for the coming

SUPREME HEADQUARTERS
ALLIED EXPEDITIONARY FORCE

Soldiers, Sailors and Airmen of the Allied Expeditionary Force!

You are about to embark upon the Great Crusade, toward which we have striven these many months. The eyes of the world are upon you. The hopes and prayers of liberty-loving people everywhere march with you. In company with our brave Allies and brothers-in-arms on other Fronts, you will bring about the destruction of the German war machine, the elimination of Nazi tyranny over the oppressed peoples of Europe, and security for ourselves in a free world.

Your task will not be an easy one. Your enemy is well trained, well equipped and battle-hardened. He will fight savagely.

But this is the year 1944! Much has happened since the Nazi triumphs of 1940-41. The United Nations have inflicted upon the Germans great defeats, in open battle, man-to-man. Our air offensive has seriously reduced their strength in the air and their capacity to wage war on the ground. Our Home Fronts have given us an overwhelming superiority in weapons and munitions of war, and placed at our disposal great reserves of trained fighting men. The tide has turned! The free men of the world are marching together to Victory!

I have full confidence in your courage, devotion to duty and skill in battle. We will accept nothing less than full Victory!

Good Luck! And let us all beseech the blessing of Almighty God upon this great and noble undertaking.

Dwight Eisenhower

onslaught. In May the Division moved to its concentration areas – 22nd Armoured Brigade to Orwell Park near Ipswich, the remainder to Brentwood and West Ham.

Order of Battle
The D-Day orbat of the Division was as follows:

22nd Armoured Brigade
1st Royal Tank Regiment
5th Royal Tank Regiment
4th County of London Yeomanry (The Sharpshooters)
1st Battalion the Rifle Brigade (Motor Battalion)
131st (Queens) Brigade
1/5 Queens Royal Regiment
1/6 Queens Royal Regiment
1/7 Queens Royal Regiment
No 3 Support Company, Royal Northumberland Fusiliers (Medium Machine Guns)

Divisional Troops
8th Hussars
Divisional Signals
Royal Artillery
3rd Royal Horse Artillery
5th Royal Horse Artillery
15th Light Anti-Aircraft Regiment
65th Anti-Tank Regiment (The Norfolk Yeomanry)
Royal Engineers
4th and 621st Field Squadrons
143rd Field Park Squadron
Royal Army Service Corps
Nos 58, 67 and 507 Companies
Royal Army Medical Corps
2nd Light Field Ambulance
131st Field Ambulance
29th Field Dressing Station
70th Field Hygiene Section
134th Mobile Dental Unit
Royal Army Ordnance Corps
Divisional Ordnance Field Park
22nd Armoured Brigade Ordnance Field Park
131st Brigade Ordnance Field Park
Royal Electrical Mechanical Engineers
7th Armoured Troops Workshop
22nd Armoured Brigade Workshop
131st Brigade Workshop
15th Light Anti-Aircraft Workshop
Royal Armoured Corps
No 263 Forward Delivery Squadron

The Great Crusade was about to begin!

A view of the Convoy. The Allied Army comprised over $3\frac{1}{2}$ million men, nearly 150 000 of which were to be put ashore on D Day alone.

Invasion

Close-up of the deck of a Landing Ship Tank en route for France. The force assembled for the invasion was gigantic and included over 4 000 landing craft and 1 600 ancillary and merchant ships.

Embarkation

The shipping plan was that the armoured brigade, less its motor battalion, would sail in assault landing craft, aiming to land on D-Day or D + 1, whilst the infantry brigade, the operational section of the echelons and the bulk of the headquarters, were to sail in Liberty ships and coasters. General Erskine recalled after the war how the plan had to be modified:

'The Division embarked from a number of different points. I went round to see them all and also units of 50th Division and 4th Armoured Brigade with whom I was likely to have to work closely on arrival at the other side. 22nd Armoured Brigade and my own Tactical HQ embarked on LSTs (Landing Ship Tank) in the River Orwell at Dovercourt. The rest of the Division embarked in Troop transports mostly at Tilbury. The salient point was that the 22nd Armoured Brigade went very light in transport and supporting arms (infantry, gunners and sappers) and there was a considerable time lag before the rest came along from Tilbury and elsewhere.

We had a lot of difficulty at Dovercourt in loading the LSTs according to the tables. Many of the vehicles were extremely awkward articulated vehicles for preparing airfields – scrapers, bulldozers and the like. They were towed equipment and difficult to load backwards into an LST. We had all practised loading but none of the drivers of these most awkward equipments had been given a chance. They nearly drove us mad and we got further and further behind in our loading schedules. Eventually Admiral Parry and myself had to scrap the programme and make one which could be carried out. Undoubtedly this earth moving equipment was necessary but it was a great embarrassment at such an early stage.

Those of us who embarked at Dovercourt collected into a convoy off Deal during the afternoon and evening of June 5th. We set forth during the night and passed through the Straits of Dover in the early hours of June 6th. We expected to receive salvos from France as we went past, but not a shot was fired. It was a bright and sunny day with a bit of wind and the sea flecked with white. It was not rough but the sea was in movement. We passed along the south coast without incident and after mid-day we began to meet LCTs and other small craft returning. The BBC was in full blast giving all the news and things seemed to be going well. This was good and in contrast to our arrival at Salerno where everything was going very badly while we were at sea. We were a large convoy and as we went westwards we joined up with other shipping. As we got off the Normandy coast the whole sea seemed to be ships. Nobody was attacked from the air or sea. It was all most orderly, except from our own bombardment

Operation 'Overlord' – 6th June 1944 and subsequent advance of 7th Armd Div

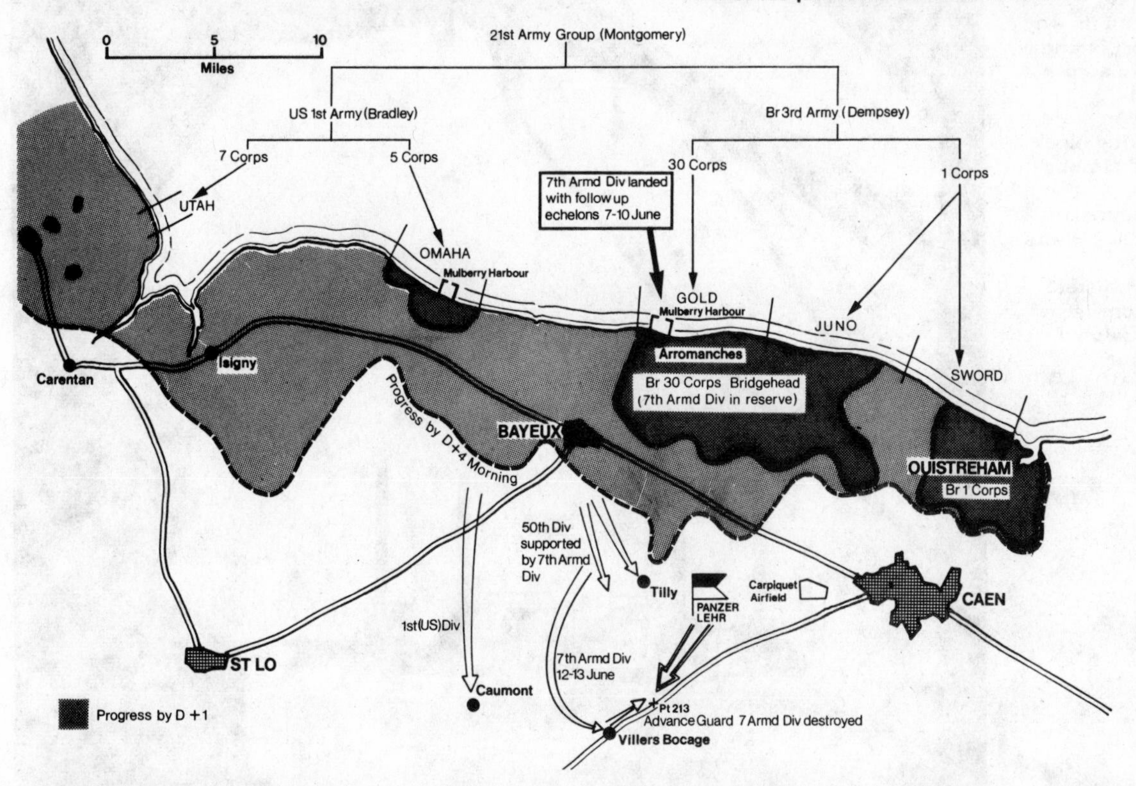

and bombing on the Normandy coast by the RAF, which increased as we moved to our positions opposite our beaches. We were in the vicinity of the beaches by the evening of D-Day, June 6th, and had anticipated landing on the tide about 2200 hours.

Very few people in our convoy landed on the 6th because the rough weather had "broached to" many of the early landing craft and the beach organisation could not handle us at the rate we were arriving.

Every LST was urgently required to do a return journey. It would have been far easier from our point of view to have sailed straight on to the beaches and unloaded. The objection to this was that the LSTs would have then lain on the beach stranded until the next tide floated them off and in the meantime they would have been sitting targets. Therefore, in theory, we were supposed to unload onto large floating platforms called Buffaloes and be towed in. It was just too rough for these Buffaloes; we could load on to them but they were too clumsy to move about. A good deal of time was wasted trying to make use of these things. Ultimately Admiral Douglas Pennant scrapped that method and ordered the ships ashore at half tide on the June 7th. I should think that was about 1100 hours. From the time of arrival we were champing at the bit to get ashore and particularly so from first light when we could not understand what was stopping us driving straight on to the beaches. When the time came we plunged into the water and drove ashore without any trouble. The waterproofing worked splendidly and directly we reached dry land we unwaterproofed ourselves according to the drill. This involved a number of things including the blowing of a "cortex" charge when was an engineer invention to achieve a quick release. It was most effective but damaged the beer and whiskey reserve carried by some people on the sides of their tanks!' (General Erskine's private papers.)

Tanks Landing on Gold Beach

Gold Beach was the chosen beach for those units of the Division landing on June 7th. As Powell Jones of 4 CLY recalls at least one tank driver had his problems:

'At the Normandy landing on D + 2, we reckoned on driving off the tank landing craft into about 3-4 feet of water, but owing to rougher conditions and heavier swell, drove off into around 6 feet or so – a very strange sensation for the driver as all he could see through his visor was dark-green. Despite the strict instructions we'd received – "Keep your foot down on the accelerator, do not change gear, and drive straight ahead", one of the tanks in our troop drove out to sea! The last we saw of it was the sea up to the top of the turret and crew standing on the

Right: A section of a Mulberry harbour on its way to the beaches. Most landings were initially made across open beaches until breakwaters could be established by sinking block ships. On Gold and Omaha beaches enormous prefabricated harbours, known under the code-name of Mulberry were constructed. The vast steel and concrete sections were towed across the Channel and then sunk off the beaches.

Above: A destroyer shepherds the convoy towards the invasion beaches. Over 1 200 warships, including seven battleships and 23 cruisers, protected the great armada.

Below: The Convoy steams majestically on. This photograph shows clearly the small barrage balloons which were attached to all landing craft as a protection against low level air attack. As it turned out there was little enemy air interference as the Allied Air Forces had already crushed the Luftwaffe's fighter strength.

top looking quite forlorn. They rejoined the squadron a couple of days later with another tank – I think somebody got another rollicking over that one!'

Personal Impressions of the Landing

What was it like to be a member of that historic invasion force? The following account written by a soldier of the Eleventh Hussars gives one a graphic impression of their feelings on that memorable day:

'Our column moved off down the road to the loading area just before first light. A few hours' sleep in a very ordinary English ditch, the sight of stolid policemen at every side-road, the thought of people still in bed and the early hour of the morning did not increase our morale. The loading onto the LCTs was accomplished surprisingly quickly and soon the craft were anchored in pairs in the middle of the estuary. From now on we had had it. No one could go ashore, no wireless was allowed and no newspapers came aboard. Movement was very limited, as to get from one end of the craft to the other it was necessary to crawl over the armoured vehicles.

After everyone had been organised into parties to cook and clean, there was nothing left to do but sit and wait; luckily the weather was good enough for sun-bathing. Amusement was provided by the small balloons attached to each craft, as in the strong wind they careered about until they got entangled with each other and then broke loose, gaining height rapidly until they burst when nearly out of sight. We thought that we should leave the next morning. Rumours went around for a time, but they soon ceased, as there was no scope for them amongst only forty people. We did not start the next morning, so had to settle down to another long day. The balloons had been tamed and, apart from sleeping, the only thing to do was

Top: A Sherman Firefly (17 pdr) belonging to the 4th County of London Yeomanry landing in Normandy. Over 320 000 men and 54 000 vehicles were landed in the first week.

Above: A column of waterproofed Sherman tanks, followed by some lorries, comes ashore through the shallows. By June 11th the Allied bridgehead was 50 miles wide by 12 miles deep.

to inspect the special rations which had been issued for use on landing. Self-heating tins of cocoa which brewed up in five minutes after being set off with a match won high praise. The weather was still good and we were lucky, as there was no shelter aboard and everyone had to sleep on the top of their vehicles or underneath them.

The following morning orders were given to pull the camouflage nets across the vehicles and interest began to rise as the craft prepared to move. Soon about fifty craft, in good order, were passing out into the open sea, which after the calm of the river seemed quite rough. Now we were definitely off and our thoughts were divided, some thinking of what was left behind, others of what they were going to, and a few too occupied to think, being ill over the side. The rest of that day was spent in readjusting ourselves to the motion of the boat, holding on to things when moving about, thinking twice before eating, and getting used to the spray which periodically dampened our ardour. Other convoys were seen, distinguished in the distance by the balloons each craft carried. All seemed to be going different ways and nothing indicated any special direction.

The night was uncomfortable and there was also the thought that the Calais guns might open up. However, we heard nothing of them, though we learnt afterwards that a later convoy was engaged. At first light we were just in sight of the Sussex coast at the same time as the first troops were landing in France. A wireless set was opened to get any news that came over the Army broadcasts, but nothing was heard. As the day progressed so more convoys were seen, all converging, and now all were going in the same direction. Later still the craft could be seen stretching in four lines to the horizon in both directions. Naval launches were moving up and down the lines shepherding the craft into position. In the distance on either side escort vessels could be seen guarding the lane down which all the landing craft were moving. Planes in formation kept passing overhead at a great height. The balloons shining in the brilliant sun showed up like silver pin-heads on the horizon.

In the afternoon another wireless set was opened up on to the frequency of the infantry division which was landing in front of us. Soon we were getting the locations of the forward troops and it was with great satisfaction that we could mark on our maps a red line showing that the infantry had achieved a substantial bridgehead. Throughout the day the columns of craft had been moving at the same speed and without any checks or alarms. There was no sign of the German Air Force. Later in the evening the order was given to roll back the camouflage nets and to run the vehicle engines for twenty minutes. Then the shackles securing the vehicles to the deck were released and all precautions taken to ensure that the vehicles would not move, as the sea was still rough enough to make the motion of the craft unpleasant. Final adjustments to the waterproofing of the vehicles were made.

After the last meal had been finished and all kit had been stowed away, there was nothing left to be done but to sit on the vehicles and wait for the outcome of the operation which had been planned for years. As the sun went down more and more ships could be seen spread over a large area in front of us, the smaller ones moving forward and the larger ones at anchor. Everything was very quiet except for the engines, and it all gave an impression of a naval review rather than an operation to defeat the Huns for all time. As we approached the mass of ships, the lines of landing craft slackened speed and it seemed now that we should not land that evening. The craft moved slowly forward and just before light failed the shore could be seen, but only as a dark, long line, and nothing could be made out except for a few fires burning. There was no thought of sleep, because we knew that, though the Luftwaffe had not appeared during the day, they would certainly come that night. Tin hats that would fit were put on and everyone sat listening while the gun crews prepared for action. Attacks came at about hourly intervals throughout the night, but only by a few planes. The amount of metal that was shot up into the air was staggering, ranging from the heavy stuff from cruisers to the small stuff from individual weapons, and the amount of spent ammunition falling all round us was much more frightening than anything else. The tracer gave a display surpassing any of Brock's Benefits. Two enemy planes were seen to fall in flames, but the noise was so deafening that it was impossible to hear them or even hear bombs falling. Little damage was done and there was no direct hits; the only ships that suffered were the ones that had near misses and were thoroughly drenched by the spray thrown up. The landing had evidently caught the German Air Force as well as the Army by surprise, as it was not until the following night that attacks became heavy.

At first light all the craft were still milling about waiting for a chance to land their vehicles. The sea was still rough enough to make the craft more uncomfortable and to bring a lot of spray aboard. There did not seem to be any future in waiting for others in front to land and so our skipper prepared to make a run for the shore, with us feeling that anything would be better than staying aboard. With everyone on their vehicles and drivers holding their brakes, the craft speeded up and rushed the sandy shore. With luck we missed the many sandbanks and, passing with cheers the craft which were stuck and would have to wait for the high tide, we ran up well and stopped, leaving only about thirty yards of water to drive through with a maximum depth of 4 feet. It was all very different from what we expected. Whereas we had been prepared to land with "one up the spout" and with shells falling all around, our only real worry was to get our kit ashore dry. Now came the time when all our efforts with the waterproofing material were to be finally tested. The ramp was lowered and the experts, testing the depth with sticks, ordered the first vehicle into the water. With cheers and facetious advice, the vehicle moved down the ramp at a steep angle with everyone quite prepared for everything to disappear under the waves. But as the water was coming up to the driver's window the sand was reached and slowly the vehicle ploughed ashore, the crew gesticulating wildly. Encouraged, the other vehicles soon followed and everyone drove across the sand past other boats stranded by the high tide and past tanks stuck in soft patches and a few blown up by mines. Moving through a safe lane, we got onto a road and soon were in a field removing some of the waterproofing which had been so successful.

And so we had landed, relieved to be away from the uncomfortable and never-still craft, relieved that all was peaceful, and happy to hear again the cry "Brew up".' (From the Victory Number of the Eleventh Hussar Journal and published here by kind permission of Home Headquarters, The Royal Hussars.)

Top: An RASC vehicle belonging to the Divisional Supply Column leaves the ramp of a landing craft on its way to the land. Over 100 000 tons of stores were landed on the bridgehead in the first seven days.

Above: Into Battle. Cromwells of 4 CLY leaving the Normandy beaches – the great advance had started!

North West Europe

Caen, 1944. Probably the most devastated town in Normandy. Caen was pounded to rubble by continual air raids. Despite this treatment the citizens showed touching examples of gratitude for liberation and kept the graves of Allied soldiers fresh with flowers.

A Class 40 Bailey Pontoon Bridge across the River Seine at Les Andelys near Louviers constructed by 6 Army Troop Engineers Aug 29th-31st, 1944 – length 440 ft.

Welcome Monty! Graffiti on the walls of Malines, Belgium which the Division reached on September 11th from Ghent after 'an extremely pleasant march – grand reception everywhere and all vehicles finished laden with fruit and tomatoes'.

Villers Bocage – scene of one of the Division's toughest encounters in Europe.

North West Europe
Route taken by
Seventh Armoured Division
June 1944 - July 1945

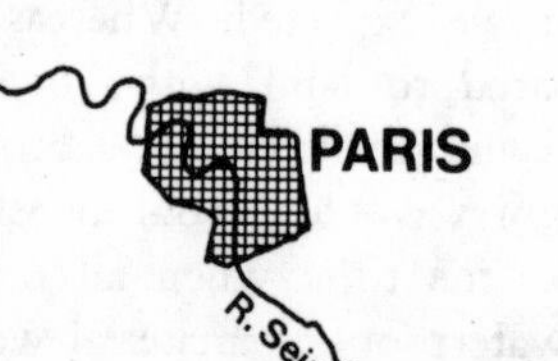

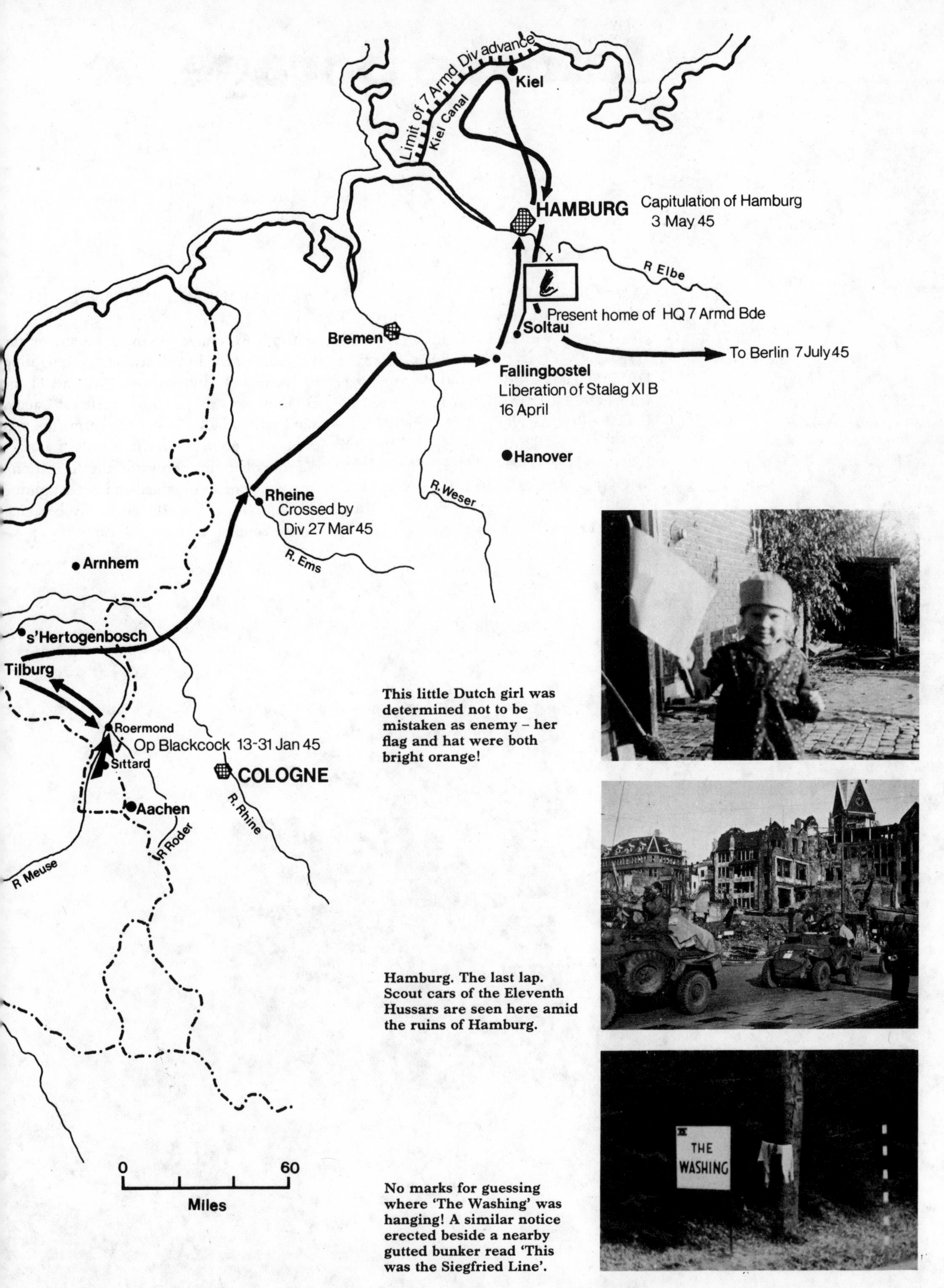

This little Dutch girl was determined not to be mistaken as enemy – her flag and hat were both bright orange!

Hamburg. The last lap. Scout cars of the Eleventh Hussars are seen here amid the ruins of Hamburg.

No marks for guessing where 'The Washing' was hanging! A similar notice erected beside a nearby gutted bunker read 'This was the Siegfried Line'.

Into the Bocage

Radio Bulletin

NOT FOR PUBLICATION, BROADCAST IN OVERSEAS BULLETINS OR USE ON CLUB TAPES BEFORE 23.30 DBST ON THURSDAY JULY 13TH, 1944 (I.E. FOR FRIDAY JULY 14TH MORNING PAPERS). NOT TO BE BROADCAST IN THE MIDNIGHT NEWS OF JULY 13TH/14TH. THIS EMBARGO SHOULD BE RESPECTED OVERSEAS BY PREFACING ANY MESSAGES FILED WITH THE EMBARGO.

7TH ARMOURED DIVISION TO JUNE 17TH 1944

'The 7th Armoured Division was among the vanguard of the British armour to be fighting in Normandy. By June 9th, elements of the Division were already concentrated at Caugy, and by the following day the formation was occupying positions in the Mendaye area.

From that time onwards the formation's story was one of sustained and bitter fighting in which it did superb service by breaking many counter-attacks and capturing positions held by powerful enemy forces. On June 11th it was in action in the Tilly area and here for several days it took part in mopping up German troops, advancing towards Hottot against stern reaction and, later, holding a line in the face of violent enemy counter-attacks.

By June 14th, the Division had established strongpoints in several villages among the low hills to the west of Villers Bocage, and here during the next few days, it repelled several enemy assaults taking a heavy toll of the German armour. On June 17th, in particular, the famous "Desert Rats" gained a remarkable success in destroying large forces of the enemy in a fierce action at Bricquessard'.

The Bocage

The brief radio bulletin above tells little of the fierce action fought at Villers Bocage in which the Division really experienced for the first time the difficulties of fighting in the dense bocage countryside with its high hedges, sunken roads, thick standing crops and orchards, where the normal battle range was likely to be under 300 yards and camouflage and concealment were all important. They also discovered the unpleasant fact that their Shermans and Cromwells were usually no match for the opposing Tigers and Panthers, being outgunned and underarmoured. Villers Bocage was therefore no great victory, but the Desert Rats fought

Top: Tank battle in Villers Bocage. A British tank (left) engaging a German Tiger muzzle to muzzle through the corner of a house. (Reproduced by kind permission of the Illustrated London News).

Above: Advancing through the Bocage.

tenaciously and with great courage throughout, suffering considerable casualties.

The Outline Plan

The main aim of the British 2nd Army at that time was to capture Caen and a pincer movement was launched with 51st Highland Division to the east of the town, and 50th Division and 7th Armoured Division to the west. Neither arm of the pincer was par-particularly successful and on June 11th the operation was temporarily halted, the German Panzer Lehr Division proving too tough a nut to crack.

Meanwhile, however, the Americans had been able to push inland some 20 miles from Omaha beach, forming a deep salient around Caumont. It was therefore decided that 7th Armoured would wheel behind 50th Division, strike south so that it was advancing parallel with the Americans around Caumont, and then turn due east again to take first Villers Bocage and then Caen from the flank. Unfortunately for the Desert Rats their vanguard, composed of the 4th County of London Yeomanry, 'A' Company 1st Rifle Brigade and 'B' Battery 5th Royal Horse Artillery, ran into 501 Waffen SS Heavy Tank Battalion shortly after leaving Villers Bocage on the road to Caen. This battalion was equipped with Tiger and Panther tanks which were occupying good fire positions in the close bocage countryside and wrought havoc amongst the British armour. The story of this engagement is told by Major Christopher Milner, MC, who was at that time second in command of 'A' Company, 1RB.

Christopher Milner

'As we passed through the small town of Villers Bocage we were greeted with interest rather than enthusiasm by the small groups of people standing about: "Les pompiers", (the fire brigade) I recollect, being much in evidence in one area; they might have warned of trouble if one had had time to stop, but I was on my way in my half track

Left: Carriers of the Queens take to a cornfield to bypass enemy opposition.

Below: Jerry shells here. Fine weather brought clouds of dust along the unmetalled roads, and the dust in its turn brought German shells – hence this common roadside sign to limit vehicle speeds.

Bottom: A Sherman Firefly. The 17-pounder of the Firefly was one of the few tank guns capable of dealing with German Tigers and Panthers. This one belonged to 4 CLY.

from the rear to the front of the company, picking up the platoon commanders and the mortar sergeant en route, in response to an urgent 'O' group summons from my company commander, James Wright. He in turn had just been briefed by Arthur, Viscount Cranley, commanding 4 CLY, at Point 210, the top of the low hill about 1½ miles east of the town – and our objective.

We were motoring rapidly along the straight road, past the dismounted riflemen and their evenly spaced half-tracks, but not past the scout platoon because Alan Mather's carriers had been shipped in a different vessel and they had not yet caught up with us. As this officer proved subsequently before he was killed, he was a particularly able and resourceful carrier commander and the outcome of the battle might have been very different if the force commander had had the benefit of information from this very experienced reconnaissance platoon to draw upon, in addition to that received from the tired and over-stretched armoured car squadron. As we shall see, had they been available to protect the southern flank of the regimental group as it swung from south to east, not only might the German tanks have been rumbled much earlier (since the parallel track which the enemy followed would have provided even better cover for the low-slung carriers) but one can even speculate upon a

fantastically different outcome of the Normandy battle if only this break-through had been successful enough to enable the Queen's Brigade to follow through the gap and dig in behind the German lines on this exceedingly important feature.

Things would also have been different had the platoon commanders been with their men – or even at a pinch, if I had been available at the rear of the company to rally them – either forward on to point 210 (the German tanks would have been terribly vulnerable to intelligent soldiers behind those thickly-banked bocage hedges, as our own tank commanders would readily testify) or back into the town, where their presence could have made all the difference to the CLY, who were trapped in the narrow streets without the riflemen stirrup-hangers who had been trained to work with them in just such conditions. Anyway, none of these things happened; instead, when my truck had just

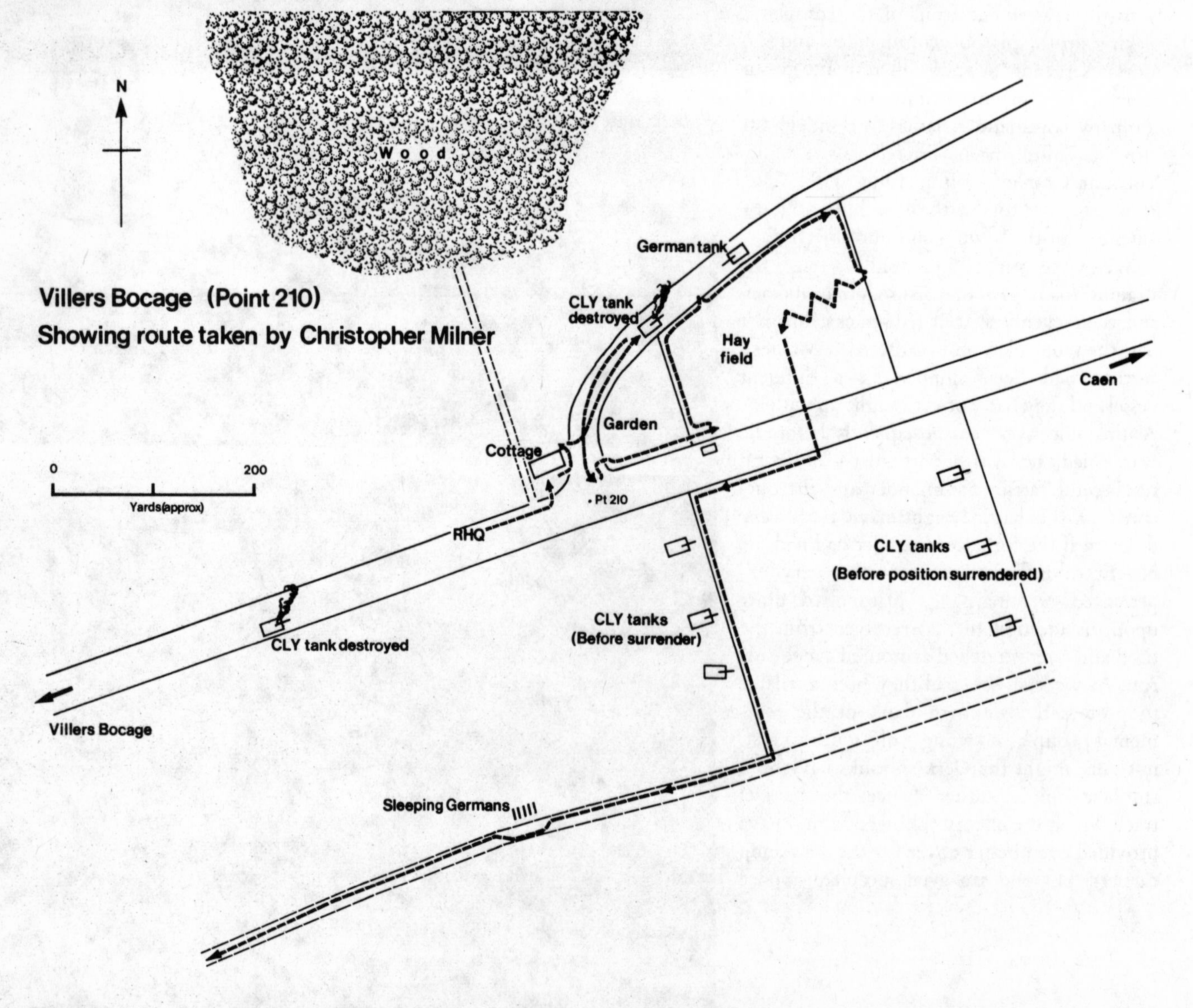

Far left, top: Villers Bocage in ruins after the battle.

Above: A Panther burns.

passed the rearmost CLY tank (which was facing forward, suspecting nothing) at the foot of the rise, the tank was hit and burst into flames. As we passed the next one (it had a high turret and was a 17 pounder) perhaps a 100 yards further on, it swung round and began to engage whatever had shot-up its neighbour from the south. A minute later we dismounted by the cottage at the lane junction which lies at point 210, to join a shaken 'O' group in circumstances which had changed utterly since it had been called.

There followed a period of physical inactivity on point 210, whilst the enemy attended first of all to the three motor platoons by cutting the road behind us and then trundling back towards Villers Bocage, shooting up vehicles and riflemen section by section, with only the company's two 6 pounder anti-tank guns able to offer even a measure of resistance; which, I learned afterwards, they did with considerable bravery but with little effect upon the German Tigers and Panthers which joined battle with the two CLY squadrons in the town.

The force on point 210 consisted, then, of Colonel Cranley and his Tac HQ, one depleted squadron of Cromwells, a gunner OP officer, OC 'A' Company (James Wright) and all his officers (except the one commanding the leading platoon, who had run back to his men and was, I think, killed with them), the mortar section and one section only of riflemen. The CLY tanks had fanned out a little, but apart from intermittent harassment by shellfire, the Germans left us to our own devices whilst they dealt with the main body of the regimental group. We were stonked at intervals during the morning and suffered one particular casualty which grieved us very much – a young officer who had only just joined and as I recall it, one whose mother later could never really accept that he had no chance to live because he was captured still alive and for months afterwards she wrote the most tragic letters to me, trying to believe that he had not died. Anyway, the infantry section I put on the southern side, covering what I discovered afterwards was the track parallel to the main road along which the German tanks had been shadowing us, though no more appeared on our particular high point until a little later. I set myself to cover the lane running east north east from point 210 and the mortar sergeant covered the track leading into and out of the wood directly to our north. I was behind a small cottage. It was along this track that a peasant woman walked up to us, was detained as a possible spy, but after an hour or so she slipped away. Was she a spy?

Not long after, a CLY tank, edging forward around the bend along my lane, was hit and the wounded crew baled out having suffered the driver killed. They seemed to be pinned down so I crawled along the road and helped them to get back to the comparative safety of the cottage. I then lay on watch again, armed with a sten gun, my pistol and, I half remember, a German Luger without

Normandy Obstacles. Taking every advantage of the natural defensive features of the Normandy countryside, the Germans make dugouts in hedgerows, build concrete strong points for mortar crews in orchards, use farm workers as decoys and employ many other tricks in an attempt to trap Allied troops and armour or to hide from our observers their strengths and dispositions. (Reproduced by kind permission of the Illustrated London News).

any ammunition. Suddenly there was a rumble of tanks from the east and as I darted round to the front of the cottage I was astonished to find that the tank shooting seemed to have ended and that some officers in black berets were standing about talking to one or two of our officers in the middle of the main road. Since there had been no shooting and everyone seemed very friendly I took them to be members of the Royal Tank Regiment and stepped out to join in the conversation, only to be frozen in my tracks when I realised that they were German tank crews.

I immediately turned and didn't run back where I'd come from but ducked into a little garden to the left and ran up inside the hedge in the direction of the enemy, not of our own people in Villers Bocage. I went through a little gate beyond the garden still just inside the hedge with one of the German officers running along the road parallel to me shouting "Englishman surrender! Englishman surrender!" Fortunately he stopped after about fifty yards and talked to another officer who'd just arrived from the German side in a Volkswagen and at this stage I decided that it was about time I died a hero's death and so I stood up and levelled my sten gun at the two of them, at pretty well point blank range over the top of the hedge, took careful aim and pressed the trigger. But of course, like so many sten guns, it decided not to work and just had the effect of sobering me up! I concluded that perhaps it wasn't a good thing after all to draw attention to myself in this way; so I turned left up the inside of a hedge, which was actually running due north, and crept quietly along until to my horror I saw a German boot sticking out of it; I thought my number was up. However, creeping up very carefully and slowly I was relieved but disconcerted to find that the leg in the boot belonged to a dead German soldier.

Keeping low down under the lee of the hedge (which like most in the Bocage was on top of a three foot high bank) I turned right, round the northern edge of this little hayfield, found a gap and decided that the best thing to do was to make a break for it, since I could memorise the map of the district. If I could cut across this lane (which was the same one that I had been guarding previously) I could then make my way back to our own lines through the large wood which lay to the north. I gingerly let myself down the bank on the other side feet first and peeked to my right, only to find that I was about twenty yards from the muzzle of a German tank's gun which, had I thought a bit more care- carefully, would have been the one which knocked out the Cromwell whose crew I had helped a little earlier. Very fortunately (and

The GOC, Major General Verney, in his scout car near Lille.

not for the last time that day) nobody seemed to notice me, so I pulled myself back up the bank, through the hedge, and crouching down, thought again. I had now been on three sides of the hayfield and it only left the fourth side. I had a brain-wave that perhaps the best thing to do was to climb up into one of the trees which grew out of the bank and make myself inconspicuous there until darkness fell and perhaps I could then get out and return to our lines.

So I crawled, by this time on my belly, round the outside of the field and found a suitable place to lever myself up to the bank top and look through the bottom of the hedge to see what was happening the other side, that is to say in the direction of the German lines – only to find that I was frustrated yet again, because in the middle of that field there had just arrived a German troop of guns, which was busily digging itself in and would obviously make my life uncomfortable from the noise and the blasts, or might take it upon itself to notice me and that would be that.

All this time there had been rumblings and shouts along the main road, but for some extraordinary reason, although the hedge on the main road side was not very high, no one seemed to look into my field. Anyway, it seemed the only thing to do was to somehow stay there and remain inconspicuous, so I gradually wormed my way along a zig-zag course, in order that someone passing by the end of my track in the hay (which wasn't very high – about one foot six) wouldn't be able to look along my little belly track and see where I was. I stopped in about the middle of the hayfield and lay still to think things over. By this time, I suppose, it must have been early afternoon and I started wondering what had happened to everybody else.

Not very surprisingly I wasn't the only person thinking along these lines, because I hadn't been in this position very long when there was a wizz and an explosion and a smoke shell landed quite near me, followed by another one and then a whole smoke screen laid itself across the middle of my little field, probably some excellent RHA gunners who were obviously doing their best, although rather too late, to give us some protection behind which we could withdraw. Anyway the shells landed and it was difficult not to cough an awful lot, they gradually gave up and all was peaceful. It was a nice fine afternoon, the sun was shining and I suppose I went to sleep for a bit. The only snag was that I was incredibly hungry and not a little thirsty, because I don't remember if I had a water bottle; if I had, there was precious little in it. At any rate I survived this tedious afternoon and evening and at last it began to get dark and I started to crawl slowly towards the main road again, that is to say towards the south side of the field. My plan was now to wait until all was clear, dash across the main road, over the intervening field to the parallel track (that is to say the Panther tanks' track) and, once again remembering the map, turn back in a westerly direction towards Villers Bocage and try to take a course which would bring me round the south side of the town instead of the north – or into the town itself if that was where our own troops were.

At last, perhaps around midnight, when the Germans decided that they might as well have a rest, there was a lull with no vehicles passing and fortunately it was dark without, as far as I can remember, much in the way of a moon. So I was able to sprint across the road, dive into the hedge on the far side and creep along the inside of the hedge until I hit the track. No one seemed to have spotted me or took any notice so I stood up and walked gingerly along the grass track, back towards the town, which was perhaps a mile and a half away. Suddenly I heard a very odd noise, surprisingly like several people snoring and in point of fact I was quite right, it was snoring and it came from a section of German soldiers who had dug a broad shallow trench, wrapped themselves in their blankets and, having piled their arms beside the trench, were all sound asleep. I had no idea where their sentry was but I was lucky because I didn't spot the piled arms until I was perhaps twenty five yards away. Anyway, I crept past and after a while found myself coming into a farm-yard. I don't think that even a dog barked, if it did it didn't take much notice of me and the great thing was that I found a trough full of drinkable water and I remember taking off my beret (which had been rendered pretty well waterproof by the combination of grease and sweat in my hair over a year or two) and it held water remarkably well. I had an extremely good drink.

It was still uncanny to find no one about. However, I pressed on and came to the railway sidings on the south side of the town, across which I had to go in order to reach the far side and take the road back the way we had come early the previous morning. Then another astonishing thing occurred, because a number of shells started to fall on the British side of the town, followed not long afterwards by a number of shells on the German side of the town, yet so far as I could tell neither army had any troops there by way of targets. After a while things calmed down and I continued on my way unmolested, across the railway tracks and would certainly have been spotted immediately if there had been anybody about, but there didn't seem to be any civilians around either. At last I reached the western side of the town and I remember walking judiciously along the side of the road until I came to some tank tracks leading into a field. So I turned into it, not quite knowing whether they were our tracks or those of the enemy and tried to work out which they were without coming to any clear decision. At any rate there were no tanks or vehicles around, so I went back on to the road and continued walking along the south side where at this point there seemed to be a fairly high bank which provided a certain amount of shadow, because I had a feeling that there was a moon getting up by now.

Below: Aunay-sur-Odon from the south.

Above: Cromwells of the Skins being prepared for battle.

Suddenly (as they say in the books) I froze to the ground because I was challenged, and to this day I can't be sure whether it was a German or a British soldier, because the words if you drop an "H" are absolutely identical if you want someone to stop – "alt"! After a second call I still wasn't sure, so I scrambled as fast as I could up the bank, through a fence, dashed down the side of a hedge and was just in time to fling myself into it as a Verey light went up and obviously the soldier had called one of his mates and they were starting to investigate where I was. Having lain in this spot for a little while and having decided that they were going back to

Orders Groups were held to pass on the details of 'Operation Bluecoat'.

their sentry post, I went on back towards our lines, aiming to get on to the main road at a suitable distance along it – alternatively lying up for a quarter of an hour and then creeping along and listening very carefully in case I heard any sounds. Then, as dawn was really starting to break, I heard some noises in a farm house and so gave it a wide circuit and eventually came on to the blessed road, by which time it was daylight. Still no one saw me apparently, or challenged me and, rounding a bend, at last I saw what I had been looking for and that was part of our own brigade and its vehicles. I remember that I turned off down a side track and the next thing I found that I was amongst a regimental cook-house and was cadging a large billy-can full of bacon, plus a mug of tea.

So that was my battle of Villers Bocage, not very glorious I'm afraid and yet of any twenty-four hours in my life I can think of none which I can recall so clearly as I can those hours, which photographed themselves in my mind so that now, telling the story God knows thirty years later, I can see every yard of the route which I followed and every episode as clearly as if it had happened last year'.

The Enemy

The Tiger tank which caused the initial carnage was commanded by Ober Sturmfuhrer SS Michel Wittman, who knocked out 25 vehicles in that one engagement to add to his already incredible tally of 119 Soviet tanks destroyed during his service on the Russian front! It was an exploit which 'almost made a legend of the man who held up an entire armoured division and contributed not insignificantly to the events which followed' Wittman was killed shortly after this engagement. (Profile *AFV Weapons Book No 48* by P. Chamberlain and C. Ellis.)

The 'Skins' join the Division

'Fare thee well Inniskilling! Fare thee well for a while
To all your fair waters and every green isle!
And when the war is over we'll return again soon
And they'll all welcome home the Inniskilling Dragoon'.

(Last verse of 'The Inniskilling Dragoon').

On July 29th the 4th County of London Yeomanry were transferred to 4th Armoured Brigade to amalgamate with their sister regiment the 3rd CLY, because there were no longer enough reinforcements to keep both Regiments up to strength. 4th CLY had been with the Division since 1942 so it was a sad parting. Their place was taken by the 5th Royal Inniskilling Dragoon Guards newly arrived from England. They were soon to be in action as Operation 'Bluecoat' was about to begin. The initial aim of the British 2nd Army was to capture Mont Pincon, south of Aunay-sur-Odon, so within two days of joining the Division the 'Skins' were in battle for the first time since Dunkirk. As their Regimental history explains they felt very much the new boys:

'The column of new tanks bearing the freshly painted divisional and brigade signs, the desert rat and the stag's head, made their way into harbour about Juaye Mendaye, some four miles to the south of Bayeux, to take over from the Sharpshooters. "What mob are you?" inquired a bearded and grimy visage looking over the top of a scarred and battered turret, "Never 'eard of yer!" remarked the face after explanations had been offered, and with that devastating comment it sank back into the dark and oily depths. In this distinguished company, where highly coloured corduroy trousers, brilliant pullovers and gaudy scarves were de rigeur – where, it was rumoured, the sand of the desert still lurked in shoes and ears – the 5th Royal Inniskilling Dragoon Guards still had their spurs to win'. (The 5th Royal Inniskilling Dragoon Guards, by Maj Gen R. Evans, CB, MC.)

A Troop Leader's View
What was it like to be a troop leader in that newly joined regiment? Brigadier Henry Woods, MBE, MC, who was then a young troop leader in 'C' Squadron, recalls his first action:

'After the breakout from the Normandy beaches 7th Armoured Division advanced almost due north from the area of St Pierre-sur-Dives (SW of Caen). The movement began on August 16th 1944, and the divisional axis of advance was developed through Livarot, Lisieux and Montfort, being directed towards the lower reaches of the Seine. During the night 26th/27th 5 Innis DG harboured in the area of Bonneville Appetot, and during the morning of the 27th, C Squadron attempted to advance north on Bonneville in thickish country very like the bocage of the beach head fighting. Tiny fields and orchards, thick hedgerows and small copses made the country very small, and in many of the fields were fine herds of cattle. Alive, they suggested rich milk, fine butter and Camembert cheese as a welcome addition to compo rations. Dead, the sickening stench from their bloated bodies permeated everything even the tea one drank and the food one ate. To all who fought in Normandy, the smell of death lives longest in the memory.

B Squadron of the Skins forming up for an attack near Aunay-sur-Odon.

Between noon and 2 pm B Squadron passed through C and advanced into the village of Bonneville Appetot and out on two routes leading north and north west. About a mile out on the northern route 3 Tp, B Sqn ran into trouble. Picture them moving forward across a large open common, with a long wood on the right and some small fields and farm buildings on the left, beneath a bright summer sky. The trees, hedgerows and grass are lush in the late summer, and looking north the country slopes gently downwards in a series of wooded ridges. Beyond one of these – in fact about six miles away, the River Seine flows between Rouen and Le Havre. As the leading tank rumbles to the corner of the hedgerow near the farm house – the driver's next bound – the white dust streams away from the tracks and seems to float momentarily before dispersing on the wind. Suddenly, there is a sharp crack like a large nutcracker smashing an enormous walnut. At the same moment the leading tank lurches, a bright flash winks on the right front of the turret. With gathering speed the tank jinks off the road, crashes through the hedgerow to the left and then right to the corner of the orchard by the farm.

On the radio the set phrases of a SITREP uttered in staccato tones reveal the urgent crisis of the moment. Though the leading tank has been hit on the corner of the turret which is jammed, the crew are unhurt. The rest of the troop have also moved rapidly to

Above: Held up by mines – a group of German POWs can be seen behind the half track on the left of the photo.

Top right: A Panther which was knocked out by C Squadron of the Skins south of Canville whilst supporting the 5th Wiltshires (part of 43rd Division) in their attack on Mt Pincon, August 14th, 1944.

Bottom right: POWs.

fire positions in the same area. Tank commanders are busy searching the area whence the fire came, but at this stage of the war, the enemy are still highly skilled in the tactical siting and camouflage of their fearsome 88mm anti-tank guns, and in the hot summer afternoon, there is no indication of exactly where the gun which fired is or where its inevitable companions might be. A lull descends temporarily while the troop and squadron leaders wrestle with the problem of whether to risk another tank brewed up by moving into the open and drawing fire. The CO is involved and decides that the risk is too much without fire support and covering fire. 2 Lt Bradfield and his crews sit watching.

Meanwhile 1st Tp C Sqn, which I commanded was still just south of the village. Since noon, we have had a hasty sandwich of bully beef and a brew of tea, and I have found time to purchase a chicken, cheese, fresh milk and butter from a small farm. These are now stowed in the left-hand bin above the tracks of my tank. Like soldiers throughout the ages, stowage diagrams and instructions, whether covering personal or vehicle equipment, are more honoured in the breach than the observance, and much of the kit which should be in that bin is festooned around the rear of the turret. Being on a squadron net, we have heard only very garbled and summary reports of what has occurred to B Sqn. But the pause now ends and as C Sqn Leader, Major Ward-Harrison speeds back from the CO's Tac HQ, we troop leaders are summoned over the radio to an 'O' Group. Clutching map-boards, chinagraph pencils and notebooks we double across to the Sqn Leader's scout car. The gist of the orders for me is that 1st Tp is to reinforce B Sqn at once, and to move forward and join up with 3 Tp B Sqn, at which stage I will come under command. A quick glance at the small scale maps (all we have) does not give me the truth about the lie of the land north of the village, and with hindsight I did not then realise than 3 Tp B Sqn was well over the crest and on a forward slope. Urged on by an angry demand from Sqn HQ to know why I am not on the move, I give very hasty orders to my crew commanders, shout "mount" and 1st Tp are soon rolling in column through the village. As we clear the houses I order the troop to deploy "two up", which means two Cromwells supported in the second rank by one Cromwell and the Sherman 17 pdr Firefly. My tank is left forward, and we are almost shaken out into formation as we cross the crest.

There is a violent flash on the front of the right forward Tp Cpl's tank, and it stops. Within seconds it is clearly "brewed up", as smoke wraiths trickle from the engine and the turret. The crew pop out like champagne corks, seeming to flow down the front and sides to the ground as though diving feet first. We all realise our exposed position, but luckily I am able to halt the rear two tanks so that they are hull-down on the crest. I switch onto the inter-comm and order the driver to wheel hard left and get back behind the crest, jinking as we go. We are almost back to the crest, when suddenly there is a jarring thud,

the driver reports that all his controls have gone and I look down to see smoke wisping through the engine covers. We are also "brewed up", and there is nothing for it but to bail out. As I leap from the turret which is still traversed over the rear, my beret comes off, but I catch it on my little finger before I reach the ground. My Tp Cpl's crew are under cover behind a small bank beside the road, atop of which is a wayside wooden Calvary and we double across to join them. As we go the crackling hiss of machine gun bullets spurs us on. Panting, we fling ourselves down behind the tank, and for a few seconds there is peace, shattered by first of all my Tp Cpl's tank and then my own roaring into flames. No one has yet spotted where the enemy guns are, but at least except for two minor wounds, we are all alive.

Apart from my rage at losing two tanks in less than a minute, all those excellent farm supplies have gone west, and the chicken is burnt beyond recall. Now it is time for more action, and I evict my troop sergeant from his tank, and he takes the dismounted crews back into the village to Sqn HQ. The CO decides not to try to advance due north by the obviously well-covered approach, but to develop a thrust on the other route and outflank this opposition. The sun is well down in the west by the time that the opposition has withdrawn and the Regiment finally reaches Bonneville. At that stage our advance to the lower Seine finished, and 7th Armoured Division was pulled out to rejoin 12 Corps for the great swan up to Belgium. We never did taste that chicken!'

Belgium ~ 'You are Quite Welcome'

General Verney, GOC 7th Armoured Division, arriving in Ghent in a Staghound Armoured Car, September 8th, 1944.

F225524

Monty gives his orders. Gen Verney GOC, Seventh Armoured Division is on the right of the picture.

An Even Greater Welcome
The wonderful welcome which the British troops had received in France was even more enthusiastic when they crossed the frontier into Belgium. As the War Diary of the 3rd Regiment, Royal Horse Artillery commented: 'Even more flowers, larger and better fruit – an even greater welcome'. There were flags everywhere, on the churches, on the houses and many banners hung across the roads with such inscriptions as 'Vive les Anglais!' Welcome!', 'Well Done!' and even one which must have been the understatement of the war, reading 'You are quite welcome'! I have chosen two incidents from this period of the advance, first the liberation of the old city of Ghent by tanks of A Squadron, 5th Royal Tank Regiment and second, the defence of the bridge at Wetteren over the River Schelde, by 4th Field Squadron, Royal Engineers. Both have in common the tremendous friendship shown to the Desert Rats by Belgian civilians everywhere. What is equally heart-warming is the way in which this friendship has stood the test of time and is still as strong today as it was over thirty years ago.

Full Speed for Ghent! The Ghent Force
At mid-day on September 4th, 1944, General Verney, GOC 7th Armoured Division, warned a special force to prepare for what he hoped would be 'the last long gallop for Ghent'. The size of the force to be sent had to be worked out very carefully as the petrol used by the Division had been averaging over 70 000 gallons a day – that was seventy lorry loads. So it was out of the question to move more than a composite brigade on that final seventy mile dash. The Ghent Force, as it was called, was commanded by a reduced Main Divisional HQ and comprised the 11th Hussars, Main HQ 22nd Armoured Brigade, 5th RHA, 5th Innis DG, 5th RTR, 1/6th Queens and 'A' Company 1st RB. Extra petrol lorries from 8th Hussars, 1st RTR and the Rifle Brigade accompanied the force. The remainder of the Division stayed in their positions around Bethune and did their best to keep the Centre Line open.

The Force Advances
That afternoon the Cherry Pickers led the force out, their initial objective being to secure a crossing over the river at Audenarde, scene of Marlborough's famous battle. Whilst the force was advancing members of the Belgian resistance were themselves in action. One of these resistance fighters, 'From' Fromont, takes up the story:

'Tanks on the way to Ghent from Audenarde, September 4th, 1944 at 1600 hours. We of the Belgian resistance had had some days of hard work before then rounding up pro-German civilians and taking them to a safe place called "The Pinte" where they could be protected from the rest of the population and also to stop them from giving information to the Germans about Allied troop movements, as it soon became well known to the civilian population that the British were on their way.

I return for a moment to the day before – September 3rd at about 1900 hours – when a large German patrol consisting of one officer, two sergeants and about 60 troopers, all on bicycles and heavily armed with automatic weapons and hand grenades, passed through St Denis-Westrem on the main road from Ghent to Courtai. We, the resistance men, only had revolvers and we were only seven in all, but we had a very fast car. The driver, a resistance officer, a sergeant of the Belgian Army and myself, followed the Germans at a safe distance. After a while they turned back, so we quickly had to leave the main road and take a side track into Lathem–St Martin, where to our great surprise we saw a company of about three hundred Germans, all armed, taking a rest in a field. No need to say that we passed them at full speed! We returned to St Denis-Westrem that night and had to send many civilians home, they were still standing along the road carrying flowers and fruit for the incoming Allied forces!

The next day we took some German soldiers prisoner as well as more pro-German civilians and moved all of them to "The Pinte". At about 1300 hours I went to take a rest in the house of a friend – Madame de Volqelaire. Her first husband had died during the 1914-1918 War and her second husband died in 1940 in action; he was a major in the Belgian Army. She herself, although not a full time member of the Resistance, helped us whenever she could. She woke me up at about 1600 hours telling me the best news I had ever received, the news that we had been waiting for all of those last four years – "The English are here!" I ran out of the villa, down the lane, onto the main road, and there they were! Tanks were taking up positions to defend the cross roads – The Pinte – St Denis – Westrem. I remember very well that there were only seven tanks, later I got to know that this was all that was left of "A" Squadron, 5th Royal Tank Regiment, the rest being out of action along the road from Audenarde.

The first officer I spoke to – my English was all right since my late mother was a Scot and we always spoke English at home – was Lt Roy Dixon, now Director of British Army Aviation. I offered my services, he took me down to a Cromwell tank with a short gun-barrel and introduced me to Captain Stuart Jones. All the men were dirty and very tired. Captain Jones accepted my services, but I felt he did not trust me! Quite right too, I would not have done so in his place, but I thought "Time will tell".

September 5th. Our work as resistance men went on as before. The civil population from Ghent about 5 miles away came down to greet the liberators! That afternoon a motorised German 88 came from Courtai. One of the tank commanders, Lt Zoeftig, tried to fire at it, but as civilians were running about all over the place he could not do so without harming them. After a while the 88 came back along another road and later its crew destroyed it and escaped.

On the morning of September 6th a German railway gun fired one shell which struck a pole next to the tank belonging to the Squadron Sergeant Major of "A" Squadron who was very badly hurt and died that same afternoon. Lt Zoeftig, having been told that 300 German troops were camped at Lathem-St Martin got permission to go and get them – but only with one tank. I went with him and Lt Zoeftig arranged with a Belgian Major named Ham, for the capitulation of these Germans. Their small arms went to the Resistance and the Germans were marched down the road to St Denis–Westrem, parked in a field and later were marched to the nearby village of Nazareth. The Resistance patrolled the road to Ghent, but no Germans were to be seen. Captain Stuart Jones risked his own tank and a Humber

THE TOWN COUNCIL
and THE CITIZENS
of GHENT

express their real veneration and gratitude to the gallant

Officers and Men of the 7th Armoured Division

who, on the 6th September 1944, delivered our City from the bold and odious German enemy.
Glorify the heroic war-acts of the 7th Armoured Division on the African and the European continent,
Bow deeply for the sacrifices brought by the 7th Armoured Division for the liberty of our City and our Country,
Salute in the 7th Armoured Division the spirit of freedom and opposition against all kind of tyranny of the English people, who, alone resisted, in 1940, the strongest enemy and so made possible the final victory.

Long live the 7th Armoured Division !

Ghent, the 6th September 1945.

Burgomaster:

Town Council:

Town Secretary:

The Ghent Citation. Presented to the 5th Royal Tank Regiment in honour of their being the first Regiment to enter Ghent.

The Ghent Medallion, presented to the Division, now on show in the RAC Tank Museum, Bovington Camp, Dorset.

Scout car to go into Ghent. I went with him on the tank, he riding on the "Dingo" driven by Sergeant Harry Hampton. We went as far as the Town Hall where he drank champagne with the town officials, whilst we stayed outside trying to keep the people away. After that we returned to the crossroads at St Denis–Westrem. We took some more prisoners and that same day the seven tanks of "A" Squadron, all went into Ghent to take up positions at St Pieters station and other important places on the north side of the city. The day after, September 7th, the tanks went up to the industrial area named "Rabot". There Captain Butler was badly wounded and died later in a Military Hospital at Eeklo and was buried at the Canadian Cemetery in Odeqem and still rests there. In that industrial area the 51st Highland Division joined in to fight the Germans.

Many people think that it was the Poles who liberated Ghent, but the real liberator was Captain Stuart Jones with his "Dingo" and his one tank'.

Recollection of the Liberation

One of the seven tank commanders, Lt Ted Zoeftig also recalls the first moments of liberation:

'My own special recollections – for what they are worth – concern that time as we came towards the centre of the town. People were lining the streets in thickening numbers. Flowers were beginning to heap up over our blanket rolls and over the engine plates, the lap-gunner's gun and against the turret. But the stream of people swished forward like a stream of silver sound which flowed and surged into the square, behind us and around us. It surged and swirled with a single continuous sound of happiness and joy, a chorus of exhultation which focussed on us, around us and now so it seemed, above us. The bells were ringing. In our sorry clothing, oil stained and petrol washed; tank track guards dented and holed, tow ropes hanging loose, scarecrow replicas of regimental dress, we tried desperately to be "The Liberators". We kept our positions, we remained alert for an unlikely sniper, the gunner at his gun, the driver cautiously keeping the tank moving, the wireless operator on watch and the troop leader vigilant. But this swelling silver sound was music. This must indeed have been the music that returning victorious legions of Rome had heard. A momentary approbation to forget, for a space, our soldiers' role. Now all the simple plain young men crewing the tank were enveloped – embraced – possessed, by the God-sent thanks. The tracks squeaked and stopped rolling. The surges of golden faces and hands swept up to us, and, for a moment, over us. Then for a short while the spirit of this brooding antique town claimed the five of us. Bedecked like natives of Hawaii, gifts were thrown, kisses given, treasured bottles of liqueurs, kept from the dark days of 1940 for just this longed for moment, were thrust home into our hands. Small wonder that none who experienced it

Lt Ted Zoeftig's tank with German officer prisoners sitting on the back. It led the column of some 300 German soldiers whom he captured at Lathem St Martin.

can forget or escape one single facet of that crystallised moment of glory'.

The Defence of the Wetteren Bridge, Belgium (September 5-6, 1944)

Fighting Soldiers First
In any phase of war the Royal Engineers are worth their weight in gold, because there are always far too many jobs to be done which call for the sappers' special know-how and expertise. Therefore, it is unusual for them to be required to fight as infantry soldiers. They are of course trained for this task first and foremost and have on numerous occasions proved their prowess. The defence of the important bridge at Wetteren, over the River Schelde, was one such occasion.

The Battle in Outline
Wetteren lies to the east of Ghent and the bridge there had been partly damaged by a German demolition party. 4th Field Squadron, Royal Engineers, was given the dual task of repairing the bridge and of defending it. They started work, but hardly had they begun, when they were attacked by a reinforced company of SS troops, supported by heavy mortars and anti-tank guns. A fierce fight ensued which lasted all night and most of the next day. Tanks of C Squadron, 5th Royal Inniskilling Dragoon Guards finally arrived on the scene to tip the scales, but in the meantime the sappers had fought magnificently, defending the bridge against repeated enemy attacks. This is the story of their battle.

September 5th, 1944
A Squadron 5DG reached Wetteren at about midday on the 5th and at once approached the bridge. It was a three span affair on timber piles, the centre span being a lifting span, pivoting at the near bank with the aid of a counter weight. This span was found to be raised and the enemy were evidently intending to demolish the bridge, indeed, they had already made two unsuccessful attempts.

Major Fitzgerald, DSO, the OC of 4th Field Squadron, was with the tanks and quickly realised that the bridge must be lowered so that our infantry could get across and clear the enemy from the far bank. So, whilst the tanks put down covering fire, he dashed across the open square, together with some local civilians and climbed on to the raised portion of the bridge – their combined weight caused the span to drop into place. This bold move was carried out under the very noses of the enemy who were taken completely by surprise. Sappers then rushed forward and put some timber on to the damaged superstructure of the bridge, which allowed the infantry to cross and to clear the immediate area around the bridge taking a good many prisoners. The sappers then repaired the bridge sufficiently so as to allow the tanks and some armoured cars of the Eleventh Hussars to cross and to carry on with the advance.

The commander of 22nd Armoured Brigade then decided that, because of a drastic shortage of infantry, the sappers

General Verney arriving at the Ghent Town Hall, September 8th, 1944.

would have to defend the bridge as well as reinforcing it sufficiently so that it would take all the remaining Divisional traffic. Major Fitzgerald wirelessed back for his squadron and they motored up to Wetteren. Later, at his Orders group, he detailed a party to repair the bridge and then decided to take his troop leaders out on a recce to look for suitable defensive positions – it was now about 1600 hours.

Civilians Report 'Enemy!'

Civilians began to report that masses of German troops were approaching Wetteren from all directions, so Major Fitzgerald sent out recce parties down the various approach roads to the town. Sergeant Eric Morrall, MM, BEM, was in command of one of those recce patrols and now takes up the story:

'Once the centre span of the bridge had been lowered into position by Major Fitzgerald with the assistance of some brave local civilians, my troop, 1 Troop, under the command of Lt Jim Turpin (better known as "Dick") was called forward to defend the bridge.

I was first ordered by Lt Turpin, to recce the main road running north east from Wetteren and parallel with the river, where it had been reported by the local inhabitants that an enemy patrol was approaching the town. After about a mile or so we sighted the enemy by the river bank, heading in our direction. Small arms fire was exchanged and they withdrew, with the loss I believe of one killed. Later I was re-called by Lt Turpin, to the bridge where our Troop were digging in.

That evening all was quiet and everyone apart from the usual lookouts and guards were getting a little shut-eye. I was with Dicky Turpin in our troop headquarters in an old brickworks, bedding down between piles of bricks and chimney pots. Suddenly, during the night, small arms fire opened up and shortly afterwards two wounded sappers were brought in, one, the youngest lad of the troop, had been shot several times. I placed the poor lad in my Jeep, telling the driver, Tich Bader, to cross the bridge and take the casualty as quickly as possible to a Mobile Dressing Station (MDS) several miles out of Wetteren. A little later, still in the dark, Tich returned with the wounded lad, saying he couldn't find a way out of the town. The casualty was now asking for me, so Dicky Turpin ordered me to get him urgent medical attention. With the aid of a local civilian, we managed to find our way out of the town by travelling back the way we had come in the afternoon before. After a while we found what we were looking for in the darkness, on the side of the road, the MDS sign lit up in an upturned petrol can. I drove up the drive to a large building with this young lad sprawled across my lap and still losing blood. We got him into the building and to the on-duty Medical Officer only to find that he had just died.

Back at troop headquarters I was reporting the sad news when the enemy attacked again, almost overrunning our forward positions. However, Cpl Crutchley took a Bren gun and dashed forward firing from the hip which completely disorganised the enemy attack and forced them to withdraw. Unfortunately he was hit by a bullet in the head and fell in the open, so Lt Bob Warren, the troop second in command, took the recce car forward and drove it round in front of where L/Cpl Crutchley lay. Whilst he gave covering fire his recce corporal, Cpl Stuckfield and Lt Turpin dashed forward and pulled the wounded man to safety.

Shortly after this the enemy started shelling the bridge area and the town to our rear, but we could not be sure of their gun positions, so I climbed up the stone spiral steps inside the church tower and managed to spot the gun flashes, before beating a hasty retreat down the steps again as the tower received some direct hits! The enemy next opened up with mortar fire and again we were unsure of their location. Lt Turpin went up to 3 Section, to take personal command and to direct their fire. Unfortunately a mortar bomb landed in the section position causing several casualties, Lt Turpin lost a leg and three others were wounded. The next mortar bomb caused even more casualties, virtually writing off the section. Lt Turpin gave orders to find medical attention for his men, saying that a civilian doctor was in attendance at the convent on the south side of the river. These casualties were evacuated under heavy enemy fire with the exception of one sapper, who was rushed into the cellar of a nearby house for safety and left with the women and children who were sheltering there. The enemy were now attacking in greater strength, also their snipers were very active, keeping us pinned down. It looked as if we were going to be completely over-run and were being driven back house by house. Lt Warren had taken command by now and did a great job directing our fire and forming new defensive positions, but we were really fighting for our lives. Cpl Stuckfield was doing magnificent work with his Bren gun and rallied the defence heedless of personal danger. He moved from house to house firing at the enemy from the hip and it was chiefly due to his courage and determination that their attacks were broken up.

I made an attempt to recover the man from the cellar before it was over-run by the enemy, but the fire, chiefly from snipers, made it impossible. Just as things were looking really bad, a troop of tanks from the 5DG arrived. Lt Bob Warren placed them in position and I dashed forward with one of the tanks and brought back the injured sapper from the cellar. He was also taken to the convent for medical attention.

Things were looking a little brighter now, we had some tanks for support and the houses on the far side of the sports ground where the remaining enemy were located

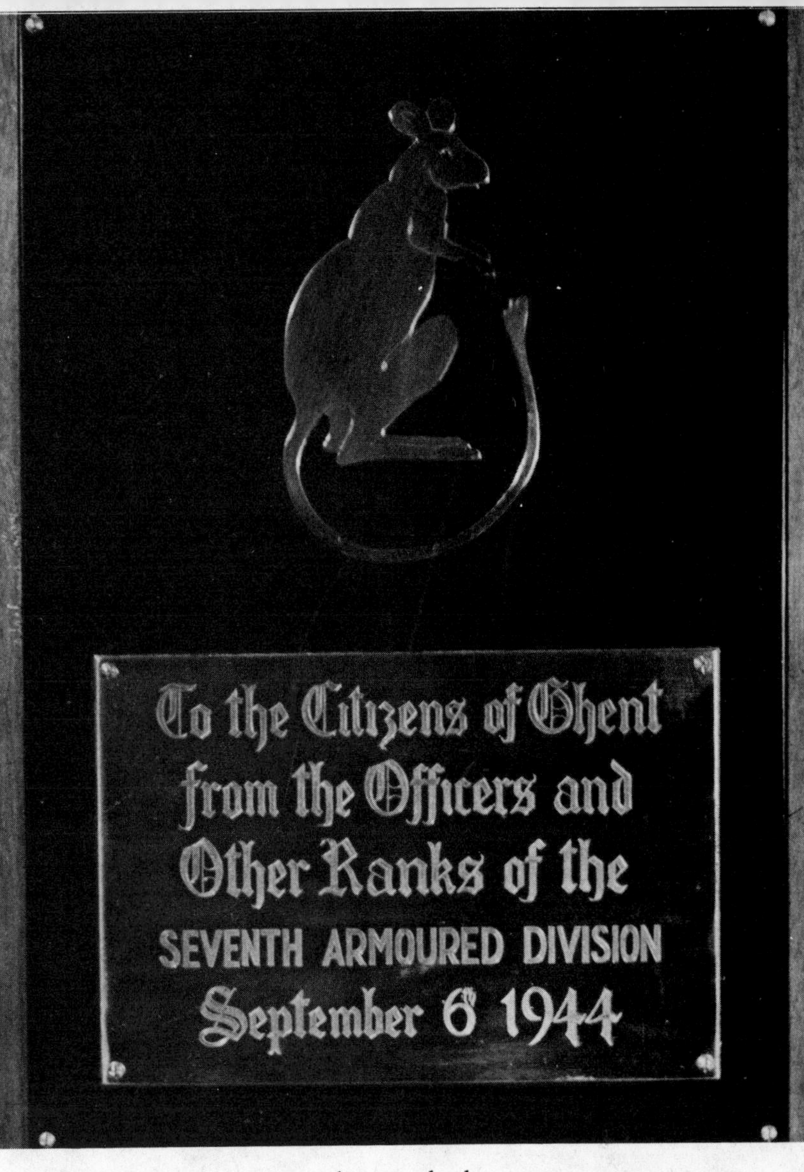

Plaque presented to the citizens of Ghent by the Desert Rats.

Below: A tank of 5 DG at Wetteren – the bridge can be seen to the left rear.

were now under intense fire from our guns. Corporal Stuckfield with 1 Section, some men of Troop headquarters and a sergeant from the anti-tank gun crew, now worked their way in a right flanking movement up to the houses, under the covering fire of the tanks and the recce car and assaulted, wounding two Germans who were in the garden. The majority of the rest of the Jerries were in the cellars and asked to surrender. The first man came out with his hands up, but as the second came out he threw a stick grenade, which fortunately hit the ceiling and did no damage. Meanwhile Lt Warren brought up 2 Section and some men of 3 Troop and we cleared the whole area. In the back of the houses we found twenty-two Germans and nine more were taken from the cellars. These were sent back to Squadron Headquarters. Three heavy mortars were also captured in the garden.

At this point, a company of the Queens arrived, and we combined forces and attacked the final enemy strong point in a powder factory, which was on fire from our earlier efforts. The tanks gave covering fire and the whole area was cleared. A further twenty eight prisoners were captured including the company commander and the pay clerk.

The OC then recalled the troop and we consolidated in our original positions. The infantry returned and thickened up our defences. The time was then about 1500 hours on the 6th. No further trouble occurred after this.'

Aftermath

The story does not end there, for Eric Morrall was destined to meet the brave inhabitants of Wetteren again:

'It had always been my wish to return one day to Wetteren to see if I could recognise any parts of the town which holds such vivid memories for me. An opportunity came my way in August 1970 when my wife Jennie, and I were driving to Germany to spend a holiday with our daughter, Deirdre. So, whilst on the way between Ostend and Brussels, we drove a few miles off our route to visit Wetteren, planning to briefly look around for about half an hour.

Above: A Comet tank of A Squadron 5 RTR outside the Town Hall, Ghent on the first anniversary of the liberation September 6th, 1945. 'From' Fromont is one of the crew (left rear).

Another view close to the bridge in Wetteren.

On arrival in the centre of the town, I asked a Belgian youth if he spoke English and he led me a few yards to his parents' cafe where his mother, Mrs Gisella van de Velde, who spoke good English, invited us in for a chat. After this, we made our way back to our car when we saw a man walking briskly towards us. He introduced himself in very good English as Gustaaf van den Berge, another cafe owner, who had spotted the Desert Rat badge on my car. He asked the purpose of my visit to Wetteren and I said I just wished to see the town again, since I had been there briefly during the war. Once he knew the purpose of our visit, we were invited into his cafe, where we continued our talk over a cup of coffee. During our conversation he said he was about 14 years old when the town was liberated and he mentioned that the British Royal Engineers had been one of the first units to enter Wetteren and then had a battle on their hands to liberate the town from the enemy.

At my request we visited a spot on the other side of the canal where several 1 Troop lads were killed. I located the very spot, showing Gustaaf shrapnel and shrapnel marks still in the side of a house. I then recognised another house where our wounded had been put in the cellar for attention. Gustaaf made enquiries from the lady of the house, who said that they had no cellar, so with that I thought I must have been mistaken. Then this lady's husband appeared at the doorway. He said they had a cellar during the war, but that it had been filled in for safety reasons just after the war. Strangely enough this man asked Gustaaf questions about me and said he had seen me before. So we questioned each other using Gustaaf as an interpreter. He said he was only 13 years old at the time of the fighting when he lived in the cellar of this house with his mother and grandmother. He could remember me coming to the cellar to remove the wounded at the height of the battle.

After this most surprising meeting, we set off to visit the "Kliniek" (Hospital) known to me in 1944 as "The Convent", where a young Belgian doctor and several nuns did wonderful work caring for our wounded, even performing amputations in the middle of the night, also taking care of our dead comrades. On entering the hospital with Jennie, Gustaaf left us inside the main entrance, very soon to return with a nursing

The Last Post being played by the band of Wetteren's Fire Brigade.

nun; we instantly recognised each other – it was Sister Emanuel. Her first words were "You are the English Sergeant who brought your wounded comrades here during the night of the fighting". We had quite a long chat, talking about what happened to this soldier and that soldier. The sad thing was that the young doctor had since died when still quite young. The last I saw of Sister Emanuel during the war, before moving on, was when I was requested to return to the "Kliniek" to identify our dead comrades and good friends, my lads of 1 Troop.

To Gustaaf and Jennie all this was becoming unbelievable, the brief story which I had mentioned only an hour or so earlier, was now unfolding with remarkable evidence. Gustaaf was flabbergasted to think I could remember and select this particular house with the cellar, also remember other points and places of interest after so many years had passed and with the rebuilding of all damaged buildings. Now we were taken back to Gustaaf's cafe to continue our talk and Jennie and I were introduced to several other friends, so our intended half-an-hour's visit developed into an overnight stay as guests of Gustaaf and his family.

Later on I had the pleasure of meeting a young man by the name of Jacques de Vos, an historian, who was obtaining material for a book he was writing about events which took place during the war in the area of Wetteren and Ghent. He said he knew of a Sergeant Morrall of the Royal Engineers, by name only, through a British military book he possessed, which gave an account of the defence and liberation of Wetteren in 1944. Jacques produced the book – Yes! this was it. I did not know it existed, this is still more unbelievable I thought, so I produced my passport to prove to him that I was the ex-Sergeant he was hoping to meet.

Some time after returning home from our holiday, I received an invitation to attend Wetteren's Armistice Church Service on November 11th, 1970. I replied saying that I would do my utmost to attend and on November 10th I left home for Wetteren, informing Gustaaf only a couple of days in advance that I was coming. He was most kind and met me at the railway station in Ghent. Little did I know what the following day had in store for me. It was a most memorable day – a day I shall never, never forget. The photographs show some of the events.

Eric Morrall laying a wreath of Flanders Poppies from the Christchurch British Legion, at the War Memorial in Wetteren.

Programme of Events on November 11/12th 1970 in brief:

08.30 Parade formed up at the Railway Station, consisting of: The Mayor and Members of the Council, Town Band, Fire Brigade and Wetteren's Legionnaires.
08.45 March through the town to the church in the Market Square.
09.15 Laying of Wreaths
09.45 Church Service
10.30 March Past
11.00 Presentation by the Mayor in his Council Chambers
12.00 Champagne Party at Mr L. Van Laey's house
13.00–17.30 Presentation Lunch with the Legionnaires.
19.00 Private Dinner Party (guest of Mr and Mrs Van Laeys)
21.30–02.30 Party at Gustaaf's Cafe.

The end of a most memorable day with very hospitable and friendly people, many whom I am pleased and proud to call my friends. Gustaaf being one of the Very Best, always out to do someone a good turn of a helping hand, a really wonderful chap.

Each year ever since on Armistice Day, I have returned to join my many Belgian friends in paying homage to our fallen comrades. To lay a wreath of "Flanders" poppies on the town's Cenotaph, whilst the "Last Post" is played by the buglers of the Fire Brigade, followed by the one minute's silence, is a very touching and memorable moment. All these ceremonies and parades have a large following led by the Mayor and with members of the Belgian Parliament, the Town Council and officials, representatives from various organisations and departments, with of course a large contingent of ex-service members, the Legionnaires complete with brass band and colourful banners. The dignity and sincerity of the people of Wetteren and their remembrance of the fallen British soldiers is really wonderful. To see the "Flame of Peace" brought forward to the Cenotaph, brought specially from The Unknown Warrior's Tomb in Westminster

Left: Visiting the graves of members of 4th Field Squadron who died in the defence of Wetteren and are buried at the British War Cemetery, Heverlee, near Brussels.

Below: 'Nurse Nightingale' – Sister Emanuel, who is now matron of the hospital at Wetteren and who did such wonderful work looking after the wounded during the battle.

Abbey, makes one feel proud as well as humble.

The next day, I also find very touching as with the help of my very good friend, Jacques de Vos, I visit the British War Cemetery at Heverlee, situated in a beautiful area to the south east of Brussels, to lay a Remembrance cross and poppies on the graves of my comrades, killed in action in the defence and liberation of Wetteren.

In 1971 on one of my visits, I had great pleasure in presenting to the Mayor and the people of Wetteren, a plaque, on behalf of the ex 4th Field Squadron RE, which I made myself and bearing my treasured RE cap badge, which I wore at the time of Wetteren's liberation. Also in 1974 I made another plaque to present to Sister Emanuel (now the Matron of Wetteren's Hospital) better known as "The Angel of Wetteren", to show our appreciation for her wonderful help in attending to our wounded comrades.

To me it is always a great pleasure to return for this special occasion and to be with such generous and good friends.'

Holland~Winter Operations

Men of 9th Battalion, The Durham Light Infantry, fighting in the village of Bakenhoven, the first village to be taken in the attack on January 16th, 1945.

Right: Members of the Tank Troop of Tac HQ 7th Armoured Division taken in Holland during the winter 1944/45.

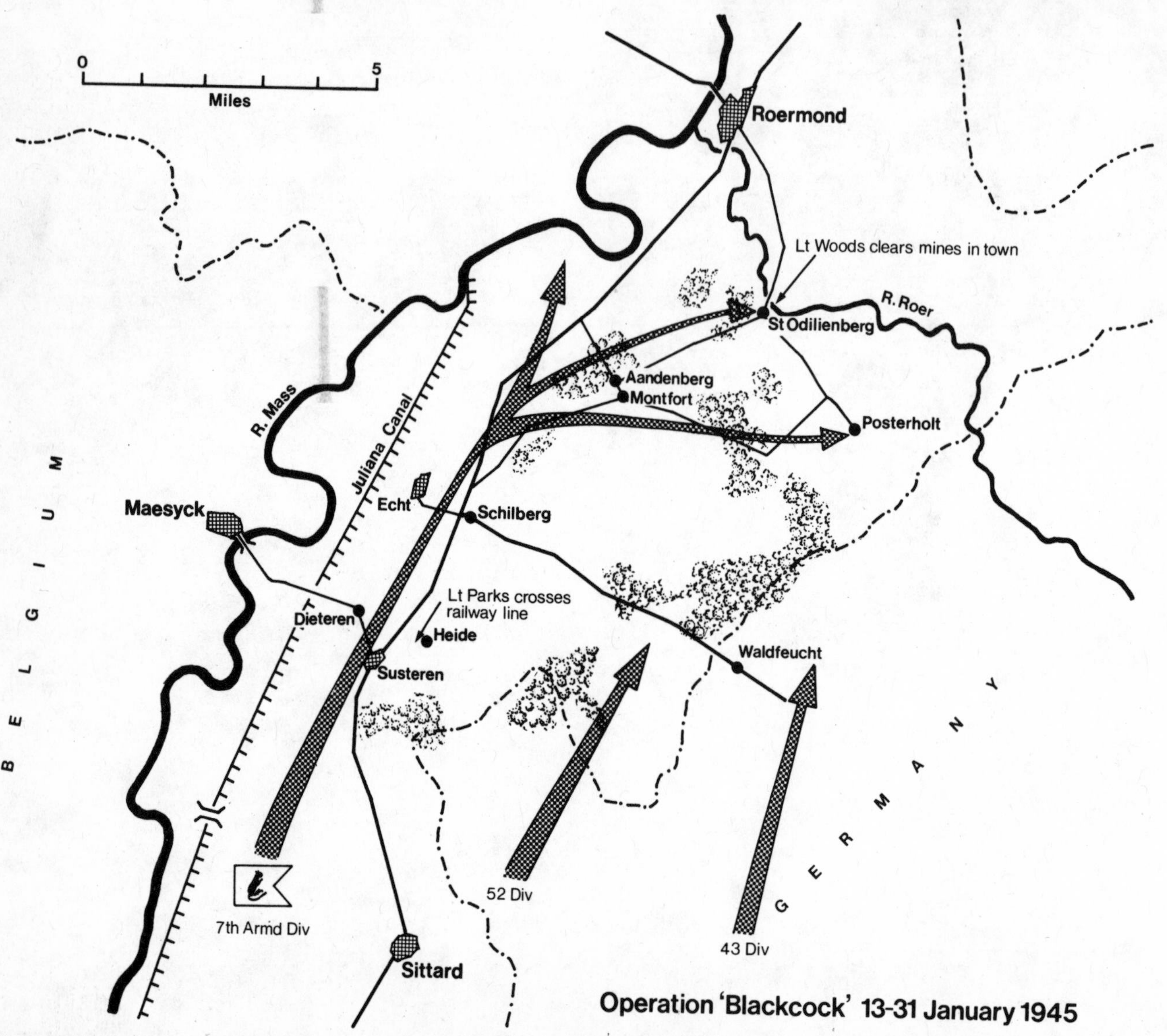

Reorganisation of the Division
In November 1944 the Division was reorganised. 131 Lorried Infantry Brigade lost both the 1st/6th and 1st/7th Queens in exchange for the 2nd Battalion, The Devonshire Regiment and the 9th Battalion, The Durham Light Infantry, both from 50th Division. Also the Division changed commanders and General Verney, who had been GOC since August 4th, 1944, was succeeded by General L O Lyne, DSO. 'Lou' Lyne continued to command the Desert Rats for the remainder of the war.

The Victory of the Roer Triangle – Operation 'Blackcock' (January 16th–24th, 1945)
One of the essential preparations before the final drive to the Rhine was the clearing of the area between the Rivers Maas (Meuse) and Roer by 12 Corps (7th Armoured, 52nd and 43rd Divisions) in an offensive operation called 'Blackcock'. The area, known as the Roer Triangle, was held by two strong German Divisions with at least 160 guns, their defensive positions being both heavily mined and well camouflaged. The weather was dreadful; bitterly cold, snow and ice, indeed the operation had to be delayed for twelve hours due to dense fog – caused by a smoke screen, which had been put down to cover movement on the left flank, freezing in the air!

The Division opened its attack on January 16th and there followed nine days of very fierce fighting before the Triangle was finally cleared. To illustrate the battle I have chosen two excellent sketches from contemporary issues of the *Illustrated London News*, together with two accounts of the action written by troop leaders in 1 RTR and 5 Innis DG.

Alan Parks, now a Lieutenant Colonel commanding HQ Rheindahlen Garrison in the British Army of the Rhine, was then a troop leader in C Squadron 1 RTR.

'During the early part of January 1945 the 1st Royal Tank Regiment had been resting when it became clear that something was afoot. The weather was extremely cold and there was snow about. Each tank was issued with some whitewash and the crews were told to paint their vehicles with it as camouflage. There was not enough whitewash to go round, and this, plus a shortage of brushes, made it an interesting task.

On about January 16th, we were told that the Regiment was to take part in 'Operation Blackcock' which was intended to clear the remaining Germans from the triangle formed by the Rivers Roer and the Maas. A quick look at the map told us that it was rather unattractive tank country with woods, small fields and ditches with plenty of water. On January 18th the Regiment attacked and took Susteren. It was bitterly cold, the tanks slid about on the ice and there was very little protection for the crews. It was a long and tedious day but by nightfall we were in the town which was being shelled by the enemy. As it was intended to push on up the main road to Echt and Schilberg the following day, we all went for orders after dark. On returning I was extremely hungry, but as there were no fires I had to be content with a cold tin of M and V (meat and veg) which my gunner handed to me – there were no electric boiling vessels on tanks in those days.

One of the Signals' lorries of Div HQ in Echt in January 1945. Note the slogan left by the retreating German forces.

The gallant fight at Susteren. B Company 1/5 Queens hanging on grimly in the northern part of Susteren village as they waited for 1st Royal Tanks to get across the Vloed Beek to support them. They were attacked by a battalion of infantry supported by six tanks, but managed to knock out two of them and to hold on until our tanks arrived. (Reproduced by kind permission of the Illustrated London News).

The first spoonful gave me quite a shock as the contents were frozen solid and did not really go down terribly well!

My orders were to take my troop and capture a small village called Heide, just to the east of Susteren and across a railway line. This was to be done at the same time as A and B Squadrons were moving north to Echt and Schilberg. We slept very little that night because of the cold and by first light I was approaching the railway ready for a quick dash through a tunnel under the line which led straight into the village. We were on our own with no infantry, so our intention was to go hell for leather down the lane running through the village. I was surprised when my point tank suddenly came to a grinding halt at the entrance to the tunnel and the commander waved his arms as if something was wrong. A quick look showed me that the whole of the subway under the line was flooded and quite impassable. There seemed nothing for it but to cross over the line on top, so I rushed at the embankment and suddenly found that I was on the line with a vast open space all around me. I realised that I was very vulnerable to any enemy in the area, so decided that I would cross over the line as quickly as possible with my other tanks following. It was an interesting and unusual sensation with the tank tracks catching in the railway lines and me wondering if they would break. Luckily due to the age of our vehicles the tracks were stretched and we soon found ourselves roaring down the far embankment into the comparative safety of an orchard south of the village. Not a living soul or animal was in sight and the thatch of the odd farmhouse was burning merrily as we raced down the village street and took up our posts at the far end. We were pleased to be joined by some infantry shortly afterwards which gave us the opportunity for a long-overdue meal and a brew up.

Subsequently, after Echt and Schilberg had been captured, we moved on towards Posterholt which dominated the River Roer. From a tank man's point of view it was not a great battle, but the closeness of the country offered protection to the enemy and this exercised one's judgement and tactics. Rearguards were left in the form of the odd SP or anti-tank gun together with mining of the roads. One had to be especially alert and all members of the crew played their own vital part. It is interesting to remember that it was my driver, who although driving fast down a road, spotted a string of mines laid across it; pressed hard on the brakes thereby causing the tank to stand on its nose but undoubtedly saved all our lives'.

Another troop leader who took part in Operation 'Blackcock' was Henry Woods, now a Brigadier, who was then commanding 4th Troop in C Squadron of the 'Skins' (5th Royal Inniskilling Dragoon Guards).

'During the Christmas period the Division held their sector with 131 Lorried Infantry Brigade garrisoning the villages on the old Dutch/German border as a line of stray outposts. Elements of the armoured regiments also took part as infantry; B Sqn, 5 Innis DG, garrisoned Susteren/Papenhaven for a week and my troop spent one of the coldest nights I can ever recall as an infantry guard on a bridge site beside the Juliana Canal, the bridge being a jumble of twisted snow-covered steel which disappeared into the ice on the surface of the canal. When the sun rose, red rimmed in the morning, we were numb with cold, and sober, despite the consumption of a jar of rum among twelve men throughout the night. It was a very bitter winter and houses and barns were used for cover and warmth wherever we went. The infantry of the Division started the attack on January 16th, a process of classic "crumbling" to gain the German outpost villages opposite our own. It was not until January 22nd that 5 Innis DG were ordered to advance through the infantry to seize the important road junction town of Montfort, more or less in the middle of the salient, after spending a week at Susteren guarding the right flank of the left hand thrust astride the Sittard-Roermond road. The orders to the Regiment also said that 1/5th Queens would come under command late on January 22nd, to assist the advance and consolidate the gains. A and B Squadrons, each with a motor rifle platoon of A Coy 1 RB, a sapper section and a Valentine scissors bridge, moved off on two axes, B on the left towards Aandenburg and A on the right towards Montfort. C Squadron moved in reserve to the area of Echt. The wind was still bitter and the landscape of black trees in stark contrast to the white snow, appeared gloomy and malevolent. Our column jerked forward in fits and starts, reaching the Echt area soon after dark.

The left forward squadron were already closely engaged with the enemy in Aandenburg, a small village commanding the north approach of any enemy reinforcements to Montfort. The German parachutists who faced us were fighting skilfully and contesting every advance with grim determination, especially the British move into Aandenburg. It was clear that, for the time being anyway, this was the critical area, and our CO, Lt Col Swetenham, lost no time in pushing forward reinforcements to B Sqn. The rest of A Coy 1 RB, and the remaining troops of B Squadron were got forward but still the situation in Aandenburg was touch and go. Not until close on midnight did the 1/5th Queens arrive at Echt, and with great haste A Coy was mounted on C Squadron tanks to be moved to an area as close to Aandenburg as possible without becoming involved in the battle. There were enough tanks there already, and the need was for infantry to cope with the street battle.

The infantry clung on as best they could, looking very cold and miserable, even though the ones on the engine decks were warmer than they had been for many days and nights. The column of tanks without lights, and under a fitful moon often hidden by clouds, lurched into the night along an inferior shell-pocked road through St Frost. This place had been the scene of a short, sharp fight earlier in the day, and amid smouldering houses lay the wreckage of a Rifle Brigade Bren carrier (of the Scout Platoon) and a half-track, as well as a German half-track with four heavy anti-aircraft machine guns

Below: Preparations for Op Blackcock. Crews whitewashing their vehicles to match the snow – not easy with a shortage of both brushes and whitewash!

Bottom: Moving up for Op Blackcock. Tanks of the Division move up complete with whitewash to blend with the snow.

Top: The artificial moonlight battle for Montfort. Tanks and infantry of the Division attacking Montfort seized the outskirts but came up against fierce enemy resistance. The village was eventually occupied during the night of January 23rd/24th, 1945. (Reproduced by kind permission of the Illustrated London News).

Above: Troops of 2nd Battalion, The Devonshire Regiment clearing the town of Echt of German rearguards, January 18th, 1945.

mounted on it. From St Frost our route took us along a forest track, the low branches of the trees which swept over the heads of tank commanders and operators, proving an additional and nerve-wracking hazard to the infantry. In a thin wood about a mile from Aandenburg the column halted and the weary infantry clambered down, soon to disappear into the darkness towards the glow which, with the regular but intermittent crackle and explosion of small arms, grenades, mortars and shells, showed where the fight was at its height.

Meanwhile, for what was left of the night, C Sqn remained in position, peering anxiously to the north, and thus ready to secure the left flank, and our lines of communication to the Montfort/Aandenburg area. In the morning, and in company with A Coy 1 RB, C Sqn carried out a limited advance on the same flank in support of the attack on Montfort carried out by 5 RTR and another battalion of 131 Lorried Infantry Brigade. The tanks and infantry moved forward slowly, as due to the wooded and close nature of the country, with more small fields and groups of farm buildings, it was not easy to deploy, or when the enemy resisted, to bring full fire support to bear. However, in our case there was little enemy resistance.

On January 26th the advance to the Roer continued, and C Sqn were ordered to advance at first light from the Montfort area to St Odibenburg on the Roer itself. We were led by two troops of Recce Squadron and the scout platoon of A Coy 1 RB, on whom the brunt of that day's activities fell. By late afternoon it was clear that an enemy rearguard was well ensconced, aided by extensive minefields around the town. A formal attack was laid on for the following morning, in which the advance was led by two troops of Flails from the Lothian and Border Horse and C Squadron, together with a company of 2 Devons, advanced on the right towards the town. The Flails moved off over the Start Line, about 600m from the first houses, with artillery and tank covering fire, and successfully breached the minefield. 1st and 4th Tps of C Squadron then moved through, with the Devons, and while 1st Tp went straight towards the centre of the town, my 4th Tp swung right down to the road running into the town along the banks of the Roer River.

The infantry slipped quickly along the street, using all the cover, from garden to garden, house to house, room to room, and, with my tank leading, we followed along the road, taking advantage of what cover there was from garden walls. I had not gone more than 200m, when I observed, at the same time as my driver, that the next 100m of road had many little hummocks of snow. That instant we realised that these were mines, and the armoured element halted. Attempts to contact the Devon's platoon on the separate tank/infantry radio were not successful, and so the platoon went on ahead before we could warn them of our (and as it turned out their) predicament. Having reported the reason for delay, I dismounted myself, my driver and co-driver, and ordered the driver and co-driver of the next tank (my Tp Sgt) to come too. On scraping away the snow, we found the dreaded Schu-mines – anti-personnel rather than anti-tank – underneath. We therefore, cleared a gap one tank wide and returned to move the troop through the gap. Meanwhile, enemy mortars and machine guns on the east bank of the river Roer had reacted to our presence and the operation of clearing the mines, in which the rear platoon of the Devons had now joined, was not without adventure. The Germans could see and shoot between the houses, and the infantry had I think two casualties from this fire. It is strange how even in a cumbersome tank winter oversuit one could run at high speed when the Spandaus spoke.

At length the troop moved forward and rejoined the leading Devons platoon in the centre of the town, at the same time meeting the leading tank of 1st Troop which had driven into the town from the south west. It was now plain that the German rearguard, minus a few dead, a few casualties and a small group of very sullen prisoners, had escaped across the river. As we watched the black waters of the Roer sliding past the houses at the end of the street, even an ordinary troop leader could tell that this operation was over. At last we could hope to return to warm barns and houses away from the bitter cold for a short while. We did not of course know that Operation Blackcock was to be our only winter campaign and that our next operation would be across the Rhine itself in the early spring'.

Soon after the successful completion of the Blackcock operation, the Corps Commander, General Ritchie, wrote to GOC Seventh Armoured Division and said:

'I cannot tell you how I admire the really dogged and fine fighting qualities the Division has displayed throughout "Blackcock". Yours was the most important role, for unless you created the breach, the operations could not have developed so well as they did. The Division did many really good things in this operation, but none which I admire more than the determined fighting spirit displayed by both armour and infantry in the operations leading up to the securing of Echt; operations forced through by hard fighting to a successful conclusion in the most adverse conditions of weather in which Blackcock started'.

The Desert Rats certainly had every reason to be satisfied with their efforts. They had destroyed one German division, badly mauled a crack paratroop battle group and gained all their objectives. They could now enjoy a brief rest period before the battle for Germany itself began.

Below: Two surprised Germans are caught in the village of Dieteren by a soldier of 9 DLI, January 16th, 1945.

Bottom: Men of 9 DLI moving through Schilberg together with a column of Churchill tanks January 20th, 1945. Some Churchills were fitted with a flame gun in place of the bow machine gun. The 'Crocodile', as it was called, was a fearsome weapon capable of directing accurately a stream of burning fluid for about 90 yards.

Continental Living

War-torn buildings provided some shelter, although these Riflemen preferred to eat outside.

Where the Living was Easy

It might be imagined by those who fought only in the empty inhospitable deserts of North Africa or the dripping jungles of Burma, that the advantages of combat in civilised surroundings were considerable. But it was not so, civilians are out of place on a battlefield and quickly become homeless refugees. Buildings are reduced to piles of impenetrable rubble prohibiting constructive movement, indeed, the very pattern of civilisation hinders the whole business of war.

What was it like to fight in Europe? I hope that the photographs on the following pages will give some idea of how the Desert Rats fared in their new surroundings.

Homes Various

An armoured division is by definition a mobile formation, constantly on the move, so the vast majority of Desert Rats continued to make their vehicles their homes as they had done so before in the Desert. From time to time it was possible to use buildings but never for very long in any one place.

Food Glorious Food

The introduction of the composite ration pack was probably the most useful addition provided for the Army by the Supply branch, because it made certain that, on most days anyway, every soldier could be guaranteed an adequate, appetising and balanced meal, whether he was in or out of action. The proposal to produce ration packs originated with the BEF in 1939 and by the end of the war most of our Allies were producing similar rations.

Keeping Clean and Tidy

As anyone who has done any camping will tell you the open air life make you lose your inhibitions especially as to where you perform such everyday acts as bathing or having a haircut.

Top left: Some ruins took on a strange beauty such as can be seen in this striking photograph of Aunay-sur-Odon near Mt Pincon in Normandy.

Above: Happy smiles all round on the faces of these French women and children who have just been liberated by the Skins.

Top right: Dead and bloated cattle were another unsavoury feature of war in a civilised environment.

Above: A tank harbour in daylight. Not a manoeuvre to be attempted for any length of time without air superiority, however, on occasions it was essential for refuelling, replenishment or reorganisation.

Miscellany

The photographs which follow are a mixture of people, places and animals which, I believe, speak for themselves in portraying some of the good and some of the bad aspects of soldiering in Europe.

Beer, Glorious Beer!

So that we keep the proper perspective in this survey of Continental living, I have included some photographs dedicated to that most serious subject dear to the hearts of all Desert Rats – strong drink, for example; beer, vino or even zbib. The latter was a lethal, inflammable, corrosive and explosive beverage, popular in Sergeants' Messes. It was normally 95 per cent wood alcohol and burned with a fierce blue flame.

The Charlie Love

Finally, to close this short account of life in war torn Europe, here is a description of that strange phenomenon known as 'The Charlie Love':

'The expression "Charlie Love" (in other words the "Centre Line") wasn't in vogue much in the Desert, because there was no restriction to one's movement. "C" Squadron, Eleventh Hussars, of course, did have a field day on the Bardia–Tobruk road in June 1940, but this was merely classed as an ambush. It is, however, worthy of note, because in present times it would class as a Gold Cup winner. Another important feature was that throughout the early stages of the war it was played the wrong way round; on this occasion the bag was ninety puggled Wop Met, (Mixed Enemy Transport) and their occupants, a real live general, the local outpost brothel truck, with three women, and an officer, his wife, who was heavy with child, and the nurse, who immediately drank a bottle of iodine, but had to give it back again owing to the sharpness of the medical orderly. The next opera-

Members of Div HQ Staff (tank crews and signallers) make themselves at home in a half-destroyed house in Echt, Holland.

tion was at Sidi Saleh, which produced an even larger bag.

On neither of these occasions was the way for the enemy restricted. There was unlimited desert to go on and the success of the performance was due to the helplessness of the Italians and their refusal to leave the only road that existed.

I give these examples to remind you that this new and interesting game, known throughout the Army as "chewing up the Charlie Love" was only a concentrated form of "smartening up the loha". Like many other things, it appeared in its true light in Europe.

The game consists of two parties – Ours and Theirs. We always make the first move (because they make the necessary countermeasures preventing the game being reversed): this consists of pushing our chin well out into the virgin country up front, where there seem to be no enemy. When nicely placed and everyone is "brewing up", they move in behind us and prepare to put in the bag the SQMS, the Echelon, RHQ DR and the odd Tech Armd Car (with only a driver) which are bumming down the Charlie Love, their occupants nodding in peaceful slumber.

The first staccato burst of Spandau, or the sickening thud of HE wakens the dreamers, and from that moment things begin to move sharpish. Milling sets in as they try to turn round (except for the water truck, which opens the throttle and pushes on into the bag), and there are collisions, and vehicles at all angles across the road, many of which can't face the pressure any longer and subside, groaning, into the ditch.

The true situation is, of course, not known at RHQ, who merely state that the echelon must be held up by traffic blocks. The news of the chewing arrives by rumour first. Someone was talking to a water-truck driver who said there were a hundred Tigers chewing up the Charlie Love, and that out of forty vehicles all were "brewed" except himself, and he only escaped because, as luck would have it, the brakes wouldn't work (the Tech hadn't got any fluid) and he was out the other side before things really got going. This rumour gets stronger as each new arrival comes in. The enemy force grows to an army corps, and the devastation to the most fantastic proportions. Nothing more is heard until, sensing that there must be something up, a troop is sent back down the Charlie Love to investigate. Yes, it's true, there are Moffer (German soldiers) messing about fifteen miles back. And so it goes on.

The first match was played within seventy-

Above: These White half tracks belonging to 65th Anti-Tank Regiment (Norfolk Yeomanry) are parked outside a very desirable residence, the local pub!

Centre left: This 'saloon' bodied half track was specially built up by 1 RHA, REME for the Signals Section – the proud 'owner' (C Davis) told me that he once did 45mph in it!

Bottom left: Another 'home on wheels' in Normandy, 1944.

Left: Most vehicle convoys would try to get under the cover of hedgerows etc and take advantage of natural camouflage to augment vehicle camouflage nets.

Top: 'If you know a better 'ole, go to it!' Looking reminiscent of Bruce Bairnsfather's World War I character Old Bill, these soldiers of 1 RB make the best of very difficult living conditions.

two hours of landing in Normandy, on the Villers Bocage–Briquessard road. The chewing lasted about fourteen hours, but as both sides were inexperienced, only one lorry was "brewed". The second round was at Oudenarde, where the enemy were treated as conquering heroes by the flag-waving and flower-throwing civies, until the latter were soundly trounced by machine-gun fire, which was how the SS often introduced themselves.

The greatest chew of all came on the only road between the troops at Nijmegen and Eindhoven. For miles lorries were lying three abreast waiting for someone to remove the enemy so that they could get on. On this occasion it took a large part of the division to clear the Charlie Love and four tanks were destroyed. The scene on the road showed it had been a good match. About fifteen

lorries were "brewed up" and a Sherman tank. This was the biggest match played, as latterly it has consisted of "brewing up" the OP places with bazookas, and other rather childish things.

The Charlie Love, I should explain, is the road, probably the only road usable, which must carry all the soft stuff as well as tanks, transporters, and so on. In most cases, whether out of the amusement it affords to the onlooker in a jeep or out of ignorance, the Charlie Love seldom is a road where you can pass another car without drawing in your elbows and knees. Often it is a cart track with 2-foot deep boggy ruts, caused by the tanks, and everyone gets stuck. When the Charlie Love is well established, many painted signs appear, such as "When in doubt BREW UP"; "If you must stop, get off the road" and then a little later, "If you can't get off the road, don't stop" (even if all the tyres are flat!) At bridges you get "Step on it if you want to live" (when under fire) and in one place "Russians! Don't Shoot!"

Yes, the Charlie Love produces a host of interesting views. Now there are no more of them, and the only time we get chewed up on a road is for proceeding at 30.2 mph in England. This will cost you a fiver and your licence endorsed, and there will be nothing funny about it either, because you won't have a fiver, and thus will be going to the "cooler" for a week. When you come out you'll be courtmartialled for going AWOL! Such is life".*

*First published in the Victory Number of the Eleventh Hussar Journal and reprinted here by kind permission of Home Headquarters, The Royal Hussars.

Far left, top: Unpacking Composite Rations – The 'Compo' ration pack was designed to give a good breakfast, a dinner and a substantial evening meal, plus some items which could be used as snacks during the day. There were seven types of packs which included such firm favourites as rice pudding, mixed-fruit pudding, red salmon and tinned fruit. Cigarettes, matches and soap were also included.

Far left, centre: The contents of 'Compo' packs was designed to be eaten cold if no means of heating was available. However, all AFVs carried small cookers (two seen here in right foreground). The enamelled white coffee pot must have been a treasured item 'acquired' en route to Berlin!

Far left, bottom: Armoured soldiers clearly had to be able to eat their meals on the move, as demonstrated by these tank crewmen of the Skins.

Left: General 'Lou' Lyne, GOC of the Division, takes tea with some of his officers in 'A' Mess in a Dutch farmhouse near Echt, Holland, January 1945.

Left: Cows to milk. Cows which happened to still be alive in the battle area were fair game (can you see the bucket?)

Above: Bath time in a tank leaguer.

Top right: Sheep to steal. It is anybody's guess where this 'Prisoner of War' finished up!

Right: A haircut 'in the field' for Commander R Signals, 7th Armoured Division.

EDITH

Above left: Whiskey, friend and companion of the late Douglas Boggie, Norfolk Yeomanry, posing on his 'Kennel'.

Above centre: This enthusiastic supporter of 'Compo' ration packs containing Grade 3 salmon unfortunately got stuck in the tin and had to be helped out!

Centre left: Amateur musicians of 22nd Armoured Brigade Workshops 'at play' – (note the bicycle strategically placed for a quick getaway if anyone complains of the noise!)

Bottom left: George Formby and his 'Uke' entertaining the troops in his own inimitable manner.

Top right: Mind my Bike!

Right: Well armed members of 22nd Armoured Brigade Workshops out hunting.

Far right: Even mundane jobs like typing orders take on a new meaning 'in the field'.

Above: Favourite pastime of all Desert Rats!

Below: Obviously a vintage year!

Far right: War's over, so now we can get down to the really serious business.

Into the Fatherland

Men of 9 DLI engaged in clearing the village of Weseke.

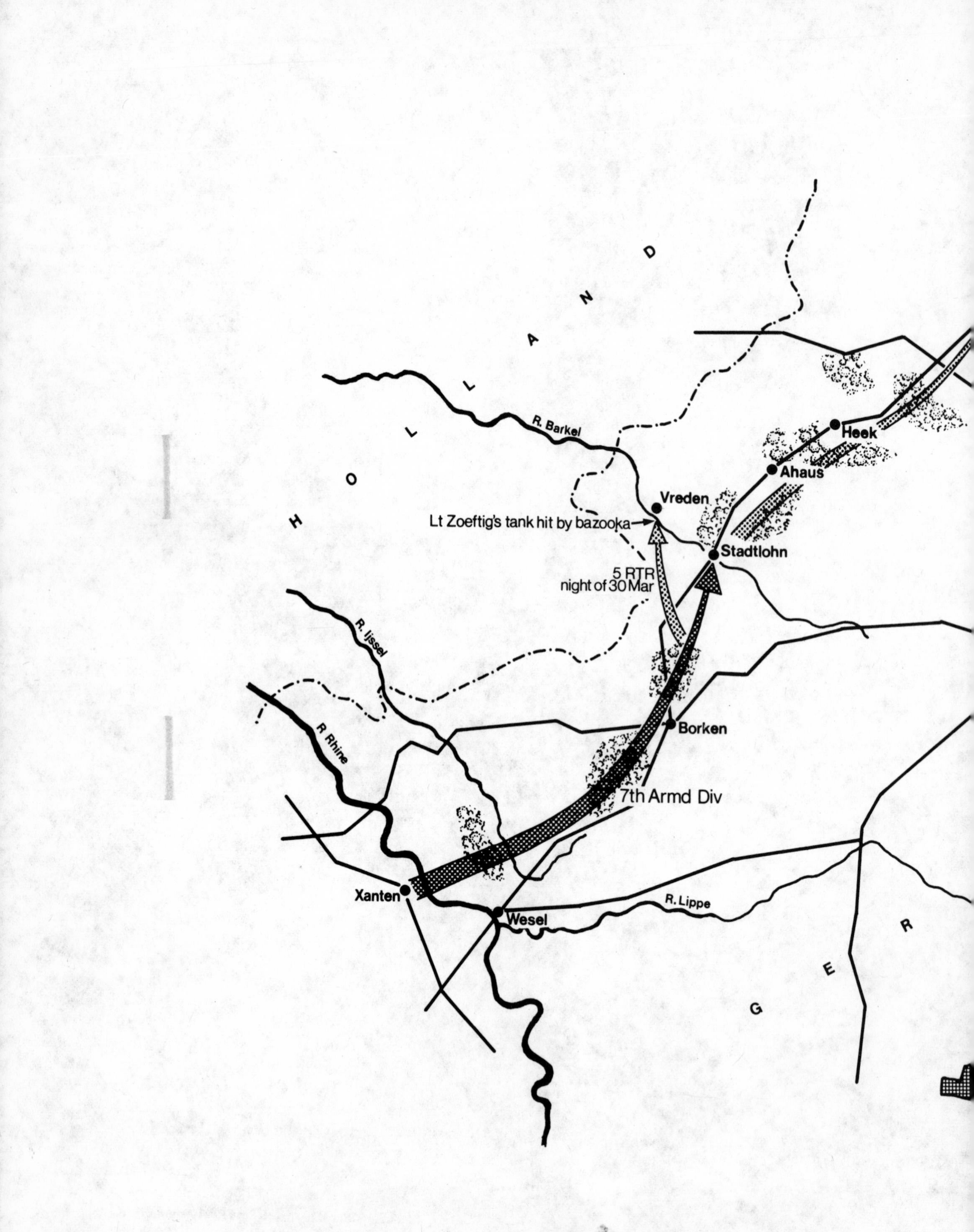
H O L L A N D
R. Barkel
Heek
Ahaus
Vreden
Lt Zoeftig's tank hit by bazooka
Stadtlohn
5 RTR
night of 30 Mar
R. Ijssel
Borken
R Rhine
7th Armd Div
Xanten
Wesel
R. Lippe
G E R

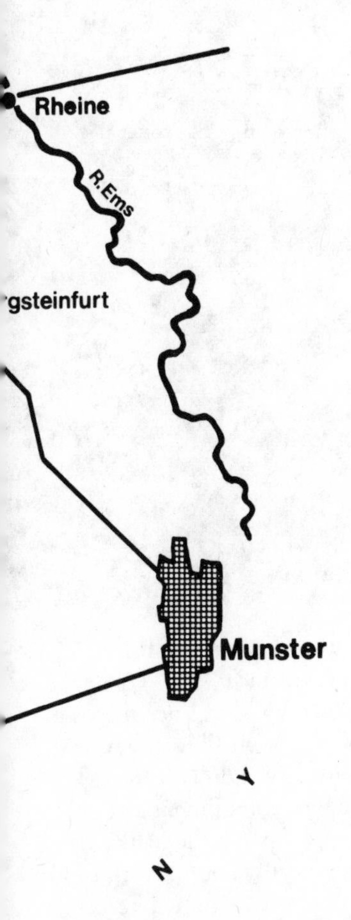

Tanks in Line!
(To the tune of 'Tales from the Vienna Woods')

'Tanks, Tanks, Tanks in Line,
Sweeping, on towards the Rhine,
The First, the Fifth, the Skins and Guns
We're out to b . . . up the Huns!
Cromwells, Shermans, Fireflies too
A floating punch to see us through,
The Engineers with Scorpions
And a troop of Bofors, half a dozen loafers,
And the Navy nice and wavy,
RAF umbrella, nothing could be sweller,
Deutschland here we come!'

This was the first verse of a song which had its beginnings in the Desert days when the tanks of the Division were 'Sweeping on to Alamein'. The European version was composed in Holland during October 1944 by some officers of 'C' Squadron, 1st Royal Tank Regiment, after operations north of Tilburg. The second verse goes on:

'The First are always at the front,
"C" Squadron picked to bear the brunt,
The "iron ring" well at the back
The SergeantMajor's thrown a track,
Tom Stacey he will do the trick
But only with his usual tick.
The 95's are wanging,
88's are banging
Johnnie Dingwall slanging
Office staff are lazy
Tank Commanders hazy
It's about time that we had a brew
– Too true!'

This verse does perhaps need some explanation – The 'iron ring' refers to Squadron Headquarters; Tom Stacey was 'C' Squadron fitter sergeant, who continued to serve in the First, with distinction, for many years after the war: two of the Cromwells in SHQ were armed with 95mm howitzers instead of the normal 75mm, whilst the deadly accurate German 88mm gun was both well known and respected by all; finally Johnnie Dingwall, a famous 1 RTR character of World War 2, was then commanding 'C' Squadron. 'Tanks in Line' is still sung lustily after dinner nights in the First's officers' mess and is now as much a part of their regimental tradition as their black berets and ash plants.

Operations in Germany

In order to give some idea of the operations which the Division carried out in Germany I have chosen three stories, all by armoured soldiers, but each very different. The first concerns the feelings of a tank troop leader, Lt Ted Zoeftig of 5 RTR, during a night operation in which he was bazookered. The second is an extract from the diary, for early April 1945, of Captain Richard Brett Smith of the Eleventh Hussars and is typical of the slow progress and bitter fighting which characterised the early days of the final campaign. Finally, I have finished on a more cheerful note with the liberation of a British Prisoners of War camp near Fallingbostel, by Captain (now Brigadier) Tim Pierson of the Eighth Hussars.

Night Attack March 30th, 1945

Anyone who has driven in the dark along unfamiliar country roads knows the feeling of relief when that all important road junction which your navigator has been telling you for the past ten minutes is 'just around the next bend', finally appears and your headlights are able to pick out the strange sounding place names on the signboard. Imagine, therefore, how much more difficult it is when one is perched on top of a noisy, lurching steel monster, without lights, only able to glance furtively at your map from time to time with the aid of a flashlight, exposed to the elements and constantly on the alert for trouble. It is, I believe, one of the most severe tests of a tank commander, particularly if he is also spearheading an important advance into enemy held territory.

This was the case in the story which follows. 7th Armoured Division had crossed the Rhine a few days before near Xanten, as Corps reserve. Now they were leading on the Corps' right flank, making for an important enemy airfield complex around Rheine. There had been only minor enemy interference until Stadtlohn (see sketch map) where fierce fighting was even now taking place. A patrol of the 11th Hussars, operating on the left, managed to get to within about a thousand yards of Vreden – north of Stadtlohn, and reported that the bridge there appeared undamaged. To be able to capture Vreden and the bridge over the River Berkel would cut the enemy's line of retreat. 5th Royal Tank Regiment, with infantry support, was therefore despatched that night to capture the bridge. They set off, first moving over some bad tracks until they reached the main road, where a road block caused them some delay but was finally successfully re-

Tanks in Line! Tanks of the Division massed across the Rhine at Brunen, awaiting orders to continue the chase.

moved. Although enemy were present in the woods all round no serious opposition was encountered until the leading tank reached the outskirts of Vreden. Here it was hit by a bazooka and knocked out. The next tank was also ditched and surrounded by enemy infantry. The infantry who had been with the two tanks suffered casualties, but were able to fight their way back to the main body where a plan was made to deal with the enemy strong point. However, before this could be put into effect the enemy withdrew and 5 RTR were able to enter Vreden, only to have the enemy blow the bridge as the leading tank approached. The column then returned to Stadtlohn after destroying an enemy self-propelled gun on the far side of the river at the blown bridge.

That is the bare factual outline of this minor incident in the Division's progress through North West Europe, but it was an incident which was anything but trivial for Lieutenant Ted Zoeftig of 5 RTR, who was commanding the leading tank troop in the column and was at the receiving end of the enemy bazooka rocket. Here is his story:

'My troop was leading. Lieutenant Doug Smith was my Baker.* My Firefly (a Sherman fitted with a 17 pounder, instead of the normal 75mm) had thrown a track about five minutes before the advance. The "A" set radio net was a bit "blabby" but since the attack was so imminent no possible harm could come of it. It certainly didn't disturb me. Some remarks were even complimentary! We had Canadian troops up on the tanks with us. We all felt comfortably confident in a subdued comradely manner. I remember agreeing the Verey signals with the Canadian officer and then lending him my Verey pistol because he didn't have one of his own. An 11th Hussar recce car purred up and had an encouraging word. "Yes, it was clear up to a small road block – No, there didn't seem to be anyone there." We paused, the "A" set chatter was dreadfully loud. No moon of course, just a clear sky with some shady warning of pre-dawn glow. "Yes! We'll come up the road block with you – *and* move it if you'll cover us". Wonderful chaps the 11th Hussars. Now we are well past the block. Over to the "B" set. "Baker – take the lead". A not exactly cheerful "Wilco – out" in reply. Head down just below the turret for a few seconds – to map read.

*A tank troop normally consisted of three tanks – the troop leader plus two others designated for use on the radio 'Able' and 'Baker'.

Tanks and vehicles of the Division passing through Brunen in pursuit of the enemy.

"We're coming up to the wood's edge. About 1 200 yards short of the little town. There's open ground after that".

I request over the "A" set to drop my infantry and work forward in concert – flushing the road as we proceed – "No", the answer comes back "You're late already, speed up if you can". I call up Douglas Smith on the "B" set. "I'll take the lead now Doug". "Roger – out". I see the blur of a shadow of small building on the right. Head down for a second to read the map – the torch doesn't seem too bright – only about 300 yards to go to the "blue" (the river), "Slow down a bit, driver". Head down for another quick glimpse of the map and there's the bridge ahead. Then a massive vibration of thick, light and dark grey lines. I feel very heavy and find that I am being pressed down to the bottom of the turret. I feel as if I'm swimming under water. In strange slow motion I start to move up. No one is near me. The tank seems to be pointing up in the air. A high pitched screaming whistle persists in my ears. I find myself sliding over the back of the engine decks to fall and roll over onto the road. There is a spitting, crackling sound – rather sharp – but not loud – round about me. One pace and I flop into a shallow ditch. A grey lump is level with my right eye. I have just tripped over someone. Sticky feeling in my mouth. My nose is bleeding or something is. I feel all right. A sizzling sound is in front of me and what seems like lighted matches spurt up from the ground about nine inches from my head. A realisation that this is tracer, seemingly aimed directly at me, rapidly clears my sleepy thinking. But something is definitely wrong with my hearing. That machine gun is doing nothing but Squeak!

Now I realise that my tank has been heavily fired on. The Canadian troops who had clung so eagerly to the turret have scattered – one or two, probably many more, are lying on the road; my protectors in death. What had happened to my crew? Have I failed them? Where was Doug? – God – he must have got it as well! What was to have been the first firm, speedy, sure-footed thrust to the Elbe had been tripped. The machine gun stopped. I was becoming alert. I must do something – what a bloody mess. Can I get back into the tank to use the "A" set? I turn my head slowly sideways. The nose of the tank and turret seemed to appear mountainously high on the dark skyline. Must be careful or they'll see me. A dreadful sense of guilty failure is beginning to envelop me. Had I left my crew? Where were they? Still in the tank – wounded – smashed? "Do something! At least you're not afraid. Think clearly! Determined? This is

A Cromwell passing through Borken, March 30th, 1945.

easy – make a dash – ready? Now!" – Straight into a group of about eight Jerry paratroopers – all young. Their marksmanship was appalling. They missed at point blank range, but I was moving fast – straight into them, that's what spoiled their aim. Then the kicking, struggling and shouting started – but that was nothing, *anything* was better than the dreadful sense of failure. What was the waiting regiment going to do? The bitter taste of defeat and the chagrin of fallen pride remains until today.

They dragged me off – over the bridge and then blew it up – I heard something go off with a bang. Later, shortly afterwards, I got away. There seemed to be hundreds of them and they appeared rather sorry for knocking me about, as if they knew the war was finished. All I received were split eardrums, a bloody nose, split lips and a small cut on my head. I made my wobbly way back to the Regiment about three or four days later.'

Extract from the Diary of Captain Brett-Smith of the Eleventh Hussars March 31st, 1945

'Through Stadtlohn (a completely ruined and war-wrecked town, smelling horribly of death and burning) and then by country tracks to rejoin the main road, Stadtlohn-Ahaus. Apparently the 1st Tanks had made a real cavalry charge in the night from Stadtlohn to Ahaus, and got through the hordes of bazookamen with amazingly light casualties. A terrific show and they were played out when we reached them in Ahaus.

Ahaus was also badly devastated, and there were still a few last-ditchers sniping, and a good number of mines holding up further progress. (Nigel Campbell, of D Squadron, had two Daimlers bown up). However, I was informed that the Recce Troop of 1st Tanks was through Ahaus and pushing on, so I told Van (Major W V Burdon, MC, my Squadron Leader in "C") this and followed them up. About half a mile out I met an RHA OP, who told me to move off a bridge I was on, which was being shelled every five minutes, and directed me on to the tanks (two Honeys) who were just a little way on. As I came up to them they were firing spasmodically at the woods on both sides of the main road, which was banked up on each side. One of the Honeys had to turn back for more gas, so I left Sgt Palmer and the others well back, as I expected trouble, and closed up the first Honey, telling the troop leader that I would follow him at about thirty yards and watch the left. Actually I volunteered to take over the lead and the patrol, as I thought it my duty, though it was his show, and after a

Ram Kangaroo Armoured Personnel Carriers loaded with men of 9 DLI wait to enter Weseke.

good-natured argument we agreed that I should do this when we got to a certain point. We never did, and I still have rather a guilty conscience about it. We met in Berlin after the war, and he was most generous and kind about it, and we had quite a party to celebrate his and our escape.

Sure enough, we had not gone more than another 300 yards down this very straight road, when an anti-tank gun at the end of it opened up, and brewed the Honey with its first shot. Simultaneously bazookas on the left of the road fired at him and me, and I reversed sharpish. By the grace of God the Honey made so much smoke and such a good brew-up that the German gunners were unsighted: but five or six 88mm AP shots whistled past very close to my Daimler, and caused considerable consternation amongst the half tracks and some more tanks further back! Mercifully we got off the road after a hectic bit of reversing into a farmhouse forecourt, then I collected the troop and sat in observation. The troop leader of the Honeys had got out with his operator – as I had seen, but the driver was killed. We crawled up the ditches on both sides of the road to get them, and were relieved and surprised to meet them returning on the way. The operator was wounded, and their own people got both away to safety. Then I and Sgt Palmer with some of the men from the half tracks tried to get close to the 88 along the ditches, but we couldn't get close enough to spot it because of small arms fire from the wood and to our left. In any case it had probably moved already. We smartened up the likely areas with small arms but with what effect I cannot say.

I not unnaturally decided to take it very steady, and sat in observation most of the day. We got the RHA on to where we thought the gun was from the original flashes (finding out later that we were wrong, of course) and waited for the tanks to find a way cross-country. There was some heavy plough on the left but goodish going on the right. This they did very well. I had tried the plough in my Dingo, not daring to show it on the road, but very nearly got bogged down and had to give it up. They negotiated it, as I say, well, but met trouble, so were unable to go fast. Although I thought that the gun had probably baled out, I was not taking any chances. (Windy!) In the evening a mobile column composed of 1st Tanks, Crocodiles and Bren carriers swept up the road to prove that it had moved, helped by the information of the tanks who had got ahead on the right, after a sticky time in the

Left: A Cromwell passes a road block left by the enemy in Stadtlohn, March 31st, 1945.

Below: Tanks of the Division driving through Ahaus.

GERMANS FLEEING, AND DELIRIOUS BRITISH AND AMERICAN PRISONERS CHEERING FROM THE ROOFS OF THEIR PRISON HUTS, AS AN 8TH HUSSARS TANK SQUADRON OF THE 7TH ARMOURED DIVISION ROLLS UP TO THE MAIN GATES OF STALAG 11B IN THE EARLY-MORNING LIGHT OF APRIL 16.

The Liberation of Stalag XIB drawn by Captain Bryan de Grineau. Reproduced by kind permission of the London Illustrated News.

woods. The column finished up near Heck, where we joined them.

Entry (part) for April 5th
A day of pouring rain and constant Luftwaffe attack. (Visibility too bad for RAF, and Luftwaffe only dare come up when its like this – first time since January 1st I have come up against them). To Dielingen then on to Lembricht, where 5th Tanks and RHA did very well, and took the place. Following up we took two POW (both wounded by their guns). Through the burning village and took lead while RB's were still clearing it; 4-5 mile patrol up to a railway bridge. Shortly before this a roadblock had held us up for some little time, and Sgt Palmer and myself had both been sniped by a sniper when we were least prepared for it. However, we brewed up a farm, and the Germans withdrew, assisted by the Colonel of 5th Tanks, always well up (Lt Col A R Leakey) tore down the road block after some of his tanks had had a go at it. Took four more POW on the CL. Also lost face slightly by asking the infantry to deal with a battery of AA 88's on my right, which turned out to be dummies, when I thought them merely deserted! Saw best sight of the war on this day – a Focke Wolf 190 hit its wing against the tree-tops, crashed into a field, bounced literally 200 yards and brewed. We put up considerable small arms fire against 'Schmitts and FW and I think Sgt Palmer hit one though he didn't bring it down within our sight. Unpleasant day'.

The Liberation of Stalag XI B, Fallingbostel – April 16th, 1945
Perhaps one of the happiest achievements of the Division's operations in April 1945 was the liberation of the great prison camp in the woods south west of Fallingbostel. Some prisoners had been there since the Fall of France, amongst others more recently arrived were members of 4 CLY and 'A' Company, 1 RB, who had been put into the bag at Villers Bocage nearly a year before (see 'Into the Bocage'). Newest of all was a leave party from the Norfolk Yeomanry whose truck had taken a wrong turning near Ibbenbüren only a fortnight previously! As well as British and American prisoners there were some twelve thousand other allied nationalities many of whom had suffered appalling hardships. Here is how Tim Pierson who was then commanding the reconnaissance troop of the Eighth Hussars remembers that wonderful day:

'Nosing its way cautiously along sandy tracks that skirted or went through the many pine-woods that were the main feature of this country, the leading section of Honeys started off slowly. Though there was no sign of any enemy, similar woods had produced quite a few the day before, and the leading tank occasionally raked the edges of the trees and suspicious hollows or clumps of grass to discourage any panzer-faust expert that might be waiting hopefully for us to get within range of his very useful weapon. The afternoon before, when he had been missed three times, Lieutenant Anstey, the leading tank commander, confessed to feeling like a goalkeeper in a football match, but this particular sunny morning there was, much to our relief, no sign of them.

A wide clearing confronted us, obviously man-made, cut at right angles through the woods, its sandy surface covered with tufts of grass, stretching dead straight to the right as far as we could see, and to the left turning out of sight through two small mountains of earth. This must be the autobahn, though scarcely what we had expected, the maps have given no hint of this rudimentary stage in its construction.

We turned left, came to the huge heaps of earth and halted while the leading commander, Corporal Spencer, dismounted to have a look at what lay round them out of sight. No more woods, but a flat open expanse of grass bounded, some thousand yards away, by a long uneven line of low buildings, out of which, further to our left, rose what looked like half a dozen tall warehouses. Binoculars showed that the main mass of low buildings lay behind a high wire fence – and people, at first we saw one or two moving about, then made out groups of a dozen, and finally realised that the thickening of the bottom half of the fence was in fact a solid mass of them. At this moment the leading tanks of "C" Squadron, approaching on a different route, came up behind us, and without waiting to see any more we jumped into our tanks and shot out into the open. In high spirits we crossed the grass as quickly as the ground would allow, but as the distance between us and the fence grew less we noticed that the predominant colour of the mass that was streaming out of the gates towards us was grey, dark grey. At the same moment we saw a French flag – or was it Dutch – which in our excitement we had not noticed before, fluttering behind the main gate. Our hopes sank; these were not British prisoners, but another of the camps full of all nationalities of Europe that we had come across so many times before. Perhaps there were some British amongst them, then again perhaps there was no British camp at all, and the Germans have moved XIB as they had moved so many others out of the way of the armies advancing from east to west.

The leading tank came to a stop as the first of the breathless, shouting stream of humanity surrounded it, and Corporal Spencer, still clinging to a faint hope, lent down and yelled "English soldaten?" He repeated himself in a moment's hush and then a hundred hands pointed to his left, and the clamour of the excited crowd broke out with increased intensity. As he looked round for someone out of whom he could get some sense it seemed that every nation was represented, women as well as men, the majority in civilian clothes, with but two things in common; they were all happy, and all indescribably dirty.

Noticing one persistent man who seemed to have a smattering of English he hauled him up on to the tank and asked which way. The fellow pointed, and as the tank moved slowly forward the crowd melted away in front. He glanced over his shoulder and noticed that he was still leading, the Cromwells of "C" Squadron were as uncertain as he had been as to the route, but were now following hot on his heels. It was going to be

General 'Lou' Lyne inspects the Jordan Bridge across the River Weser at Nienburg. The bridge (a Class 40 Bailey Pontoon) was built by the Division's sappers on April 13th, 1945 and was called 'Jordan' as there appeared to be only one more river (the Elbe) to cross. In fact the very next obstacle encountered by the Division when the advance was resumed beyond the Aller was a brook called Jordan, near Kirchboizen!

Top: Headquarters 22nd Armoured Brigade at Syke, on the southern approaches to Bremen, April 1945.

Above: Divisional Headquarters staff sorting through some of the enormous numbers of maps which were required during the rapid advance through Germany.

a close thing who reached the Camp first.

Parallel to the fence, which he had now reached, ran a concrete road, and turning left along this, to the accompaniment of cheers from the waving smiling crowd of prisoners and DPs that thronged its entire length, he soon passed the tall warehouses that had first been noticed in the distance. The fellow on the turret pointed excitedly forward, but Corporal Spencer could see nothing, except a road, tree-lined on both sides, that met ours at right angles. We halted at the junction; to our left the road went under a stone bridge built to carry the autobahn, but with no autobahn to carry looking comically like a piece from a child's set of toy bricks. A quick glance to the right revealed nothing more than an empty road. But the guide was tugging at Spencer's sleeve and jabbering away – and following with our eyes the direction of his pointing arm we saw across the road through a gap between two trees a khaki-clad figure wearing a maroon coloured beret, clinging to a wire fence beyond and jumping up and down, obviously shouting his head off, though not a word reached us over the noise of the engines and earphones.

And then all the way down to the right we could see between the tree-trunks more figures racing along the wire. We'd got there, and before the Cromwells, which came up behind just as we moved off down the road giving the glad news over the air. Three or four hundred yards down the road was the main gate to the camp and as we approached the sound of welcome from the crowd that lined the wire and covered the roofs of the camp buildings grew to a roar that penetrated our earphones above the noise of our engines. Inside the main gates was an open space packed with British prisoners, and beyond another wire fence, what looked like an inner enclosure was black with figures. This was Stalag XI B.

Quite staggering was the contrast between this scene and that which we had seen at other camps containing prisoners of the Allied nations. Despite the enthusiasm of the men inside you could see at a glance that here was order and discipline. The remarkable RSM Lord, Grenadier Guards, of the 1st Airborne Division had already taken charge and was busily engaged in his office giving peace-time orders to his Orderly Warrant Officers. Camp MP's, each with a red armband, policed the gates, and as the crowd came out to meet us there was no ugly rush but a steady controlled stream that surrounded each tank as it stopped, a stream wearing the headgear of what looked like every unit in the Army. The Airborne beret predominated – men of D-Day, Arnhem, even the Rhine crossing who had only been inside for a few weeks – but you could pick out the hats, caps, berets and bonnets of a score of others. And under each one was such a look of happiness and thankfulness that made us as happy to be the cause of it. It was a quiet crowd that thronged round us; they had had their cheer, and now when the moment came for words, few words came. Mostly they were too moved to speak, men who could only grin broadly and clasp your hand as the tears ran down their cheeks. You couldn't speak yourself, only shake as many as possible of the hands that stretched towards you, and grin back, trying to take it all in, and marvel. For these men didn't look like prisoners; the battle-dresses were pressed and clean, here and there web belts and gaiters were scrubbed white and the brasses gleaming, they might have been off duty in a town at home instead of just walking out of prison wire behind which they had been for anything from five weeks to five years.

Memories of that scene leave a picture of a healthy and, if not overfed, certainly not starving crowd, of apologetic requests for cigarettes and one man turning green with his first puff, having given up the habit for his three years inside; of the creases in the tartan trews and the shining buttons on the jacket of a CSM in the 51st Highland Division, who admitted having marched five or six hundred kilometres from East Prussia and who didn't look as if he had been more than five or six hundred yards from his own front door; of the Camp MO indignantly denying cases of typhus; of the German Commandant and a few of the camp guards standing apart in a small group watching unmoved the reversal of his role, and handing over his automatic with an offer to show us over the nearby storehouses; scraps of conversation "I've been waiting five years for this day" – "Three days ago we expected you", and in contrast, "You've come too soon, my jacket's still wet", this from one who had washed his battledress specially for the occasion; and from one as impressed by our appearance (we hadn't washed or shaved for nearly forty-eight hours) as were we by theirs. "You look like real soldiers". There were several requests to see a Jeep, which we could not unfortunately produce at that moment; much signing of autographs on both sides and nearly always the first question "What's your mob?" and finding several members of the Regiment in the camp, taken at Sidi Rezegh in 1941; and finally, on asking news of their erstwhile captors, being told that they were not long gone and were carrying panzerfausts. This was more serious, with all these fellows about, and on asking the police to clear the road we got the first startling proof of the state of the camp discipline. For at a word from a tall figure wearing the Airborne beret, RSM Lord, the Camp MP's went round, and in a very few moments and without a murmur these scores of men, some of whom were tasting freedom for the first time in more than five years, made their way back behind that same barbed wire and netting that to them must have been a symbol of all that was hateful and depressing of this life.

Tanks Advance! Lt Col (now Maj Gen) A R Leakey giving the orders over the radio to the 5th Royal Tank Regiment during the advance on Bremen.

We left as the vanguard of visitors was arriving, the VIP's and the not so VIP's, the Press and the frankly curious, all wishing to to get a first-hand glimpse of the first large predominantly British camp to find itself in the path of the British Army of Liberation. And we left taking with us an impression that will never fade; of men whose courage and hope had been kept alive through long years of boredom and privation by their faith in their comrades and their country; and whose behaviour in their moment of triumph when faith had been rewarded was an example of the highest traditions of the Army to which they belonged.

And that might have been the end of our part in the proceedings of what was for all of us a great occasion. But later on that day we happened to pass that way again when things were more normal; erstwhile prisoners strolling about in groups, or sitting in the sun enjoying a smoke and waving contentedly at the passing traffic. But all was not quite normal, for as we came up to the main gates where we had received such a reception a few hours earlier, we saw a troop of armoured cars obliging some movie-cameramen by driving slowly past a group of wildly waving and shouting ex-prisoners; and for a brief moment, as we beheld the scene as spectators and not actors, we felt again all the emotions of that most memorable day.'

Surrender. Brig John Spurling entering Hamburg Town Hall, May 3rd, 1945, accompanied by Captains Mitchell (GSO3) and Lewisohn (IO) with mapboard.
General Alwin Wolz, Commander Hamburg Garrison is saluting. The smiling German officer standing next to him is his Intelligence Officer who was educated at Oxford University and is wearing a Christchurch scarf. The mayor is standing behind in civilian clothes.

Above: Scout Cars of the Eleventh Hussars crossing the Elbe bridge into Hamburg.

Top right: Squadron Headquarters, D Sqn, 11th Hussars outside Hamburg Town Hall, May 3rd, 1945.

Centre, bottom right: Hamburg – The extent of the damage caused by months of air raids can be seen in these photos of the desolation in the streets of the city.

The Final Act

During late April 1945 it became very clear that the total defeat of Germany was not far off. Indeed, there were really only two outstanding questions to be answered – firstly, who was willing to surrender the German Armed Forces and secondly, would they obey a call to lay down their arms. The build up towards final capitulation on the 21st Army Group front began with minor local surrenders and parleys and ended with the negotiations for the surrender of Hamburg.

Throughout this confused period the commander of Hamburg Garrison, Major General Alwin Wolz, was wrestling with his conscience, trying to decide whether or not he should surrender the city. Certainly the influential and realistic members of the Hamburg Chamber of Commerce wanted it in order to prevent further destruction to their already much battered city. However, some elements of the German armed forces, still displaying fanatical devotion to the Fuhrer, were against it. Clearly General Wolz was afraid that he might become a scapegoat. Nevertheless he began secret negotiations. By May 1st his troubles were virtually over as General Keitel had ordered him to surrender on behalf of Admiral Doenitz. He was further told that a delegation of general and admirals from the German High command would be arriving the following morning en route to see the British Army Group Commander. So, whilst General Wolz was agreeing at his level with GOC 7th Armoured Division to allow British troops to enter Hamburg, General Admiral von Friedeburg was leading a delegation to negotiate a complete surrender with Field Marshal Montgomery.

Let us start our examination of the final act at a slightly lower level with the thoughts of a young captain of the Eleventh Hussars, Richard Brett-Smith (as recorded in his book *Berlin '45*) as he waited with the leading British troops to enter Hamburg, the largest city ever to surrender to the British Army . . .

'We did not know, when we waited on our armoured cars that afternoon of May 3rd, 1945, ready to enter Hamburg, whether we would have to fight our way up Schleswig-Holstein and into Denmark, or not. Naturally we hoped that we would not have to, but we knew that our entry into Germany's second city and the events of the subsequent day would settle our doubts one way or the other.

We were supposed to lead in the 7th Armoured Division at three o'clock. It was a grey, depressing sort of day, and for some

reason we were held up. It started to rain, and for hours we waited in the drizzle, moving forward by slow degrees with an enormous and seemingly never-ending column behind us. Already a few tanks and some infantry had gone forward to secure the Elbe bridges, and a number of unauthorised explorers and joy-riders had penetrated into the city by design or by mistake.

At last, when it was nearly seven o'clock in the evening, we led the Division through Harburg and over the Elbe into Hamburg itself. Harburg had prepared us a little for what we were to see, but even so Hamburg was a terrible sight. Yet it was miraculously tidy. A few people lined the streets in quiet wonder, but there was hardly a sound as we passed through, except for the slight whine of our gears changing and the buzzing and whistling of our wireless sets. Scores of Hamburg policemen in their bright-green uniforms directed us on our way, most of them middle-aged or elderly men, for nowhere did one see a young man not in the Wehrmacht, unless he was a cripple or a physical weakling.

There was something unnatural about the silence, something a little uncanny. As we drove up to that last great bridge across the Elbe, the final obstacle that could have held

Radfahren

us up so long, it seemed impossible that we had taken Hamburg so easily. Looking down at the cold grey waters of the Elbe swirling far beneath, we sensed again that queer feeling that came whenever we crossed an enemy bridge, and it would have been no great surprise if the whole structure had suddenly collapsed and our cars plunged headlong into the river. But no, it did not blow up, and we found ourselves safely across, and so apparently did those behind us. Now at last we could heave a sigh of relief, for we were across the last obstacle, the Elbe, and there were no more rivers to cross, at worst only the Kiel Canal!'

Brett-Smith's Squadron made straight for the Atlantic Hotel on the shores of the Grosse Alster where until recently Himmler had had his headquarters. Meanwhile, in the centre of the city the surrender ceremony had taken place that afternoon in the Adolf Hitler Platz. Here General Wolz, together with his officers, had paraded to wait for the arrival of the 'British General'.

'But the General was denied the pomp and ceremony that he thought the occasion demanded. He and his officers had paraded in their smartest uniforms and full decorations in the otherwise deserted main square, to await the British General. But the first British vehicle to arrive had been a "waterbug" (15 cwt water truck) of the 7th Queens, which had flashed through the square, irrepressibly shabby and obviously miles off its route. Its unperturbed driver grinned at the Germans and shouted some ribald remarks at them. They stiffly ignored him.

The next arrival promised better. He was, in fact, our Colonel, in a Daimler scout car. The Germans sprang to attention, and General Wolz, a rather fat man with spectacles, advanced towards Colonel Wainman, whom he took to be the Divisional commander, figuratively waving the keys of Hamburg in his face. The Colonel, who was dressed in an American combat jacket and a pair of Bedford cords, climbed briskly out of his car, totally ignored the General, and walked over to the only other occupants of the square, some tame pigeons who lived there, whom he began to feed with Army biscuit.'

Below: A half track belonging to 3 RHA approaching the bridge over the Kiel Canal.

Right: After VE Day – Vehicles of D Squadron 11th Hussars in the main square of Tonning, a pleasant seaside town on the Eiderstadt Peninsula. Brigadier Spurling, Commander 131 Brigade, can be seen in the background going into the Military Goverment offices with a German officer.

Bottom right: Officers of D Sqn 11th Hussars receiving the surrender of a small German town.

First Desert Rat into Hamburg

Although the Eleventh Hussars were the first unit to enter the city, the prize for being

the first British soldier to enter Hamburg officially must be given to a staff car driver from HQ 7th Armoured Division who, when General Wolz's own Mercedes broke down, was lent with his car to the Hamburg commander to return him to the Town Hall in time to prepare for the official entry ceremony. However, I have heard about an officer who claimed that he came into Hamburg from the Lauenburg direction early in the morning of the 3rd, believing that British troops were already in the town. He found the streets empty, apart from German police at every road junction who waved him forward, but no British troops. As the truth dawned on him he beat a hasty retreat!

The Surrender of the City Takes Place

'At 1800 hours on May 3rd, Brig Spurling, guided by Major Andrae and accompanied by Captains Mitchell and Hodson, reached the main entrance to Hamburg Rathaus. Here he was met by General Wolz, accompanied by Burgermeister Burchard-Motz and Hauptmann Dr Link as interpreter. General Wolz made formal transfer of the military command. The Brigadier was then conducted upstairs to the Burgermeistersaal. Here Gauleiter Kaufmann stood alone in the middle of the room, behind him a group of senators and members of the party. Brigadier and gauleiter greeted each other and walked to a table in the corner of the room. As a matter of history it was round that table that the act of civil surrender took place. Brigadier Spurling, as civil administrator until a military governor should take over, charged the German officials present to be responsible to him for law and order in the city. It was nearly seven o'clock on the evening of May 3rd. The surrender of Hamburg had taken place.

These weighty matters having been settled, Gauleiter Kaufmann told Brigadier Spurling that he, the gauleiter, had already arranged for the British commander and his staff to be accommodated at the nearby Atlantic Hotel, where they would find dinner prepared for them. Such was in fact the case. Major Morrison, the leading Military Government officer, had meanwhile reached Hamburg and was discussing detailed matters of administration with Rathaus officials. Later that evening, the commander and staff of 8 Base Sub-Area came into the city and lodged in the "Vier Jahreszeiten' (The Four Seasons Hotel). They had come straight up from Ostend and were charged with the vitally important task of opening up the port of Hamburg.

General Lyne himself established his caravan headquarters on the evening of May 3rd on the shores of the Aussen Alster. This was, however, an overnight stop; he and his division were destined to move further north into Schleswig-Holstein. It is General Lyne's testimony to General Wolz's efficient telephone communications and the discipline of his anti-aircraft division that not one single shot was fired at the British troops as they moved into the city, nor was there any breakdown in command. The population remained in their houses. No white flags

were visible anywhere. For Hamburg the war was over. The rest is the story of Military Government.' (Taken from *The Capitulation of Hamburg 3rd May 1945* by Dr J K Dunlop published in the RUSI Journal February 1954.)

Another young captain of the Eleventh Hussars who also witnessed these eventful happenings was Richard Moore. Shortly afterwards he wrote the following letter home:

'Dear Mother,
We do live in stirring times. The events of the last two days from our angle will interest you.

After some days of the Hamburg negotiations and standing by for more all the time; finally after delays and hitches, "on a much, much higher level" as they say on the wireless, in we went. Then yesterday after a night spent in a bank, of all places (no money but primuses on the counter brewing up!) and the Moffer (German soldiers) coming by in their hundreds, a message to expect a big cheese and later on other messages to me on the rear link to alert people to meet the big

The End of the German Army. Some of the thousands of German soldiers, men of every conceivable age and unit who jostled one another in complete disorder as they came to give themselves up. Some could hardly walk and plodded along with the aid of sticks, their arms long since thrown away. The motley collection of vehicles they had collected towed each other along (the record seen by the 11th Hussars was eight cars being pulled by one lorry!)

Right: Men of the Eleventh Hussars show off a captured Swastika.

Below: 'D' Squadron Eleventh Hussars' Bonfire on VE-Day May 8th, 1945. 'That wonderful night will never be forgotten by anyone who was there with hordes of strange fur-coated figures swigging rum punch and singing their hearts out. Verey lights ricochetting all over the place and the Colonel going round each squadron in turn, and each squadron striving to produce a bigger and better 'brew-up' for him than the last and succeeding only too well'(1)

(1) 'The Eleventh at War' p.479.

Bottom: Vehicles of Tac Divisional HQ near the shores of the Aussen Alster in Hamburg. The houses they occupied temporarily had been vacated by the Gestapo.

cheese. By and by up came our people and we all (SHQ and the representatives from 21st Army Group) went up to the leading troop on the road to Kiel.

By now the Moffer were coming past in their thousands, lorries, carts, bicycles, buses and everything, but mainly walking not marching and looking unbelievably lost, every vestige of discipline and smartness gone. There, we with the colonels waited – the classic scene being an MP looting some eggs, he in immaculate redcap, the whitest of belts and shiniest of boots and us in fur coats, corduroys and God knows what, all eating fried eggs and drinking char.

Finally along came Admiral Freideberg to negotiate the surrender, as you know, in a car by himself and soon after a Wehrmacht staff officer in another; the cameras clicked and they talked for a few minutes. I thought Toby was going to loot the admiral's car, he was chatting away to him and looking into it! Then off they went and we settled down to the business of raking in and organising several thousand POW, the local police and so on, including several hundred Russian, Polish, French and God knows what else, in ancient vehicles of all sorts, mostly run on wood and coal and *all* on tow, off to a camp one of the other squadrons is running, and so on again until after midnight and early next morning (today) again still as thick as ever. More big cheeses from the other side, including two who came in and more or less offered us the Luftwaffe and later on Admiral Hoffman from Doenitz who wanted to get rid of the Fleet. They all came along and asked for Field Marshal Montgomery most correctly – get shown in to Toby and me who usually give them tea and/or cognac and pass them on. The reaction from asking for the Field Marshal and getting two buckshees, in pretty rough kit, is worth seeing. Next the BBC, Vaughan Williams or some one arrived to see the Moffer coming in; so they had tea and cognac, then went up to Reggie and did a recording. The real highlight of the day was Tom Suggitt, the signal sergeant, with a news flash from the BBC – "Huddersfield has won the Rugby Cup" and as an afterthought later on "two Moffer armies have surrendered somewhere!"

Unconditional Surrender

The delegation under General Admiral von Freideburg signed a document of unconditional surrender at 1820 hours on May 4th, 1945. This related only to the forces in Holland, the Fresian Islands, Heligoland, Schleswig Holstein and Denmark who were facing 21st Army Group. It was not until May 6th that the final unconditional surrender of all Land, Sea and Air Forces of the Third Reich was made.

It is fitting that we should close this chapter with the Special Order of the Day issued by the GOC 7th Armoured Division:

SPECIAL ORDER OF THE DAY
by
Major General L O LYNE CB, DSO
Commander, 7 Armoured Division
(To be read out to all troops on parade)

The war with Germany is won. It has ended with the complete and final defeat and destruction of the German Armed Forces.

No Division in the British Empire has contributed more to this result than the 7th Armoured Division.

Through the long years of fighting in the Middle East, in Tunisia, in Italy and throughout the campaign in North West Europe, our Division has always been in the thick of it.

Your rapid advance from the Rhine to the Elbe, and the hard fighting which made this possible, contributed very greatly to the brilliant success of the whole campaign.

I wish to congratulate every officer and man in the Division upon their fine achievements, and to thank them personally for their loyalty and unflagging enthusiasm.

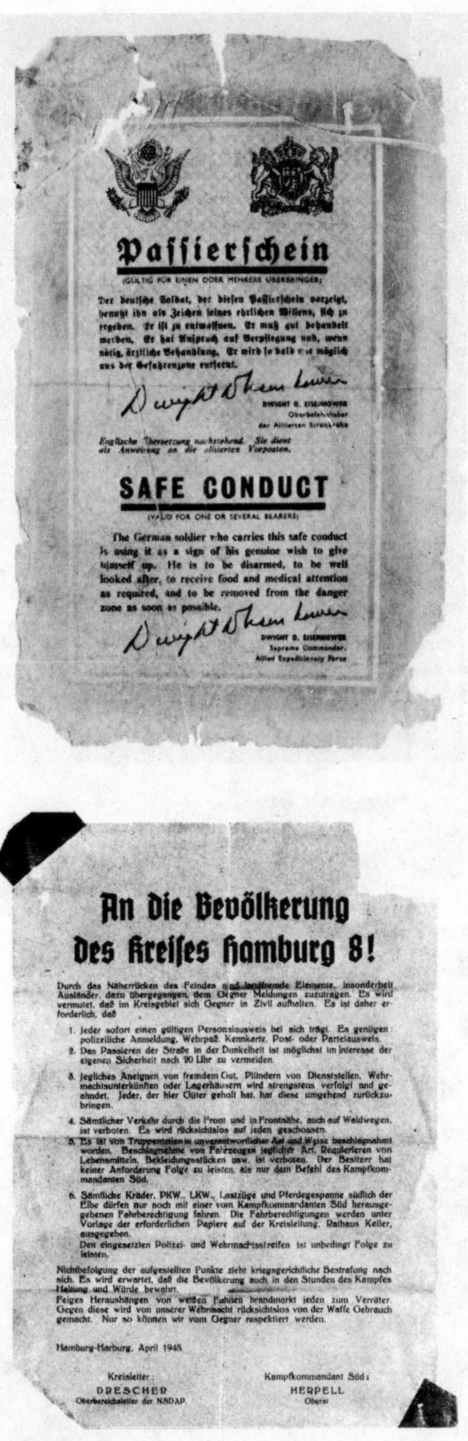

Passierschein

(GÜLTIG FÜR EINEN ODER MEHRERE ÜBERBRINGER)

Der deutsche Soldat, der diesen Passierschein vorzeigt, benutzt ihn als Zeichen seines ehrlichen Willens, sich zu ergeben. Er ist zu entwaffnen. Er muß gut behandelt werden. Er hat Anspruch auf Verpflegung und, wenn nötig, ärztliche Behandlung. Er wird so bald wie möglich aus der Gefahrenzone entfernt.

DWIGHT D. EISENHOWER
Oberbefehlshaber
der Alliierten Streitkräfte

Englische Übersetzung nachstehend. Sie dient als Anweisung an die alliierten Vorposten.

SAFE CONDUCT

(VALID FOR ONE OR SEVERAL BEARERS)

The German soldier who carries this safe conduct is using it as a sign of his genuine wish to give himself up. He is to be disarmed, to be well looked after, to receive food and medical attention as required, and to be removed from the danger zone as soon as possible.

DWIGHT D. EISENHOWER
Supreme Commander,
Allied Expeditionary Force

An die Bevölkerung des Kreises Hamburg 8!

Durch das Näherrücken des Feindes sind landfremde Elemente, insonderheit Ausländer, dazu übergegangen, dem Gegner Meldungen zuzutragen. Es wird vermutet, daß im Kreisgebiet sich Gegner in Zivil aufhalten. Es ist daher erforderlich, daß

1. Jeder sofort einen gültigen Personalausweis bei sich trägt. Es genügen: polizeiliche Anmeldung, Wehrpaß, Kennkarte, Post- oder Parteiausweis.
2. Das Passieren der Straße in der Dunkelheit ist möglichst im Interesse der eigenen Sicherheit nach 20 Uhr zu vermeiden.
3. Jegliches Aneignen von fremdem Gut, Plündern von Dienststellen, Wehrmachtsunterkünften oder Lagerhäusern wird strengstens verfolgt und geahndet. Jeder, der hier Güter geholt hat, hat diese umgehend zurückzubringen.
4. Sämtlicher Verkehr durch die Front und in Frontnähe, auch auf Waldwegen, ist verboten. Es wird rücksichtslos auf jeden geschossen.
5. Es ist von Truppenteilen in unverantwortlicher Art und Weise beschlagnahmt worden. Beschlagnahme von Fahrzeugen jeglicher Art, Requirieren von Lebensmitteln, Bekleidungsstücken usw. ist verboten. Der Besitzer hat keiner Anforderung Folge zu leisten, als nur dem Befehl des Kampfkommandanten Süd.
6. Sämtliche Kräder, PKW., LKW., Lastzüge und Pferdegespanne südlich der Elbe dürfen nur noch mit einer vom Kampfkommandanten Süd herausgegebenen Fahrberechtigung fahren. Die Fahrberechtigungen werden unter Vorlage der erforderlichen Papiere auf der Kreisleitung, Rathaus Keller, ausgegeben.

Den eingesetzten Polizei- und Wehrmachtsstreifen ist unbedingt Folge zu leisten.

Nichtbefolgung der aufgestellten Punkte zieht kriegsgerichtliche Bestrafung nach sich. Es wird erwartet, daß die Bevölkerung auch in den Stunden des Kampfes Haltung und Würde bewahrt.
Feiges Heraushängen von weißen Fahnen brandmarkt jeden zum Verräter. Gegen diese wird von unserer Wehrmacht rücksichtslos von der Waffe Gebrauch gemacht. Nur so können wir vom Gegner respektiert werden.

Hamburg-Harburg, April 1945

Kreisleiter: DRESCHER, Oberbereichsleiter der NSDAP
Kampfkommandant Süd: HERPELL, Oberst

Left: Safe Conduct Pass – A rather tattered but still legible copy of an Allied Safe Conduct Pass.

Bottom left: This photograph shows an original German poster which was displayed on the walls of houses in Hamburg.

To the inhabitants of the Sector Hamburg 8

Because of the proximity of the enemy, alien elements particularly foreigners have deserted taking messages to the enemy. It is surmised that in the sector there are members of the enemy in civilian clothes it is therefore necessary that:

(1) The current personal identity cards must be carried. The following will suffice, police notification, serviceman's papers, identity cards, post office or party identity cards.

(2) Use of the streets after dark is to be avoided after 2000 hours as much as possible in the interests of personal safety.

(3) Every appropriation of alien goods, pillage from offices, Army accommodation or warehouses will be strictly followed up and punished Anyone who has taken these goods must immediately bring them back.

(4) All traffic through and near the front, even on forest paths, is forbidden. Those who do so will be shot without mercy!

(5) Sections of troops are appropriating goods (looting) in an inexcusable manner. Appropriations of vehicles of any sort, requisitioning of food, articles of clothing etc. is forbidden. The owner is under no obligation to obey except by the command of Camp Commandant South.

(6) All transport, private motor vehicles, lorries, heavy trucks, horse drawn vehicles, south of the Elbe may only travel with one of the travel permits issued by Camp Commandant South. These permits will be given out from the District Command in the Town Hall Keller on production of the necessary papers. The lanes set up by the police and army must be used.

Those who do not follow the above orders will be court martialled. It is hoped that the population even during action will maintain dignity and bearing. The cowardly hanging out of white flags brands one as a traitor. Those who do this will be ruthlessly executed by the army. Only like this can we be respected by our enemies.

Hamburg-Harburg April 1945.
Head of District
DRESCHER
Region leader NSDAP*
Camp Commandant South
HERPELL, Colonel

*(National Sozialistische deutsche Arbeiter partei) German National Socialist Workers Party.

Difficult days may lie ahead of us in the transition period from war to peace, but you will overcome these as you have overcome all difficulties in the past.

It will be a great honour in the future to be able to say "I was a Desert Rat".

Main Headquarters,
7 British Armoured Division
7 May 45

L. O. LYNE
Major-General
Commander

Above centre: Victory Parade. Vehicles of the Division moving towards the saluting base.

Berlin~The Greatest Day

MONS TO BERLIN

"Well, the boys have got there at last."

On June 14th, 1945, whilst the Division was busy settling down to the job of occupational duties north of Hamburg, orders came from 21 Army Group that the Desert Rats must stand by to move to Berlin. Unfortunately it was impossible to take the whole Division due to lack of accommodation there, and so on June 16th orders were issued that the following units would stand by at 48 hours notice to move:

Tactical Divisional Headquarters
Headquarters 131 Infantry Brigade
3rd Royal Horse Artillery
8th Hussars
11th Hussars
1st/5th Queens
2nd Devons
4th Field, 621st Field and 143rd Field Park Squadrons, Royal Engineers.

In addition, in order to make the force as fully representative as possible 21 Army Group placed under command 1st Battalion Grenadier Guards from the Guards Armoured Division and a composite Canadian Battalion from the 1st Canadian Army. One can imagine how much excitement the prospect of the move created. Here is how Sergeant Joseph Lodge of 2nd Devons remembers it: 'When we first heard of our move to Berlin I think every man from private soldier to officer were so elated that it would be really impossible to describe or even guess at each man's thoughts. I know for myself and the

forty or fifty men nearest to me we looked upon it as a great honour to think we were to be stationed in the very heart of Germany. The actual move I do not remember all that much about. I know that it was a very slow process what with the large numbers of troops and vehicles involved, also the bloody-mindedness of the Russians when it came to entering their sector. When we did eventually reach our destination (Spandau Barracks) we thought that under the very difficult circumstances they met, our advance party had done a good job.

The first few weeks were spent cleaning up and trying to make life a little more pleasant. The non-fraternisation with the German population came very hard to us all, seeing the utter destruction of Berlin one had to have just a little feeling of pity for the civilian population and, as everybody knows, the hardest thing for a British soldier once he comes in contact with anybody is not to be friendly. Our Brigadier visited us after a very short time, a really bull parade – all went well until our company was ready for inspection, eyes front, was given in turn by all platoon sergeants. Support Company (mine) was head of the parade, I gave the final eyes front and then instead of stepping off I froze to the spot – got a bit of a ripping from the RSM it had been a terrible night in the Mess the night before as I'm sure all 2nd Devon sergeants will remember!

After a while everybody seemed to get themselves organised, what we would now explain as "doing their own thing". Some took up football, horseriding, many went on different courses, I think more for a rest than anything. I went on an anti-tank course in which funnily I had specialised for the last two years of the war – no change but very enjoyable.'

The main body of the Division arrived on July 4th, which began with a deluge of rain but fortunately cleared up later. Led by 'C' Squadron 11th Hussars, the Division reached the saluting base on Pichelsdorfer Strasse about half past six that evening, where the GOC was waiting to greet them. There followed a period of intense activity cleaning and repairing their accommodation and rehearsing for the many ceremonial parades which took place over the next few days.

The first of these was on July 6th when the Union Jack was hoisted on the biggest flagpole which could be found, at the foot of the Franco-Prussian War Memorial in the Grosse Stern. The GOC had charged the commander of 131 Brigade, Brigadier (now Major General) John Spurling, with the task of finding the flagpole and his resourceful sapper field squadron commander decided to 'borrow' one from the Olympic Stadium, some four miles away. Transportation proved a problem and eventually the Berlin Fire Brigade had to be called in to help move the enormous pole. The sappers then set to work making a hole in the pavement to set in the pole. They were so busy getting it erected and concreting it into the floor of a conveniently

Far left, top: Mons to Berlin. 'Well the boys have got here at last' (E H Shepherd drawing from Punch, July 11th, 1945 and reproduced here by kind permission of the proprietors).

Far left, bottom: The last leg. Vehicles of the Division on the autobahn en route for Berlin from Helmstedt.

Centre bottom: Passing Russian troops on the autobahn en route for Berlin from Helmstedt.

Below: Magdeburg Bridge. On July 1st, 1945 the Div Recce party started to cross the Elbe by the autobahn bridge built by the Russians alongside this one which had been blown. The GOC was leading the column and after the first few vehicles had crossed a Russian sentry appeared on the far side and said that his orders were to allow no vehicles of any type or nationality over and that all traffic should use the temporary 'Friendship' bridge in Magdeburg. Arguments and persuasion by the GOC proved to no avail and the column had to turn around and use the other bridge.

placed underground public loo, that they forgot to paint it. Resourceful to the end, however, Brigadier John Spurling obtained the services of a Japanese acrobat from the Hamburg Circus, to shin up the pole with a pot of paint! The same acrobat was required to perform again later that day when the French decided they wanted the Tricolour flying on top of the Franco-Prussian War Memorial.

The Greatest Day

Finally the greatest day of all arrived and at 10 o'clock on the morning of July 21st, 1945, a roar of guns broke out over the ruins of Berlin, as the 3rd Regiment Royal Horse Artillery fired a 19 gun salute in honour of the Right Honorable Winston Churchill who was to take the salute at the Victory Parade.

The programme of events for the Parade was as follows:

1000 hours – The Prime Minister accompanied by the Commander-in-Chief arrives at the Saluting Base. Met by GOC British Troops, Berlin. Salute by guns of 3RHA.
1005 hours – The Prime Minister, accompanied by Distinguished Visitors, drives round and inspects the Parade.
1030 hours – The Prime Minister returns to the Saluting Base.
1035 hours – March Past begins.
1110 hours – March Past ends.
1115 hours – The Prime Minister departs.

As the guns, tanks, armoured cars and carriers thundered past the saluting base, followed by the marching troops, the feelings of all those taking part in this great cavalcade would have been well worth recording. One can only speculate, however, as did General Verney in his history of the Division:

'What thoughts must have passed through the minds of the veterans as they saluted their great war leader! Of that first venture through the wire of the Egyptian frontier and the overwhelming victory of Beda Fomm and Sidi Saleh; of Sidi Rezegh in November 1941; and the desperate fighting in that same area a few months later; Alam Halfa and Alamein; Tripoli and Tunis; the crossing of the Volturno; the bloody fighting in the Bocage and the Plains of Caen; the exhilarating scenes of "Liberation" on the long road to Ghent; the harsh winter battles and the last long advance into the heart of the enemy's country.

So many scenes, good times and bad, savage heat and extreme cold, sand storms and snow, rain and sunshine and perhaps, too, so many names – O'Connor and Creagh the first architects of victory: Gott and Campbell; Pinney, Ward Gunn and Beeley; Holliman and Wainman and all those others whose names find no written records but who gave their whole endeavours to their comrades and their Regiments, who died in battle or afterwards, who will be honoured and remembered for all time by those who served with them' (*The Desert Rats, North Africa*, page 282.)

Top left: Poster on the road into Berlin.

Top centre: Berlin at last! Tanks of the Division entering Berlin July 4th, 1945.

Above: The GOC taking the salute in the Pichelsdorfer Strasse as the Division enters Berlin 1825 hours, July 4th, 1945. (Nobody seems to have noticed that the Union Jack was upside down).

Left: The entrance to the Reich Chancellery in the Wilhelmstrasse. The balcony on the right of the building was used by Hitler for making speeches and reviewing troops. (Note also the two Russian guards).

This series of photographs was taken by Major Christopher Milner of the Rifle Brigade using a 'looted' film which had been used before to photograph prisoners in Dulag XIB, hence the ghostly background faces

Above: Berlin 1945. The Brandenburg Tor.

Top right: Berlin 1945. Fuel shortage. Note the World War I British tank in the background.

Far right: Berlin 1945. The Brandenburg Tor, note the Red Flag draped over the statue.

Right: Inside the devastated Reich Chancellery which had been looted and disfigured with graffiti in Russian and English.

'Dear Desert Rats'

Memorable though the parade undoubtedly was, to my mind it was the moving eloquence of Churchill which really set the seal on this the greatest of days. After the parade, whilst opening the 'Winston' Club he said: 'Soldiers of the 7th Armoured Division. I am delighted to be able to open this Club and I shall always consider it a great honour that it should have been named after me.

I have, not for the first time, had the pleasure of seeing your troops march past, and this brings back to my mind a great many moving incidents in these last, long, fierce years.

Now, here in Berlin, I find you all established in this great centre, from which, as from a volcano, fire and smoke and poison fumes have erupted all over Europe twice in a generation. And in bygone times also German fury has been let loose on her neighbours, and now it is we who have our place in the occupation of this country.

I feel I can go so far as to ask Field Marshal Montgomery to signalise this happy event of the great Victory Parade we have had today

DUL XI B
200099
DUL XI B
200097

Dul. XI B
200086

by giving a whole holiday to all the troops in Berlin, and I hope, Field Marshal, that you can accommodate this to operational and other necessities.

Now I have only a word more to say about the Desert Rats. They were the first to begin. The 11th Hussars were in action in the desert in 1940 and ever since you have kept marching steadily forward on the long road to victory. Through so many countries and changing scenes you have fought your way.

It is not without emotion that I can express to you what I feel about the Desert Rats.

Dear Desert Rats! May your glory ever shine! May your laurels never fade! May the memory of this glorious pilgrimage of war which you have made from Alamein, via the Baltic to Berlin, never die! It is a march unsurpassed through all the story of war so far as my reading of history leads me to believe. May the fathers long tell the children about this tale. May you all feel that in following your great ancestors you have accomplished something which has done good to the whole world; which has raised the honour of your own country and which every man has a right to be proud of'. (Extract from *A Short History of the 7th Armoured Division June 1943–July 1945.*)

Top left: Berlin 1945. Old armoured car.

Above: Berlin 1945. Russian soldiers using horse drawn transport.

Left, far left: Bomb damage in Berlin 1945. The capital of the Third Reich had been devastated by bombs and weapons of all types before suffering the crowning indignity of being occupied by enemy forces.

Above: Berlin 1945. The Russians erected enormous copies of photographs of the Allied War leaders on the Unter den Linden.

Centre left: Berlin 1945. More Russian photographs, these are of some of their top generals in the Alexander Platz.

Bottom left: Berlin 1945. The Black Market flourished in the Tiergarten in front of the gutted Reichstag.

Top right: Hoisting the Union Jack at the foot of the Franco-Prussian War Memorial in the Grosse Stern, July 6th, 1945.

Right: Hand-over of French Sector. Brig John Spurling together with his French opposite number inspects the Guard of Honour of the Eleventh Hussars.

44
208337

BRITISH VICTORY PARADE

BERLIN

21ST JULY 1945

Above centre: Victory Parade. Vehicles of the Division moving towards the saluting base.

Above left: Hand-over of French Sector. Flag ceremony in progress.

Left: Cover of the programme for the British Victory Parade, July 21st, 1945.

Top right: The 3rd Regiment Royal Horse Artillery firing a nineteen gun salute in honour of the Prime Minister, the Right Honourable Winston Churchill's arrival to take the Victory Parade.

Right: Victory Parade. A scene at the Saluting base showing Mr Winston Churchill, Fd Marshal Sir Harold Alexander, Fd Marshal Sir Bernard Montgomery, Mr Anthony Eden and Mr Clement Attlee, together with GOC 7th Armoured Division, Gen 'Lou' Lyne.

"I didn't mind Churchill saying it, but the next soldier that says 'Good morning, my DEAR Desert Rat' is going to cop it."

Left: Victory Parade. The Inspection in progress. Mr Churchill, together with other VIPs in a half track, moves slowly past tanks of the Division.

Right: Victory Parade. The Colour Party of the 2nd Battalion, The Devonshire Regiment marching towards the saluting base.

Bottom left: Dear Desert Rats. As usual Giles manages to catch the humour of the moment in this cartoon which appeared in the 'Daily Express' on July 24th, 1945 and is reproduced here with his kind permission.

Bottom centre: Opening the 'Winston' Club. After the parade, Mr Churchill opened the 'Winston' Club, making his famous 'Dear Desert Rats' speech, part of which is reproduced at the end of this section.

Bottom right: Opening the Jerboa Club. Major General 'Lou' Lyne cutting the tape at the entrance to the Desert Rats new club in Berlin July 23rd, 1945.

'Roll on my Demob'

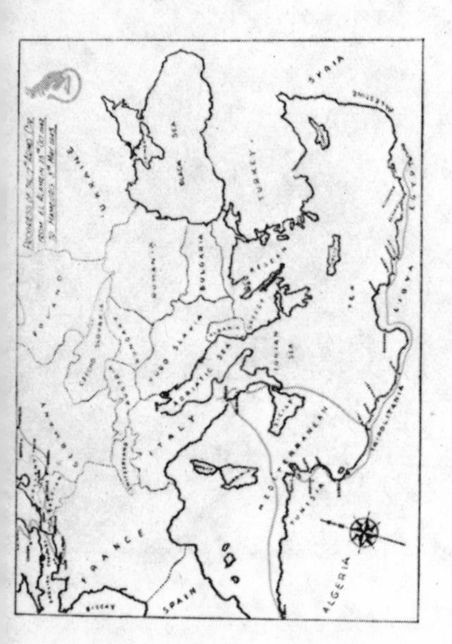

PERSONAL MESSAGE
from
COMMANDER
7th ARMOURED DIVISION
to
EVERY OFFICER AND MAN
ON DEMOBILISATION

•

MAIN HEADQUARTERS
7th ARMOURED DIVISION

You may well be very proud to have served with the 7th Armoured Division. No Division in the British Empire has contributed more to the downfall of the Axis Powers and to the total defeat of Germany.

The Desert Rats first saw service in the Middle East, when Italy declared war on us in 1940. They fought with great distinction all through the long campaign which culminated in the victory of ALAMEIN. They took a leading part in the pursuit of Rommel's defeated forces, and in the final breakthrough to TUNIS.

The Division was the first British Armoured Division to land in Europe, when it took part in the assault landing at SALERNO. It served through the Italian Campaign till brought back to England early in 1944 to prepare for the great assault on Western Europe.

Once more the Division formed part of an assault Corps and fought hard throughout Normandy and the winter campaign. Finally, the 7th Armoured Division crossed the RHINE and made history by its rapid advance to the ELBE and subsequent occupation of HAMBURG.

This is a grand and glorious record. The credit for it belongs to you, to each individual officer and man.

I think that there are three particular qualities to which we can ascribe our success:

(1) THE FIRM BELIEF WHICH WE HAVE HELD IN THE IDEALS FOR WHICH WE HAVE FOUGHT, THE RESTORATION OF CHRISTIAN CIVILISATION TO THE WORLD, AND OUR TRUST IN GOD TO GIVE US THE POWER TO ACHIEVE THIS,

(2) OUR FIGHTING SPIRIT AND THE DETERMINATION TO OVERCOME ALL DIFFICULTIES;

(3) OUR TEAM SPIRIT AND THE DESIRE THAT ALL WE ACHIEVE MAY BE FOR THE COMMON END AND NOT FOR SELFISH GAIN.

These three great guiding motives have stood out like shining beacons, not to us alone, but to all men and women of the United Nations.

We have won the war; now for the peace.

Difficult times and hard work for all of us lie ahead if we are to restore the ravages of five-and-a-half years of war. The same sterling qualities which led our country through every peril to final victory will help us again.

I hope that you will carry back to civilian life with you those three fine qualities which have played so predominant a part in the life of this Division. I am sure that if you do we shall win the peace as completely as we have won the war.

Finally, I wish to thank you for all that you have done for the Division, and to wish you happiness and good fortune in the years to come.

L. O. Lyne

Major-General,
Commander,
7th Armoured Division.

Roll on My Demob!

The road to Civvy Street and a good job was not always easy for the returning Desert Rat as is evidenced by this cautionary tale entitled 'Post War Plans' which appeared in the second issue of the 'Jerboa Geordie' published on November 15th, 1945. This was the fortnightly journal of No 3 Independent Machine Gun Company, Royal Northumberland Fusiliers, who were part of 131 Brigade throughout the North West European campaign:

'I was half way through my leave – the last one I would have in the Army – sprawled comfortably in my favourite chair, in front of a roaring fire, and feeling thoroughly at peace with the world.

Two months to go, I thought, and then I'll be a fully-fledged civvy. After six years of blood and tears, good times and bad, I'd be free once more to do as I liked. What would I do? Well, first of all there was that fortnight's holiday I had promised to have with my wife – we hadn't had a decent one during the war – then get a job and settle down.

A job! The thought brought me back to earth with a jolt. My old job had been blitzed, and anyway, I wanted something better, now that I was a family man. The more I thought of it, the more I realised that now was the time to find a job, while I had plenty of time to spare. Suiting the action to the word, I picked up the evening paper once more, and scanned the "Situations Vacant" column. There was quite a selection to choose from, and I couldn't decide which one to apply for, so I thought the best idea was to try a few of them in person in the morning.

Next morning at 0830 hours I was all dressed and ready for the fray, much to the surprise of my wife. "Where do you think you're going at this hour?" she asked. "Looking for a job" I replied. "No good waiting until I'm demobbed; strike while the iron's hot. Do It Now – that's my motto from now on".

My first port of call was a gent's outfitters – I always did fancy myself as a seller of fancy socks. Meekly I asked for the manager, and as a huge man advanced and towered over me, my knees turned to water.

"Well what can I do for you?" he rumbled. "I've come about that job you advertised in the News last night" I squeaked. "Any references?" he growled. "No, I've been six years in the Army though". "What did you do in the Army?" Here is my chance I thought, and proudly swelling my chest to its glorious 28½ inches I said "I was a driver/operator".

"Um, I've heard of them" he said in a pitiful sort of voice, "No good for anything that requires hard work. No resistance – nothing. Better try somewhere else. Good morning".

Dejectedly, I looked at the next name on the list – Smithers, grocers in High Street. Surely I could weigh a pound of sugar! Boldly I marched in and asked for the boss. This man was short and thin, and going bald on top, and had an expression of constant worry on his face. In the advanced stages of couponitis I thought, so he should be easy to handle. Going straight into the attack I said "I'm looking for a job, and thought the position which you advertised last night would just suit me. I've been six years in the Army, and rose to the rank of corporal." "So did Hitler" he barked, "And look what a mess he made of his firm. No, I couldn't take the risk. Good day". Blindly I stumbled out on to the pavement, and realising that they had just opened, I decided to have a tonic.

Looking at my list, I found my next chance lay with S. Windle & Co., jewellers. Just in my line, selling watches and rings was the easiest thing in the world, or so it seemed as I watched the transactions in Berlin. I opened the shop door and walked in, and immediately an oily individual oozed towards me, rubbing his greasy palms together. "Vat can I get der chentlmans?" he blubbered, in a voice which made me feel bilious. "You advertised last night for an assistant and I'm just the man you want". "Vat other jobs have you did" he wheezed. "Guard commander, i/c reliefs, and orderly corporal, so you will see that I'm a man of great initiative and highest integrity. Why, many's the time the Sergeant-Major has left me in complete charge of a brand new order board".

"Vat part of Chermany did you occupy?" asked the oily one. "Berlin", I answered proudly. "Ah! You are a Rat! The chap I just sacked vos also a Rat, he took seven watches and left twenty fags in der till. Once a Rat, always a Rat!"

This was too much for me, and I slammed the door behind me and I tramped home, deciding that as soon as I got back to Berlin, I would sign on – maybe they can make me permanent company runner!' (Reproduced by kind permission of RHQ (Northumberland) The Royal Regiment of Fusiliers; Journal loaned by R. Jarvie Esq.)

Far left: This card was given to all ranks of the Division on demobilisation.

Below: Cartoon reproduced by kind permission of Jon.

"Don't worry old man,
Pte. Blenkinsop assured me
he'd fix us up
with a job"

Sand at the Finish

Sand at the Finish

'The General had already made his farewell speech to the men; a fatigue party had been detailed to take down the headquarters sign-board and the guard commander had been instructed to lower the Divisional flag for the last time.

In the Sergeant's Mess at 7th Armoured Division headquarters, RSM Jack Allen, who had joined the Division in the desert as a tank commander in 1941, raised his glass and called for a last toast: "Gentlemen, here's to 7th Armoured Division – the finest in the British Army".

Sergeant Albert Saunders unhooked a fire bucket from the wall, took out a handful of sand and spread it at the feet of his comrades. It was a sentimental but fitting last gesture from one of the original Desert Rats to the memory of a division which has now been disbanded, but which will live long in the memories of all who proudly wore the famous Jerboa sign'. (Quoted from *Soldier* Magazine, March 1948).

Maj General 'Pip Roberts, GOC in 1948, toasting his Desert Rats at the first disbandment of the Division at Bad Rothenfelde.

That is how E J Grove, a reporter for *Soldier* magazine described the scene in 1948 at the first disbandment of the Division when Major General Pip Roberts, CB, DSO, MC, was commanding and Divisional Head-quarters was located in the Westphalian village of Bad Rothenfelde. General Pip had been in command since January 1946 and had guided the Division through the difficult period of occupational duties. He had com-manded 11th Armoured Division in the latter stages of the war, but was no stranger to 7th Armoured, having been a Desert Rat for most of the North African campaign, his last appointment with the Division being as Commander of 22nd Armoured Brigade at the time of the capture of Tripoli. He was described in an Army Quarterly of the day as "the living embodiment of all that has been best in the Division". In his farewell message to his Desert Rats he expressed the hope that the Division would be reformed and fortu-nately his words proved to be prophetic. About the time of the Berlin airlift and the beginning of the Cold War, the Division was reformed and went on to serve with distinc-tion for a further period in the British Army of the Rhine, until it was once again dis-banded on April 16th, 1958. On this occasion the Division was redesignated as '5th Divi-sion', which under a year later was yet again re-designated as '1st Division'.

The Times leader, published on the day following the disbandment parade, was a mark of the high esteem in which the Desert Rats were held:

'The glories of the British Army are by tradition enshrined in the permanent regi-ments and corps which go to make it up. Divisions and brigades, being essentially ephemeral formations, have not so often caught the public imagination, though there are exceptions to this rule dating back to the Light Division in the Peninsula, and the Light Brigade in the Crimea. The First World War served to build up a number of divisional reputations. In the second several divisions acquired a name first within the Army and then throughout the nation for consistent valour and prowess in different theatres of war. But it is no exaggeration to say that the 7th Armoured Division, the Desert Rats, won more renown than any division has ever gained in the history of the British Army. There are those who felt, and feel today, that this was unfair. There are other divisions which won equally glorious victories, endured equal butcheries and fought in even worse physical conditions.

Why then did the renown of the Desert Rats grow so mightily? One reason is that they were "first in and last out" of the battle. It is true that they did not fight at Dunkirk, but they were on active operations in the Western Desert from the beginning of the war, and as the only armoured division acquired a reputation in the Army equivalent to that of "the Few" in the RAF. Then there was the spectacular nature of some of their victories, the great distances covered, the masses of prisoners, and the restoration of speed to war. The news of these exploits served to hearten the Commonwealth at a time when there was not much else to be cheerful about. And they were sloggers too. At Sidi Rezegh, Knightsbridge and Alam Halfa they took fearful punishment.

The Desert Rats preserved a shining spirit. Rightly or wrongly, the concept of chivalry was retained among them in the circumstances of modern war. They were a light-hearted and happy division. Sir Winston Churchill in his memoirs recounts how, listening in London to a relay of one of the early desert battles, he heard with delight a squadron leader report "I am now at the second B in Buq Buq". They exemplified the attitude of the British to war at its most dangerous, which found a response among the British people. Some of their fame they undoubtedly owe to the inspired choice of an emblem by one of their earlier commanders, Major General Sir M O'Moore Creagh. Public relations are important, in war as in anything else. The nickname of the Desert Rats caught on. It is a lesson which the unimaginative generals who had decreed the end of this famous fighting force should take to heart.' (Published by kind permission of the *Times* Newspapers Limited.)

Third Time Unlucky?

But of course that was not the end of the story. You can't keep a good Rat down and the Jerboa went on being proudly worn by the men of the 7th Armoured Brigade who remain as the only formation with the Desert Rat emblem. Alas the demise of that tough little rodent which had been put off twice is now yet again a distinct possibility. It is fitting therefore that the present 'Chief Rat', Brigadier Martin Farndale, should have the last word:

'The Desert Rats live on in the name of 7th Armoured Brigade in Soltau, Germany. All the "Rat" property, silver, pictures and relics are there and annually the Brigade celebrates the battle of Sidi Rezegh on November 22nd. On that day a church service is held followed by a march past of the present generation of "Rats". The original battered flag of the desert days lies on the altar at the service and old comrades come out from England. It is a moving experience and serves as a reminder to each generation as it comes along, that the standards and example set in battle are not forgotten.

The Brigade in 1975 consists of two armoured regiments, 1st The Queen's Dragoon Guards and the 13th/18th Royal Hussars (Queen Mary's Own) and two mechanised infantry battalions, the 1st Battalion The King's Own Royal Border Regiment and the 1st Battalion The Prince of Wales's Own Regiment of Yorkshire. It is interesting to note that the Brigade's affiliated Squadron in the Royal Air Force, 20 Squadron (Harriers), proudly wears the Rat on the tails of its aircraft.

But alas are they to be the last custodians of the Rat? The Defence White Paper of March 1975 announced that Brigades are to be no more. Will the Rat go from the order of battle of the British Army? At the time of writing we do not know, but we do know that the Rat will never ever be forgotten. The fame of the Desert Rats has spread around the world, their exploits have never been equalled even by the marches of the Romans, Hannibal, Alexander the Great or Napoleon. No force in history has marched so far or fought so long. The Red Rat marched from Alamein to Naples and on to Berlin via Normandy while the Green Rat marched from India to Rangoon and always he marched to victory. Whatever happens the Rat will remain one of the greatest formation symbols of all time, the envy of all. Since the end of the war he has been in Germany demanding high standards from all who serve him and he remains now as bright, shiny and agile as he was when he was born in the desert of North Africa in 1941. Like the true old soldier that he is he will never die'.

Stand Down

Below: This splendid authentic bronze statue of a Jerboa was made by Brig George Davy, who commanded 7th Armoured Brigade at the Battle of Sidi Rezegh in November 1941. (His painting of the battle appears in the North African volume of this series).

Right: The End of the Road – The Divisional Axis board erected in Berlin in July 1945.

Stand Down
Here are we met upon this day
To toast the golden past away,
To hand a duty gladly done
To those whose task has just begun.
We who have taken for our charm
The Desert Rat upon our arm,
Extend our greetings firm and true,
Ring out the old – ring in the new.

And now to King of all the Rats,
Those present here take off their hats;
A welcome then to General Lyne
The leader of our desert sign
Our toast before dividing ways:
'God send him happy all his days'.

So many here, so much to say,
So many dreams to dream away.
Memory cool and crystal clear
Lives on in every moment here.
Those days – those days! We're looking back!
Down a well worn Axis track.
Cairo, Knightsbridge, Alamein,
That never changing desert scene.

The scorching sun, the midnight stars,
Those ever stretching lonely hours.
The desert stove – the desert rose!
The secrets that the desert knows.
Always the desert, desert sand,
That hellish never never land.
But there was forged this bond so true
Which lives in everyone of you.

Then over blue and summer sea
To fight again in Italy.
To England after four long years,
Wisbech girls and Norwich beers.
So the months ran swiftly by
To bring the Rat to Normandy.

Bursting through across the Seine
We chased the bloody Bosche again.
That Belgian welcome felt we all
Could never be beyond recall.

Holland! Flat with cold and damp
Bogged us down with winter cramp.
And then the spring on winter's heels
Dried the mud and loosed our wheels.
At last the greatest show was near,
The Rhine was crossed, the future clear.

So in this land of evil fame
We say goodbye, but always claim
That he who marched so in this war
Has done a deed ne'er done before.
Proudly we share this brotherhood
By strangers scarcely understood.

And those who now do stand by me
Stand thus until eternity.
Long may their spirit breathe and live
Good Speed you – Seventh Armoured Div!

Taken from the menu of the 'Hail and Farewell' dinner which was held in the Warrant Officers' and Sergeants' Mess, Headquarters, Seventh Armoured Division on November 7th, 1945.

THIS AXIS HAS BEEN LAID FROM
EL ALEMEIN TO BERLIN
VIA:-
AFRICA
TOBRUK
BENGHAZI
TRIPOLI
MARETH
TUNIS
ITALY
SALERNO
NAPLES
VOLTURNO
FRANCE
NORMANDY
THE SEINE
ROUBAIX
BELCIUM
OUDENARDE
GHENT
MALINES
HOLLAND
EINDHOVEN
TILBURC
THE MAAS
THE RHINE
CERMANY
AHAUS
SULINGEN
NIENBURG
SOLTAU
HAMBURG
ZEISS
OPTIK

Finale

Victorious Desert Rats pose with a captured trophy.

On 13th May 1943 two very important, but very different, signals were despatched by the opposing Armies in North Africa.

The first was from General Alexander to No 10 Downing Street, and read:
"Prime Minister, Sir — It is my duty to report that the Tunisian campaign is over. All enemy resistance has ceased. We are masters of the North African shores."

The second was from the Headquarters, Afrika Korps, to Army Group Africa and OKH, and read:
"Ammunition shot off. Arms and equipment destroyed. In accordance with orders received DAK has fought itself to the condition where it can fight no more. The German Afrika Korps must rise again".

Without any doubt the 7th Armoured Division, the true Desert Rats, had played a leading part in the victory. They had hardly ever been out of the battle, from the very earliest days against the Italians to the moment of final victory in Tunis. At last they could take a well-earned breather — but not for long! Round one was over and the fight had now to be taken on to Europe. It was clear that the Desert Rats would be in the thick of it again very shortly.

FLOREAT JERBOA!

Bibliography

Bolitho, Hector: *The Galloping Third,* (John Murray).
Brett-Smith, Richard: *Berlin '45 The Grey City,* (Macmillan).
Carver, Michael: *A Short History of the Seventh Armoured Division Oct. 1938-May 1943,* (Printing & Stationery Services MEF).
Chamberlain, Peter and Ellis, Chris: *Profile, AFV Weapons No. 48,* (Profile Publications Ltd.)
Clark, Dudley: *The Eleventh at War,* (Michael Joseph).
Crawford, Robert: *I was an Eighth Army Soldier,* (Victor Gollancz).
Davy, George: *The Seventh and Three Enemies,* (Heffer).
Douglas, Keith: *Collected Poems,* (Faber & Faber).
Evans, Roger: *The Story of the Fifth Royal Inniskilling Dragoon Guards,* (Gale & Polden).
Fernyhough, A.H.: *A History of the RAOC 1920-1945,* (William Clowes).
Foster, R.C.G.: *History of the Queen's Royal Regiment Vol. 8,* (Gale & Polden).
Garnet, Jack (Editor): *Wardrop of the Fifth,* (Private).
Hart, B. Liddell: *The Tanks Vol. 2,* (Cassell).
Hastings, R.H.W.S.: *The Rifle Brigade in the Second World War 1939-1945,* (Gale & Polden).
Jarrett, G.B.: *West of Alamein,* (Sentry Books).
Jewell, Derek (Editor:) *Alamein and the Desert War,* (Sphere Books).
Joly, Cyril: *Take these Men* (Constable).
Lindsay M. & Johnston H.E.: *The History of the 7th Armoured Division June 1943-July 1945,* (Printing and Stationery Services, British Army of the Rhine).
Macksey, Kenneth: *Armoured Crusader,* (Hutchinson). *Beda Fomm,* (Ballantine).
Morris, Desmond: *The Mammals,* (Hodder & Stoughton).
Military Training Pamphlet No. 41
Miller, Harry: *Service to the Services, (Newman Neame).*
Mills, Giles & Nixon, Roger: *The Annals of the King's Royal Rifle Corps,* (Leo Cooper).
Scarfe, Norman, Duncan, W.E., Ellis, H.F., and Banks, R.L., Joint Editors: *The Royal Artillery Commemoration Book 1939-45,* (G. Bell & Sons).
Thesiger, Wilfred: *Arabian Sands,* (Longmans, Green & Co.).
Verney, G.L.: *The Desert Rats,* (Hutchinson).
Woolley, A.D.: *The History of the KDG,* (Private).

Periodicals
Bir Hakim *(Editions de la Revue du Caire).*
The Illustrated London News, various editions, 1944-45
Jerboa Geordie, November 15, 1948
La 13e Demi-Brigade de Légion Etrangère, (Private).
La lre D F L Epopée d'une reconqûte, (Arts at Métiers Graphiques).
RUSI Journal, February 1954
Soldier Magazine, March 1948
The Times, April 16, 1958

Photo Credits

Major J. Alpe: 192, 198(B), 202, 320, 323(R), 326(B), 331(T), 332(TR)
APTC Museum: 120(TR), 121
Arts at Metiers Graphiques: 15(T)
A. Atkins: Title page, 51, 145(B), 147(B), 154(B), 155(B), 156(Inset), 159, 179(Inset), 197, 203(Inset), 204(T), 259, 260(T), 319, 332(B), 334(B), 336, 337
H. Auger: 14(T), 186(C), 186(B), 189(TL), 189(TR)
Major A. H. Barnes: 196(C), 198(T), 224, 226, 230, 231(B), 236, 236(Inset), 237(Inset), 238(B), 240(AC), 241(B), 246(T), 289(T), 290(TR), 290(B)
F. Black: 177(T), 314(B)
Major A.S.C. Blackshaw: 32(C), 32(B)
N. Bloomfield: 222(TL)
Mrs. D. Boggie: 85, 155(CR)
Mrs. J. Boggie: 285(T), 290(TL)
Major General B.H.W. Brind: 332(TL), 335(T)
S.A. Busby: 324(TL)
S.R. Campbell: 59(B), 71, 152(BL)
C.E. Chapman: 104, 105
Brigadier Sir F. Coates: 26, 33(TR)
The Commanding Officer, QOH: 70
Mrs. Cornford: 117(BR), 155(TR)
Brigadier M.L. Crosthwait: 220(C)
T.P. Dalton: 176(BR), 185(BR), 195
C. Davis: 285(C)
La 13e Demi-brigade de légion Etrangère: 81(B)
D. Dickson: 234, 250, 251(Inset), 252, 253, 254, 255, 280, 281(B), 286(T), 286(B), 288(L), 288(TR), 292
Editions de la Revue du Caire 1942: 81(T)
Major P.N. Erskine: 201(T), 228(B), 229
Major H. Firth: 36(CL), 38(C)
G. Forty: 263
Major I. Fowler: 6
F. Fromont: 261, 265(Insert)
Cannon K. Meiklejohn: (37)B, 120(BL)
Mrs. M. Milburn: 292(Inset)
Major C. Milner: 241(T), 264, 266, 278, 281(T), 283(Inset), 322(B), 322(BR), 326(T), 327, 328(T), 330(B)
Major F.J. Mitchell: 63(CR), 120(TL), 156, 176(TR), 189(CR)
D.C. Monday: 153(TL)
Mrs. S.M. Moore: 241(C), 310, 311(T), 312(C), 312(B), 313, 315, 316, 317, 318(C), 325(B), 330(C)
E. Morrall: 267, 268, 269
Mrs. B. Morton: 155(TL)
NAAFI: 15(B), 112, 132, 133(T), 133(B)
J.H.J. Orchard: 21(B), 110(BR), 111, 137, 143(B)
V. Overfield: 50
R. Parker: 272(T), 273, 284, 318(B)
H. Perkins: 124(BL)

Major N. Plough: 18(Inset), 19(Inset), 22(Inset), 24(B), 56(BR), 57, 63(T), 69, 84, 130, 145(CL), 145(R)
K. Popplewell: 89
A. Potter: 36(BL), 117(TL), 117(BL), 118(T), 119(B), 140(T), 140(B), 144(T), 145(TL), 184(T), 196(T), 205, 206, 206(Inset), 207(Insets), 209, 220(B)
Punch: 322(T)
RA Institution: 100, 101(TL)
RAC Tank Museum: 38(T)
RAOC Museum: 64, 65, 86, 125, 126(T), 126(B), 127(B), 128(T), 128(R), 160
RASC Museum: 113(Inset)
W. Rendall: 14(B), 128(B) 129
W.R. Reynolds: 196(B), 205(T), 222(TR), 223(T)
Major General G.W. Richards: 18, 36(T), 37(T), 142(BL), 183(TL)
Mrs. H.C.W. Richardson: 191
Royal Signals Institution: 109(Inset), 110(BL)
Royal Zoological Society: 10(T)
4 RTR: 17
Colonel S.C.F. de Salis: 20(B), 106, 186(B), 187(T)
A. Sandbrook: 282
F. Shepard: 12, 28(B), 33(TL)
H.A. Gardner: 146(T)
Brigadier J. Gilman: 124(BR)
F.H. Granger: 4, 91(Inset), 117(TR), 140(C), 142(BR), 164
G.A. Griffin: 25(T), 131(TR), 131(CR), 154(TL), 188(T)
N. Hall: 131(TL), 194, 240(BC), 240(B), 245(C), 290(C), 291, 293(Inset)
R. Hardy: 318(T)
N.C. Harper: 20(T), 21(T), 135(Insets), 136(B), 150, 152(R), 153(B)
Reverend E.G. Hazleton: 39(CR), 239(T)
Home HQ 1 The Royal Hussars: 200
Home HQ KRRC: 38(B)
Home HQ RGJ: 67, 77(T), 101(TR), 134, 137(T)
B. Hook: 24(T), 25(BR), 142(T), 152(CL), 154(TR), 182, 183(B), 186(T), 186
Illustrated London News: 74, 115, 123, 127(T), 244(T), 248, 274, 276(T), 304
Imperial War Museum: 10(B), 11, 30, 32(T), 33, 39(CL), 39(B), 39(T), 42, 44, 48, 52, 53(Inset), 54, 56(BL), 58, 60, 62, 63(B), 66, 72, 75, 76, 77(B), 78, 79, 82, 87, 90, 92, 97, 102, 108, 116, 118(B), 124, 141, 143(T), 157(Inset), 162, 163, 165, 166, 168, 169, 172, 173, 174, 189(B), 190, 199, 208, 210, 212, 213, 214, 215, 217(Inset), 218(T), 219, 220(T), 221, 222(BR), 227, 228(T), 238(T), 239(B), 242, 244(B), 245(T), 247, 249, 256, 258, 262, 270, 275, 276(B), 277, 294, 298, 299, 300, 301, 302, 302(Inset), 305, 306, 307, 308, 312(T), 325(T), 333(T), 333(B), 334(T), 334(BR), 335(B), 348
Powell Jones: 245(B)
Colonel W. Kaulback: 98, 183(TR), 184(BL), 185(BL)
J. Kinsella: 285(B)
J.S.P. Knight: 187(B)
Brigadier G.S. Knox: 287, 289(B)
L.J. Lee: 28(T), 46(B)
M.H. Leese: 311(C), 311(B)

H. Martin: 23(Inset), 25(BL), 232, 240(T), 342
John McDonnel *(Surrey Comet):* 146(BR)
Mrs. E. Sillito: 153(TR)
R.W.E. Smith: 146(BL)
Soldier Magazine: 338, 341
Major General J. Spurling: 331(B)
Colonel A.H. Stanton: 34, 36(BR), 131, 176(L), 177(B)
Lieutenant Colonel Stanton: 216
G. Stimpson: 59(T), 136(T)
Miss J. Surgey: 47, 52(Inset)
E. Thompson: 142(CL), 152(T)
H.L. Turner: 147(T), 185(T)
Brigadier P.A.L. Vaux: 36(CR), 80, 188(B)
R.D. Walls: 286(C), 324(TR), 328(B), 329, 330(T)
J. Welsby: 144(B)
F.J. Williams: 29(T)
F.W. Winborne: 180